Judging Poverty and Inequality in Brazil

Judging Poverty and Inequality in Brazil

TAINÁ GARCIA MAIA

Postdoctoral Researcher, Center for Human Rights of the University of Erlangen-Nuremberg

OXFORD
UNIVERSITY PRESS

OXFORD
UNIVERSITY PRESS

Great Clarendon Street, Oxford, OX2 6DP,
United Kingdom

Oxford University Press is a department of the University of Oxford.
It furthers the University's objective of excellence in research, scholarship,
and education by publishing worldwide. Oxford is a registered trade mark of
Oxford University Press in the UK and in certain other countries.

This project has received funding from the European Research Council (ERC) under the European Union's
Horizon 2020 research and innovation program (grant agreement No 817652).

Published in the United States of America by Oxford University Press
198 Madison Avenue, New York, NY 10016, United States of America.

British Library Cataloguing in Publication Data
Data available

Library of Congress Control Number: 2026934015

ISBN 978–0–19–899402–2

DOI: 10.1093/oso/9780198994022.001.0001

Printed and bound by
CPI Group (UK) Ltd., Croydon, CR0 4YY

The manufacturer's authorized representative in the EU for product safety is
Oxford University Press España S.A. of Parque Empresarial San Fernando de Henares,
Avenida de Castilla, 2 – 28830 Madrid (www.oup.es/en or product.safety@oup.com).
OUP España S.A. also acts as importer into Spain of products made by the manufacturer.

MIX
Paper | Supporting
responsible forestry
FSC® C013604

To all who bravely resist in order to simply exist with dignity.

Preface

Human rights can be theorized, but they are first and foremost experienced. While conducting detailed theorizations on poverty and inequality, this work recognizes the limits of any theory to fully grasp the phenomenon of oppressions, all facets of intersectionality, and the lived realities they entail. Within the inherent constraints of academic inquiry, this book pursues three main objectives.

First, it aims to explore the complex interactions and interconnections between poverty and inequality, both in theory and in practice. The study focuses on Brazil, the largest and most populous country in Latin America, whose postcolonial and post-slavery context continues to shape the manifestations of poverty today. In the first decade of the twenty-first century, Brazil became a paradigmatic example of poverty reduction, making it a compelling case for examining the interconnections between substantive equality, intersectionality, and anti-poverty public policy. Second, the book seeks to identify how law accommodates poverty and addresses its interplay with persistent and historical inequalities, not only through the positivization of rules but also through the work of courts. To this end, it centres its analysis on the work of two prominent courts with jurisdiction over the actions and inactions of the Brazilian State: the Brazilian Federal Supreme Court and the Inter-American Court of Human Rights. Through an unprecedented empirical analysis of their equality jurisprudence addressing poverty, the book identifies judicial strategies that unveil the multidimensional oppressions associated with poverty in Brazil and assesses their impact on poverty reduction from 1988 to 2023. Third, the book endeavours to enrich the critical debate on whether and how law can effectively respond to poverty and its intersectional manifestations, thereby promoting social change. Drawing on the findings of the empirical study while also incorporating a normative dimension, this analysis examines both the potential and the limitations of law and courts in promoting transformative change towards poverty eradication.

This project has received funding from the European Research Council (ERC) under the European Union's Horizon 2020 research and innovation programme (grant agreement No 817652). It is the product of years of research, supported by many colleagues and institutions, without whom this project would not have attained the depth it ultimately achieved. I am deeply thankful for the comments and input from Niels Petersen, Aziz Tuffi Saliba, Paulo de Martino Jannuzzi, Juliana Cesario Alvim Gomes, Mônica Teresa Costa Sousa, Manuellita Hermes, Carlos Gaio, Elaine Meire Vilela, Marjorie Corrêa Marona, and Bruno de Oliveira Biazatti. I am also grateful to the scholars and peers I met at various research events—including Lucía Zurita, Anne Lisa Kjær, Veronika Fikfak, Thomas Gammeltoft-Hansen, Karen Alter, Mikael Rask Madsen, Başak Çali, and Lutiana Valadares Fernandes Barbosa—whose insightful questions, sometimes brief but pivotal, helped me refine key aspects of this research. I am thankful to all the staff of the Brazilian Federal Supreme Court and its Department of Judicial Research for their methodological input and institutional insights, as well as for a visiting stay that proved profoundly relevant to this study. Lastly, I would like to thank my family for their trust, patience, and loving support throughout the lengthy process that accompanies the writing and publication of a book. I am extremely grateful to you all.

Tainá Garcia Maia, Belo Horizonte, 2025

Contents

List of Figures xi
List of Tables xiii
List of Abbreviations xv

1. Introduction **1**

PART I. INEQUALITY AND POVERTY IN THEORY

2. 'What's in a Name?' Shakespeare Asked **17**

3. How Does Law Accommodate the Socio-Economic Concept of Poverty? **61**

4. Judicializing Poverty: The Four-Prong Model for a Legal Assessment of Poverty Through Equality **93**

PART II. EMPIRICAL ANALYSIS

5. The Evolution of Poverty in Brazil (1988–2023) **117**

6. Equality and Poverty in the STF **157**

7. Equality and Poverty in the IACtHR **202**

8. A Comparative Analysis and Paths Forward **237**

9. Conclusion **266**

References 285
Index 305

Figures

2.1 Comparison of values (in R$) of the IPL and the PBF and Brazil Aid lines of extreme poverty (2011–2023) 26

2.2 Comparison of (non-extreme) poverty lines (2011–2023) 29

5.1 Extreme poverty levels in Brazil (1988–2023) 129

5.2 Monetary poverty in Brazil (1988–2023) 129

5.3 Unemployment levels in Brazil (2012–2023) 131

5.4 Undernourishment in Brazil (2000–2024) 141

5.5 School attendance in Brazil (2002–2023) 142

5.6 Higher education for persons aged 25 or over in Brazil (2016–2023) 143

5.7 Share of the population living with deprivations disaggregated by race in Brazil (2018) 147

5.8 Share of the population living in multidimensional poverty in Brazil disaggregated by race (2002 and 2015 comparison) 148

5.9 School attendance in Brazil (2019) 152

5.10 Headcount poverty rate (World Bank versus IBGE, 2012–2023) 154

6.1 Judgments on affirmative action measures and quota systems (STF, 1988–2020) 175

Tables

6.1 Success rate disaggregated by the criterion of distinction (STF, 1988–2020) 180
6.2 Dimensions of equality disaggregated by judicial strategy (STF, 1988–2020) 200
7.1 Success rate disaggregated by the criterion of distinction (IACtHR, 1979–2020) 222
7.2 Dimensions of equality disaggregated by judicial strategy (IACtHR, 1979–2020) 236

Abbreviations

ACHR	American Convention on Human Rights
ACO	Original Civil Action
ADC	Action for the Declaration of Constitutionality
ADI	Direct Action for the Declaration of Unconstitutionality
ADO	Action for the Declaration of Unconstitutionality by Omission
ADPF	Action Against a Violation of a Constitutional Fundamental Right
BPC	Continuous Cash Benefit Programme
BWEP	Brazil without Extreme Poverty
CAISAN	Interministerial Chamber of Food and Nutritional Security
CCT	conditional cash transfer
CESCR	United Nations Committee on Economic, Social and Cultural Rights
CF/88	Federal Constitution of Brazil of 1988
CONSEA	National Council on Food and Nutritional Security
ECA	Statute of the Child and Adolescent
ECtHR	European Court of Human Rights
ENDEF	National Survey of Family Expenditure
FAO	United Nations Food and Agriculture Organization
FHC	Fernando Henrique Cardoso
FIES	Student Financing Fund for Higher Education
HC	*habeas corpus*
IACommHR	Inter-American Commission on Human Rights
IACtHR	Inter-American Court of Human Rights
IBGE	Brazilian Institute of Geography and Statistics
ICCPR	International Covenant on Civil and Political Rights
ILO	International Labour Organization
IPEA	Institute for Applied Economic Research
IPL	international poverty line
LGBTIQ+	lesbian, gay, bisexual, transgender, intersex, and queer
LOAS	Organic Law of Social Assistance
MC	preliminary injunction
MDS	Ministry of Social Development and Fight Against Hunger of Brazil
MESA	Extraordinary Ministry of Food Security and Fight Against Hunger of Brazil
MPI	Multidimensional Poverty Index (UNDP and OPHI)
MPM	Multidimensional Poverty Measure (World Bank)
MS	injunction
OAS	Organization of American States

OECD	Organisation for Economic Co-operation and Development
OPHI	Oxford Poverty and Human Development Initiative
PBF	Programme *Bolsa Família* ('Family Grant')
PNAD	National Household Sample Survey (IBGE)
PNADC	Continuous National Household Sample Survey (IBGE)
PNS	National Survey of Health
PoU	Prevalence of Undernourishment
PPP	purchasing power parity
Protocol of San Salvador	Additional Protocol to the American Convention in the Area of Economic, Social and Cultural Rights
PT	Labour Party
RE	extraordinary appeal
SAGI	Secretariat of Evaluation and Information Management of the MDS
SIAPE	Integrated System of Human Resources Management
SIS	Summary of Social Indicators (IBGE)
SISAN	National System of Food and Nutritional Security
STF	Brazilian Federal Supreme Court
SUS	Brazilian Unified System of Health
UDHR	Universal Declaration of Human Rights
UN	United Nations
UnB	University of Brasília
UNDP	United Nations Development Programme
WWP	Brazil Learning Initiative for a World without Poverty

1
Introduction

My mother always sewed life with threads of iron.

—**Conceição Evaristo (2016)**[1]

In 1997, Paulo Lins published the first edition of his book *City of God*, one of the most important works in contemporary Brazilian literature. The book inspired the homonymous film released in 2002, which received worldwide critical acclaim and four Academy Award nominations. Based on real-life events, the novel depicts life in the grip of organized crime in one of the poorest communities of Rio de Janeiro, Cidade de Deus (in English, City of God).

Beyond the narrative of crime and survival, *City of God* is a distressing commentary on chronic poverty and its entanglement with racial and socioeconomic inequality in Brazilian society. One of the book's main characters is Busca-Pé (in English translations, 'Rocket'), a young man from City of God whose dream is to be a photographer. It is through his eyes that readers first see the signs of the drug war being unleashed in the community. It is also through him that Lins brings, in the first two pages of the novel, a poignant commentary on chronic poverty and social stratification. In these pages, unaware of the war that would soon take lives by the river bank in which he sat, Busca-Pé finds himself immersed in an internal dialogue about his dreams and their collision with reality: 'He tried to remember the childish joys that had died, one by one, every time he had bumped into reality, every day of hunger that lay behind him.'[2] Recalling the hopeful promises of his elementary school teachers, he contrasted these expectations with his now limited chances of getting a job to continue his studies, buy his own clothes, take his girlfriend out, and, finally, buy the camera, the lens, and the photography course he wanted. He imagined how nice it would be if things were the way his teachers had said, if occupational segregation, stigma, and marginalization could indeed be circumvented by the use of his agency. He imagined he would have a job, buy all the lenses

[1] Conceição Evaristo, *Olhos d'Água* (Pallas 2016), 'A gente combinamos de não morrer', p 109. Translation by the author.

[2] Paulo Lins, *Cidade de Deus* (2nd edn, Companhia das Letras 2002), p 12. Translation by the author.

Judging Poverty and Inequality in Brazil. Tainá Garcia Maia, Oxford University Press. © Tainá Garcia Maia 2026.
DOI: 10.1093/oso/9780198994022.003.0001

he wanted, and photograph everything that interested him. He would win a prize. At this moment, his mother's voice spoke in his mind: 'This photography thing is for folks with money! What you need is to get into the Air Force . . . the Navy, even the Army to guarantee yourself a future. Soldiers are the ones with money! I don't know what goes on in that head of yours!'.[3]

In his portrayal of the disillusionment of Busca-Pé, Paulo Lins highlights some of the social and structural hindrances faced by individuals living in poverty, including misrecognition and obstacles to equal participation in social and political life. As the opening pages of *City of God* illustrate in a fictional portrayal of a real-life reality, poverty is wider than income deprivation. Individuals living in poverty face material constraints on their opportunities to lead the life they choose and are often subjected to marginalization and stigma. These manifestations of exclusion and oppression are forms of inequality that derive from poverty and reinforce it.

This book delves into the intricate relationship between poverty and inequality, with a focus on the judicialization of poverty and its ability to unveil inequalities that derive from and reinforce socio-economic vulnerability. While equality has been defined by judges, lawyers, and legal scholars, poverty is a concept essentially defined by social sciences and economics. Nonetheless, law, understood as an evolving body constantly developed and expanded by courts,[4] accommodates the socio-economic concept of poverty. This book explores how this accommodation takes place and the role of equality in this process.

The book is centred on the case of Brazil. The country's history as a former colony structured around the plantation system and built on an enduring history of slavery manifests today through the perpetuation of structural and intersectional inequalities that still correlate with poverty. Nonetheless, in the first decade of the twenty-first century, Brazil became a paradigmatic case of poverty reduction through diverse state policies, providing a fertile ground for analysing the interplay between substantive equality, anti-poverty policy, and judicial responses to chronic poverty.

To assess the judicial strategies that have been used to address poverty in Brazil through the adjudication of the right to equality, the study analyses the jurisprudence of two pivotal courts with jurisdiction over the actions and inactions of the Brazilian State: the Brazilian Federal Supreme Court (STF) and the

[3] Ibid. Translation by the author.

[4] On the understanding of law as an evolving body, the development of which is recognized and consolidated through the work of courts, see: PC Chief Justice of Canada, *Remarks of the Right Honourable Beverley McLachlin* (Lord Cooke Lecture in Wellington, New Zealand 2005); Armin von Bogdandy and Ingo Venzke, 'On the Democratic Legitimation of International Judicial Lawmaking' (2011) 12 German Law Journal 1341.

Inter-American Court of Human Rights (IACtHR). By meticulously examining the potential and limitations of the approaches taken by these courts, it offers recommendations for overcoming these limitations and promoting a more effective response to the perpetuation of poverty cycles in Brazil. It illuminates the interplay between poverty, inequality, and the law, and enriches the critical discussions of how law can effectively respond to poverty.

The study unfolds in three stages. First, it assesses the interconnections between poverty and inequality in theory, building on theories from law, sociology, and political science. Next, it embarks on an empirical journey, tracing the evolution of poverty in Brazil from its redemocratization in 1988 to 2023. This empirical examination bridges the theoretical discussions conducted in the study's first part with the Brazilian context. Lastly, the study delves into the equality jurisprudence of the STF and the IACtHR. It meticulously analyses how these courts have addressed poverty as a matter of equality and non-discrimination law, evaluating their strategies for breaking cycles of poverty in the country. The analysis covers the equality jurisprudence of the STF from October 1988 to October 2020 (encompassing 260 collegiate decisions) and the IACtHR from its creation to the end of 2020 (comprising fifty-three judgments), as well as the collegiate decisions addressing poverty outside the realm of equality cases within the same timeframe. The shorter temporal scope of the jurisprudential analysis, compared to the study of the evolution of poverty in Brazil, allows an assessment of the impact (if any) of these two courts on poverty reduction in Brazil.

Section 1.1 introduces the study's starting point: the observation that the legal classification of poverty as a matter of equality and non-discrimination law is controversial and, according to the prevailing narrative in scholarly work, still incipient in practice. Section 1.2 explains the choice of case study and describes the methods used in the book's empirical analysis. Finally, section 1.3 provides an overview of the book's structure.

1.1 The problem: equality as a (under)utilized tool for addressing poverty?

In 2023, a staggering 690.76 million individuals lived in extreme poverty worldwide, surviving on less than US$2.15 per day.[5] Survival on such scant

[5] World Bank, '2023 in Nine Charts: A Growing Inequality' (2023) <https://www.worldbank.org/en/news/feature/2023/12/18/2023-in-nine-charts-a-growing-inequality?intcid=ecr_hp_headerA_2023-12-18-EndofYearCharts> accessed 6 january 2024.

economic resources is not only a distributive matter but also a concrete obstacle to fulfilling basic rights, many of which remain largely conditional on one's ability to pay. Therefore, behind the quantification of poverty lie collective and individual stories of constrained rights and unequal access to well-being—a narrative that finds poignant illustration in a Brazilian metropolis, the city of São Paulo.

A study conducted in 2023 compiled socio-economic indicators from different neighbourhoods of Latin America's most populous city. It showed a difference of up to twenty-three years in life expectancy between the inhabitants of the most affluent districts of São Paulo and those living in the poorest ones.[6] In Jardim Paulista, one of the city's most expensive districts, life expectancy is slightly higher than that of Denmark (82 years and 81.5, respectively).[7] In contrast, life expectancy in Anhangera is lower than that of Malawi (59 years, compared to 60 for men and 67 for women in Malawi).[8] Living in poverty is, therefore, not merely an issue of lack of income, but a matter of severely hindered rights. In the absence of distributive public policies, extreme poverty significantly undermines the enjoyment of basic levels of core human rights, such as the right to food, adequate housing, education, and health, among others, that deeply impact individuals' ability to lead their lives.

However, poverty is much wider than maldistribution of resources, as the story of Busca-Pé illustrates. It encompasses a spectrum of harms, ranging from material deprivation to social exclusion and hindered participation in society. Nancy Fraser and Axel Honneth argue that injustices can only be adequately understood when encompassing at least struggles over distribution and recognition.[9] People living in poverty face multidimensional oppressions that include maldistribution of income and material resources, as well as stigma and negative stereotyping. These processes of exclusion and marginalization not only impact one's construction of the self but also shrink the spaces for representation in the collectivity by hindering political and social participation. In conjunction, these processes reinforce poverty cycles.

Therefore, while essential, distributive strategies are insufficient on their own to eradicate poverty, leaving the structural barriers that perpetuate poverty cycles untouched. The insufficiency of distribution alone becomes

[6] Rede Nossa São Paulo, *Mapa da Desigualdade 2023* (2023), section 'Saúde, Idade média ao Morrer'.

[7] Ibid; OECD, *OECD Health at a Glance 2023 Country Note—Denmark* (2023).

[8] *Mapa da Desigualdade 2023*, *supra* note 6, section 'Saúde, Idade média ao Morrer'; World Bank, 'Life expectancy at birth, total (years) - Malawi' (2024) <https://data.worldbank.org/indicator/SP.DYN.LE00.IN?locations=MW> accessed 29 August 2025.

[9] Nancy Fraser and Axel Honneth, *Redistribution or Recognition? A Political-Philosophical Exchange* (Verso 2003).

evident in the case of historically marginalized communities disproportionately represented among those living in poverty. Kimberlé Crenshaw observes that those occupying the lower rungs of society in most countries still share a specific combination of characteristics.[10] In her words, '[t]hose who are poor, or otherwise marginal, are generally different from the elite whether by color, caste, descent, language or religion'.[11] Therefore, the persistence of poverty often intertwines with a history of segregation, marginalization, and discrimination. To effectively tackle poverty, public policies must take into consideration poverty's multiple manifestations and root causes, many of which are closely connected to historical processes of discrimination.

Despite the growing recognition of the multiple vulnerabilities attached to poverty, the road towards unveiling its deep interconnections with inequality has not always been smooth. Different legal responses to poverty have been adopted throughout history, not all based on a human rights approach. While today poverty is generally recognized as a human rights matter, it is still primarily approached in human rights papers as an issue of social and economic rights rather than one of equality. And equality, in turn, has often been read in conjunction with civil and political rights, as well as through the lens of much-needed but limited[12] identity politics. Referring to the US context, Patricia Hill Collins contends that '[c]lass is routinely mentioned across intersectional scholarship, yet it remains underutilized as an analytical category to explain complex social inequalities'.[13] In studying the jurisdictions of Britain, the US, Canada, and South Africa in 2011, Sandra Fredman finds that, while the right to equality has the potential to make a valuable contribution to addressing exclusions that arise in relation to poverty, 'it has not yet been sufficiently developed to address distributive inequalities in its own right'.[14] Seven years

[10] Kimberlé Crenshaw, 'Documento para o encontro de especialistas em aspectos da discriminação racial relativos ao gênero' (2002) 10 Revista Estudos Feministas 171, p 184.

[11] Ibid. Translation by the author.

[12] As Silvio Luiz de Almeida explains in the preface of the 2019 Brazilian publication of Asad Haider's *Mistaken Identity*: '[T]here is no racism without political and economic structures that support a continuous process of transformation of individuals into "blacks" and "whites". [...] In such a way that treating racism as the result of a vague and abstract idea of "white supremacy" without explaining the terms in which this is made possible politically and economically proves how much confusion the contemporary version of identity politics can cause. [...] Therefore, taking identity as the centre of politics is the same as trying to end capitalism by buying all existing goods until none are left. Identity politics without a horizon of transformation of the very "social machinery" that produces social identities generates a straitjacket that makes black persons, women, and LGBT persons be, at most, an improved and less suffered version of what the world has historically reserved for them.' Silvio Luiz de Almeida, 'Prefácio da edição brasileira' in Asad Haider, *Armadilha da identidade: raça e classe nos dias de hoje* (Veneta 2019), pp 12–13. Translation by the author.

[13] Patricia Hill Collins, 'Intersectionality's Definitional Dilemmas' (2015) 41 Annual Review of Sociology 1, p 13.

[14] Sandra Fredman, 'The Potential and Limits of an Equal Rights Paradigm in Addressing Poverty' (2011a) 22 Stellenbosch Law Review 566, p 567.

later, in a comparative study of the case law of Canada, South Africa, and India, Shreya Atrey observed that poverty 'remains largely unfamiliar to discrimination law'.[15]

This book's approach is innovative and timely. It challenges the often-repeated assertion regarding the incipience of equality as a legal tool for responding to poverty by noting that this assertion is strongly based on the experience of English-speaking jurisdictions. By expanding the empirical look beyond these jurisdictions, it fills a critical gap in scholarship on non-discrimination law. Furthermore, it contributes significantly to a broader understanding of the role of the right to equality and non-discrimination in the fight against poverty, particularly in Latin American countries characterized by transformative constitutionalism.[16] The latter is likely to impact courts' conceptualization of equality and their responses to poverty and intersectional discrimination in contexts of structural and persistent poverty affecting historically vulnerable groups.

1.2 The empirical study

1.2.1 The choice of the case study

Brazil was chosen as the case study because it is a typical postcolonial and former slave state in the Americas, where structural and intersectional discrimination still correlates with poverty. It is expected that conflicts derived from this interconnection have been the object of judicial controversies, making Brazil a compelling subject for an equality-based analysis of poverty. In addition, in the late twentieth century, Brazil's levels of extreme poverty, as defined by the World Bank, closely mirrored the regional average in Latin America and the Caribbean. However, in the twenty-first century, Brazil became a paradigmatic example of poverty reduction through state policies addressing monetary and multidimensional poverty. Some of these policies included affirmative action measures, while others incorporated different considerations of substantive

[15] Shreya Atrey, 'The Intersectional Case of Poverty in Discrimination Law' (2018) 18 Human Rights Law Review 411, p 439.

[16] Transformative constitutionalism is understood as the interpretation of constitutional law (including international constitutionalism) as a result-oriented body of norms, responsive to the historical and structural challenges in the region and a direct instrument for the promotion of change. See Armin von Bogdandy and René Urueña, 'International Transformative Constitutionalism in Latin America' (2020) 114 American Journal of International Law 403; Armin von Bogdandy, 'The Mandate of the Inter-American System: Transformative Constitutionalism by a Common Law of Human Rights' in IACtHR (ed), Dialogue Between Regional Human Rights Courts (IACtHR 2020).

equality and intersectionality. Therefore, it is expected that an examination of the jurisprudence of courts with competence over the actions and inactions of the Brazilian State will shed light on the interconnections between substantive equality and anti-poverty public policy. Such an analysis also allows for assessing judicial responses to chronic poverty and their impact on the delimitation and implementation of public policy aimed at reducing poverty in its monetary and multidimensional manifestations.

By selecting an apex court and a regional human rights court, the study assesses the practices of two institutions that are subject to different institutional settings and constraints, yet are interpreting the same right—the right to equality—in cases arising from the same context: manifestations of poverty in Brazil throughout the late twentieth and twenty-first centuries. The diversity inherent in comparing a domestic and an international court will likely uncover different patterns in addressing poverty through the judiciary. Therefore, it enriches the investigation by unveiling possibilities and limitations for addressing poverty through the adjudication of the right to equality.

While the STF is an apex court vested with competence over constitutional matters and composed of eleven justices nominated by the president, the IACtHR is a regional court institutionally located under the Organization of American States (OAS), mandated to interpret and apply the American Convention on Human Rights (ACHR). It is composed of seven judges who must be nationals of OAS member states, and its decisions require domestic implementation. Both courts differ in composition, structure, interpretative authority, and enforcement power. By examining the practices of these two institutions side by side—one embedded in the domestic constitutional framework and the other positioned as an external and subsidiary human rights court—the study is able not only to capture a broader range of legal strategies employed to address poverty through law and tackle the interconnections between poverty and inequality in Brazil, but also to compare them. It illuminates complementarities and tensions and assesses the extent to which each court has been able to influence poverty-related lawmaking and policymaking in Brazil.

1.2.2 Hypotheses

The empirical analysis aims to identify the different methods courts have used to address the interconnections between poverty and inequality. For this purpose, it maps the equality jurisprudence and the poverty jurisprudence of the STF and the IACtHR and develops a quantitative and qualitative analysis of their case law. The analysis considers the hypothesis that the dominant narrative on the incipience of equality as a tool for tackling poverty, generally based on the studies of English-speaking jurisdictions, is not applicable to the case of Brazil and the jurisprudence of the STF and the IACtHR.

Hypothesis A: The dominant narrative in legal scholarship on the (under)development of equality as a tool to address multidimensional exclusions and oppressions derived from poverty is not applicable to the jurisdictions of the STF and the IACtHR.

Second, the empirical analysis aims to determine whether there is an added value in analysing poverty through the lens of equality, even in jurisdictions that recognize the justiciability of socio-economic rights. In other words, how can law approach poverty cycles, and what is the added value of equality as a legal tool in this process? To answer this question, the study compares the content and scope of the courts' decisions in equality cases addressing poverty with those addressing poverty outside an equality framework. The study considers the proposition that equality offers a valuable pathway for bringing deprivations related to poverty to judicial scrutiny but expands the analysis beyond the justiciability of poverty and socio-economic rights. More specifically, it posits two hypotheses on the added value of equality as a tool for enhancing the capacity of the law to address poverty, even in jurisdictions where socio-economic rights are justiciable, such as the STF and the IACtHR:

Hypothesis B: In contexts characterized by chronic poverty, states have an enhanced duty of due diligence derived from the right to equality. This duty widens the scope of state obligations and, consequently, state responsibility for protecting and fulfilling the rights of individuals living in poverty.

Hypothesis C: Addressing poverty through the perspective of equality allows courts to identify non-material disadvantages and forms of oppression against individuals living in poverty.

Under the IACtHR's case law on gender-based violence, a special duty of due diligence emanates from the principle of equality in the context of systematic gender-based violence. The first hypothesis is that an enhanced duty of due diligence applies to other spheres of discrimination law every time a widespread and structural context of vulnerability of the rights of an identifiable historically discriminated group (including the context of chronic poverty disproportionately affecting protected groups) is known or should have been known by the state.

In any case, even if an enhanced duty of due diligence does not emanate from a context of chronic poverty and structural exclusion and marginalization against individuals living in poverty, equality may still retain its added value in addressing poverty. By assessing poverty through the lens of equality, courts are well-equipped to identify distributive harm in accessing material resources and opportunities. The link between poverty and distributive harm is clear: material disadvantage is closely connected to the conceptualization of poverty and impacts the opportunity a person has to enjoy their rights, such as the right to education, health, housing, and dignified working conditions. The study expects the redistributive dimension of equality to be the primary focus of cases concerning positive duties derived from the right to equality to address poverty, particularly in disputes concerning affirmative action to the benefit of socio-economically vulnerable groups.

Notwithstanding the importance of distributive justice for assessing and responding to poverty, the study anticipates that the equality approach has a much broader added value than merely facilitating distributive assessments, especially in disputes that extend beyond affirmative action. By assessing poverty through the lens of transformative equality, courts may broaden their assessment of disadvantages beyond maldistribution of resources to cover constraints derived from power structures that impact persons living in poverty. They may also be better equipped to assess how social structures might fail to accommodate difference and thus exacerbate the marginalization of individuals living in poverty. Moreover, by considering poverty as a matter of equality, courts may identify obstacles to social and political participation that are wider than income deprivation, such as stereotypes, stigma, non-physical violence, and forms of humiliation against individuals living in poverty or groups disproportionately represented among those living in economic vulnerability. Therefore, equality arguably provides a tool for courts to uncover and address otherwise 'invisibilized' forms of discrimination against the poor. The study anticipates that harms derived from misrecognition are not captured when poverty is perceived exclusively as a matter of social and economic rights.

1.2.3 The dataset

The study covers the equality jurisprudence of the STF from October 1988 to October 2020. October 1988 was chosen as the starting point of the analysis because it marks the promulgation of the Federal Constitution of the Federative Republic of Brazil. It represents the beginning of a new constitutional era through the resumption of democracy after the fall of the military dictatorship in the country.

Through the database of the STF,[17] I searched for collegiate decisions using the word 'equality' in Portuguese in connection to Articles 5–7; 37; 39; 40, III and §4; 150–152; 201, §1; 205; 206; 227; and 244 of the 1988 Constitution.[18] To account for possible mistakes in the categorization of cases in the database, an additional search was conducted with the words 'equality AND discrimination', unconnected to any provision of the Constitution. Based on these criteria, the investigation identified 260 cases in which the STF made a ruling addressing equality and non-discrimination, 10% of which concerned distinctions based on economic status or included an analysis of poverty or vulnerability to monetary or multidimensional poverty.

The analysis of the equality jurisprudence of the IACtHR covers all judgments and advisory opinions addressing equality published by the Court from its creation to December 2020. A search was conducted in two databases: the Court's *Jurisprudence Finder* and the Court's *Digesto*. The latter was used as a research tool for Articles 1 and 24 of the ACHR. The former was used with the keywords 'equality' and 'discrimination' in Spanish,[19] unconnected to specific provisions. Additional cases were found based on cross-references. In the last phase of the mapping, a search was conducted on the IACtHR's online catalogue and the Court's database *Thesaurus* to verify the results and account for possible errors in the *Jurisprudence Finder*.

The study identified fifty-three cases in which the IACtHR reached a merits decision on state compliance with the right to equality as protected under Articles 1(1) and 24 of the ACHR and six advisory opinions addressing this principle. Of these, 30.2% concerned distinctions based on economic status or

[17] The search tool is called 'pesquisa no banco de jurisprudência', in <https://jurisprudencia.stf.jus.br/pages/search>. The database search results do not list all decisions taken by the Court. Highly similar decisions in content, scope, and formalities (eg cases decided by the same group—full bench or one of the Court's chambers) are considered repetitive and therefore not displayed in the results provided by this search tool. The STF department responsible for the database continuously assesses which cases are considered repetitive. These cases are included in a digital document called 'mirror of the judgment', which lists the technical information of each individual case (eg doctrine and legal instruments cited by the Court, repetitive cases, etc). To avoid a biased result, the study did not include these 'hidden' cases. The assessments regarding which cases are included in the 'mirror of judgments' change over time, which causes the number of results for the same search term to vary. Variations in the number of results are also caused by delays in the publication of decisions in the database.

[18] More specifically, the search words were: (i) 'Igualdade' + 'Art. 5'; (ii) 'Igualdade' + 'Art. 6'; (iii) Igualdade' + 'Art. 7'; (iv) 'Igualdade' + 'Art. 39'; (v) 'Igualdade' + 'Art. 40, III'; (vi) 'Igualdade' + 'Art. 150'; (vii) 'Igualdade' + 'Art.151'; (viii) 'Igualdade' + 'Art. 152'; (ix) 'Igualdade' + 'Art. 201, § 1'; (x) 'Igualdade' + 'Art. 227'; (xi) 'Igualdade' + 'Art. 244'; (xii) 'Igualdade e deficiência' + 'Art. 37'; (xiii) 'Igualdade e deficiência' + 'Art. 40, § 4'; (xiv) 'Igualdade e deficiência'; (xv) 'Igualdade e discriminação'.

[19] 'Igualdad' and 'discriminación'.

included an analysis of poverty or vulnerability to monetary or multidimensional poverty.

The cases in which the STF and the IACtHR addressed poverty in connection with a finding of equality/inequality were the object of quantitative and qualitative analysis. To account for alternative methods developed by the two courts for addressing poverty other than the interpretation and application of the right to equality, the investigation looked at the case law of the two courts addressing poverty outside equality cases. This analysis was restricted to the same temporal limits as the research on the Court's equality jurisprudence and was considered only for the purposes of qualitative study.

1.2.4 Content analysis

After the study identified the equality case law concerning poverty and the broader equality jurisprudence of the two courts, every case was analysed individually and hand-coded according to a pre-defined coding system. The codebooks, coding results, and the complete list of analysed cases can be found in the data repository of the University of Münster.[20]

The analysis of the approaches used for considering poverty in the equality jurisprudence of the STF and the IACtHR is based on the categories developed by Fredman and Atrey. Fredman identifies three approaches to addressing poverty through the right to equality: classifying poverty as a prohibited ground of discrimination; challenging the inclusiveness of anti-poverty measures through the right to equality; and recognizing positive obligations in discrimination law.[21] In turn, Atrey identifies two strategies developed by courts to grasp the intersectional nature of poverty: recognizing poverty as a discriminatory context, and treating poverty as a matter of substantive equality.[22] Because of the similarities and complementarity of their studies, this book combines the two models and categorizes four theoretical approaches for considering poverty as a matter of equality: (i) recognizing poverty or economic status as a suspect category of discrimination; (ii) using equality as a tool for assessing the inclusiveness of anti-poverty measures; (iii) treating poverty as a matter of discriminatory context; and (iv) treating poverty as a matter of substantive and positive equality. These approaches may coexist with one another, and two or more can be applied simultaneously in the same case.

20 <https://data-management.uni-muenster.de/datastore> accessed 18 August 2025.
21 Fredman (2011a), *supra* note 14.
22 Atrey (2018), *supra* note 15.

In addition to assessing the approaches each court takes in addressing poverty within the framework of equality claims, the empirical investigation also analyses which, if any, dimensions of equality were recognized and applied by the courts in their assessments of poverty. It applies Fredman's multidimensional framework for assessing substantive equality, which extends beyond purely material disadvantage to encompass four dimensions of substantive equality: redistribution, recognition, participation, and transformation.

The redistributive dimension aims to break cycles of disadvantage associated with a group. Equality as recognition aims to break down stereotypes, humiliation, and verbal violence, among other forms of misrecognition. The participative dimension relates to facilitating the social and political participation of members of marginalized or otherwise oppressed groups. Lastly, the transformative dimension seeks to accommodate differences and promote structural change.[23]

Fredman's multidimensional framework allows for identifying vulnerabilities and assessing how policies, laws, and judicial decisions respect, protect, and promote equality in its multiple and interconnecting dimensions. This framework will guide the book's assessment of state policies, judicial practices, and omissions in addressing the inequalities attached to poverty in the Brazilian case study. It will also be applied in the analysis of the advantages and shortcomings of the legal approaches designed by the SFT and the IACtHR to address poverty within the framework of equality.

1.3 The book's structure

The book is divided into two parts: Part I examines inequality and poverty in theory, and Part II conducts the book's empirical analysis. Part I comprises three chapters, which assess the interconnections between poverty and equality by drawing on theories from law, sociology, and political science. Chapter 2 discusses the definition of poverty and equality, noting different conceptualizations for these terms and their potential and limitations. It argues that a multidimensional conceptualization of poverty and equality provides a foundation for recognizing their relations and interconnections.

Having defined these terms, Chapter 3 investigates how law accommodates the socio-economic concept of poverty. Through an analysis that focuses on the dimensions of race and class, the chapter contends that law has not always

[23] Sandra Fredman, *Discrimination Law* (2nd edn, Oxford University Press 2011b), Chapter 1.

addressed poverty through an equality approach or even a human rights-based approach. The chapter does not aim to provide a complete overview of the legal history of poverty in law, and the examples it introduces of regulations addressing poverty in different times and contexts are essentially non-exhaustive. The chapter explores the emergence of a human rights-based approach to poverty since the mid-twentieth century, arguing that it provides a foundation for legal systems and institutions to address poverty through the lens of equality.

Concluding Part I, Chapter 4 introduces a model for the judicial assessment of poverty through the lens of equality, laying the groundwork for the empirical analysis in Part II. More specifically, based on the studies of Fredman and Atrey, it introduces the four-prong model of judicial strategies for a legal assessment of poverty through equality.

Part II of the book—its backbone—is composed of Chapters 5–8. Chapter 5 delves into an in-depth examination of the evolution of poverty in Brazil from 1988 to 2023. The chapter unveils how the intersections between poverty and inequality discussed in theory in Part I are found in practice in the case of Brazil. This analysis provides the factual background of the case study. In addition to providing essential background for understanding the context in which the two courts that integrate the study are inserted, it also identifies points of contact between poverty and inequality in Brazil, which are expected to be explored by the STF and the IACtHR in their respective jurisprudences.

Chapters 6 and 7 present the empirical findings concerning the judicial practices of the STF and the IACtHR, respectively. They identify the extent to which the two courts have tackled poverty as a matter of equality, the judicial approaches adopted by each court to address poverty in their case law, and how effective these approaches have been in recognizing and addressing multidimensional inequalities affecting individuals living in poverty in Brazil. Through this empirical investigation, these chapters also assess the extent to which the two courts have been able to capture intersectionalities within the phenomenon of poverty in Brazil.

Chapter 8 presents a comparative analysis of the two jurisdictions and their impact on reducing poverty and shaping public policy in Brazil. It examines the potential and limitations of the studied approaches and offers recommendations for fine-tuning the accommodation of poverty in law through the right to equality and for promoting a more effective response to poverty and inequality in the country. Lastly, Chapter 9 synthesizes the book's main findings and presents concluding insights drawn from both the theoretical and empirical analyses.

PART I

INEQUALITY AND POVERTY IN THEORY

2

'What's in a Name?' Shakespeare Asked

> *If names be not correct, language is not in accordance with the truth of things. If language be not in accordance with the truth of things, affairs cannot be carried on to success.*
>
> *When affairs cannot be carried on to success, proprieties and music do not flourish. When proprieties and music do not flourish, punishments will not be properly awarded.*
>
> **—The Analects of Confucius, 13:3**[1]

The concepts of 'poverty' and 'equality' do not find a unanimous and single definition in law, economics, and political philosophy. Poverty can refer to monetary thresholds, either absolute or relative. It can also refer to multiple dimensions in which income is but a means of attaining basic needs or even to a subjective definition of what one perceives they are able to afford and economize. Quoting Niels Petersen, 'There is no one "right" way to define poverty'. 'How we define the concept', Petersen argues, 'depends on what we want to know'.[2]

Similarly, while equality has often been discussed with reference to the Aristotelian dictum of treating equals equally, the precise meaning of these words varies significantly. What are the parameters to define one as 'equal', and what does 'equal treatment' mean? Different answers have been proposed. Some propose that equality be limited to equal treatment by the law and before the law. Others argue for a right to substantive equality, including positive measures that equalize historical and structural disadvantages. Equality can refer to equal opportunities, equal results, or a multidimensional definition that includes but goes beyond distributive goods and material disadvantage. In Peter Westen's provocative essay on equality, the principle of equality has

[1] Confucius, *Confucian Analects: The Great Learning, and the Doctrine of the Mean/Translated by James Legge* (Dover Publications 1971), pp 263–264.
[2] Niels Petersen, 'Avoiding the Common-Wisdom Fallacy: The Role of Social Sciences in Constitutional Adjudication' (2013) 11 I-CON 294, p 317.

Judging Poverty and Inequality in Brazil. Tainá Garcia Maia, Oxford University Press. © Tainá Garcia Maia 2026.
DOI: 10.1093/oso/9780198994022.003.0002

even been described as an entirely circular concept and, therefore, 'an empty vessel with no substantive moral content of its own'.[3]

It is not only the conceptualization of equality and poverty that lacks unanimity. The relationship between these two concepts is also disputed. The Indian sociologist André Beteille contends that the relationship between poverty and inequality is 'neither clear nor direct'.[4] These two phenomena may vary independently. Furthermore, they are not per se a marker of the other, they do not change at the same pace, and the policies implemented to tackle one of them may have the opposite effect on the other.[5] Hence, according to Beteille, it is difficult to formulate any meaningful statement about the relationship between the two without clarifying the particular understanding of poverty and inequality being referred to.[6]

Beteille is right: defining these two terms is the first step to analysing their relationship. This chapter discusses the definition of poverty and equality in depth. By analysing the potential and limits of different conceptualizations of the two terms, it provides the basis for understanding the interconnections between them. Furthermore, by exploring the extent to which the very conceptualization of equality allows for the insertion of poverty as a relevant space for realizing equality, it lays a foundation for addressing poverty in law as a matter of equality.

2.1 What is poverty?

On 7 March 2012, *The New York Times* reported that the proportion of people living in extreme poverty fell for the first time in every developing region worldwide from 2005 to 2008.[7] In a year in which the media still discussed the ongoing adverse effects of the Great Recession, *The New York Times* reporter Annie Lawrey was the carrier of more optimistic news, announcing that even 'the biggest recession since the Great Depression seems not to have thrown that trend off course'.[8] Lawrey observed that the progress was so drastic that the United Nations' Millennium Development Goal to cut extreme poverty in half would be reached globally five years before its 2015 deadline.[9]

3 Peter Westen, 'The Empty Idea of Equality' (1982) 95 Harvard Law Review 537, p 547.
4 Andre Beteille, 'Poverty and Inequality' (2003) 38 Economic and Political Weekly 4455, p 4456.
5 See ibid.
6 Ibid, p 4455.
7 Annie Lowrie, 'Dire Poverty Falls Despite Global Slump, Report Finds' *The New York Times* (6 March) <https://www.nytimes.com/2012/03/07/world/extreme-poverty-down-despite-recession-world-bank-data-show.html> accessed 29 August 2021.
8 Ibid.
9 Ibid.

Lawrey was not wrong to qualify the global reduction in the proportion of individuals living in extreme poverty as drastic. In February of the same year, the World Bank issued a press release noting the significant decrease in poverty levels in developing regions and, more broadly, the world from 1981 to 2008. In 1981, 77% of the population of East Asia and the Pacific lived on less than $1.25 a day. By 2008, the headcount poverty ratio had been reduced to 14% of the region's population. Latin America and the Caribbean also experienced a significant reduction in their poverty rate, declining from 14% of the population to 6.5% over the same period. Even excluding China, the change in the poverty level of the so-called developing world is significant: from 41% in 1981 to 25% in 2008.[10]

Progress is even more evident if one considers more recent data from the World Bank, which applies the updated $1.9/day poverty line. In Sub-Saharan Africa, a region where more than half of the population had consistently lived in extreme poverty, the headcount poverty ratio progressed as follows: 55.1% (1990), 60.5% (1995), 48.8% (2008), 43.9% (2012), and 40.4% (2018), representing a reduction of 26.7% from 1990 to 2018.[11] The change is remarkable globally: 1.93 billion people worldwide lived in extreme poverty in 1981, a number that decreased only slightly throughout the 1980s, reaching 1.73 billion people in 1988 before rising again to 1.92 billion people in 1989. In 2008, that number was reduced to 1.24 billion people and further reduced in 2017 to 696.4 million people. In other words, 42.7% of the world's population lived in extreme poverty in 1981, 18.4% in 2008, and 9.3% in 2017.[12]

A less optimistic view is put forth by Thomas Pogge, who warns that a celebration is only due if one thinks in terms of the percentage of the population living below the international poverty line. If this line is raised or one considers the total number of persons living in poverty instead of the proportion of the population living under those conditions, one arrives at a much more austere picture of world poverty.[13] A similar caveat was raised by the World Bank, which noted that the abovementioned numbers on the progress in the fight against poverty become less striking if one adopts a higher poverty line.[14]

[10] World Bank, 'World Bank Sees Progress Against Extreme Poverty, But Flags Vulnerabilities' (2012) <https://www.worldbank.org/en/news/press-release/2012/02/29/world-bank-sees-progress-against-extreme-poverty-but-flags-vulnerabilities> accessed 29 August 2021.

[11] DataBank, 'Poverty and Equity: SubSaharan Africa' (World Bank) <https://databank.worldbank.org/reports.aspx?source=poverty-and-equity-database> accessed by 6 October 2021.

[12] DataBank, 'Poverty and Equity: World' (World Bank) <https://databank.worldbank.org/reports.aspx-?source=poverty-and-equity-database> accessed by 6 October 2021.

[13] Thomas Pogge, 'Poverty, Hunger, and Cosmetic Progress' in Malcolm Langford, Andy Sumner, and Alicia Ely Yamin (eds), *The Millennium Development Goals and Human Rights: Past, Present and Future* (Cambridge University Press 2013).

[14] For instance, $2 a day. See World Bank, 'World Bank Sees Progress Against Extreme Poverty, But Flags Vulnerabilities', *supra* note 10.

Today, a grimmer scenario appears amid the socio-economic effects of the Covid-19 pandemic. In October 2020, the World Bank announced a global increase in extreme poverty for the first time in over twenty years, as the disruption of the pandemic exacerbated the impacts of conflict and climate change, which were already impeding progress in poverty reduction.[15] Rather than seeing extreme poverty decline to 7.9% in 2020, as initially projected had the pandemic not shaken the world, the Bank estimated that 9.1 to 9.4% of the world population was living in extreme poverty in 2020, possibly surpassing the 9.2% rate achieved in 2017.[16] By the end of 2020, an additional 97 million people had been pushed into poverty.[17]

This brief overview of poverty levels worldwide brings to light two key factors for any academic assessment of poverty. First, poverty levels vary according to economic, social, and political phenomena affecting a country, a region, or the globe. Second, the history of global, regional, and national poverty changes according to the definition given to the term. Quoting Juan Carlos Feres and Pablo Vilatoro, 'poverty is a historically determined construct, which means that the standards of what constitutes poverty vary with time'.[18]

The quantitative data from the World Bank presented earlier refers to monetary poverty and, more specifically, to an absolute poverty line. Yet poverty may also be understood in relative terms and even defined in non-monetary terms as a multidimensional concept. In addition, a series of other important choices are decisive to how one presents and understands the evolution of poverty or the efficacy of public policies applied in the fight against poverty. For instance, poverty may be tracked as a percentage of a state's population or the total number of persons living under these conditions. Furthermore, it may be analysed with reference to its incidence or intensity, among other factors.

This section explains how the assessment of the evolution of poverty depends on the threshold adopted to define the term. Section 2.1.1 discusses monetary poverty, and section 2.2.1 examines multidimensional poverty. To illustrate how different definitions of poverty may lead to different conclusions

[15] World Bank, 'COVID-19 to Add as Many as 150 Million Extreme Poor by 2021' (2020) <https://www.worldbank.org/en/news/press-release/2020/10/07/covid-19-to-add-as-many-as-150-million-extreme-poor-by-2021> accessed 29 August 2021. See also World Bank Group, *Poverty and Shared Prosperity 2022: Correcting Course* (Poverty and Shared Prosperity, 2022), pp 4 and 50.

[16] World Bank, 'COVID-19 to Add as Many as 150 Million Poor Extreme by 2021', *supra* note 15.

[17] Daniel Gerszon Mahler and others, *Updated Estimates of the Impact of COVID-19 on Global Poverty: Turning the Corner on the Pandemic in 2021?* (World Bank Blogs 2021).

[18] Juan Carlos Feres and Pablo Villatoro, *A viabilidade de se erradicar a pobreza: uma análise conceitual e metodológica* (Cadernos de Estudos Desenvolvimento Social em Debate 2013), p 11. Translation by the author.

regarding its evolution, the chapter will refer to the case of Brazil and the main definitions and measurements of poverty that have been applied in that state in the last two decades.

The chapter's objective is not to settle on a specific poverty definition as the most adequate and complete. Rather, it aims to critically analyse how poverty may be defined and measured and the potential and limits connected to each conceptualization. Given the book's object, it is essential to comprehend the different conceptualizations of poverty, many of which have been employed by different courts at different times. Even one single court may rely on diverse measurements of poverty throughout its case law, as Chapters 6 and 7 will explain.

2.1.1 Poverty lines

Poverty lines are unidimensional measures that define a threshold for poverty. Persons who fall below a certain level (or, in other words, who fall below the line) are considered poor. Accordingly, the minimum level above which one is considered free of poverty is called a 'poverty line'.[19]

Every poverty line is based on a particular variable. Hence, a key question to understanding the meaning of a poverty line is to ask what dimensions that line measures. For example, is it based on the level of consumption, income, or another indicator? Does it refer to the income of the household or of the individual? The choices of a unit of analysis, which may vary in different indexes, reflect differences in the conceptualization of poverty, leading to very different results and conclusions.

2.1.1.1 International lines for monetary poverty

The World Bank sets a global poverty rate taking into consideration the costs of living, including basic food, clothing, and shelter.[20] In 1990, it introduced the global poverty threshold, also called the International Poverty Line (IPL), of US$1 per day at 1985 purchasing power parity (PPP). The $1 per day value was reached based on a study by Martin Ravallion, Gaurav Datt, and Dominique van de Walle. The three researchers compiled national poverty lines for thirty-three developing countries. Dean Jollife and Espen Beer Prydz, members of

[19] See Marcelo Medeiros, *Medidas de Desigualdade e Pobreza* (EdUNB 2012), cap 7: Mensuração da Pobreza: o ponto de partida.

[20] World Bank, 'FAQs: Global Poverty Line Update' (2015) <https://www.worldbank.org/en/topic/poverty/brief/global-poverty-line-faq> accessed 29 August 2021.

the Development Economics Research Group of the World Bank at the time, explained in a 2016 World Bank policy paper that the abovementioned compilation suggested that six of the lower lines of these thirty-three states were near a common value: that of one US dollar.[21] This absolute line became the basis for the first Millennium Development Goal, that is, '[t]o halve, by the year 2015, the proportion of the world's people whose income is less than one dollar a day and the proportion of people who suffer from hunger and, by the same date, to halve the proportion of people who are unable to reach or to afford safe drinking water'.[22]

Around the end of the first decade of the 2000s, Ravallion, Chen, and Sangraula made an enlarged compilation covering eighty-eight developing economies and gathering seventy-four national poverty lines with complete data. As expected, the study showed that more affluent countries had a higher national poverty line. On the other hand, the poverty lines of the fifteen poorest countries[23] did not appear to be correlated with average national wealth. This was interpreted as suggesting the existence of a line, or threshold, of absolute minimum needs among the poorest countries.[24] The average value of the national poverty lines of these fifteen countries was US$1.25 per day at 2005 PPP. These findings indicated that the concept of absolute poverty (ie poverty defined through a line based on a constant real value, which the study identified as $1.25/day) was more relevant in poor countries, while relative poverty (which varies according to a comparative variable, such as the mean or median income or consumption pattern) was more significant in middle- and high-income countries.[25]

By 2008, the World Bank used US$1.25 per day at 2005 PPP as the global line for poverty. In 2015, the line was updated to US$1.90 per day at 2011 PPP.[26] In September 2022, considering the study of new data from low-income countries and the median of the national poverty lines of twenty-eight of the world's poorest countries in 2017 PPPs, the World Bank updated the US$1.90

[21] Dean Jollife and Espen Beer Pryds, *Estimating International Poverty Lines from Comparable National Thresholds* (Policy Research Working Paper 7606, 2016). See also World Bank, *World Development Report 1990: Poverty* (World Development Indicators, 1990), p 27.

[22] UNGA, 'United Nations Millennium Declaration', Resolution 55/2, 8 September 2000.

[23] Those countries were Malawi, Mali, Ethiopia, Sierra Leone, Niger, Uganda, Gambia, Rwanda, Guinea-Bissau, Tanzania, Tajikistan, Mozambique, Chad, Nepal, and Ghana. They all had personal consumption expenditure per capita of less than $60 per month.

[24] Cf Jollife and Espen Beer Pryds, *supra* note 21.

[25] Martin Ravallion, Shaohua Chen, and Sangraula Prem, 'Dollar a Day Revisited' (2009) 2 The World Bank Economic Review 163, p 164.

[26] See Francisco Ferreira, Dean Mitchell Jolliffe, and Espen Beer Prydz, *The International Poverty Line Has Just Been raised to $1.90 a Day, But Global Poverty is Basically Unchanged. How is That Even Possible?* (World Bank Blogs 2015).

line (2011 PPP) to US$2.15 (2017 PPP).[27] Almost three years later, in June 2025, the IPL was updated once again, reaching US$3.00 at 2021 PPP. This last update reflected changes in price levels across the world and improvements in data on the costs of basic food, clothing, and shelter needs in low-income countries.[28]

From 2017 onwards, the World Bank constructed an additional poverty line based on the income level of countries. Marta Schoch, Christoph Lakner, and Samuel Freije-Rodrigues, from the World Bank, explain this change as rooted in the fact that the IPL was first constructed when 60% of the world population lived in low-income countries. At that point in history, constructing a poverty line based on the national lines of some of the world's poorest economies was a meaningful measurement for a large portion of the world's population.[29] However, by 2017, the situation had significantly changed: 86% of the world's population lived in lower-middle-income or upper-middle-income countries, and only about 9% lived in low-income countries, making the IPL an insufficient single measurement of poverty worldwide.[30] In this context, a need emerged to complement the IPL. Quoting Schoch et al, '[p]overty does not end when a household crosses the US$1.90 per person per day International Poverty Line'.[31] While, formally, extreme poverty does end at that point, measuring the number of persons living in (non-extreme) poverty or remaining vulnerable to returning to extreme poverty remains important.

Hence, the World Bank created three different poverty lines based on income. These were: US$3.20 per day, US$5.50 per day, and US$21.70 per day at 2011 PPP per capita for states with medium-low, medium-high, and high incomes, respectively. In September 2022 and later again in June 2025, the lines for lower-middle and upper-middle income were updated. Today, the poverty line for lower-middle and upper-middle income are US$4.20 per day and US$8.30 per day at 2021 PPP, respectively.[32] These lines establish a threshold for poverty to be applied equally to all countries that belong to

[27] World Bank, 'Fact Sheet: An Adjustment to Global Poverty Lines' (2022) <https://www.worldbank.org/en/news/factsheet/2022/05/02/fact-sheet-an-adjustment-to-global-poverty-lines#3> accessed 13 February 2023.

[28] World Bank, 'June 2025 Update to Global Poverty Lines' (2025) <https://www.worldbank.org/en/news/factsheet/2025/06/05/june-2025-update-to-global-poverty-lines> accessed 18 August 2025.

[29] Marta Schoch, Christoph Lakner, and Samuel Freije-Rodriguez, *Monitoring Poverty at the US$3.20 and US$5.50 Lines: Differences and Similarities with Extreme Poverty Trends* (World Bank Blogs 2020).

[30] Ibid. In 2017, 41% of the world's population lived in lower-middle-income countries, and 35% in upper-middle-income countries.

[31] Ibid.

[32] Deon Filmer, Haishan Fu, and Luis Felipe López-Calva, *Further Strengthening How We Measure Global Poverty* (World Bank Blogs 2025); Federica Alfani and others, *June 2025 Update to the Poverty and Inequality Platform (PIP)* (Global Poverty Monitoring Technical Note, 2025).

each income group. As such, they are still absolute lines. The Bank classifies Brazil as an upper-middle-income economy, which means that the applicable poverty line based on Brazil's income was US$5.50 per day (2011 PPP) until September 2022, and was subsequently increased first to US$6.85 per day (2017 PPP) and then to US$8.30 per day (2021 PPP).[33]

The World Bank's poverty lines coexist with other international and national poverty lines. For example, the Organisation for Economic Co-operation and Development (OECD) measures poverty as the ratio of people living with less than half the median household income of the total population.[34] The OECD measure is comparative in nature and linked to distributive justice. In other words, it measures relative poverty.

2.1.1.2 National lines for monetary poverty

The IPL is used primarily for tracking global extreme poverty and measuring progress on global goals set by the World Bank and its development partners, including the United Nations (UN). When the measurement of poverty aims to provide a basis for policy dialogue or the design of targeted programmes to reach the poorest, the World Bank asserts that national poverty lines are 'far more appropriate'.[35]

Marcelo Medeiros argues that the choice of variables used to define a poverty line is not an overzealous detail, but rather a crucial decision. After all, 'different measures may lead to completely different conclusions'.[36] Medeiros perceives the choice as a reflection of moral values that may lead to very different anti-poverty policies.[37] Sometimes, a country may institute several measures to fight poverty, each with a different objective. Different measurements of poverty may thus be necessary to provide each programme with adequate tools to monitor its effectiveness and impact on the target population. In other words, different poverty lines may be required for different strategies. Medeiros provides a very clear illustration of this situation:

> A policy aimed at reducing the intensity of poverty may distribute resources equally among the poor; [on the other hand,] a policy that aims at reducing the incidence of poverty must, necessarily, prioritize the less poor; if [. . .] [the aim is tackling] the

[33] World Bank, 'World Bank Country and Lending Groups. Country Classification' <https://datahelpdesk.worldbank.org/knowledgebase/articles/906519> accessed 31 August 2021.

[34] OECD, 'Poverty Rate' <https://data.oecd.org/inequality/poverty-rate.htm> accessed 31 August 2021.

[35] World Bank, 'Fact Sheet: An Adjustment to Global Poverty Lines', *supra* note 27.

[36] Medeiros (2012), *supra* note 19. Translation by the author. See also Paulo de Martino Jannuzzi, *Indicadores Socioeconômicos na Gestão Pública* (Universidade Federal de Santa Catarina 2009); Ministério do Desenvolvimento Social e Combate à Fome, *Questões metodológicas acerca do dimensionamento da extrema pobreza no Brasil nos anos 2000. Estudo técnico No 08/2014* (MDS 2014).

[37] Medeiros (2012), *supra* note 19, p 157. Translation by the author.

greatest severity of extreme poverty, this policy should prioritize the poorest [in the society].[38]

The link between national poverty lines and anti-poverty policies is clear in the case of Brazil. In June 2011, the Brazilian federal government, headed by President Dilma Rousseff, launched the plan 'Brazil without Extreme Poverty' (BwEP).[39] The BwEP was instituted through Decree 7,492 (2011), with the aim of eradicating extreme poverty in Brazil.[40] Yet, to attain this aim and launch adequate public policies, the BwEP had first to define extreme poverty.

Extreme poverty was defined under Decree 7,492 as a monthly income equal to or below 70 Brazilian *Reais* (R$) per capita. This national line for extreme poverty was updated in 2014,[41] 2016,[42] and 2018, reaching R$89.00/month per capita. It was used between 2011 and 2021 to establish eligibility for social benefits for extreme poverty included in the Programme *Bolsa Família* (PBF).[43] Hence, to simplify the language, the lines for extreme poverty and poverty determining eligibility for the PBF will be referred to hereinafter as the '*Bolsa Família* lines' (or PBF lines).

The Programme *Bolsa Família*, translated by the International Labour Organization (ILO) as 'Family Grant',[44] is a government programme of conditional cash transfers, created in 2004, directed towards families living in extreme poverty or poverty in Brazil. Under the programme, poverty was defined as twice the value of extreme poverty. When the BwEP was launched setting the extreme poverty line at R$70 per month, the PBF poverty line was at R$140 per month. The latter was updated in 2014, 2016, and 2018, reaching R$178 per month per capita.[45]

At its creation, the national line for extreme poverty established under the BwEP set a threshold 10% higher than the World Bank's IPL: while the PBF line for extreme poverty was R$70 in 2011, the then-applicable US$1.25 per day (2005 PPP) was equivalent to R$67.[46] However, as the 2010s unfolded,

[38] Ibid.

[39] In the original, 'Brasil sem Miséria'.

[40] Brazil, 'Decree No. 7,492', Plan Brazil without Extreme Poverty, 2 June 2011.

[41] To R$77.00.

[42] To R$85.00.

[43] As Chapter 5 will explain in more detail, the PBF was created in 2003, extinguished in early November 2021 (around the final year of the Bolsonaro government), and reinstituted in early March 2023, approximately two months after the end of the Bolsonaro mandate.

[44] Janine Berg, *Brazil. Conditional transfers as response to the Crisis: the Bolsa Família Programme* (ILO Notes on the Crisis, 2009).

[45] Brazil, 'Decree No. 5,209', 17 September 2004, Article 18.

[46] Tereza Campello, Tiago Falcão, and Patrícia Vieira da Costa (Org), *O Brasil sem Miséria* (MDS 2014), p 75. See also Giordano Benites Tronco and Marília Patta Ramos, 'Linhas de pobreza no Plano Brasil Sem Miséria: análise crîtica e proposta de alternativas para a medição da pobreza conforme metodologia de Sonia Rocha' (2017) 51 Revista de Administração Pública 294.

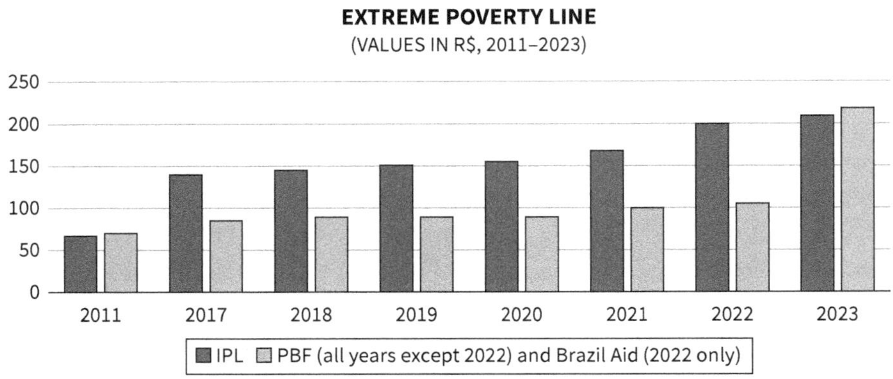

Fig 2.1 Comparison of values (in R$) of the IPL and the PBF and Brazil Aid lines of extreme poverty (2011–2023)

Source: Based on data from: MDS 2014 and SIS 2018–2024/IBGE (for the IPL); Decree No 7,492 (2011), Law No 14,284 (2021), and Law No 14,601(2023) (for the PBF and Brazil Aid line).[a]

[a] The table compiles the historical values applicable in each year to the IPL, PBF, and Brazil Aid programmes. Detailed information on the sources and methodology used in preparing each figure and table in this book is available in the supplementary material uploaded to the data repository of the University of Münster: <https://data-management.uni-muenster.de/datastore>.

the situation became significantly inverted. Under the Brazilian Institute of Geography and Statistics' (IBGE) calculations, US$1.90 per day (2011 PPP) was equivalent to R$151 in 2019.[47] Nonetheless, the PBF line for extreme poverty remained R$89. This represents a significant discrepancy and leads, as Medeiros had estimated *in abstracto*, to very different conclusions concerning the state of poverty in Brazil. See Figure 2.1, in which the Y axis refers to the values of the poverty lines in Brazilian currency (*Reais*, R$) to allow for comparison from 2011 (the year of the promulgation of Decree 7,492) to 2023.

In August 2021, during the third year of the Bolsonaro government and amid the Covid-19 pandemic, an executive measure announced the discontinuation of the PBF and its replacement by the Programme *Auxílio Brasil* (in English, 'Brazil Aid').[48] Four days before the measure entered into force, the government increased the lines for extreme poverty and poverty of the PBF to R$100 and R$200, respectively.[49] Despite the adjustment, the national line for extreme poverty still lagged behind the IPL, which was equivalent to R$168 in 2021 according to the IBGE's calculations.[50] These values continued to be

[47] IBGE, *Síntese de Indicadores Sociais: Uma Análise das Condições de Vida da População Brasileira 2020* (Estudos & Pesquisas Informação demográfica e socioeconômica, 2020), p 64, Quadro 1.

[48] Brazil, 'Provisional Measure No. 1,061', 9 August 2021.

[49] Brazil, 'Decree No. 10,851', 5 November 2021; Brazil, 'Decree No. 10,852', 8 November 2021.

[50] IBGE, *Síntese de Indicadores Sociais: Uma Análise das Condições de Vida da População Brasileira 2022* (Estudos & Pesquisas Informação demográfica e socioeconômica, 2022), p 61, Table 6.

used during the Covid-19 pandemic to determine eligibility for Brazil Aid until March 2022, when they were updated to R$105 for extreme poverty and R$210 for poverty.[51]

It was only in 2023 that Brazil's national line for extreme poverty once again surpassed the IPL. This occurred through Provisional Measure No 1,164 (2023), enacted in the first semester of Lula's third non-consecutive mandate, following his 2022 electoral victory over Jair Bolsonaro. The measure reinstated the *Bolsa Família* programme, discontinued the short-lived Brazil Aid Programme, and introduced a single monetary threshold for being entitled to the PBF benefit: a family income equal to or less than R$ 218,00 per capita.[52] For comparison purposes, the IPL was equivalent to R$209.00 in 2023.[53]

In addition to the PBF lines for poverty and extreme poverty, it is important to note two other absolute lines set out by the state. Law No 8,742 (1993), known as the Organic Law for Social Assistance (LOAS), regulates access to a programme of unconditional cash transfers (hereinafter called the Continuous Cash Benefit Programme[54] (BPC)) to older persons[55] and persons with disabilities living below a certain monetary line. The BPC's target group are individuals belonging to these two groups who do not have the necessary economic means to maintain themselves or their families.[56] The LOAS adopted the monetary line of family income equal to or less than a quarter of the minimum wage per capita to determine the specific beneficiaries of the BPC. In 2025, the minimum wage in Brazil was R$1,518.00. Therefore, under the 2025 parameters, families eligible for the BPC were those living on R$379.50 or less a month per capita. The line adopted by the BPC is thus higher than the PBF poverty line (R$218.00). Hence, more people will be classified as poor in Brazil if one adopts the BPC line rather than the PBF line, as the latter stood in the 2018 update. At the time of the creation of the BwEP, the opposite was the case in the comparison between the two lines.[57]

[51] Brazil, 'Decree No. 11,013', 29 March 2022.

[52] Families receiving more than this but less than half the minimum wage/month per capita can still receive the benefit for twenty-four months, a period in which the benefit will be reduced to 50% of its value. Brazil, 'Law No. 14,601', 19 June 2023, Article 6.

[53] IBGE, *Síntese de Indicadores Sociais: Uma Análise das Condições de Vida da População Brasileira 2024* (Estudos & Pesquisas Informação demográfica e socioeconômica, 2024), p 53, Table 5.

[54] In the original language, 'Benefício de Prestação Continuada'.

[55] In this book, the term 'older persons' is preferred in relation to the 'elderly'.

[56] Together with the *Bolsa Família*, the BPC is one of the most important federal programmes of social assistance against poverty. As the Brazilian Secretary Office for Evaluation and Information Management (SAGI) indicates, 13.1 million people were beneficiaries of social assistance programmes in Brazil in 2019. Out of those, 74.3% received the *Bolsa Família*, 22% received the BPC, and the remaining 3.7% were beneficiaries of other programmes.

[57] In 2011, a quarter of the minimum wage was equivalent to R$136.25, while the poverty line established for the purposes of the *Bolsa Família* was R$140.00.

Finally, the Brazilian government maintains a registry of low-income Brazilian households, which is called *Cadastro Único* (literally translated to 'Single Register'). The per capita threshold for inclusion in the *Cadastro Único* is half the minimum wage per capita.[58] The Brazilian government explains that the *Cadastro Único* allows it to 'know who the low-income families in Brazil are and how they live' and operationalize social assistance programmes, including the PBF.[59] The IBGE's Summary of Social Indicators (SIS) explicitly recognizes the *Cadastro Único* threshold of half the minimum wage as a national poverty line, along with the PBF and BPC lines.[60]

Figure 2.2 compares the values of each of these poverty lines (in R$) from 2011 to 2023. It shows that the threshold for accessing the BPC largely coincides with the World Bank's poverty line for lower-medium-income countries. The *Cadastro Único* line (half the minimum wage) surpasses all other poverty lines depicted in Figure 2.2 and is now virtually identical to the World Bank's poverty line for higher-medium-income countries. In contrast, the PBF line showed less responsiveness to new social and economic conditions, as indicated by its flatter trajectory compared to the other lines. Its 'responsiveness lag' persisted until March 2023, when Provisional Measure No 1,164 (2023) was enacted. While the updated PBF poverty line surpasses the value of the IPL, as converted by the IBGE (see Figure 2.1), the PBF line remains the lowest among the poverty lines presented in Figure 2.2.

The poverty lines examined so far in this chapter refer to monetary poverty, that is, monetary measurements of poverty. These measurements track the level of income or consumption and set a line that serves as the threshold for characterizing a situation of poverty. Common measures of monetary poverty are the incidence and intensity of poverty, although a myriad of other measures also exist.[61] Monetary concepts of poverty coexist with (and arguably complement) non-monetary conceptualizations of poverty, or multidimensional poverty. The latter is the subject of section 2.1.2.

[58] gov.br, 'Inscrever-se no Cadastro Único' (2021) <https://www.gov.br/pt-br/servicos/inscrever-se-no-cadastro-unico-para-programas-sociais-do-governo-federal> accessed 30 August 2021. The target groups of the *Cadastro Único* are: (i) those that have a monthly income of up to half the minimum wage per capita (ie R$550,00); (ii) those that have a total household income of up to three minimum wages per month (R$3.300,00); (iii) homeless persons living in the streets; and (iv) persons that are applying for a social benefit or social service that requires registration in the *Cadastro Único*.

[59] Ibid.

[60] See IBGE, *Síntese de Indicadores Sociais: Uma Análise das Condições de Vida da População Brasileira 2017* (Estudos & Pesquisas Informação demográfica e socioeconômica, 2017), p 63, Table 1; IBGE, *SIS 2020*, *supra* note 47, p 64, Figure 1.

[61] Medeiros (2012), *supra* note 19, p 156.

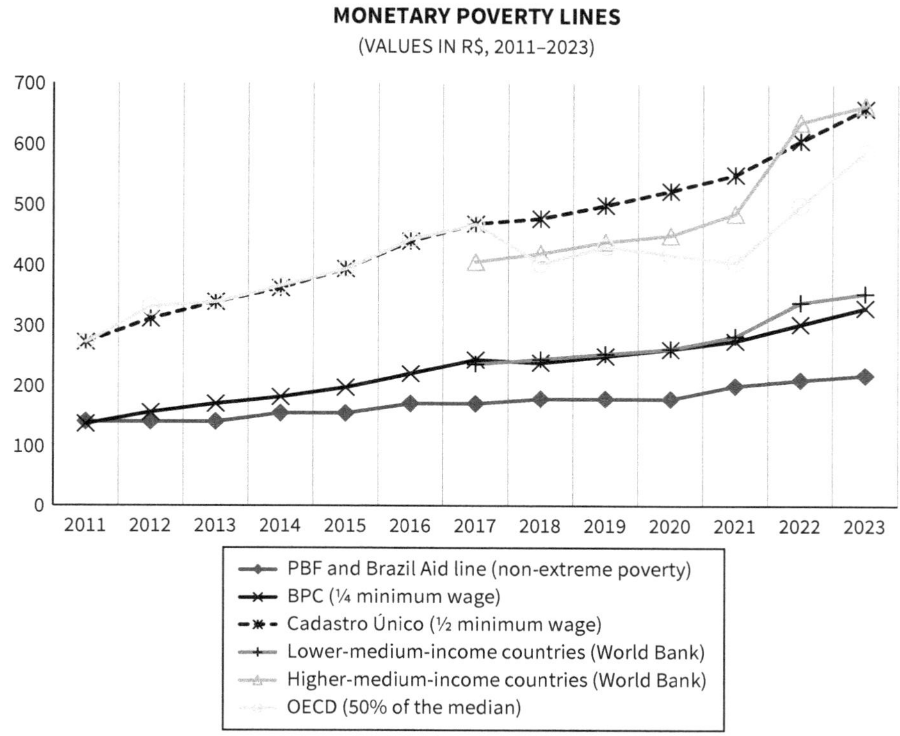

Fig 2.2 Comparison of (non-extreme) poverty lines (2011–2023)

Source: Based on data from: Decree No 5,209 (2004), Law No 14,284 (2021), and Law No 14,601(2023) (for the PBF and Brazil Aid line); IPEA (for the lines calculated based on the minimum wage); and SIS 2012–2024/IBGE (for the OEDC line and the World Bank lines).[a]

[a]The lower-medium-income poverty line and the higher-medium-income poverty line were only created in 2017 by the World Bank. Hence, that year marks their starting point in this figure.

2.1.2 Multidimensional poverty

In *Development as Freedom*, Amartya Sen discusses poverty as a capability deprivation. He argues for an understanding of poverty as 'the deprivation of basic capabilities', that is, deprivations of the substantive freedoms an individual enjoys to lead the kind of life they have reason to value.[62] While income is a relevant indicator of poverty, Sen notes that it is but a means to generate capabilities. In his words, income 'is only *instrumentally* significant'.[63] Instead of focusing on the means, the capability approach shifts attention to 'ends that

[62] Amartya Sen, *Development as Freedom* (Random House 1999), p 87.
[63] Ibid.

people have reason to pursue, and correspondingly, to the freedoms to be able to satisfy these ends'.[64]

To illustrate his theory, Sen notes that certain groups of people have less ability to earn an income. He provides the examples of disabled persons and older persons. I add to his example the experience of persons of colour, women, and trans people, who face not physical but socially constructed obstacles to earning an income in many societies. In addition, these groups may face more difficulties in converting income into capabilities. A person with a disability may need more income for medical treatment, for example.[65] And, here I add, groups particularly oppressed in society may, for instance, need more income to receive a level of education that would allow them to compensate for scarcity of social capital and/or overcome societal symbols that represent them as poor candidates for certain types of work.

As these examples show, poverty may be more intense than statistical data on income might reveal. Additionally, certain groups may face significant deprivations in their ability to lead a good life, despite having an income above the IPL. Sen illustrates this with the premature mortality of African American men and women in the United States of America (US).[66] Level of income may also be insufficient to explain or tackle significant deprivations. An example is the preference for boys in the allocation of household resources, including food and health care.[67]

In *Development as Freedom*, Sen does not propose an aggregated measure of deprivations. Instead, he analyses features of deprivation of basic capabilities, such as premature mortality, undernourishment, and illiteracy. However, indexes on multidimensional poverty have emerged since his book was published.

Adriana Stankiewicz Serra, Gaston Isaias Yalonetzky, and Walter Belik explain that, while we find consensus on the multidimensional character of poverty, the same does not occur with how we should measure it.[68] One method to identify poverty as a multidimensional concept has been the measurement of deprivations. This is exemplified by the global Multidimensional Poverty Index (MPI), an international measure of acute multidimensional poverty developed by the Oxford Poverty and Human Development Initiative (OPHI)

[64] Ibid, p 90.
[65] Ibid, p 88.
[66] Ibid, p 96.
[67] Ibid, pp 88–89.
[68] Adriana Stankiewicz Serra, Gaston Isaias Yalonetzky, and Walter Belik, 'Pobreza Multidimensional no Brasil, 2000/2010' (45o Encontro Nacional de Economia - ANPEC), p 3.

together with the United National Development Programme (UNDP). The index was presented by Sabina Alkire and Maria Emma Santos and follows the methodology proposed by Alkire and James Foster. The MPI is based on three dimensions (health, education, and living standards) and ten indicators.[69] The Index was first developed in 2010 for the UNDP's flagship Human Development Reports.[70] In 2018, the two institutions responsible for developing the MPI revised and unified its methodology.[71] The UNDP observes that, today, the index is expected to be updated at least once a year to include newly published data.[72]

Inspired by the MPI, the World Bank developed the Multidimensional Poverty Measure (MPM), which goes beyond (but also considers) monetary poverty. This index differs from the MPI developed by OPHI and the UNDP because it includes the IPL as one of its dimensions. Its dimensions are education (measured by educational enrolment and completion of primary education), basic infrastructure (measured by access to sanitation, electricity, and drinking water), and the monetary headcount ratio at the global poverty line.[73]

Ravallion, whom the readers will remember as one of the authors of the studies that guided the World Bank in establishing the IPL, also conducted work on multidimensional indexes of poverty. In a World Bank Policy Research Working Paper from 2011, he recognizes that poverty is multidimensional and agrees it is possible to form what he calls 'mashup indices'.[74] However, the provocative question he presents is 'whether it is useful to do so'.[75]

Ravallion argues that the answer to that question is negative. First, this is because of the limited number of dimensions selected for the MPI. Second, there is no consensus on how the different dimensions that compose such an index should be weighted. To quote the author,

> '[w]e can all agree that reducing child mortality is a hugely important development goal, but how can one contend—as the Alkire-Santos index does, for example—that

[69] Nutrition; child mortality; years of schooling; school attendance; cooking fuel; sanitation; drinking water; electricity; housing; and assets. For more information, see OPHI, 'Global Multidimensional Poverty Index' (*Oxford Poverty & Human Development Initiative*) <https://ophi.org.uk/multidimensional-poverty-index/> accessed 31 August 2021.

[70] UNDP, 'Frequently Asked Questions—Multidimensional Poverty Index (MPI)' <http://hdr.undp.org/en/faq-page/multidimensional-poverty-index-mpi#t410n3222> accessed 6 September 2021.

[71] Ibid.

[72] Ibid.

[73] World Bank, 'Multidimensional Poverty Measure' <https://www.worldbank.org/en/topic/poverty/brief/multidimensional-poverty-measure> accessed 31 August 2021.

[74] Martin Ravallion, *On Multidimensional Indeces of Poverty* (Policy Research Working Paper 5580, 2011), p 3.

[75] Ibid.

avoiding the death of a child is equivalent to alleviating the combined deprivations of having a dirt floor, cooking with wood, and not having a radio, TV, telephone, bike or car?'.[76]

Ravallion thus advocates for a set of multiple indices (such as the model adopted for the United Nations' Millenium Development Goals) rather than a single multidimensional index.[77] In other words, he argues for a 'dashboard' approach to multidimensional poverty.

Regardless of which approach is used to measure multidimensional poverty—be it the dashboard approach or an index—the central notion behind this concept is that the measurement of income or consumption levels is insufficient to capture the phenomenon of poverty. As Paulo de Martino Jannuzzi, Enrico Moreira Martignoni, and Baiena Feijolo Souto explain, this analytical perspective allows for the consideration of dimensions that are structurally connected to poverty.[78] Income, which is one of these dimensions, can be understood as a consequence of the other structural dimensions.[79]

In conclusion, poverty may be defined in different ways. It may be conceptualized as referring only to monetary thresholds or to multiple dimensions. When conceptualized as monetary, it may be defined by establishing an absolute poverty line (eg the IPL, the PBF line, the BPC line, and the *Cadastro Único* line) or in relative terms (eg the OECD line). When conceptualized as multidimensional, it may be assessed as a dashboard or an index that compounds and quantifies selected dimensions. Different conceptualizations and the choice of different units of measurement often lead to very different results and conclusions about the state of poverty in a certain region or state.

This multiplicity of conceptualizations is not in itself a weakness of the definition of poverty, as different definitions serve different purposes, such as guiding the development of anti-poverty policies that focus on the intensity of poverty or assessing the effectiveness of an anti-poverty policy aiming at reducing the incidence of poverty. What is necessary is that administrators, researchers, and other agents engaging with the phenomenon of poverty, including courts, be mindful of the choices they make when adopting a certain conceptualization. One must consider the purpose and limitations of

[76] Ibid, p 16.
[77] Ibid, p 17.
[78] Paulo de Martino Jannuzzi, Enrico Moreira Martignoni, and Baiena Feijolo Souto, 'Programa Bolsa Família e sua contribuição para redução da pobreza no Brasil' (2012) 4 Revista Brasileira de Monitoramento e Avaliação, p 44.
[79] Ibid, p 44.

the adopted conceptualization and exercise caution when comparing results and conclusions reached by other agents, who may have adopted a different conceptualization.

2.2 What is equality?

In 1982, Peter Westen wrote that the definition of equality as treating likes alike is empty of content.[80] First, it does not clarify who should be considered alike. If the expression 'being alike' refers to complete identity in each and every respect, it excludes every human being from its application, because no one is alike another person in every aspect. On the other hand, if it is understood as referring to people who are alike in some respects and different in others, it includes every person in the world and accordingly leads to absolute egalitarianism. Second, as with the definition of who should be considered 'alike', the definition of a 'like treatment' for the purposes of the principle of equality is similarly fuzzy. The likeness of treatments demands the establishment of standards of comparison or, in the words of Westen, 'reference to some moral rule'.[81] In this sense, Westen claims that equality is entirely circular—in other words, a simple tautology.[82]

Westen is correct to indicate that applying the Aristotelian principle of treating likes alike demands the incorporation of external standards that specify the comparisons inherent to a discussion of equality. Different theories of justice have attempted to provide these standards and accordingly specify the content of equality.

This section discusses three contributions to the conceptualizations of equality. The first is the delimitation of spaces for the application of equality, proposed by Amartya Sen. The next is the identification of classifications historically associated with discrimination, marginalization, and oppression, such as gender and race. Lastly, the section discusses the content of equality by distinguishing between formal and substantive equality. It brings forth Iris Marion Young's analysis of forms of oppression and proposes that the multidimensional concept of oppression provides a relevant tool for transcending the limits of understanding inequality solely in terms of material disadvantage.

80 Westen (1982), *supra* note 3.
81 Ibid, p 547.
82 Ibid, pp 547–548.

2.2.1 Delimiting spaces in the formula 'treating likes alike': equality of what?

Human beings are diverse from each other in their personal characteristics. Furthermore, each is subject to different constraints and opportunities derived from the social and natural environment in which they live or have lived. Because they are subject to different external and personal characteristics, different persons and groups face different opportunities and obstacles in their lives and have different needs. In this context, not only do the conditions of life among different individuals vary, but so does their capability to convert the same resources into well-being.[83] For example, the same income level might not allow for the same capabilities—such as leading a healthy life, freedom to take part in cultural life, achieving mobility—to a person with a serious illness compared to a healthy person.

This variation of comparative advantages and disadvantages among individuals can be assessed and judged through a myriad of variables. In other words, human diversity—covering both natural and socially constructed differences—implies a broad range of focal variables to evaluate equality.[84] In the example above, if income is set as the variable to evaluate whether equal treatment is provided to a person with a serious illness compared to a healthy person, the conclusion would be that both are subject to the same treatment. However, if the focal variable switches to capabilities, the answer would differ. Understanding equality thus demands answering the question of 'equality in which respects' or 'equality of what?'.

Equality may refer to an infinite list of variables—income, wealth, happiness, autonomy, access to basic goods, level of schooling, or any other parameter. Different theories focus on different parameters or, in the words of Sen, on the choice of 'space' in which the subjects are compared. In *Inequality Reexamined*, Sen argues that the qualification of a proposition as egalitarian demands the delimitation of a space. He contends that all enduring normative theories of social arrangements are necessarily egalitarian in certain aspects and inegalitarian in others. Quoting the Nobel Prize laureate in Economic Sciences, '[t]he justification of inequality in some features is made to rest

[83] Cf Amartya Sen, *Inequality Reexamined* (Oxford University Press 1992), pp 19–20. Similarly, the diversity in resources and vulnerabilities among groups and individuals implies that even rights may empower different social groups in different ways, 'depending upon their ability to enact the power that a right potentially entails', as Wendy Brown explains. See Wendy Brown, 'Suffering Rights as Paradoxes' (2000) 7 Constellations 230, p 232.

[84] See Sen (1992), *supra* note 83, p 20.

on the equality of some other feature, taken to be more basic in that ethical system'.[85] Accordingly, Sen concludes, 'the battle is not, in an important sense, about 'why equality?', but about 'equality of what?'.[86] Income-egalitarians call for equal income, welfare-egalitarians call for equal welfare levels, pure libertarians—as Sen calls them—call for equality of liberty, and so on. In each case, the demand for equality in the space qualified as central is accompanied by the acceptance of inequality in what is taken as a more remote 'peripherical' space.[87] Hence, Sen's conclusion that '[t]he disputes reside ultimately in locating the central social arrangement'.[88]

Guided by the same understanding, Norberto Bobbio contends that an assessment of equality implies an analysis of three aspects: first, the subjects among whom a distribution takes place; second, the benefits or obligations to be shared; and third, the criteria by which those benefits or obligations are to be shared.[89] Based on these criteria, various outcomes may be proposed, all of which, Bobbio argues, could be named egalitarian. At one extreme, he identifies the maximalist egalitarian principle, which he calls egalitarianist and which reflects a rigid conceptualization of formal equality as granting the same to everyone. Doctrines not located at the egalitarianist limit can be more or less egalitarian. Bobbio proposes that the degree to which a doctrine is egalitarian should be assessed based on the number of subjects involved, the quantity and worth of the benefits to be distributed, and the criteria used.[90]

In summary, an equality analysis demands establishing a 'space'. This delimitation provides content to equality and allows for its assessment. A good illustration of the relevance of choosing spaces and the impact of this choice on an investigation is found on the very object of this book. When the chosen space is income, the interconnections between poverty and inequality are clear, but they are also limited. The income space unveils a clear interconnection

[85] Ibid, p 19. This statement is further explained by Sen on p 21: 'If a claim that inequality in some significant space is right (or good, or acceptable, or tolerable) is to be defended by reason (not by, say, shooting the dissenters), the argument takes the form of showing this inequality to be a consequence of equality in some other—more centrally important—space. Given the broad agreement on the need to have equality in the "base", and also the connection of that broad agreement with this deep need for impartiality between individuals (discussed earlier), the crucial arguments have to be about the reasonableness of the "bases" chosen. Thus, the question: "equality of what?" is, in this context, not materially different from the enquiry: "what is the right space for basal equality?" The answer we give to "equality of what?" will not only endorse equality in that chosen space (the focal variable being related to the demands of basal equality), but will have far-reaching consequences on the distributional patterns (including necessary inequalities) in the other spaces. "Equality of what?" is indeed a momentous—and central—question.'

[86] Ibid, p 16.

[87] Ibid, preface p x.

[88] Ibid.

[89] Norberto Bobbio, 'Igualdade e desigualdade' in *Direita e Esquerda: razões e significados de uma distinção política* (UNESP 2001).

[90] Ibid, point 1.

between poverty cycles and disproportionate impacts on vulnerable income groups. Take, for example, the World Bank assessment of the impact of the Covid-19 pandemic on poverty levels in thirteen countries across Latin America and the Caribbean, Europe, and Central Asia. The World Bank identified large income losses among the bottom 40% of the population in these countries during the pandemic, reaching an average of a quarter of their income between 2019 and 2020 in some states, such as Peru and Colombia.[91] Furthermore, across countries, it found a correlation between larger initial losses in employment and slow recoveries, on the one hand, and gender and level of education, on the other.[92] Accordingly, the report shows that poverty cycles and poverty triggers do not affect all equally. Instead, they may disproportionately impact vulnerable groups, including the bottom-income groups. This case illustrates how the space of income may unveil vulnerabilities and related inequalities. However, that space remains limited for the purposes of an assessment of the interconnections between poverty and inequality. First, it focuses on income and capital distribution only. Second, one may find a state without absolute poverty but with a very high level of economic inequality. On the other extreme, one might find a state with very high levels of absolute poverty but very low levels of inequality based on income and capital.

When the choice of space shifts from income to an individual's freedom to lead their life, further interconnections between the two concepts are brought to light. Extreme poverty generally reduces the opportunities for achieving well-being in a significant manner. Poverty limits the real opportunities for a person to choose a job with adequate safety standards, live in suitable housing, and choose to continue their studies, among other choices on what to do or to be.[93] In other words, access to spaces that, taken together, impact one's well-being is granted differently to poor individuals compared to individuals not living in poverty. These limitations on the freedom to lead one's life are brought to the spotlight when the choice of space is capabilities. In addition, the space of capabilities unveils vulnerabilities and their impact on one's possibilities to escape poverty, in contrast to the income space, which remains an incomplete factor for such an assessment. As Sen explains:

> the adequacy of the economic means cannot be judged independently of the actual possibilities of 'converting' incomes and resources into capability to function. The person with the kidney problem needing dialysis (in the example discussed

[91] *Poverty and Shared Prosperity* 2022: *Correcting Course*, *supra* note 15, p 75.
[92] Ibid, p 76.
[93] The judgment from the IACtHR in *Firework Factory* addresses some of these effects. See Chapter 7.

> earlier in this chapter) may have more income than the other person, but he is still short of economic means (indeed of income), given his problem in converting income and resources into functionings. If we want to identify poverty in terms of income, it cannot be adequate to look only at incomes (i.e. whether it is generally low or high), independently of the capability to function derivable from those incomes. Income adequacy to escape poverty varies parametrically with personal characteristics and circumstances.[94]

In conclusion, delimiting spaces is a necessary step in providing meaning to equality. As such, it becomes essential for the analysis of the interconnections between poverty and equality. However, providing an answer to the question 'equality of what' still leaves open the question of 'equality between which groups?', which is relevant for all but completely egalitarianist theories.

2.2.2 Cognate, suspect, or protected groups: equality to whom?

Equality does not equate to identity. Given the inevitable existence of differences among humans, requiring identity would lead to the inapplicability of the principle of equality in human collectivity. Because of human diversity, the principle of equality does not demand complete identity between subjects but rather a sufficient degree of similarity in certain respects.

The assessment of similarity can take place between individuals or groups. In any case, equality theories imply a classification of similarity and dissimilarity. Such a classification requires the determination of factors of differentiation, or, in other words, clear criteria to determine a cognate group of people for the purposes of applying the principle of equality.

Sen explains that the assessment of equality often proceeds in terms of groups rather than specific individuals.[95] The focus is then on intergroup variations. The focus can be made even more specific by concentrating on grounds that have historically been used to justify systematic and pervasive disparities (eg race, sex, or gender). When one group sharing these characteristics is more likely to suffer disadvantages, the ground in question may be qualified as 'suspect' or 'protected'. This is illustrated in Tarunabh Khaitan's analysis of the classification of sex as a protected personal attribute in law, which he explains

[94] Sen (1992), *supra* note 83, pp 110–111.
[95] Ibid, p 117.

is based on a necessary trigger: the greater likelihood of women suffering disadvantages in our societies.[96]

This approach to equality based on protected classifications is closely related to the emergence of discrimination law. Some jurisdictions, such as the IACtHR, treat equality and non-discrimination as two sides of the same coin. However, scholars have proposed a distinction between the two concepts. Khaitan notes that constitutions usually safeguard a right to equality through a vaguely framed provision.[97] In contrast, the right against discrimination is generally understood as an aspect of the right to equality or related to the latter.[98] While equality is a concept applied to every group and a right of every person, the concept of discrimination is more specific.

Khaitan proposes that discrimination law comprises duty-imposing norms that fulfil four characteristics: (i) there is a connection between the act or omission prohibited or mandated with certain attributes of persons ('grounds'); (ii) the ground classifies persons in groups; (iii) members of one group are 'significantly more likely to suffer abiding, pervasive, and substantial disadvantage than the members of at least one other cognate group';[99] and (iv) the design of the duty-imposing norm is likely to distribute what Khaitan calls 'non-remote tangible benefits'[100] to some, albeit not all,[101] members of the beneficiary group.[102]

Sandra Fredman also proposes a definition of the scope of discrimination law. Taking a sociological approach to the definition of discrimination, she explains that the political and social context in which discrimination law developed greatly influences the determination of which distinctions should be outlawed as illegitimate and unacceptable.[103] She explains that race and sex are notable illustrations of categories that, in the twentieth century, became recognized as protected grounds in many constitutional and international texts.[104] From the second half of the twentieth century into the early twenty-first century, key international documents included other categories

[96] Tarunabh Khaitan, *A Theory of Discrimination Law* (Oxford University Press 2015), p 63.
[97] Ibid, p 63.
[98] Ibid.
[99] Ibid, p 31.
[100] That is, concrete distributive benefits, such as education and employment, and not merely procedural opportunities to acquire these benefits. See ibid, pp 39–41.
[101] The requirement that the measure benefits some, but not all, members of the protected group can be better understood through an example. When a non-discrimination norm prohibits discrimination based on gender, it does not impose an obligation to hire all persons of the oppressed group. However, this norm makes employment available to some members of this group, who are *a priori* excluded based on their gender. See ibid.
[102] Ibid, Chapter 2.
[103] Sandra Fredman, *Discrimination law* (2nd edn, Oxford University Press 2011b), p 110.
[104] Ibid, pp 9 and 110.

as protected against discrimination, such as national origin, disability, age, religion, and economic condition.[105] Sexual orientation and gender identity are recent additions in many parts of the world, and there is an ongoing debate about the inclusion of further categories as protected grounds, such as HIV status, socio-economic disadvantage, and poverty.[106]

There is no consensus on the formulation of protected grounds of discrimination. International instruments, constitutional texts, and statutes have adopted different models. One model is the enunciation of an exhaustive list of grounds. Fredman calls this the 'fixed category' approach.[107] At the other end of the spectrum, she identifies a second model: a broad and open-textured equality guarantee, which simply states that all are equal before the law and, therefore, leaves it to judges to determine when a given classification is prohibited.[108] The third model stands in the middle. It adopts a non-exhaustive list of grounds of discrimination. This approach gives judges a certain level of discretion while shaping their discretion by recognizing certain enumerated grounds.[109]

Suppose a country or an international human rights system adopts a 'fixed category' approach that excludes poverty and economic and social status from its exhaustive list of grounds. In that case, the spaces for a court to analyse the interconnections between poverty and equality are curtailed, though not eliminated.[110] In turn, if a legal system adopts the second or the third model, a court may recognize poverty as a prohibited criterion of classification between groups for the enjoyment of rights. In this case, discrimination may be found specifically and explicitly on this ground.

The recognition of protected groups in legal texts and the study of the models of equality clauses are relevant for the delimitation in law of the content and scope of equality. Engaging in this analysis provides tools for determining when two or more parties to a dispute should be considered alike for the purposes of being granted a like treatment. However, as Fredman explains, this is only part of the solution, because, even when race, sex, or another classification

105 E.g. UNGA, 'International Covenant on Civil and Political Rights', United Nations, Treaty Series, vol 999, 16 December 1966, Article 2(1); OAS, 'American Convention on Human Rights, "Pact of San Jose"', 22 November 1969, Article 1(1); UNGA, 'Convention on the Rights of Persons with Disabilities', A/RES/61/106, Annex I, 13 December 2006.

106 Cf Fredman (2011b), *supra* note 103, pp 9, 109 and 110.

107 Ibid, p 112.

108 Ibid.

109 Ibid.

110 As the book's Part II will explain, courts may still identify poverty as one of the disadvantages to which a protected group has been historically and persistently subjected. In other words, poverty may be assessed as relevant context to a finding of discrimination, the latter covering one or more of the protected groups enumerated in the exhaustive list of the non-discrimination clause.

historically linked to societal disadvantages are recognized as prohibited grounds of discrimination, the principle of equal treatment only goes as far as prescribing like treatment.[111] However, likeness of treatment might be of little value, as the requirement of consistency of treatment may be fulfilled by levelling up or down.[112] Furthermore, equal treatment may entrench difference and perpetuate marginalization and exclusion.[113] This equality conundrum is the focus of section 2.2.3.

2.2.3 The content of equality: a 'like' treatment?

2.2.3.1 From formal to substantive equality

Having answered the questions of 'equality in which spaces' and 'equality to whom', this chapter will now assess the content of equality. Two conceptualizations of equality delimit the scope of this right differently. The first is formal equality, and the second is substantive equality.

A myriad of scholars and courts have discussed the historical roots of these two conceptualizations. In C-410/94, when analysing the constitutionality of differences in retirement age based on sex, the Colombian Constitutional Court explained that, at its origins, formal equality was 'one of the most valuable achievements of the classical liberal state, which reacted against the privileges of the *ancient régime*, proclaiming the similar position of all before the law'.[114] Similarly, in his vote in ADPF 186 (2012), STF Justice Luiz Fux recalled the historical roots of the principle of formal equality, relating it to the liberal achievements of the eighteenth-century Enlightenment.[115]

Formal equality delimits the content of equality as the sameness of treatment in the creation and application of the law. Therefore, it depends on identifying an appropriate comparator and requires consistency of treatment.[116] In this conceptualization, equality aims to guarantee sameness of treatment before the law. Accordingly, the legislature and courts become the main venues for implementing and enforcing the right to equality.[117]

[111] Sandra Fredman, 'Substantive Equality Revisited' (2016a) 14 I-CON 712, p 717.

[112] Ibid, p 717. For examples, see: US Supreme Court, *Palmer v Thompson*, 403 US 217, 14 June 1971; House of Lords, *A v Secretary of State for the Home Department*, [2004] UKHL 56 (HL), 16 December 2004.

[113] Ibid, p 718.

[114] Colombian Constitutional Court, *C-410/94*, 15 September 1994, p 15; see also Colombian Constitutional Court, *C-044/04*, 27 January 2004, para 3.

[115] Vote of Justice Luiz Fux in STF, Judgment, *ADPF 186/DF*, 26 April 2012. Rapporteur: Ricardo Lewandowski, p 109.

[116] Martha Albertson Fineman, 'The Vulnerable Subject: Anchoring Equality in the Human Condition' (2008) 20 Yale Journal of Law and Feminism 1, pp 2–3.

[117] Ibid.

With the rise of the social state, formal equality increasingly became the object of confrontation with the emerging notion of substantive equality.[118] Substantive equality developed from the recognition of the limitations of formal equality, as the latter is satisfied with the abolition of privileges between estates and identical treatment before the law. However, equal treatment may entrench difference and perpetuate marginalization and exclusion. After all, equality as consistency disregards antecedent disadvantage. To quote Amartya Sen, 'the effect of ignoring the interpersonal variations can, in fact, be deeply inegalitarian, in hiding the fact that equal consideration for all may demand very unequal treatment in favour of the disadvantaged'.[119]

Furthermore, equality as consistency may perpetuate oppressions as the dominant group is set as the adequate comparator. As Fredman eloquently explains, 'like treatment can only be judged against the treatment accorded to a similarly situated comparator, who, far from being universal, is clothed with the attributes of the dominant gender, culture, religion, ethnicity, or sexuality'.[120] When the comparator is the dominant group, neutrality in relation to suspect classifications (eg gender neutrality and racial neutrality) is based on the reproduction of the dominant group as 'the measure of all things'.[121] When this occurs, a veil of equality might merely constitute a legal validation of the perpetuation of inequalities.

Substantive equality emerges as a tool for tackling these challenges. It transcends the limits of the prohibition of discrimination, which is the essence of formal equality, to proclaim that normative equality is devoid of value without factual implementation and social effectiveness.[122] In other words, substantive equality embodies the positive dimension of the right to equality. It requires states to remedy, compensate for, and correct social and economic obstacles that manifest as factual inequalities to the detriment of certain groups, thus aiming at the emancipation of those groups and individuals subject to historical segregation and marginalization.[123]

Fredman identifies the growing recognition of the concept of substantive equality as a new phase in the development of the legal principle of equality. She divides the development of this principle into three phases. The first two are the dismantlement of formal legal impediments (eg abolition of slavery

[118] Ibid; *C-410/94* (1994), *supra* note 114, paras 15–16; *C-044/04 (2004), supra* note 114, para.4.
[119] Sen (1992), *supra* note 83, p 1.
[120] Fredman (2016a), *supra* note 111, p 719.
[121] See Catharine A Mackinnon, *Feminism Unmodified. Discourses on Life and Law* (Harvard University Press 1987), p 34.
[122] *ADPF 186/DF* (2012), *supra* note 115.
[123] *C-410/94* (1994), *supra* note 114, para 16.

and suffrage) and the enactment of anti-discrimination legislation prohibiting discrimination by public or private actors (eg statutory restrictions on discrimination in education, services, or employment).[124] I argue that these two phases can be categorized as emanating from the principle of formal equality. The third phase originates from the recognition that decades of anti-discrimination legislation have not been sufficient to address entrenched discriminatory structures. The third phase thus moves from an essentially negative prohibition of discrimination to the recognition of positive obligations to promote equality.[125]

Different theories have emerged to delimitate the object of substantive equality. Substantive equality has been read as equality of opportunities, equality of results, and the promotion of dignity, among others. This book adopts the conceptualization of substantive equality as a multidimensional concept.

2.2.3.2 Substantive equality as a multidimensional concept

Fredman asserts that a single principle, be it equality of results, equality of opportunities, or dignity, is insufficient to capture substantive equality.[126] Equality of opportunity aims to equalize opportunities to allow individuals to be judged based on individual merit. However, this conceptualization of substantive equality may be captured by a notion of merits that disregards enduring structural discrimination based on redistributive injustices, cultural dominance, and stigmatization. In other words, a procedural rather than a substantive understanding of opportunities might simply require agents to adopt assessments based only on merit, while leaving unchanged structures that prevent historically oppressed groups from developing and fostering the 'merit' valued in their respective societies.[127] Furthermore, it may be that the very criteria used in a community or institution for evaluating merit are based on the dominant group as the standard, thereby failing to accommodate difference. In any case, quoting US President Lyndon Johnson:

> You do not take a person who, for years, has been hobbled by chains and liberate him, bring him up to the starting line of a race and then say, 'you are free to compete with all the others,' and still justly believe that you have been completely fair.

[124] Fredman (2011b), *supra* note 103, p 6.
[125] Ibid, p 7.
[126] Ibid, pp 7 and 25.
[127] See Bob Hepple, 'Discrimination and Equality of Opportunity—Northern Irish Lessons' (1990) 10 Oxford Journal of Legal Studies 408, pp 412–414; Fredman (2016a), *supra* note 111, pp 723–724; Fredman (2011b), *supra* note 103, pp 18–19.

> Thus it is not enough just to open the gates of opportunity. All our citizens must have the ability to walk through those gates.
>
> This is the next and the more profound stage of the battle for civil rights. We seek not just freedom but opportunity. We seek not just legal equity but human ability, not just equality as a right and a theory but equality as a fact and equality as a result.[128]

Given these limitations, equality of opportunity has been met with demands for equality of results. Yet, equality of results also suffers drawbacks as a definition of the scope of substantive equality. It does not offer a sufficient response to the levelling down problem, it may stagnate at a minimum by focusing on absolute entitlements, and it does not necessarily require re-examining structures that perpetuate discrimination.[129] Similarly, dignity also offers an insufficient alternative for delimiting the content of substantive equality. Not only is the meaning of dignity fuzzy in law, but it may also establish an undue burden on applicants by requiring them to prove that the impugned difference of treatment equates to a lack of respect for them as a person.[130]

Equality is better understood as a multidimensional concept closely connected to the promotion of social justice. It requires identifying and addressing material disadvantages and other forms of oppression. To explain the multifaceted nature of equality and the multiple manifestations of inequality and discrimination, this section examines Nancy Fraser's theory of social justice. Subsequently, it discusses Fredman's four-dimensional analytical framework for substantive equality.

i. Moving beyond distribution: a theory of social justice

In the Tanner Lectures on Human Values at Stanford University in 1996, Fraser noted an increasing tendency to divide social justice claims into two types: the politics of redistribution and the politics of recognition. The former focuses on socio-economic injustices, presumed to be rooted in distributive failures found in the structure of society. Responding to these injustices would then require distributive remedies.[131] In turn, the politics of recognition target injustices presumed to be rooted in social patterns of representation,

[128] Lyndon B. Johnson, 'Commencement Address at Howard University: "To Fulfill These Rights." ' (*The American Presidency Project,* 1965) <https://www.presidency.ucsb.edu/documents/commencement-address-howard-university-fulfill-these-rights> accessed 2 May 2023.

[129] See Fredman (2016a), *supra* note 111, pp 720–723; Fredman (2011b), *supra* note 103, pp 14–17.

[130] See Fredman (2016a), *supra* note 111, pp 724–727; Fredman (2011b), *supra* note 103, pp 19–25.

[131] Nancy Fraser, *Social Justice in the Age of Identity Politics: Redistribution, Recognition, and Participation* (Stanford University 1996), pp 6–7.

communication, and interpretation (eg cultural domination), which render a group invisible and stereotype the representation of this collectivity.[132] The required remedy would then be the promotion of cultural or symbolic change.[133] To use the terminology of the two founders of sociology, the victims of redistributive injustices would be closer to Marx's notion of class, while the victims in the politics of recognition would be closer to the Weberian notion of status groups.[134]

However, the persistent opposition between redistribution and recognition misses the mark. Fraser argues that 'virtually all real-world oppressed collectivities are bivalent', in the sense that the axes of oppression (such as class, gender, race and sexual orientation) face harms that comprise both distributive injustices and misrecognition.[135] She explains that certain collectivities lean more heavily towards the distribution end of the spectrum (eg class), others towards the recognition end of the spectrum (eg race in more egalitarian societies), and others remain at the centre of this bivalence. In any case, even collectivities that lean more heavily towards one end of the spectrum will still experience bivalent oppressions.[136] I argue that this can be illustrated by analysing collectivities living in poverty.

Individuals and groups living in poverty face a clearly distributive harm, derived from economic structures and the perpetuation of exclusion from the enjoyment of resources and goods. An essential remedy to break cycles of poverty is, therefore, distributive. However, poverty does not only derive from economic injustices. Furthermore, it does not only cause harm in the form of maldistribution of recourses and goods that can be remedied through the politics of redistribution. Recognition injustices are both a root cause of the perpetuation of poverty and a by-product of it, as persons living in poverty are often subject to stereotyping, stigmatizing social hierarchies, and invisibilization, which in turn reinforce poverty in a continuous cycle. Therefore, remedies for poverty should include, but not be limited to, redistribution. Addressing injustices against persons living in poverty requires cultural and symbolic change—for example, by challenging cultural norms,

132 Ibid, p 7.

133 Ibid.

134 Ibid, p 8. See Max Weber, 'Class, Status, Party' in David B Grusky (ed), *Social Stratification: Class, Race, and Gender in Sociological Perspective* (4th edn, Westview Press 2018); Max Weber, 'Status Groups and Classes Social Stratification: Class, Race, and Gender in Sociological Perspective' in David B Grusky (ed), *Social Stratification: Class, Race, and Gender in Sociological Perspective* (4th edn, Westview Press 2018); Karl Marx, 'Class in Capitalism and pre-capitalism' in David B Grusky and Szonja Szelényi (eds), *The Inequality Reader: Contemporary and Foundational Readings in Race, Class, and Gender* (2nd edn, Routledge 2018).

135 Fraser (1996), *supra* note 131, pp 10–23.

136 Ibid, p 22.

institutionalized practices of verbal violence and stigmatization, and other forms of oppression that reduce parity of participation for persons living in poverty.

Therefore, the distribution–recognition bivalence is present in the case of poverty. This conclusion is maintained even if one understands poverty as a class-only manifestation. After all, class itself is best understood as a bivalent collectivity. In the words of Fraser:

> Class, too, is probably best understood as bivalent, in spite of my earlier discussion. The economistic ideal-type I invoked for heuristic purposes occludes the real-world complexities of class. To be sure, the ultimate cause of class injustice is the economic structure of capitalist society. But the resulting harms include misrecognition as well as maldistribution. Moreover, cultural harms that originated as byproducts of economic structure may have developed a life of their own. Today the misrecognition dimensions of class may be sufficiently autonomous in their operation to require independent remedies of recognition. Left unattended, moreover, class misrecognition may impede the capacity to mobilize against maldistribution. To build broad support for economic transformation today may require first challenging cultural attitudes that demean poor and working people: for example, 'culture-of-poverty' ideologies that suggest that the poor deserve what they get. Likewise, poor and working people may need a counter-'identity politics' to support their struggles for economic justice; they may need, that is, to build class communities and cultures in order to neutralize the hidden injuries of class and forge the confidence to stand up for themselves. Thus, a politics of class recognition may be needed both in itself and to get a politics of redistribution off the ground.[137]

I argue that recognition injustices are not only resulting harms of class injustices—which would ultimately derive from maldistribution—but also one of the root causes of class injustices. One of the explanations for the fundamental division between productive and superfluous work and the related consequences on wage distribution can be found in occupational prestige. When responding to the well-known article by Kingsley Davis and Wilbert Moore called 'Some Principles of Stratification',[138] Melvin M Tumin claimed that a generalized theory of social stratification must recognize that a whole range of possible systems of motivation is capable of working in human society,

[137] Ibid, pp 19–20.

[138] Kingsley Davis and Wilbert E Moore, 'Some Principles of Stratification' in David B Grunsky and Katherine R Weisshaar (eds), *Social Stratification: Class, Race, and Gender in Sociological Perspective* (4th edn, Routledge 2018).

at least theoretically. The prevailing system of inducements and rewards is simply one of them. Tumin considers the proposition by Davis and Moore according to which certain positions in society are more functionally important than others as the first step in explaining the system of rewards and distribution and, accordingly, stratification. However, unlike Davis and Moore, Tumin argues that the judgment of how indispensable or replaceable a specific segment of skills within the population is encompasses a prior judgement about the bargaining power held by that segment.[139] In his understanding, 'this power is itself a culturally shaped consequence of the existing system of rating, rather than something inevitable in the nature of social organization'.[140] I argue that this culturally shaped system of rating results in culturally shaped occupational prestige and the interconnected system of rewards that takes the form of high wages, wage gaps, and other material benefits. In any case, whether or not one adopts the understanding that culturally shaped prestige materializes not only in status but also in material distribution, class is best understood as a bivalent mode of collectivity. After all, even if occupational stratification and wage distribution are interpreted as rooted purely in economic reasons (eg a supply and demand explanation), class injustice still produces both maldistribution and misrecognition.

In conclusion, justice must go beyond the distribution of goods and rights to include an examination of 'patterns of cultural value'.[141] A bivalent conception of justice encompasses these two perspectives on, and dimensions of, justice without reducing either to the other.[142] The need for this 'two-pronged approach' to social justice, as Fraser names it, becomes even more evident considering intersectionalities, that is, cases in which the axes of injustices do not have clear boundaries in one single collectivity but rather in mutually intersecting collectivities.[143] Once again, the case of poverty offers a valuable example. Poverty does not affect all collectivities in society equally. Certain collectivities (based on race, gender, and gender identity, among others) are often disproportionately represented among those living in poverty in different societies. Poverty or vulnerability to poverty may be perpetuated by social, economic, and cultural exclusions; marginalization; and other forms of oppression—hence maldistribution and misrecognition—based on membership to these collectivities.

139 Melvin M Tumin, 'Some Principles of Stratification: A Critical Analysis' in David B Grunsky and Katherine R Weisshaar (eds), *Social Stratification: Class, Race, and Gender in Sociological Perspective* (4th edn, Routledge 2018), p 32.

140 Ibid.

141 Fraser (1996), *supra* note 131, p 28.

142 Ibid, p 30.

143 Ibid, p 22.

ii. The two-dimensional approach to classifying injustices

Fraser identifies parity of participation as the core of the bivalent conception of social justice. Parity of participation would be its ultimate aim, the fulfilment of which depends on both distribution of material resources (named by Fraser as the 'objective precondition of participatory parity') and recognition (the 'intersubjective condition').[144]

Distribution addresses material inequality and economic dependence, thereby fostering independence, autonomy, and more capability for a person to exercise their agency. Therefore, quoting Fraser, distribution precludes 'social arrangements that institutionalize deprivation, exploitation, and gross disparities in wealth, income, and leisure time, thereby denying some people the means and opportunities to interact with others as peers'.[145]

In turn, recognition addresses institutionalized and often internalized patterns of interpretation and evaluation that depreciate and stigmatize certain groups, express cultural dominance, or are based on the dominant group as the standard norm. In the words of Fraser, the intersubjective condition of parity of participation precludes 'institutionalized value schemata that deny some people the status of full partners in interaction—whether by burdening them with excessive ascribed "difference" from others or by failing to acknowledge their distinctiveness'.[146]

In this sense, participation would not be a dimension independent of redistribution and recognition but the normative core of this 'two-prong' conception of justice, to be realized by responding to redistribution and recognition injustices. Only recently did Fraser discuss certain aspects of participation—most notably the political dimension of justice—as an independent dimension. In *Scales of Justices*: *Reimagining Political Space in a Globalizing World*, she identifies in globalization and current disputes about justice a relativization of what she calls the 'Keynesian-Westphalian frame'.[147] In the latter, disputes of justice were normally situated within modern nation-states and referred to relations among citizens. In contrast, decisions made today within one state will often impact individuals living in other states (eg climate change). In addition, myriad actors beyond the state have emerged as relevant agents in contemporary discussions of the mechanisms for promoting justice in a globalized world, including transnational companies, investors, and international organizations.[148] Amid this new context, Fraser contends that

[144] Ibid, p 31.
[145] Ibid.
[146] Ibid.
[147] Nancy Fraser, *Scales of Justice: Reimagining Political Space in a Globalizing World* (Columbia University Press 2009).
[148] Ibid, pp 12–14.

the Keynesian–Westphalian frame of justice has been questioned. She argues that the conceptualization of social justice must now go beyond the discussion of 'what' justice (distribution v recognition) to encompass justice to 'whom' and 'how'.

This new dimension, emerging from the age of globalization, questions the very frame of justice. In other words, it questions the delimitation of who has moral standing as the subject of justice.[149] While, in a Westphalian frame, the answer to the question of 'who' is given (ie the citizens of a domestic jurisdiction), in a globalized world, this question becomes the object of democratic contestation. Fraser identifies in this phenomenon the third dimension of justice. It is the dimension of representation, which concerns the 'political' in a very specific framing of the word: the scope of the space of contestation and the rules that structure this space, that is, the procedures to receive and adjudicate claims, which frames not only the 'who' but also the 'how' of social justice.[150] It is important to emphasize that this third dimension of Fraser's social justice theory refers to a specific aspect of political participation in the context of globalization and relativization of the Keynesian–Westphalian frame of social justice.[151] It does not negate that participation, in its broad sense, is not reduced to one single dimension of social justice.[152] While discussing representation as an independent dimension of justice is undeniably thought-provoking, this book focuses on the manifestations of poverty and inequality domestically and the resulting judicial responses, which remain state-centred in the studied courts. For this reason, it adopts Fraser's two-prong conception of social justice.[153]

iii. The four-dimensional approach as an analytical framework

While Fraser moves beyond the distribution–recognition opposition in her analysis of social justice, Fredman moves beyond material disadvantage and the frequently found focus on redistribution to examine equality, arguing that equality, to be transformative, must be assessed through broader dimensions.

[149] Ibid, p 24.

[150] Ibid, pp 16–18.

[151] Fraser explains that 'this two-dimensional understanding of justice still seems right to me as far as it goes. But I now believe that it does not go far enough. Distribution and recognition could appear to constitute the sole dimensions of justice only as long as the Keynesian-Westphalian frame was taken for granted. Once the question of the frame becomes subject to contestation, the effect is to make visible a third dimension of justice, which was neglected in my previous work—as well as in the work of many other philosophers.' Ibid, p 17.

[152] Ibid, p 21.

[153] In turn, a discussion of *global* inequalities is expected to benefit significantly from transcending the borders of distribution and recognition to include Fraser's proposed dimension of representation and its resulting analysis of manifestations of 'misframing' in misrepresentation.

As mentioned earlier, the need to move beyond distribution without abandoning it as a standard of justice had already been proclaimed by Fraser, who is a key reference in Fredman's work on multidimensional equality. However, unlike Fraser, Fredman proposes not a two-dimensional but rather a four-dimensional framework for substantive equality. More specifically, she proposes that equality be seen as a multidimensional concept pursuing four overlapping aims: (i) breaking cycles of disadvantage; (ii) promoting recognition by taking into consideration interpersonal affirmation and the impact of society and social norms on identity; (iii) facilitating full participation in society; and (iv) accommodating difference by achieving structural change.[154] These four aims capture the four dimensions of substantive equality: redistribution, recognition, participation, and transformation.

The redistributive dimension of substantive equality aims to break cycles of disadvantage, and it finds its object in the distribution of resources, income, opportunities, and capabilities.[155] The recognition dimension aims to promote respect and dignity while going beyond this by expressly recognizing that a person's identity is impacted by social relations and how others recognize them.[156] This dimension tackles stereotypes, stigma, and further obstacles to the recognition of one's basic humanity and individual value.[157]

The participative dimension aims at full inclusion in society, finding its object in the forms of political and social participation and the manifestations of social and political exclusion.[158] Lastly, the transformative dimension aims at accommodating differences by promoting structural change. The object of the transformative dimension is structural harm and structural obstacles to autonomy and substantive freedoms.[159] The transformative dimension does not treat difference as inherently negative, addressing pressure for assimilation and accommodating difference through structural change. It aims to expand the range of one's feasible options.[160] Quoting Fredman et al, 'the need for structural change entails 'a redistribution of power and resources and a

[154] Fredman (2011b), *supra* note 103, p 25; cf Sandra Fredman, Jaakko Kuosmanen, and Meghan Campbell, 'Transformative Equality: Making the Sustainable Development Goals Work for Women' (2016) 30 Ethics & International Affairs 177, p 180.

[155] See Shreya Atrey, 'The Intersectional Case of Poverty in Discrimination Law' (2018) 18 Human Rights Law Review 411, p 429

[156] According to Fredman, 'recognition and dignity differ because of the former's essentially relational format: rather than regarding each person as an isolated individual to whom dignity is attached, it regards individuals as constructed in many ways by society and social norms.' See Fredman (2016a), *supra* note 111, p 724

[157] Atrey (2018), *supra* note 155, p 429; Fredman (2011b), *supra* note 103, p 25.

[158] Atrey (2018), *supra* note 155, p 429.

[159] Ibid, p 429.

[160] Fredman (2016a), *supra* note 111, p 738.

change in the institutional structures that perpetuate [...] subordination'.[161] As this dimension addresses obstacles to autonomy, the analysis of power relations in the context of institutional change—understood as requiring institutions and not individuals to change—is considered, for the purposes of this book, to fall under the assessment of transformative equality.

Fredman acknowledges Fraser's conceptualization of social justice and, in fact, adopts her theory as one of the main sources for understanding the recognition dimension of her model of assessment of substantive equality.[162] Nonetheless, Fredman's four-dimensional model separates participation as one specific dimension of substantive equality. Were Fredman's model aiming to define substantive equality, its classification of four dimensions would reveal inconsistencies. First, if the criteria used for this classification are the types of targeted injustices and required remedies, the participative and transformative dimensions would not qualify as independent dimensions. Targeting unequal participation will often be equivalent to targeting the distributive disadvantages or recognition obstacles that hinder parity of (social and political) participation, at least when the assessment of participation remains constrained to a Westphalia frame. This objection is strengthened by the fact that Fredman does not explain the extent to which the injustices targeted by the participative dimension could not simply be classified as derived from maldistribution or misrecognition. In addition, there is no explanation of whether the participative dimension requires remedies that transcend distributive justice and the politics of recognition. A more debatable question is whether the transformative dimension would similarly fail to meet the abovementioned requirements, as it could be argued that the promotion of structural change does not perfectly fit the definition of distributive remedies and remedies derived from recognition.

Another objection to conceptualizing substantive equality as a four-dimensional concept is the link between the transformative dimension and accommodation. Should difference always be accommodated, or may difference itself be a social construct that is the product of forms of oppression and reproduces the latter? Phrasing this question differently, equality requires distribution in all cases in which there is a distributive injustice based on discriminatory grounds. It also requires recognition in all cases that reveal interpersonal harm to respect, dignity, and self-esteem. Parity of participation is similarly a universal demand. Yet is accommodation similarly a universal requirement for equality? This objection may be illustrated in the context of

161 Fredman, Kuosmanen, and Campbell (2016), *supra* note 154, pp 180–181.
162 Fredman (2016a), *supra* note 111, pp 730–731.

women's rights. Accommodation of difference may derive from an essentialist definition of women, thereby remaining unresponsive to intersectionalities. It may also entrench stereotyped roles assigned to women. As Wendy Brown explains, '[t]he problem surfaces in the question of when and whether rights for women are formulated in such a way as to enable the escape of the subordinated from the site of that violation, and when and whether they build a fence around us at that site, regulating rather than challenging the conditions within'.[163]

While accommodation might be a sufficient and even necessary response in specific cases of inequalities, this is not universal. Equality may instead require challenging the very identities and notions of sameness and difference upheld in discourse, politics, and law. In other words, the promotion of substantive equality may require an epistemological change that questions the very opposition between identities and breaks down binary classifications of groups (eg based on sex, race, and sexual orientation). As Guacira Lopes Louro explains when analysing queer theories and identities, '[t]he affirmation of identity always implies the demarcation and negation of its opposite, which is constituted as its difference'.[164] In contrast, a deconstructive perspective recognizes these oppositions and their implications and questions the processes through which the characteristics of the dominant collectivity (eg heterosexuality) become the norm and come to be regarded as 'natural'.[165] Hence, queer theorists point to a post-identity theory and politics, finding that 'identity politics can become an accomplice of the system against which it intends to rise up'.[166]

The conundrum of difference and equality was the object of analysis by Fraser in the Tanner Lectures on Human Values. Fraser recognized the relevance of the question of whether the recognition of individual or group distinctiveness could be required by justice as an element of the intersubjective condition of participatory parity.[167] She finds that the answer depends on the specific context, notably on the assessment of the obstacles to participatory parity and the needs of a group or individual to participate as a peer in social life.[168] When misrecognition manifests itself as the negation of the common humanity of the group, the remedy would be what Fraser calls 'a universalistic recognition'. In turn, when misrecognition manifests as the denial of an

[163] Brown (2000), *supra* note 83, p 231.
[164] Guacira Lopes Louro, 'Teoria queer—uma politica pós-identitária para a educação' (2001) 9 Estudos Feministas 541, p 549. Translation by the author.
[165] Ibid. In the words of Lopes Louro: 'The denied identity is constitutive of the subject, providing the latter limits and coherence and, at the same time, hunting them with instability.' Translation by the author.
[166] Ibid. Translation by the author.
[167] Fraser (1996), *supra* note 131, pp 32–35.
[168] Ibid, p 35.

individual or a group's distinctiveness (eg through requirements of assimilation) or the false presentation of the dominant group's particularity as universal, the required remedy could be the recognition of difference.[169]

In summary, whether one reads equality through a deconstructive approach (eg through the lens of queer theory) or not, the accommodation of difference is not universally applicable as a requirement of equality. A case-by-case analysis of differences and proposed accommodations contributes to avoiding reinforcing stereotypes and possible identity traps. The accommodation of difference is, therefore, not always transformative.

For these reasons, from a normative-philosophical standpoint[170] and within the constraints of a Westphalian frame, the classification of inequalities appears to be better described by a bipartite division between redistribution and recognition. Parity of participation, and ultimately transformative equality, is achieved by identifying the multidimensional oppressions faced by marginalized collectivities as products of redistributive and recognition injustices, and by implementing appropriate remedies that take into account the specific oppressions faced. Depending on the circumstances of the case, one such remedy may be the accommodation of difference, which may take place through redistributive measures or through protecting and promoting recognition.

Hence, the conceptual integration of redistribution and recognition advocated by Fraser and discussed in the previous section offers a methodologically solid basis for conceptualizing substantive equality. However, recognizing the normative adequacy of the two-pronged approach to social justice does not displace Fredman's model of substantive equality. While the bipartite understanding of social justice offers a solid basis for the classification of injustices and, here I argue, inequalities, Fredman's model serves a different purpose. The latter does not intend to define substantive equality. It rather aims at providing an analytical framework. As Fredman explains, the four-dimensional approach to equality is not a 'definition as such, but an analytic framework which can be used to assess and assist in modifying policies and practices to better achieve substantive equality'.[171] In her words, '[d]rawing attention to all the dimensions and insisting on resolving conflicts and building complementarities can move us positively towards ensuring

[169] Ibid, pp 32–33.

[170] The use of this nomenclature derives from the work of Fraser, who distinguishes between normative-philosophical issues (eg the relationship between recognition and distributive justice), social-theoretical issues (eg the relationship between economy and culture), and practical-political issues (eg tensions arising when seeking to promote redistribution and recognition simultaneously). See ibid, p 23.

[171] Fredman (2016a), *supra* note 111.

that laws, policies or programs can be formulated in ways which further substantive equality'.[172]

Fredman's model offers a framework for a detailed analysis of laws, policies, and practices of state agents, institutions, and non-state agents, including their impact on different and interlocking facets of inequality. By including accommodation and participation as analytical dimensions, Fredman offers a model to assess in detail how policies, laws, and practices address different facets of equality. Her model also sheds light on possible conflicts between these different facets. Therefore, it is a useful analytical map for assessing how equality is protected in law, in the actions and policies of the state, and in the work of courts.

For these reasons, while this study acknowledges the limitations of the quadripartite approach for conceptualizing the dimensions of equality, it recognizes the usefulness of this approach as an analytical and evaluative framework. The four dimensions of substantive equality will be the language used in the book to clarify the content and scope of the equality assessment applied by the STF and the IACtHR in disputes concerning poverty. Therefore, the book will refer to the redistributive dimension, the recognition dimension, the participative dimension, and the transformative dimension. Yet, for the reasons explained earlier, it considers the participative and transformative dimensions to be 'accessory-dimensions', accompanied by the redistributive dimension, the recognition dimension, or both. By pursuing these four overlapping and coexisting dimensions, states pursue what Fredman calls 'transformative equality'.

Furthermore, this study interprets the transformative dimension of equality more broadly, not as a universal requirement of accommodation of difference but as a need for structural change. The latter includes the reaffirmation and accommodation of difference in some cases, and, in others, it may require challenging the social construction of difference and adopting a deconstructive perspective. By applying these adjustments, the investigation responds to the objections discussed earlier while preserving the added value of the four-dimensional framework.

The four-dimensional model extrapolates an individualistic approach to the assessment of inequalities by covering cultural and symbolic patterns of collective misrecognition and addressing systemic and structural obstacles to equality. These dimensions coexist with one another in a process of constant interaction. For example, addressing stigmatization and stereotypes may

[172] Ibid.

impact not only the promotion of recognition but also contribute to overcoming social obstacles to participation. Similarly, when representativeness and diversity are promoted, the social symbols attributed to a group will often change progressively and may lead to the reduction of stereotypes and negative stigma in a society. This constant interaction between the dimensions of equality is also clear with regard to the transformative dimension. The likelihood of achieving structural change and accommodating differences increases by addressing stigma against traditionally marginalized groups, modifying cultural patterns and symbols that value assimilation instead of recognition of difference, distributing resources that contribute to equality of opportunities and even equality of results, and accordingly increasing political and social participation of the group in question.

While these examples refer to a harmonious interaction between the dimensions of substantive equality, this will not always be the case. As discussed above, accommodating difference may naturalize social constructs of otherness and leave untouched structures of oppression. A different conflict might arise from distributive justice, as a given distributive measure may reinforce stereotypes. Another example is the increase of participation of an oppressed group in an institution in cases in which this advancement of participation is correlated with explicit or implicit requirements for assimilation. In this case, the increase in the participation of a group in political and social life and decision-making may leave behind individuals who retain the characteristics of the oppressed group, as well as individuals facing multiple or intersectional discrimination.

Both the harmonious interactions and conflicts between dimensions can be identified through the application of this evaluative framework of equality when assessing a law, a policy, or a court decision. Therefore, this framework amplifies the possibilities of approaching substantive equality and, as Fredman argues, assessing practices and policies 'in ways that can be more responsive to real social wrongs'.[173]

2.2.3.3 The scope of substantive equality: beyond disadvantage

The conceptualization of equality as multidimensional, together with the adoption of a four-dimensional evaluative framework, shows that the scope of substantive equality transcends disadvantage as maldistribution of resources and benefits. This section relies on Iris Marion Young's analysis of forms of oppression to further clarify how equality transcends the limits of material disadvantage.

[173] Ibid, p 728.

i. Oppression and discrimination: synonyms or complementary concepts?

In 'Five faces of oppression', Young notes that philosophical discussions of justice and injustice use the term 'discrimination' to refer to what radicals call 'oppression'. While recognizing that discriminatory practices frequently serve as instruments of oppression and are part of some forms of oppression, she argues that the two concepts do not coincide with one another and should not be reducible to the other.[174]

One of the grounds for such a differentiation resides in Young's understanding of discrimination as relating to intentional actions and policies that exclude members of a group from institutions or confine them to inferior positions.[175] Young was a US scholar, and, in the US, discriminatory intent can be relevant in certain equality cases. However, a myriad of other legal systems, such as the Inter-American System of Human Rights and Brazilian constitutional law, do not include intent as an element of the definition of discrimination. Nonetheless, the proposed differentiation between discrimination and oppression remains useful, as it is based on additional arguments.

Young argues that discrimination presupposes the identification of individual victims and an identifiable agent who discriminates (be it the state, a juridical entity, or individuals). In turn, oppression is systemic. It manifests through disadvantages and injustices that are not caused 'because a tyrannical power intends to keep them down', as Young eloquently explains, but because of 'everyday practices of a well-intentioned liberal society'.[176] In other words, oppression is 'part of the basic fabric of a society'.[177] Therefore, it is not contingent upon the choices or policies of a few individuals. Similarly, it is not solved by selecting new rulers or making new laws, because it is reproduced in major economic, political, and cultural institutions systematically.[178] In a similar line of reasoning, Marilyn Frye explains that oppression relates to 'an enclosing structure of forces and barriers which tends to the immobilization and reduction of a group or category of people'.[179]

The difference between the concepts of oppression and discrimination is reduced when equality moves from a strictly formal concept to substantive equality. As we have seen in this chapter, substantive equality can be interpreted as a multidimensional concept pursuing the overlapping aims of

174 Iris Marion Young, 'Five Faces of Oppression' (1988) 19 The Philosophical Forum 270, p 272.
175 Ibid.
176 Ibid, p 271.
177 Ibid.
178 Ibid.
179 Marilyn Frye, 'Oppression' in Anne Minas (ed), *Gender Basics: Feminist Perspectives on Women and Men* (2nd edn, Wadsworth 2000), p 13.

redistribution, recognition, transformation, and participation. A strict distinction between discrimination and forms of oppression is thus blurred by the emergence of substantive equality as a multidimensional concept. When this multidimensional understanding of equality is adopted, manifestations of oppression can be, per se, manifestations of inequalities. Hence, understanding forms of oppression becomes a tool for identifying disadvantages to which groups that are structurally marginalized or segregated are subjected. In other words, Young's proposed categorization of forms of oppression becomes relevant to unveiling different forms through which discrimination materializes.

ii. The five categories of oppression

Young identifies five categories of oppression: exploitation, marginality, powerlessness, cultural imperialism, and violence.[180] The first refers to relations of power and inequality in which the energy and labour of a group benefit another in a systematic and continuous process.[181] One example of exploitation is that described by Marxist theories as class oppression and surplus value.

Marginalization, as conceptualized by Young, refers to the exclusion of certain categories of people from the labour market and participation in social life. The application of marginalization in equality cases involving poverty is made clear through exemplifications. Older people are often subject to marginalization in the labour market. This can lead to material deprivation and deprivation of fundamental rights derived from stigmatization and patronizing attitudes.[182] Another example relates directly to our case study. As Chapter 5 will discuss in detail, black and brown people constitute a little over half of the labour force in Brazil. Yet they are marginalized as a group in the Brazilian labour market, forming two thirds of the persons living in unemployment.

The third manifestation of oppression is powerlessness. It refers to the lack or reduction of one's autonomy, a person's or a group's negative experiences with commanding respect, expressing themselves—particularly in state or bureaucratic settings—and exercising their own judgement at work.[183] In this conceptualization of power, the latter is linked to privileges in social relations and influence. While the element of power and autonomy is analysed in sociological studies of status, it is often invisibilized by an understanding

[180] Young (1988), *supra* note 174.
[181] Ibid, pp 276–280.
[182] Ibid, pp 280–283.
[183] Ibid, pp 283–284.

of inequality restricted to an analysis of material disadvantage. Still, courts have not remained completely oblivious to the third category of oppression in their equality analysis. In ADC 41 (2017), the STF examined the constitutionality of racial quotas for admission through public examinations to positions as public servants in the Brazilian federal public administration. In analysing the constitutionality of the quota system, the STF cited statistical data on social stratification of black and brown persons in Brazil. The Court noted that, among public servants, the majority of black people occupy positions with lower qualification, prestige, and remuneration compared to white public servants with the same level of education.[184] Therefore, the third category of oppression was an element used by the STF to assess the extent to which a positive measure realized the principle of equality.

The fourth category of oppression is cultural imperialism. It refers to the degree to which one's experience is made invisible, while, at the same time, stereotypes created by a dominant perception are reinforced. The invisibilized group is marked as 'the Other', and their experiences and perspectives are read through the lenses of the dominant group's own references. In turn, those references form symbols that impact the experiences of the invisibilized groups. This gives rise to what Young defines as a 'paradoxical oppression', in which victims of cultural imperialism found themselves 'both marked out by stereotypes and rendered invisible'.[185] The invisibilization of the oppressed group and the stigmatization of their experiences and identities are internalized by members of the vulnerable group themselves, with such internalization at times reframed as resistance to and negation of these projections. Even the recognition of persons with certain shared characteristics as a social group can result from social processes of oppression.

Lastly, the category of 'violence' refers to systematic forms of violence that are legitimate in the sense that they are no longer surprising to the general population and are often met with impunity. The IACtHR recognizes violence against a person because of their belonging to a historically vulnerable group, as well as violence that disproportionately affects the group, as one of the most extreme forms of discrimination.[186] According to the Court's jurisprudence *constante*, judicial ineffectiveness fosters an environment of impunity, thereby facilitating and promoting the repetition of violent acts. This sends a message

[184] STF, Judgment, *ADC 41/DF*, 08 June 2017. Justice Rapporteur: Roberto Barroso.
[185] Young (1988), *supra* note 174, p 286.
[186] See IACtHR, Judgment (Preliminary Objections, Merits, Reparations and Costs), *Azul Rojas Marín and other v Perú*, 12 March 2020. Series C No 402; IACtHR, Judgment (Merits, Reparations, and Costs), *Guzmán Albarracín and others v Ecuador*, 24 June 2020. Series C No 434.

that violence against a vulnerable group can be tolerated and accepted, ultimately encouraging its perpetuation and social acceptance. It also fosters the perception and sensation of insecurity within the affected group and opens the door to an ongoing lack of trust in the justice system.[187]

The categories of oppression allow for an understanding of social benefits and burdens among the members of society that go beyond the distributive paradigm. They also evidence the need to move beyond purely distributive remedies. In conclusion, they are a tool for unveiling forms of inequality that are not confined to the allocation of resources or individual choices and isolated policies. Understanding oppression, in its multiple manifestations, unveils forms of inequality that derive from social structures and relationships of power imposing constraints on individuals because of their status. Therefore, this tool is significant for assessing the interconnections between poverty and inequality beyond the space of income. As Caroline Sweetman explains when discussing poverty in the context of women's rights, 'this is as much about agency compromised by abuse, stress, fatigue, and voicelessness as it is about lack of resources'.[188]

2.3 Concluding remarks

Defining equality and poverty is not a mere question of semantics. Poverty and inequality are both matters of foremost evaluative concern in most societies. Defining those terms and identifying their manifestations in society is a substantive issue for governments, scholars, and courts, among others.

This chapter explained that poverty can be defined in different ways. It also showed that different measurements of poverty coexist and sometimes even complement one another. Some measurements reveal the incidence of poverty, and others measure the intensity of poverty. Some measurements establish a poverty line based on absolute values (eg the IPL and the PBF line). Others use a comparator (eg OECD's line of 50% of the median household

[187] IACtHR, Judgment (Preliminary Objections, Merits, Reparations and Costs), *Véliz Franco et al v Guatemala*, 19 May 2014. Series C No 277, para 208; IACtHR, Judgment (Preliminary Objections, Merits, Reparations and Costs), *Espinoza Gonzáles and others v Peru*, 20 November 2014. Series C No 468, para 280; IACtHR, Judgment (Preliminary Objections, Merits, Reparations and Costs), *Gutiérrez Hernández and others v Guatemala*, 24 August 2017. Series C No 339, para 176; IACtHR, Judgment (Preliminary Objections, Merits, Reparations and Costs), *VRP, VPC et al v Nicaragua*, 8 March 2018. Series C No 350, para 291.

[188] Caroline Sweetman, 'Editorial' in Caroline Sweetman (ed), *Gender and the Millennium Development Goals* (Oxfam GB 2005), p 3.

income in a society). The existence of these various measurements is not a problem in itself. On the contrary, it is important in light of the needs, objects, and targets of different social programmes and institutions. What matters is that those conducting an analysis of poverty levels over time pay attention to the specific types of measurement used, their object, aim, and limits. The need to pay attention to the potential and limits of the concept adopted is important for every actor, including courts. When relying on statistical data in cases concerning poverty, courts must be aware that the word 'poverty' assumes different definitions, is measured in different ways, and serves different purposes depending on the definition adopted.

Similarly, equality can be assessed through different lenses depending on the definition adopted. Law often determines that equals shall be treated equally. However, it does not explain what 'equals' or 'being treated equally' means, thus making equality a tautology in the absence of external standards. The otherwise empty concept of equality finds external standards in theories of justice and socio-legal studies. The word 'equality' may refer to economic equality, equality in the distribution of resources, equality in the enjoyment of an existencial minimum, and equality of libertarian rights, among others. Different theories propose a focus on different spaces, highlighting the importance of a certain space over another. Therefore, the assessment of equality in a certain society depends on the delimitation of this variable.

In addition to requiring the delimitation of spaces, the principle of equality requires the determination of cognate groups or external standards for evaluating whether two or more individuals are to be considered similar for the purposes of being granted equal treatment. Some legal systems adopt an open equality clause, leaving the analysis of which classifications are allowed and which are prohibited to courts alone. Others adopt a non-discrimination clause through an exhaustive or a non-exhaustive list of protected grounds. The focus is then on intergroup variations.

Having determined those two standards, the law may still approach equality through different models. It may refer to formal equality, to substantive equality while still being restricted to the assessment of material disadvantage, or it may go beyond material disadvantage to cover multidimensional forms of oppression against groups. The analysis of oppression unveils different manifestations of disadvantages that are systematic and go beyond the distributive paradigm. As with poverty, inequality too can be conceptualized as multidimensional, notably when it moves beyond the distributive paradigm.

The link between poverty and inequality becomes more evident when these two concepts are understood as multidimensional phenomena. A headcount measurement of monetary poverty in a given state says little about inequality if seen in isolation.[189] Furthermore, if poverty is a question of simply reaching a minimum level of income above the poverty line, it could be argued that it can be tackled and resolved regardless of the extent of inequalities in a society.[190] By contrast, when poverty is understood as deprivations that affect an individual's ability to lead the life they choose, inequalities in the distribution of basic goods and opportunities to realize rights, as well as stereotyping and patronizing, are brought to the spotlight. In the words of Beteille, 'where relative deprivation is central to the conception [of poverty]', the latter 'is tied closely, if not inextricably, to inequality'.[191]

Similarly, when understood as a multidimensional concept, inequality unveils interconnections with poverty. Persons living in poverty may face a persistent and significant disadvantage in accessing infrastructure, adequate housing, and fundamental services, such as health treatments and education. These are indicators of both multidimensional poverty and inequality in the realization of fundamental rights. In addition, particularly vulnerable groups may be disproportionately represented among those living in monetary and/or multidimensional poverty. Finally, when inequality is understood as a phenomenon not only informed by material disadvantage but also by the unequal distribution of symbolic capital, it may unveil the processes through which certain groups living in poverty face different forms of oppression, which may, in turn, reinforce the very phenomenon of poverty.

Having shown that the very conceptualization of poverty and inequality allows for identifying interconnections between the two phenomena, the book now turns its lens to the accommodation of poverty in law. Chapter 3 explores how law addresses poverty and the role of equality in shaping its legal treatment. It will show that law has not always addressed poverty through the lens of equality or even through a human rights-based approach.

[189] Cf Beteille (2003), *supra* note 4, p 4462.

[190] For a critical discussion of this argument, see Sandra Fredman, 'The Potential and Limits of an Equal Rights Paradigm in Addressing Poverty' (2011a) 22 Stellenbosch Law Review 566, pp 568–569.

[191] Beteille (2003), *supra* note 4, p 4460.

3

How Does Law Accommodate the Socio-Economic Concept of Poverty?

> *[The poor] have to labour in the face of the majestic equality of the law, which forbids the rich as well as the poor to sleep under bridges, to beg in the streets, and to steal bread.*
>
> **—Anatole France (1894)**[1]

Chapter 2 resorted to economics and social science studies to define poverty. It showed that the IPL derives from studies on national poverty lines worldwide to identify an approximate common value for a poverty threshold. It also explained that, just as the World Bank lines, national lines for monetary poverty are based on a variable (such as per capita family income or household consumption expenditure), a unity of analysis (eg the individual or a household), and a measurement of monetary poverty (eg the incidence or the intensity of poverty). Similarly, multidimensional poverty requires a choice of spaces (such as consumption, access to health services, or education); the quantification of access to these spaces; and the socio-economic delimitation of significant deprivations to identify a situation of multidimensional poverty.

Accordingly, the definition of poverty does not derive from law. Law utilizes the definitions provided by socio-economic studies and regulates subjective rights and state obligations connected to poverty. For example, it utilizes poverty lines to identify target groups to which it grants the right to a given anti-poverty measure. It also utilizes the conceptualization of monetary and multidimensional poverty to establish duties for the state to eradicate poverty. In other words, law does not define, but rather 'accommodates', the socio-economic concept of poverty.

Different legal strategies have been used when accommodating a concept imported from other fields of knowledge. This chapter analyses how this

[1] Anatole France, *Le Lys rouge* (Calmann-Lévy 1906), p 118. The book was first published in 1894.

Judging Poverty and Inequality in Brazil. Tainá Garcia Maia, Oxford University Press. © Tainá Garcia Maia 2026.
DOI: 10.1093/oso/9780198994022.003.0003

accommodation takes place. Its purpose is not to provide a complete overview of the legal history of poverty in law but to explain that poverty has not always been incorporated into law through a rights-based approach. In making this argument, it introduces examples of regulations addressing poverty in different contexts and times. These examples are intrinsically non-exhaustive and focus on two of the pillars of this study: race and class.

Section 3.1 discusses the punitive treatment of poverty in law. Numerous historical examples could have been included to examine how law may perpetuate poverty traps or explicitly grant different legal protection to lives based on economic and social status—for example, the criminalization of women engaged in prostitution[2] or the Iberian Union's Philippine Ordinances (applied in Brazil from 1603 until their gradual revocation after Brazil's independence), which, among other criminal law regulations, provided authorization for a husband to kill his wife and her lover in case of adultery, provided the lover was of a lower social class than the husband.[3] Yet, considering the object of the book, this section focuses on vagrancy provisions, which are key illustrations of the criminalization of poverty. Section 3.2 discusses the consolidation of a human rights approach to poverty in law. Lastly, section 3.3 explains how equality constitutes one such approach and argues that it provides significant added value to addressing poverty through law.

3.1 The 'deserving' and the 'undeserving' poor: treating poverty punitively

3.1.1 A legacy of marginalization: vagrancy laws in Brazil

The inclusion of poverty as a topic addressed by law is not a novelty. In the Late Middle Ages, criminal law was an instrument used by public authorities to respond to poverty. The case of England is illustrative of this development. In the fourteenth century, the population of England had been significantly reduced by the Black Death. Amid concerns of labour scarcity and an increase

[2] On the legal treatment of prostitution in the early years of the Republic of Brazil and its connection with vagrancy laws, see Manuela Abath Valença, 'A Construção Social da Vadiagem nos Discursos Jurídicos do Início da Era Republicana' (2014) 1 Revista Brasileira de Sociologia do Direito 98.

[3] Iberian Union, 'Ordenações Filipinas' (1603) <https://www2.senado.leg.br/bdsf/item/id/242733> accessed 31 January 2024, book V, Title XXXVIII, M-liv 5 t 16 pr, p 1188.

in wages, the government approved the 1349 Ordinance of Labourers, compelling every 'able-bodied'[4] man and woman under the age of 60 years old who did not live by trade, exercise a craft, have assets or land, or serve another person to work. Wages for those individuals were set to match the values commonly found from 1340 to 1346, a measure aimed at preventing the rise of wages due to the scarcity of labour force following the loss of lives to the Plague. Failure to work would justify detention in strict custody until the individual found surety to serve in the aforementioned form.[5] Further punishment was institutionalized through the 1572 Vagabonds Act. The Vagabonds Act authorized the physical punishment of unlicensed vagrants and beggars, who could be whipped and burned through the ear.[6]

During the reign of Elizabeth I, the 1601 Poor Relief Act determined that children whose parents could not maintain them should be set to work as apprentices.[7] The Act was amended in 1834, one objective being to compel individuals to work and reduce demands for public funds.[8] On the one hand, the amendment established that the 'able-bodied poor' were to be placed in workhouses, clothed and fed, and that the children living in the workhouses could enjoy some level of schooling. On the other hand, the poor were required to wear a uniform in the workhouses, follow a specific and strict diet, and work under harsh conditions.[9]

The legal treatment of poverty was thus established based on whether one qualified as an 'able-bodied poor' or an 'impotent poor'. If qualified as the former, poverty was perceived as a reality linked to one's incorrect personal choices and moral flaws. Persons falling under this category were to be treated punitively. In other words, law provided different treatment for the poor based on an assessment of 'able-bodiedness'[10] and stereotyped views of poverty. When perceived as capable of working, the poor were considered to possess a level of agency that allowed them to work and take steps out of poverty. Failure to do so was to be treated punitively.

[4] Language of the law, which speaks of 'able in body'. To analyse the historical examples provided in this section, the chapter will retain the language of the law.

[5] The Statutes of the Realm, 'The Statute of Labourers', 23 Edw III, 1349, p 307.

[6] UK Parliament, '1601 Poor Law' <https://www.parliament.uk/about/living-heritage/evolutionofparliament/2015-parliament-in-the-making/get-involved1/2015-banners-exhibition/rachel-gadsden/1601-poor-law-gallery/> accessed 10 July 2022; BBC, 'Life in Elizabethan England' <https://www.bbc.co.uk/bitesize/guides/zxjgqty/revision/3> accessed 10 July 2022.

[7] Cf W Ivor Jennings, 'Poor Relief in Industrial Disputes' (1930) 46 Law Quarterly Review 225, p 226.

[8] UK Parliament, 'Poor Law reform' <https://www.parliament.uk/about/living-heritage/transformingsociety/livinglearning/19thcentury/overview/poorlaw/> accessed 10 July 2022.

[9] Cf The National Archives, '1834 Poor Law: What did people think of the new Poor Law?' <https://cdn.nationalarchives.gov.uk/documents/education/poor-law.pdf> accessed 10 July 2022.

[10] See note 4 for an explanation of the use of this term.

A similar punitive treatment of the poor, labelled as vagrants by law, was also adopted in continental Europe, including France[11] and Portugal[12] in the fourteenth century.[13] However, the criminalization of poverty was not a phenomenon restricted to the Global North. In Brazil, it withstood colonial independence and revealed a markedly racial perspective, as the following paragraphs will explain.

Chapter IV of the 1830 Criminal Code of the Brazilian Empire was titled 'Vagrants and Beggars'. Article 295 imposed the penalty of deprivation of liberty and prison labour for persons capable of working who did not have an 'honest and useful occupation' or sufficient income.[14] In addition, vagrancy was the object of the slow and gradual abolition of slavery in Brazil, as revealed by three key moments in the process of abolition of slavery in the country.

In 1871, Law No 2,040 ('Law of the Free Womb') granted freedom from slavery to all children of enslaved mothers born from the date of the promulgation of that law onwards. While the child was freed from slavery, their parents were not. Children could stay under the care of their mother until aged 8, in which case they would be subject to the authority of their mother's enslaver. Thereafter, the enslaver could choose between two alternatives. The first was to receive monetary compensation from the state for allowing the child to continue living in his[15] property. The second was to use the child's work without paying remuneration until they turned 21.[16] The second alternative was the standard one under the terms of the law, to be applied every time the enslaver did not explicitly opt for the first alternative. On the other hand, if the enslaved mother decided to give away or abandon her children, they would be delivered to an association which could use their labour for free

[11] Emanuel Chill, 'Religion and Mendicity in Seventeenth-Century France' (1962) 7 International Review of Social History 400.

[12] Portugal, 'Lei contra a vadiagem' <https://cctic.ese.ipsantarem.pt/red/hist/ficha_documento.php?cod=48> accessed 31 January 2024. See also Portugal, 'Livros das Leis e Posturas - Lei pela qual se reprime a vadiagem' <http://www.governodosoutros.ics.ul.pt/?menu=consulta&id_partes=43&accao=ver&pagina=20> accessed 31 January 2024. For a detailed analysis of the Portuguese case, see: Laurinda Abreu, 'Beggars, Vagrants and Romanies: Repression and Persecution in Portuguese Society (14th–18th Centuries)' (2007) 6 Hygiea Internationalis - An Interdisciplinary Journal for the History of Public Health 41; Daniel Tomazine Teixeira, 'Enquadramento da Pobreza em Portugal do Baixo Medievo: Assistencialismo e Repressão Estatal (séculos XIV/XV)' (Universidade Federal Fluminense 2011).

[13] For more examples, see Paul Ocobock, 'Introduction: Vagrancy and Homelessness in Global and Historical Perspective' in A L Beier and Paul Ocobock (eds), *Cast Out: Vagrancy and Homelessness in Global and Historical Perspective* (Ohio University Press 2008).

[14] Brazil, 'Criminal Code of the Empire of Brazil', 16 December 1830, Article 295. The penalty was applied after a warning.

[15] At that time, society was legally organized around patriarchal structures and symbols. Because the head of the household and the legal owner of the household's possessions at that time was generally the man, the use of the male pronoun has been adopted here. Furthermore, the use of the male pronoun in this paragraph reproduces the language of Law No. 2,040 of 1871.

[16] Brazil, 'Law No. 2,040', 28 September 1871, Article 1, § 1.

until they turned 21. In exchange, the association would raise the minors and look for an occupation for them after they reached 21.[17]

The Law of the Free Womb also recognized additional categories of enslaved individuals as freed, such as those, and here I quote, 'abandoned by their masters'.[18] The individuals falling under these additional categories who had been freed from slavery by virtue of the Law of the Free Womb were to remain under the government's inspection for five years. During that time, they were obliged by law to provide evidence that they had found work. If living in vagrancy, the law required them to conduct mandatory work in public institutions.[19]

Vagrancy was thus treated punitively. Furthermore, the gradual abolition of slavery in Brazil constituted a tool for prolonging forced or compulsory labour—including unpaid work at the household of the enslaver of the child's family or at the association providing care to abandoned children of enslaved parents. In addition, by requiring recently freed enslaved individuals—who accordingly lacked formal education and faced racial and social stereotyping, among other forms of oppression that qualified their skills and knowledge as less worthy and valuable—to immediately find work under the threat of being classified as vagrants, the law contributed to the perpetuation of poverty cycles and the institutionalization of patterns of domination.

Fourteen years after the Law of the Free Womb, Brazil adopted Law No 3,270 (the 'Dantas-Saraiva-Cotegipe Law' or 'Sexagenarian Law'). This was the final imperial anti-slavery law before the complete abolition of slavery in Brazil. The Sexagenarian Law freed enslaved individuals who had reached the age of 60 as long as they continued to work for three years to pay compensation for their freedom.[20] The Sexagenarian Law determined that freed individuals were to continue living with their 'former masters' after those three years,[21] who would feed, clothe, and treat them in case of disease in exchange for their unpaid work. The requirement to perform this compulsory work could be lifted if the recently freed individual preferred to obtain other means of subsistence and if a judicial authority considered that the individual would be capable of doing so.[22] In any case, an individual freed under this law who was found without an occupation would be 'obliged to get employed or hire their services out by the deadline set by the Police', in the words of the provision.[23] The freed sexagenarians were also obliged to remain for five years in the same municipality where

[17] Ibid, Article 2, § 1.
[18] Ibid, Article 5, § 4.
[19] Ibid, Article 5, § 5.
[20] Brazil, 'Law No. 3,270', 28 September 1885, Article 3, § 10.
[21] Language of the law. In Portuguese, 'seus ex-senhores'. Ibid, Article 3, § 4.
[22] Ibid, Article 3, § 13. Translation by the author.
[23] Ibid, Article 3, § 17. Translation by the author.

they had been freed. If they were to leave the municipality, the law determined that they should be considered vagrants and thus be detained by the police and taken to work for the state or in 'agriculture colonies'.[24]

The same considerations concerning the poverty trap instituted through the Law of the Free Womb apply to the Sexagenarian Law, with an addendum. In the case of the Sexagenarian Law, the obligation to find work was established for individuals aged 60 years or more, and work was to be found in the very same municipality where the individual had been enslaved. Racial bias thus intersected with age-based stereotypes and the omission of the law to accommodate the situation of older persons. In addition, it is relevant to recall that the life expectancy of a person born in 1910 in Brazil was 33.4 years for men and 34.6 years for women.[25] This figure would likely have been considerably lower for individuals enslaved throughout their lives. The possibilities for an individual in this situation to reach 60 years or more, be freed, and find work in one specific municipality were limited, and the work found likely restricted to socially undervalued occupations.

The Law of the Free Womb and the Sexagenarian Law created and validated conditions likely to perpetuate a poverty trap. Individuals who until then were enslaved and lacked formal education and monetary, social, and political capital, in addition to being subjected to stigmatization and marginalization in society, were to acquire an immediate occupation, often in the same municipality where they used to be enslaved. The logical consequence is the perpetuation of vulnerable labour relations and precarious conditions of work for the recently freed population of Afro-descendants.

The fragile nature of the abolition of slavery in Brazil is even more evident when one recalls that the Sexagenarian Law determined that freed sexagenarians could continue working for their 'former masters' (to use the language of the regulation) and receive food, clothes, and basic health care in exchange for their work. If the sexagenarians did not want to avail themselves of this possibility, they would have to find work in the same municipality in which they used to be enslaved; otherwise they would be considered vagrants and sent to mandatory work. Paulo Cruz Terra identifies in this provision the objective of immobilizing the freed individuals in the municipality where they used to work, keeping them subject to the power of their former enslaver.[26] The gradual abolition of slavery was thus more formalistic than substantive.

[24] Ibid, Article 3, § 15. Translation by the author.

[25] IBGE, *Estatísticas do Século XX* (2006).

[26] Paulo Cruz Terra, 'Racismo, trabalho e ociosidade no processo de abolição: o Brasil e o Império Português numa perspectiva global (1870-1888)' (2021) 41 Revista Brasileira de História 155, p 170.

The complete abolition came with Law No 3,353 (the 'Golden Law or Áurea Law') on 13 May 1888.[27] Three months after the promulgation of the Golden Law, the Chamber of Deputies of the Brazilian Parliament engaged in discussions concerning a bill for the repression of vagrancy, introduced by the then Minister of Justice of the Empire of Brazil, Ferreira Vianna.[28] The 1888 Annals of the Chamber of Deputies indicate that the parliamentary discussions were carried out in the context of the abolition of slavery.

Congressman Rodrigues Peixoto, who had been a supporter of the abolition, nonetheless called for the need to repress vagrancy in what he qualified as a context of the 'more or less clumsy effects [of the Golden Law], which disorganized work in farms and disturbed all economic relations'.[29] He recalled the vagrant regulations of France, England, and Switzerland as examples of the importance of fostering the 'spirit of initiative' and work habits of vagrants, in contrast to focusing on poverty relief, given that the latter could augment misery and make the poor 'discouraged with life'.[30] He argued that some of the root causes of the difficulties faced by Brazil and the high number of vagrants in the country lay in the natural richness and abundance of the Brazilian soil, as well as the amenities of the weather, which, by themselves, could fulfil the needs of vagrants and therefore reduce their incentives to foster work habits. Given this context, a repressive law compelling the non-disabled poor to work should be adopted, Congressman Peixoto claimed.[31]

A repressive treatment of the poor who were physically capable of working was also defended by Congressman Mac-Dowell. The Congressman stressed what he perceived as valuable effects of the proposed law given the recent abolition of slavery:

> I voted for the usefulness of this project, convinced, as we all are, that *today, more than ever*, it is necessary to repress vagrancy, *unnecessary* begging [...] etc. In the current circumstances in the country, this measure of repression is useful and needed. [...] I say this by recalling that the Minister [of Justice] appears to refer to the new law of 13 of May [the Golden Law] only in the justification of the project,

[27] Brazil, 'Lei Áurea', 13 May 1888.

[28] Sidney Chalhoub, *Trabalho, lar e botequim: o cotidiano dos trabalhadores no Rio de Janeiro da belle époque* (Editora da Unicamp 2012), p 66; Flávio Raimundo Giarola, 'Trabalho e combate à vadiagem: representações da mão-de-obra nos discursos dos periódicos de São João del-Rei (1871-1888)' (2012) 4 Temporalidades 278, p 281.

[29] Brazil. Câmara dos Srs Deputados, 'Annaes do Parlamento Brazileiro', vol VI, 1–31 October 1988, p 150. Translation by the author.

[30] Ibid, pp 150–151. Translation by the author.

[31] Ibid, p 152.

> when he referred to the need to provide support to the invalids of slavery. [Yet] this very generous, commendable, and just need [. . .] implies a corresponding *imperative duty on the part of the State to repress* and put a dam to all *the vices that the freedman brought back from his former state*, and which the miraculous effect of law could not make disappear, because law cannot, from one moment to another, *transform what comes from nature*.
>
> [. . .] [The vagrancy law] will produce the desired effects, suppressing vagrancy and compelling the idle population to honest work, reducing *the disastrous effect that is fatally foreseen as a consequence of the liberation of an enormous mass of slaves*, thrown into the midst of the civilized society; *slaves without incentives for good*, without education, *without the noble feelings* that only a free population can acquire. Finally, the education of minors will be regulated, the latter becoming instruments of intelligent work [. . .] and serving as examples for the edification of others in the same social class.[32]

Repression of vagrancy was justified as a measure to educate and reduce criminality and poverty. Yet, this punitive treatment relied on and perpetuated stereotypes based on race and economic condition. Furthermore, it preserved a poverty trap for the black and brown population in the country. The racial dimensions of parliamentary discussions on vagrancy, already evident in discussions prior to the bill introduced by the Minister of Justice, were denounced at the time by the newspaper *Gazeta da Tarde*. In a piece published on 7 May 1888 (ie eight days before the adoption of the Golden Law), the newspaper criticized the government's association of the soon-to-be freed enslaved individuals with threats against public order and labour. In this criticism, it presented the following question: 'Does the government want to free black people to put them in jail? [Does it want to] arm violent and despotic rural police at the service of the former bad lords who do not know how to adapt to the new working conditions?'.[33]

With the proclamation of the Republic in Brazil in 1889, the criminalization of vagrancy was taken to the new Criminal Code. The 1890 Criminal Code criminalized vagrants and *capoeiras*.[34] Individuals who did not have

[32] Brazil. Câmara dos Srs. Deputados, 'Annaes do Parlamento Brazileiro', vol VII, 1–31 October 1988, p 259. Translation by the author. Italics added by the author.

[33] 'Semana Parlamentar' *Gazeta da Tarde* (7 May 1888) <http://memoria.bn.br/pdf/226688/per226688_1888_00103.pdf>, 1st edn, Issue 103. The original text is in Portuguese.

[34] The word *capoeiras* refers to individuals engaging in the Afro-Brazilian martial art *capoeira*. This martial art was created by enslaved individuals of African origin in Brazil. On the criminalization of *capoeiras*, see Brazil, 'Criminal Code', Decree No 847, 11 October 1890, Articles 399–402. The practice of *capoeira* in public spaces could lead to detention of up to six months or double the time for the leader of the *capoeira* group. See ibid, Articles 402–403.

an occupation, means of subsistence, or housing, or who received an income from an occupation prohibited by law or 'manifestly offensive to morals and good customs' were to be imprisoned for fifteen to thirty days.[35] The criminalization of the absence of occupation and housing by the non-disabled poor impacted in a significant manner the black population in the Republic, who only two years earlier had been freed from slavery without compensation or other forms of reparation. The explicit criminalization of *capoeiras* further intensified the indirect impact of criminal law on this racial group.[36]

3.1.2 The punitive treatment of poverty and its impact on equality

The historical examples of the Elizabethan and Victorian eras in England and nineteenth-century Brazil demonstrate that law has not always addressed poverty and inequality as interconnected concepts. Law did not tackle the correlations between the two phenomena, and the remedies to respond to poverty resulted in violations of what is now codified as the right to equality.

The measures adopted under those regulations to overcome poverty did not reveal an institutional aspiration to accommodate equality. On the contrary, the law established a different treatment—including physical punishment, compulsory work, and detention—based on one's economic status and classifications of 'able-bodiedness'. These classifications apply and reinforce stereotypes. As Fredman explains, the poor regarded as capable of working are attributed more power and agency than they might have, given societal constraints and manifestations of oppression. In turn, when regarded as incapacitated for work, a poor person is often deprived of all agency.[37] This stereotyped differentiation manifested in law in a divide between the 'deserving' and the 'undeserving' poor,[38] which permeates the historical examples of the legal regulations discussed earlier. As Fredman explains with reference to nineteenth-century Britain, punitive treatment was provided to the 'undeserving poor',

[35] Ibid, Article 399.

[36] Today, vagrancy is no longer the object of regulation by the Criminal Code of Brazil, even though it is still addressed by the Code of Criminal Contraventions. The Code of Criminal Contraventions penalizes idle persons who have the capability to work but do not have sufficient means of subsistence with deprivation of liberty for fifteen days to three months. See Brazil, 'Law on Criminal Contraventions', Law-Decree No. 3,688, 3 October 1941, Article 59.

[37] Sandra Fredman, 'The Potential and Limits of an Equal Rights Paradigm in Addressing Poverty' (2011a) 22 Stellenbosch Law Review 566.

[38] Ibid, p 580.

whereas the 'deserving poor' were deprived of their qualification as individual agents and 'protected' as objects of charity.[39]

The insertion of poverty as a matter of criminal law exemplifies how law may institutionalize measures that aim to address poverty by establishing a detrimental treatment to particularly vulnerable groups. In this case, poverty is not perceived as an issue of equality, and the law does not treat equality as a means to reduce poverty. Through the punitive approach, law assumes a repressive role. It also reinforces stereotyped perceptions of the poor, in particular certain categories of poor individuals, in a confluence of factors of discrimination. This repressive treatment of poverty has had a disproportionate impact on historically vulnerable groups and, at times, targeted these groups directly, as the nineteenth-century case of Brazil shows. In the latter, the criminalization of poverty gained a racial perspective, notably in the gradual abolition of poverty and the post-slavery context of the first republic.

Decriminalization of poverty is still ongoing in the twenty-first century. In 2012, the United Nations Special Rapporteur on extreme poverty and human rights, Magdalena Sepúlveda Carmona, called states to repeal and reform laws that criminalized life-sustaining activities conducted in public spaces by persons living in extreme poverty, including sleeping, begging, eating, and performing personal hygiene activities.[40] The Rapporteur also called attention to the possible disproportionate effects of criminal sanctions and incarcerations on persons living in poverty, including homeless persons.[41]

Despite these challenges, how states approach poverty through regulations and institutions has gradually changed. A human rights approach to poverty has been progressively incorporated into constitutional, international, and statutory law worldwide. The very existence of the abovementioned UN report calling for decriminalization of homelessness and extreme poverty and the designation of a Special Rapporteur at the UN on poverty are examples of tools for incentivizing a human rights approach to poverty derived from international instruments. These mechanisms, in turn, raise the costs of noncompliance with rights-based standards.

[39] Ibid.

[40] Human Rights Council, 'Final draft of the guiding principles on extreme poverty and human rights, submitted by the Special Rapporteur on extreme poverty and human rights, Magdalena Sepúlveda Carmona', A/HRC/21/39, 18 July 2012, para 66.

[41] Ibid, paras 65–66.

3.2 The emergence of a human rights approach to poverty

In 2009, Beth A Simmons asserted that human rights had been 'one of the most powerful normative concepts of the past half century'.[42] They have served as the language of action for the international community against manifestations of oppression, in discourses within and among states themselves, and by groups to mobilize and make subjective claims before governments. The language of human rights brought about a new approach to rights and their legitimacy before governments, and it gradually consolidated throughout the twentieth century through the development of national and international institutions and legal frameworks.

However, the emergence and consolidation of such an approach and its responsiveness to structural societal challenges is neither a smooth nor a stable path. Taking this debate to the realm of poverty, Thomas Pogge brings forth a provocative reflection on the persistence of poverty despite great progress in moral and legal norms, unprecedented technology, and global economic growth. He identifies a tension in the process of consolidation of moral and legal norms. On one side, Pogge locates moral norms as being designed to safeguard the dignity and livelihood of those who are vulnerable.[43] On the other side, he identifies influential players upon whom burdens of commitment are placed and who are compelled to compliance. Pogge argues that those agents, consciously or unconsciously, act towards 'arranging their social world so as to minimize their burdens of compliance'.[44] If successful, compliance is possible while still enjoying the benefits of their dominance.[45] As a result, compliance costs[46] are generally reduced, and so is the level of protection afforded to the vulnerable communities.[47] Quoting Pogge, such a process gravitates towards an equilibrium between a mode of organization that gives the influential players 'as much as possible while still allowing them to be in compliance with their moral norms'.[48]

[42] Beth A Simmons, *Mobilizing for Human Rights: International Law in Domestic Politics* (Cambridge University Press 2009), p 112.
[43] Thomas W Pogge, *World Poverty and Human Rights. Cosmopolitan Responsibilities and Reforms* (Polity Press; Blackwell Publishers 2002), p 6.
[44] Ibid, p 5.
[45] Ibid.
[46] Including direct costs of compliance and what Pogge calls 'opportunity costs'. Ibid, p 6.
[47] Ibid.
[48] Ibid, p 6.

This section provides an overview of key legal factors in the development of a human rights approach to poverty. This analysis does not intend to be exhaustive but rather to explain with key examples the process through which a human rights approach was incorporated into the legal treatment of poverty. It shows, in the establishment of commitments to sufficiency, instances of the tensions to which Pogge referred. Notwithstanding these tensions, the emergence of a human-rights approach to poverty amplifies the opportunities for law to address poverty through the right to equality and non-discrimination. It also amplifies the costs of non-compliance with equality in the legal treatment of poverty.

3.2.1 The incorporation of social rights into the constitutional text

In the interwar period, there was a growing tendency to incorporate social rights into constitutional texts. At the time, the idea of promoting sufficiency through distributive measures was flourishing.[49] An early case of the incorporation of social rights in the constitution comes from Latin America. The 1917 Mexican Constitution guaranteed labour rights, including the right to a minimum wage that was 'sufficient, considering the needs of each region, to satisfy the normal life needs of the worker, his[50] education and honest pleasures, taking into consideration his role as the head of the family'.[51] The 1917 Mexican Constitution also prohibited discrimination based on a series of factors, including social status.[52]

Roberto Gargarella identifies in the 1917 Mexican Constitution a novel version of the social contract, one that integrates renewed social demands into the foundations of the traditional liberal-conservative agreement.[53] He explains that leaders of the liberal-conservative alliances[54] across Latin

[49] Samuel Moyn, *Not Enough: Human Rights in an Unequal World* (Harvard University Press 2018), p 35. For examples, see the 1917 Mexican Constitution and the 1919 Constitution of the Weimar Republic.

[50] Language of the law.

[51] Mexico, 'Constitution of Mexico', 5 February 1917, Article 123.A.VI. The text has been modified and now safeguards the right to a minimum wage that is 'sufficient to satisfy the normal material, social, and cultural needs of a family, and to provide the compulsory education of children'. See México. Cámara de Diputados, 'Constitución Política de los Estados Unidos Mexicanos', last update on 18 November 2022, 5 February 1917.

[52] Constitution of Mexico (1917), ibid, Article 1.

[53] Roberto Gargarella, *Latin American Constitutionalism, 1810-2010: The Engine Room of the Constitution* (Oxford University Press 2013), p 106.

[54] The term 'liberal-conservative alliance' or 'liberal-conservative compact' in Gargarella's book refers to the cooperation between liberals and conservatives in the mid-nineteenth century in Latin American

America, drawing inspiration from Mexico, came to recognize that expanding the scope of the traditional constitutional compact was both feasible and necessary. As a result, they began to advocate for new constitutions to accommodate previously omitted social demands.[55]

Throughout the twentieth century, Latin American constitutions increasingly incorporated what Gargarella calls 'the social question', one after the other. In Brazil, for instance, the 1934 Constitution guaranteed labour rights, classified interference with the enjoyment or legal exercise of social rights as a crime of responsibility by the Head of State, and guaranteed equality regardless of social class, wealth, and a person's profession or that of their parents, among other grounds.[56] Within this context, Gargarella argues that a new type of constitutionalism emerged in the region between 1930 and 1980, with socially committed constitutions and a reorganization of constitutional rights.[57]

In the European context, Orsola Razzolini cites the 1919 Weimar Constitution as the first commitment to socio-economic rights in constitutional law in Continental Europe.[58] Razzolini interprets this early incorporation of socio-economic rights in the constitutional text as reflecting an attempted compromise between the nineteenth century's individual liberalism, on the one hand, and the twentieth-century's aspiration of social justice and social solidarity that followed 'the rise of capitalism and collective movements and the shift away from a homogeneous (bourgeois) structure toward a pluralist social structure', on the other.[59] In her words, 'the idea of a "social-democratic constitution" reflects an abandonment of the laissez-faire approach for a new and different understanding of the relationship between state and economics, law and politics'.[60]

countries. Their alliance forged what Gargarella calls 'the basic matrix of Latin American constitutionalism', grounded on limited political liberties and ample economic liberties that left untouched crucial aspects of the countries' economic structure. Ibid, p 198.

[55] Ibid, p 106.

[56] Brazil, 'Constitution of the Republic of the United States of Brazil', 16 July 1934, Articles 57.d, 113 and 121. The 1934 Constitution was substituted by the 1937 Constitution upon the commencement of the dictatorship of Getúlio Vargas (1937–1945). The 1937 Constitution guaranteed the right to equality in Article 122, but without specifying any protected group. It also made no reference to the expression 'social rights', thereby significantly reducing the explicit protection of rights, including those related to labour. See Brazil, 'Constitution of the Republic of the United States of Brazil', 10 November 1937. However, in 1943, Vargas adopted the Compilation of Labour Laws, which remains in force today. Three years later, social rights were once more the object of explicit constitutional protection in the 1946 Constitution. See Brazil, 'Constitution of the Republic of the United States of Brazil', 18 September 1946.

[57] Gargarella (2013), *supra* note 53, Chapter 6.

[58] Orsola Razzolini, 'Constitutionalization of Socio-Economic Rights at the EU Level: Some Critical Notes' (2015) 98 Critical Quarterly for Legislation and Law 284.

[59] Ibid, p 284.

[60] Ibid.

While Razzolini stresses the search for compatibilization between individual liberalism and social justice as a mark of the early incorporation of socio-economic rights in constitutional texts, Samuel Moyn notes a different pattern. He argues that the emergence and multiplication of welfare states in the first half of the twentieth century pointed to a search for the compatibilization between freedom from want and equality.[61] Moyn finds that different welfare states, while starting with sufficiency, ultimately constrained inequality more and more, eventually making equality an aim in itself. In other words, welfare states established a floor and a ceiling, the latter through measures such as increased taxation.[62]

Moyn identifies that, by the late 1940s, entitlements for sufficient provision had almost become 'a constitutional orthodoxy' under both capitalism and communism.[63] Still, the increased incorporation of social rights in constitutions and the expansion of public policies towards sufficiency were generally not matters for judicial scrutiny. Moyn finds that next to no one at the time viewed these entitlements as standards for judicial enforcement.[64] Hence, sufficiency was hindered from full recognition as a subjective and justiciable right. Similarly, looking at the Latin American context, Gargarella explains that, despite the emergence of a new type of constitutionalism, social rights remained dormant in constitutional practice, set aside by judges across the region who viewed them as unenforceable or merely programmatic.[65] As social rights fell into a 'constitutional slumber' during most of the twentieth century,[66] criticism emerged, denouncing the disconnection from real-world implementation and portraying the new constitutions as poetic and generous but ineffective.

3.2.2 Post-1945 codification of international human rights law

After World War II, the codification of international human rights law brought a legally binding international obligation for states to respect, protect, and fulfil fundamental rights. This obligation emanates to all state actions. Accordingly, it also emanates to state policies and laws, including those

[61] Moyn (2018), *supra* note 49, p 6.
[62] Ibid, *supra* note 49, Chapter 2.
[63] Ibid, p 46.
[64] Ibid, p 47.
[65] Gargarella (2013), *supra* note 53, p 144.
[66] Ibid.

addressing poverty or impacting individuals living in poverty and groups particularly vulnerable to poverty. Therefore, the expansion of international human rights law raised the costs of failure to incorporate a human rights perspective into domestic responses to poverty.

In 1948, the Universal Declaration of Human Rights (UDHR) guaranteed equal entitlement to all rights and freedoms enshrined therein 'without distinction of any kind', mentioning a non-exhaustive list of prohibited grounds of discrimination, including social origin and property.[67] In Article 22, the UDHR safeguarded the rights to social security and to the realization of the economic, social, and cultural rights indispensable for one's dignity and the free development of their personality, through national effort and international cooperation.[68] Article 23.3 guarantees the right to 'just and favourable remuneration ensuring for himself and his family an existence worthy of human dignity, and supplemented, if necessary, by other means of social protection'.[69] Next, Articles 24 to 28 safeguard a series of social, economic, and cultural rights and entitlements to a social order in which the fundamental rights listed in the Declaration could be realized. Among the rights guaranteed are the right to rest and leisure, including paid annual holidays; the right to an adequate standard of living in terms of health and well-being; and the right to free education, at a minimum in the elementary and fundamental stages.[70]

A human rights approach to poverty was further developed during the mid- to late-twentieth century, with international social and economic rights expanding amidst a global justice debate. In 1966, the United Nations General Assembly adopted the International Covenant on Economic, Social and Cultural Rights.[71] Three years later, the delegations in the Inter-American Specialized Conference on Human Rights adopted the American Convention on Human Rights, protecting a myriad of civil and political rights and establishing an obligation for the States Parties to adopt measures to progressively achieve the full realization of economic, social, cultural, and environmental rights.[72] From the 1960s to the first decade of the twenty-first century, the UN adopted a series of treaties protecting specific groups while also safeguarding

[67] UNGA, 'Universal Declaration of Human Rights', 217 A (III), 10 December 1948, Article 2.
[68] Ibid, Article 22.
[69] Ibid, Article 23.3. The use of the male pronoun is the language of the Declaration.
[70] Ibid, Articles 24–29.
[71] UNGA, 'International Covenant on Economic, Social and Cultural Rights', United Nations, Treaty Series, vol 993, 16 December 1966.
[72] OAS, 'Inter-American Convention on Protecting the Human Rights of Older Persons', 15 July 2015, Article 26.

economic, social, and cultural rights. Examples include the International Convention on the Elimination of All Forms of Racial Discrimination, the United Nations Convention on the Rights of the Child, the International Convention on the Elimination of All Forms of Discrimination against Women, and the Convention on the Rights of Persons with Disabilities.[73] In 1981, the African Charter on Human and People's Rights ('Banjul Charter') was adopted to protect civil, political, social, economic, and cultural rights.[74] Seven years later, the OAS adopted the Additional Protocol to the American Convention on Human Rights in the Area of Economic, Social and Cultural Rights ('Protocol of San Salvador').[75]

With the expansion of international human rights law, social rights were put centre stage. Furthermore, galvanized by the context of decolonization, a discussion on global poverty was born, promoting the debate of sufficiency and distributive justice as a matter of global justice.[76] This culminated in the proposals for the so-called 'New International Economic Order' (NEIO), advocated by developing countries and aimed at restructuring the international economic order towards the promotion of economic justice.[77]

3.2.3 The emergence of a human right to development

The emergence of a human rights-based approach to poverty intertwines not only with the incorporation of social rights in constitutional texts and the post-1945 codification of international human rights law, but also with the consolidation of a human rights-based approach to development. Traditionally, the term 'development' had been predominantly framed in economic terms as economic development and growth. This conceptualization underpinned the work of international organizations, such as the World Bank[78] and the

[73] UN General Assembly (UNGA), 'International Convention on the Elimination of All Forms of Racial Discrimination', United Nations, Treaty Series, vol 660, p 195, 21 December 1965; UNGA, 'Convention on the Elimination of All Forms of Discrimination Against Women', United Nations, Treaty Series, vol 1249, p 13, 18 December 1979; UNGA, 'Convention on the Rights of the Child', United Nations, Treaty Series, vol 1577, p 3, 20 November 1989; UNGA, 'Convention on the Rights of Persons with Disabilities', A/RES/61/106, Annex I, 13 December 2006.

[74] Organization of African Unity (OAU), 'African Charter on Human and Peoples' Rights ('Banjul Charter')', CAB/LEG/67/3 rev 5, 21 ILM 58, 27 June 1981.

[75] OAS, 'Additional Protocol to the American Convention on Human Rights in the Area of Economic, Social and Cultural Rights ("Protocol of San Salvador")', A-52, 16 November 1999.

[76] Moyn (2018), *supra* note 49, pp 7–8, and 119. See Mônica Teresa Costa Sousa, *Direito e Desenvolvimento* (Juruá 2011), Chapter 3.

[77] UNGA, 'Resolution 3201 (S-VI)', A/RES/3201(S-VI), 1 May 1974.

[78] See Katie Willis, *Theories and Practices of Development* (2nd edn, Routledge 2011), p 3.

UN during the first UN Development Decade (1960–1970).[79] This economic-centric view was prevalent until the mid-1960s.[80]

Hence, development as a right was still an incipient concept. Daniel J Whelan et al locate, in the discourse of the Senegalese diplomat Doudou Thiam at the twenty-first opening session of the UN General Assembly (UNGA) in 1966, the first articulation of the right to development.[81] Thiam, at the time Minister of Foreign Affairs of Senegal, reflected on the failure of the international community to meet the goals set out in the Development Decade and addressed the growing frustration with persistent economic imbalance between developed and underdeveloped nations.[82] He called attention to the rising inequality between nations, noting the increasing gap between the income of developed and underdeveloped nations.[83] Arguing that poverty and underdevelopment were not predeterminate states caused by determinism but rather consequences of the historical structure of international trade, Thiam reaffirmed the right of developing countries to development.[84]

The frustration with the international trade order voiced by Thiam was not exclusive to Senegal. Rather, it became the object of a series of deliberations that eventually culminated in the NIEO. Whelan et al observe that the word 'poverty' appeared in the official statements of twenty-five representatives in the second session of the UN Conference on Trade and Development (UNCTAD), in 1968.[85] Four years later, by ninety votes in favour, no votes against, and nineteen abstentions (the abstentions coming mainly, but not exclusively, from States of the Global North), UNCTAD established a working group to prepare a charter on economic rights and duties of states.[86]

[79] Sousa (2011), *supra* note 76, pp 185–186. See UNGA, 'Resolution 1710 (XVI)', A/RES/1710 (XVI), 19 December 1961; and UN Secretary-General, 'The Emergence of the Right to Development' in OHCHR (ed), *Realizing the Right to Development* (United Nations 2013), p 7.

[80] UN Secretary-General (2013), *supra* note 79.

[81] Daniel J Whelan, Mihir Kanade, and Shyami Puvimanasinghe, 'The Right to Development: Origins, History and Institutional Development' (*E-Learning Module on Operationalizing the Right to Development in Implementing the Sustainable Development Goals. OHCHR, UPEACE, UNU-IIGH*) <https://www.ohchr.org/en/training-materials-online-course-right-development-and-sustainable-development-goals> accessed 2 February 2024, p 2.

[82] UNGA, 'Official Records, Twenty-first Session', 1414th Plenary Meeting, 23 September 1966, paras 180–230.

[83] Ibid, paras 213–214.

[84] Ibid, paras 216–228.

[85] Whelan, Kanade, and Puvimanasinghe, *supra* note 81, p 5. See UNCTAD, 'Proceedings of the United Nations Conference on Trade and Development, Second Session', New Delhi, 1 February to 29 March 1968.

[86] The states abstaining were: Australia, Austria, Canada, Denmark, the Federal Republic of Germany, Finland, Ireland, Italy, Japan, Liechtenstein, New Zealand, Norway, Paraguay, South Africa, Spain, Sweden, Switzerland, the United Kingdom of Great Britain and Northern Ireland, and the United States of America. UNCTAD, 'Proceedings of the United Nations Conference on Trade and Development, Third Session', Santiago del Chile, 13 April to 21 May 1972, Annex I.A, pp 58–61.

The Charter was adopted by the UNGA on December 1974, by 115 votes to 6,[87] with 10 abstentions.[88] The votes against and the abstentions, once again, came from the Global North. The Charter recognized the economic, social, and cultural development of peoples as the primary responsibility of their state, while also stressing the duty of all states, individually or collectively, to cooperate in eliminating obstacles that hinder the mobilization and use of resources.[89] In the same year, the UNGA approved the Declaration on the Establishment of a New International Economic Order, noting that:

> 1. [. . .] The developing countries, which constitute 70 per cent of the world's population, account for only 30 per cent of the world's income. It has proved impossible to achieve an even and balanced development of the international community under the existing international economic order. The gap between the developed and the developing countries continues to widen in a system which was established at a time when most of the developing countries did not even exist as independent States and which perpetuates inequality.
> 2. The present international economic order is in direct conflict with current developments in international political and economic relations. [. . .].[90]

Therefore, at the origins of the right to development was a postcolonial critique of the dominant approach to development—an approach that maintained that national economies would pass through a series of stages in their process towards modernization.[91] The postcolonial critique questioned that assertion, shedding light on international structures that hindered underdeveloped nations from transitioning away from the manufacture and trade of primary goods.[92] At that historical moment, this criticism was still a movement by states and mainly centred on states,[93] with no explicit recognition of development as a human right.

Still, the framing of development was undergoing a gradual shift, moving from the conventional development approaches, which largely framed development in economic terms, to a human rights-based approach.[94] In 1979, the

[87] Denmark, the Federal Republic of Germany, Luxembourg, the United Kingdom of Great Britain and Northern Ireland, the United States of America, and Belgium. See <IBT>UNGA, 'Official Records of the Twenty-Ninth Session of the UNGA', A/PV2315, 12 December 1974, pp 1372, para 99.
[88] France, Ireland, Israel, Italy, Japan, the Netherlands, Norway, Spain, Austria, and Canada. Ibid.
[89] UNGA, 'Resolution 3281 (XXIX)', 12 December 1974, Article 7. See UN Audiovisual Library of International Law, 'Charter of Economic Rights and Duties of States', UNGA resolution 3281 (XXIX).
[90] Resolution 3201 (S-VI) (1974), A/RES/34/46, 1 May 1974, operative paras 1 and 2.
[91] Whelan, Kanade, and Puvimanasinghe, *supra* note 81, p 3.
[92] Ibid.
[93] See Moyn (2018), *supra* note 49, pp 117–118.
[94] Dan Banik, *Poverty and Elusive Development* (Universitetsforlaget 2010), pp 122–126; Willis (2011), *supra* note 78, pp 3–5.

UN recognized development as a human right and a prerogative of nations in conditions of equality through UNGA Resolution 34/46.[95] In 1986, the UN Declaration on the Right to Development was adopted, recognizing development as 'an inalienable human right by virtue of which every human person and all peoples are entitled to participate in, contribute to, and enjoy economic, social, cultural and political development, in which all human rights and fundamental freedoms can be fully realized'.[96] The Declaration's Preamble frames development as a 'comprehensive economic, social, cultural and political process, which aims at the constant improvement of the well-being of the entire population and of all individuals on the basis of their active, free and meaningful participation in development and in the fair distribution of benefits resulting therefrom'.[97]

Amid this context, the Human Development Index (HDI) was created and has been featured in the United Nations Development Programme's (UNDP) Human Development Report since 1990. Created by the Pakistani economist Mahbub ul Haq with the collaboration of Amartya Sen, the HDI emerged from the recognition that the economic metrics of development were far too narrow and limited.[98]

Despite these developments, Dan Banik explains that the integration of human rights and development faced resistance. The Declaration on the Right to Development was met with controversy[99] and remained largely disregarded in its initial years. It was only in the late 1990s that the Declaration began to gain momentum.[100] While the Declaration had been adopted with one vote against[101] and eight abstentions,[102] by the 1990s the right to development was reaching increasing consensus. The adoption by acclamation of the Rio Declaration on Environment and Development,[103] which recognized the right to development and reaffirmed it as sustainable development,

[95] UNGA, 'Resolution 34/46 (1979)', A/RES/34/46, 23 November 1979, operative para 8. See Sousa (2011), *supra* note 76.

[96] UNGA, 'Declaration on the Right to Development', A/RES/41/128, 4 December 1986, Article 1(1).

[97] Ibid, Preamble.

[98] Willis (2011), *supra* note 94, p 7.

[99] For a brief overview of the difficulties of the drafting process of the Declaration, see Whelan, Kanade, and Puvimanasinghe, *supra* note 81, pp 12–13.

[100] Banik (2010), *supra* note 94, p 126.

[101] The United States of America. See UNGA, 'Provisional Verbatim Record of the Nineth-Seventh Meeting', A/41/PV97, 4 December 1986, p 64.

[102] Denmark, Finland, the Federal Republic of Germany, Iceland, Israel, Japan, Sweden, and the United Kingdom of Great Britain and Northern Ireland.

[103] UN, 'Report of the United Nations Conference on Environment and Development, vol.II, Proceedings of the Conference', A/CONF151/26Rev1 (Vol II), p 16. The Declaration was endorsed by the United Nations in resolution 47/190 (1993). See Dag Hammarsjöld Bibliothèque, 'Résolutions adoptées par l'Assemblée générale à la 47ème session' <https://research.un.org/fr/docs/ga/quick/regular/47> accessed 2 February 2024.

and of the Vienna Declaration and Programme of Action, which reaffirmed the right to development as a 'universal and inalienable right and an integral part of fundamental human rights',[104] are notable examples of the changing scenario.[105]

In the first decade of the twenty-first century, rising criticism of conventional development strategies and their relative failure led to a growing consensus about the interdependence of human rights and human development.[106] With the framing of development as a right, the right to live free of poverty can be seen as a subjective right and an obligation of the State. According to Irene I Hadiprayitno, the right to development is a framework in which poverty is a human rights concern.[107] It provides a focus not only on the outcomes to be achieved in terms of human development but also the process through which this achievement should take place, which entails the full realization of human rights and fundamental freedoms.[108] As Whelan et al eloquently summarize, this conceptualization of the right to development and its convergence with economic and human rights perspectives tackles the 'what' and the 'how' questions.[109]

However, the emergence of a right to development does not guarantee, on its own, judicial protection to deprivations related to poverty, and its application to poverty may still fall short of tackling inequalities that both derive from and cause poverty. First, the framing of poverty as a human rights problem inserted in the right to development has limited practical effect if the right to development is not interpreted as justiciable and within the competence of national and international courts. Second, if development is interpreted through the lens of basic needs, the rights of individuals living in poverty become subject to the significant limitations that will be discussed in section 3.3.1 below. Lastly, a development approach to poverty does not equate to an equality-based approach. Banik observes that, while poverty has become a buzzword among development actors, inequality faces a different reception. In his words, development actors 'continue to feel uncomfortable

[104] UNGA, 'Vienna Declaration and Programme of Action', A/CONF157/23, 12 July 1993; World Conference on Human Rights, 'Report of the World Conference on Human Rights. Report of the Secretary-General', A/CONF157/24 (Part I), 14–25 June 1993, p 19; Whelan, Kanade, and Puvimanasinghe, *supra* note 81, p 15.

[105] See Whelan, Kanade, and Puvimanasinghe, *supra* note 81, p 15.

[106] Banik (2010), *supra* note 94, p 128.

[107] Ibid, p 126; Irene I Hadiprayitno, 'Poverty' in OHCHR (ed), *Realizing the Right to Development* (United Nations 2017), pp 146–147.

[108] See Arjun K Sengupta, 'Study on the current state of progress in of the right to development submitted by Mr. Arjun K. Sengupta, independent expert, pursuant to Commission resolution 1998/72 the implementation and General Assembly resolution 53/155', E/CN4/1999/WG18/2, 13–17 September 1999, para 37.

[109] Whelan, Kanade, and Puvimanasinghe, *supra* note 81, p 17.

about speaking of "inequality reduction" as it involves confronting the power of national, regional and local elites'.[110] He finds that, although many development actors acknowledge inequality as a problem, there is rarely a concerted endeavour to address it.[111]

3.3 An unfulfilled promise?

As the previous sections showed, during the twentieth and early twenty-first centuries, new imperatives emerged for states on a spectrum of intervention. Sufficiency was to be implemented through a human rights perspective, notably through the realization of socio-economic rights. It would be through the latter that scholars would generally discuss and approach the issue of poverty. At the same time, development was being gradually framed as an international human right, with implications for the treatment of poverty as a human rights issue.

However, tension persisted between different accounts of human rights. Pogge explains that, on one side, libertarians defended a minimalist account of human rights according to which only negative duties would emanate from them. A different account identified both negative and positive duties as derivatives of all human rights.[112] While the second account is now prevalent in international human rights law,[113] not every court is equally active in finding violations of human rights in their positive dimension compared to the negative dimension. A court more prone to finding a breach of the positive dimension of human rights is expected to have more space and opportunities to address poverty.

Furthermore, the traditional human rights tools for addressing poverty appear insufficient to respond to the persistence of poverty in its multiple manifestations. This chapter identified a shift in the legal treatment of poverty, moving beyond the punitive dimension to cover poverty vulnerabilities as an issue to be approached through the perspective of human rights, notably socio-economic rights. While this evolution signals a reframing of poverty domestically and internationally, its potential is still limited by the disputed justiciability of socio-economic rights. As Fredman explains, socio-economic

[110] Banik (2010), *supra* note 94, p 14.
[111] Ibid.
[112] Pogge (2002), *supra* note 47, p 64.
[113] Ilias Bantekas and Lutz Oette, *International Human Rights Law and Practice* (2nd edn, Cambridge University Press 2016), Chapter 2, section 2.3.4; Olivier de Schutter, *International Human Rights Law* (2nd edn, Cambridge University Press 2014), Chapter 3, section 1.1.

rights continue to struggle for full recognition within the human rights sphere.[114]

In any case, even when a positive account of human rights is maintained and socio-economic rights are justiciable, additional challenges emerge for an effective and comprehensive legal response to poverty in its multiple dimensions. This section highlights two key challenges: first, the delimitation of basic needs for the promotion of sufficiency (section 3.3.1); and second, limitations of social rights adjudication to the eradication of poverty in its structural and collective dimensions (section 3.3.2).

3.3.1 The 'basic needs' discussion

The general context of optimism post-1945 towards egalitarian ways of promoting sufficiency was met with obstacles. Moyn observes that, throughout the 1970s, the aspiration for a broader social justice in a welfare world was put on 'indefinite hold'.[115] With the expansion of brutal dictatorships in Latin America and the then Communist Eastern Europe and the unveiling of enforced disappearances, torture, curtailments of freedom of expression and assembly, and political imprisonments committed by those regimes, the focus of transnational activism turned to egregious violations of personal freedoms.[116] Moyn highlights the resistance of two leading human rights organizations—Human Rights Watch and Amnesty International—to include the issue of poverty and social justice in their agendas in the twentieth century.[117] The focus of activism by these leading Northern human rights organizations was on state repression and persecution, rather than distributive justice and poverty.[118]

This does not mean that a discussion on social justice was dropped altogether. As Moyn explains, social rights and their minimum core were reconceptualized along the lines of a global subsistence ethic.[119] To explain this development, the author highlights the early encounter of human rights with development thinking and a relatively minimalist understanding of basic needs.[120]

114 Fredman (2011a), *supra* note 37, p 566.
115 Moyn (2018), *supra* note 49, p 120.
116 Ibid, pp 120 and 123.
117 Ibid, pp 122, 123, and 193.
118 Ibid.
119 Ibid, p 120.
120 Ibid, p 145.

Moyn identifies risks associated with this redefinition. He argues that, while it is possible to hope that sufficiency leads to equality, it is equally conceivable that the poor will move closer to sufficient provision while the rich accumulate ever greater gains.[121] A different concern with the basic needs approach is offered by Fredman, who analyses the disadvantages of understanding poverty through an absolutist definition. She argues that an absolutist definition of poverty, based on a predetermined notion of the minimum needs to sustain life, can entrench inequality and ignores the central relationship between the latter and poverty.[122] In addition, a focus on an absolute notion of bare minimum defines the needs of those living in poverty on their behalf. It may also make these assumptions based on stereotypical roles assigned to individuals and, as a result, legitimize the continuing rise of inequality.[123]

At the same time, Fredman warns that a minimum threshold of needs should not be wholly disregarded, as it establishes a direction for realizing distributive equality. If there is no requirement for basic needs, distributive equality could be arguably realized by levelling down access to resources.[124] As an alternative to the potentially paternalistic approach of the existential minimum and the dangers of complete independence from minima, Fredman proposes a combination of absolute basic requirements for survival, on the one hand, and requirements relative to what others have, on the other.[125] I add that a tool that can be valuable in promoting this combination is reading the progressive realization of sufficiency in light of the multidimensional aims of substantive equality, encompassing redistribution, recognition, participation, and transformation. Under this four-dimensional analytical framework, distributive justice requires breaking down disadvantages in a way that increases equal participation and remains consonant with the promotion of recognition and, when appropriate, the accommodation of difference.[126] This multidimensional assessment avoids a levelling down strategy, as the latter fails to integrate these multiple aims. After all, while a levelling down strategy might effectively reduce distributive gaps, it is insufficient to reduce disadvantage, as it universalizes it and remains unresponsive to structures

[121] Ibid, p 5.
[122] Fredman (2011a), *supra* note 37, p 570.
[123] Ibid.
[124] Ibid, p 574.
[125] Ibid.
[126] A certain degree of levelling down may be inevitable in the distribution of limited material opportunities and goods. For Khaitan, such an indirect and gradual levelling down 'is an acceptable and necessary price to pay to secure freedom for all'. However, he argues that a threshold must be met on how much levelling down may be acceptable in a theory of non-discrimination law. In his words: 'the opportunities of the members of the dominant group should not fall below the adequacy threshold either'. Tarunabh Khaitan, *A Theory of Discrimination Law* (Oxford University press 2015), p 133.

perpetuating material, cultural, and symbolic disadvantage. In conclusion, the four-dimensional approach to substantive equality provides a relevant tool in human rights for addressing freedom from want by limiting the risks faced by the basic needs approach of stagnating at a minimum and reinforcing misrecognition, while simultaneously responding to the levelling-down objection. This will be discussed in more detail in section 3.4.

3.3.2 Social rights adjudication as a self-sufficient strategy?

An increasing number of jurisdictions today recognize the justiciability of socio-economic rights, with social rights litigation taking place in regional and international bodies as well as domestic courts. In Latin America, around the end of the twentieth century, judges started accepting and addressing claims for enforcing or implementing constitutionalized social rights.[127] Gargarella attributes this development to different factors, including the expansion of international human rights law, the emergence of larger suits, legal reforms that improved access to courts by disadvantaged groups, and the efforts of progressive jurists.[128] More recently, Latin America has moved beyond these early developments to become a global leader in the constitutionalization and judicial enforcement of socio-economic rights, offering both doctrinal innovations and concrete examples of enforcement—a development that Daniel M Brinks sees as eclipsing other regions.[129]

In Brinks's view, even if judicial interventions related to social and economic rights in Latin America are at times contentious or dismissed as ineffective, there is no doubt that they have reshaped the politics of resource distribution and influenced the strategies of social movements in numerous countries throughout the region.[130] Brinks is right to highlight the contribution of social rights litigation to the politics of provision. Turning our lenses to poverty specifically, social rights codification in constitutional and international human rights law and their judicialization undoubtedly constitute important tools to address sufficiency and poverty deprivations. However, notwithstanding their potential, if detached from an equality approach, they

[127] Gargarella (2013), *supra* note 53, p 144; Daniel M Brinks, 'Social Rights Constitutionalism' in Conrado Hübner Mendes, Roberto Gargarella, and Sebastián Guidi (eds), *The Oxford Handbook of Constitutional Law in Latin America* (Oxford University Press 2022), pp 747–749.

[128] Gargarella (2013), *supra* note 53, pp 144–145.

[129] Brinks (2022), *supra* note 127, p 744.

[130] Ibid.

remain a limited mechanism for tackling poverty in its structural and collective dimensions.

When justiciable, social, economic, and cultural rights run the risk of addressing core symptoms of poverty but not always its structural root causes. If not coupled with an analysis of oppressions and inequalities that sustain social injustices (distributive or not), socio-economic rights may leave untouched systems of dominance and subordination, as well as the power dynamics that perpetuate the exclusion of historically vulnerable groups from the enjoyment of rights (including socio-economic ones) and thereby reinforce poverty and marginalization.

When left unaddressed, structural inequalities also hinder one's ability to access, establish, or maintain the structures needed to implement otherwise formal rights.[131] To effectively address poverty and its related deprivations of rights, one must confront the participatory harms experienced by vulnerable groups. More specifically, persistent inequalities impact what Brinks and Sandra Botero call 'legal agency', that is, the probability that one's rights will be denied, the likelihood of obtaining redress for the violation, and the ability to actively and effectively engage with law and legal procedures to pursue legally sanctioned life goals.[132] Groups that face continued marginalization and exclusion face hindrances in the development and exercise of their legal agency and in benefiting from support structures for their legal claims. For these groups, rights—including core socio-economic rights eroded by poverty—are more likely to remain an unfulfilled promise, operating as symbolic formal rights rather than effective and concrete substantive rights.

Furthermore, if addressed by law as purely individual entitlements without a collective dimension, social rights litigation, while necessary, may fall short of being truly transformative. As Brinks explains, '[i]t remains an open question whether judges will find a way to balance the understandable impulse to simply enforce the law as they understand it in the context of the case at hand, with the equally understandable need to consider the effect of their decisions on the many others who depend on the same public services'.[133]

The application of the right to equality to socio-economic deprivations has the potential to bridge individualized fulfilment of fundamental rights and the promotion of structural change. The case of the right to food in Brazil offers a compelling example. Odaleia Barbosa de Aguiar and Susana Moreira Padrão

131 See Daniel Brinks and Sandra Botero, 'Inequality and the Rule of Law: Ineffective Rights in Latin American Democracies' in Daniel Brinks, Marcelo Leiras, and Scott Mainwaring (eds), *Reflections on Uneven Democracies: The Legacy of Guillermo O'Donnell* (Johns Hopkins University Press 2014).

132 Ibid, p 218.

133 Brinks (2022), *supra* note 127, p 755.

explain that food insecurity in Brazil has intricate interconnections with poverty and socio-economic inequality in the country.[134] While the possibility for individuals and civil society to claim the enforcement and fulfilment of the right to food is a positive development, Aguiar and Padrão highlight the importance of identifying the structural barriers that hinder access to this right—barriers that they trace to an economic system that has historically promoted poverty and inequality.[135] Understanding and tackling these systemic barriers is key to reducing vulnerability among the population through state-led policies that are both enduring and inclusive, with an immediate focus on redistributing income, generating employment, and ensuring food and nutritional security.[136]

When disconnected from an equality approach, adjudication of social rights before domestic courts may leave untouched or even entrench disparities and vulnerabilities to the detriment of marginalized communities, including those living in poverty and socio-economic vulnerability. Octávio Luiz Motta Ferraz's studies on right-to-health adjudication in Brazil are illustrative. Ferraz speaks of 'two Brazils' within the same country: one with socio-economic indicators comparable to highly developed nations, and another still marked by exclusion and severe vulnerability.[137] Amid this context of profound disparities, the Brazilian Judiciary has been framed by scholars and activists as a key forum for implementing constitutional transformative promises, including equitable and universal access to the right to health. However, Ferraz's research suggests that the boom in right-to-health litigation in Brazil was not matched by improvements in health equity. On the contrary, the current model of Brazil's right-to-health litigation has exacerbated health inequities. This surprising outcome has two main reasons. First, the right to health is currently interpreted by the Judiciary as an individual entitlement, as opposed to a right constrained by limited resources in which individual access to the most advanced health treatments cannot come at the expense of universality. Second, access to court is easier for individuals with higher economic and social status. Ferraz shows that those more frequently able to access the courts to claim the highest attainable health treatment (at an individual and not collective level) are individuals whose socio-economic status already contributed to improved health conditions and greater access to key social determinants of

[134] Odaleia Barbosa de Aguiar and Susana Moreira Padrão, 'Direito humano à alimentação adequada: fome, desigualdade e pobreza como obstáculos para garantir direitos sociais' (2022) Serviço Social & Sociedade 121, p 133.

[135] Ibid, pp 135–136.

[136] Ibid, p 136.

[137] Octávio Luiz Motta Ferraz, 'The Right to Health in the Courts of Brazil: Worsening Health Inequities?' (2009) 11 Health and Human Rights 33.

health.[138] He concludes that the routine approval of claims for medication by the Brazilian courts benefits privileged litigants while pulling the budget away from the universal public health system, thereby entrenching health inequalities and disproportionately impacting the poor.[139]

Ferraz argues that inequality of distribution remains the main obstacle to the implementation and consolidation of social rights.[140] In his understanding, addressing intractable issues of distributive justice and achieving consensus on them, even if extremely difficult and arguably utopian, is crucial for making the nature and content of social rights more concrete and implementing these rights effectively.[141] Tackling distributive—and, here I add, recognition—injustices is necessary for the effective implementation of social promises, including sufficiency and freedom from poverty.

If disconnected from the principle of equality, social rights litigation may fail to reduce gaps and may even increase disparities. This pitfall can be avoided by an equality approach to poverty which recognizes the impact of inequitable resource distribution on the realization and implementation of human rights, thereby approaching poverty not only as income deprivation but also as unequal opportunities for the realization of rights. In addition, the equality approach to poverty provides a normative basis for the justification of distributive remedies independent of a specific use of agency, shifting the focus from the latter to an analysis of the structural pillars that maintain persistent exclusions and marginalization of certain collectivities. Finally, the equality approach complements a socio-economic rights approach to poverty by shedding light on power relations, marginalization, and vulnerabilities that interconnect, enable, and reinforce the denial of social rights in the context of poverty. As section 3.4 will explain, the equality approach constitutes a valuable pathway for law to address poverty in its multiple dimensions.

3.4 Equality as a legal tool for addressing poverty

Equality is a well-established justiciable right domestically and internationally. It emerges as a key means for bringing a human rights-based approach

[138] Ibid. See also Octávio Luiz Motta Ferraz, 'The Right to Health in the Courts of Brazil: Still Worsening Health Inequities?' (2017) 5 Revista del Centro de Estudios Constitucionales 195.

[139] See also Octavio Luiz Motta Ferraz, 'Harming the Poor Through Social Rights Litigation: Lessons from Brazil' (2011) 89 Texas Law Review 1643.

[140] Octávio Luiz Motta Ferraz, 'Inequality, Not Insufficiency: Making Social Rights Real in a World of Plenty' (2014) 12 The Equal Rights Review, 77, p 78.

[141] Ibid, p 78.

to poverty in jurisdictions in which socio-economic rights are not integrated into the constitution, the bill of rights, or ratified international treaties.[142] Furthermore, even where socio-economic rights are protected domestically, approaching poverty as an equality issue still retains great relevance, for four main reasons.

First, if interpreted as a monetary concept, poverty causes deprivation in the enjoyment of rights, including, but not limited to, unequal access to socio-economic rights. If interpreted as a multidimensional concept, poverty is these very deprivations. Therefore, when poverty is understood in multidimensional and relative terms, its very definition becomes interconnected with aspects of inequality. However, to affirm that the root causes of poverty are the very deprivation of rights it causes is a circular argument that does not sufficiently clarify its historical causes. Maldistribution sits at the heart of the history of poverty, but a thorough explanation of the latter must consider intersectionalities, power structures, and oppression. Equality offers a tool to do so. It provides a tool for addressing the root causes of poverty,[143] not merely its manifestations.

Second, maldistributions can arguably be solved by guaranteeing social, economic, and cultural rights. However, as argued in section 3.3, the social rights approach to poverty might leave misrecognition untouched and fail to promote structural change. In contrast, a multidimensional understanding of substantive equality brings to judicial scrutiny not only maldistributions but also misrecognition. When understood as a multidimensional concept, the right to equality unveils stigmatization, exclusion, and differentiation affecting persons living in poverty. It recognizes these multidimensional oppressions as forms of inequality derived from poverty.

When discrimination takes place because one belongs to a group living in poverty, the stigma and marginalization that are produced reinforce poverty. An equality approach is thus important as a strategy to respond to intra- and intergenerational cycles of poverty reinforced by exclusion and marginalization. By transcending the focus on material disadvantage[144] and the space of income distribution, a multidimensional understanding of equality allows institutions, including courts, to address discriminatory consequences of poverty, such as misrecognition and structural obstacles to parity in participation.

[142] Fredman (2011a), *supra* note 37.

[143] For a deeper analysis of this point, see Gwen Brodsky and Shelagh Day, 'Beyond the Social and Economic Rights Debate: Substantive Equality Speaks to Poverty' (2002) 14 Canadian Journal of Women and the Law 184.

[144] On the insufficiency of the disadvantage approach, see Sandra Fredman, *Discrimination Law* (2nd edn, Oxford University Press 2011b), pp 26–27.

Therefore, even jurisdictions resistant to discussing equality in the space of income distribution may still apply an equality approach to poverty, by identifying harms derived from misrecognition as products of the treatment of the poor and as root causes reinforcing poverty cycles.

Third, the analysis of poverty through the lens of equality requires assessing whether poverty disproportionately affects certain protected groups. Breaking historical cycles of inequality cannot leave aside the context of monetary and multidimensional poverty to which certain social groups have been historically subjected. By addressing poverty through equality, law is not only better able to respond effectively to poverty but also unveils otherwise invisibilized forms of inequality. After all, considering poverty—in its monetary and multidimensional dimensions—in equality cases may unveil multiple and intersectional discrimination.

Finally, an equality assessment impacts the state's positive obligations to address poverty. Equality limits the risks of stagnating at the minimum, which could occur if poverty is assessed exclusively through a basic needs approach. Furthermore, it provides a framework to challenge positive measures for being underinclusive or reinforcing stigma and stereotypes. It can also be used as a legal argument in favour of recognizing a positive obligation—that is, an obligation to act—towards addressing material disadvantage and other forms of oppression connected to living in poverty. When this takes place, an assessment of social, educational, and labour stratification, among other forms of marginalization and exclusion, become particularly relevant.

3.5 Concluding remarks

Law has not remained oblivious to the phenomena of poverty and inequality. Beteille asserts that, in pre-industrial societies, law not only accepted but also recognized estates or caste-type divisions in society. With the advent of industrial organizations, society gradually changed from hierarchy (where inequalities among estates or castes were legally recognized) to stratification (where inequality between social strata is a matter of factual reality, and not an essential component of the law).[145] However, the move from hierarchy to stratification should be looked at critically, as industrial states coexisted with systems of slavery and colonization for a long time.

[145] Andre Beteille, 'Poverty and Inequality' (2003) 38 Economic and Political Weekly 4455, pp 4461–4463.

In systems of hierarchy, estates and castes reinforce poverty and forms of deprivation through institutions, social practices, and the law. In turn, in systems of stratification, the incorporation of the right to equality before the law and the legal recognition of social entitlements as rights derived from citizenship gradually changed the logic of hierarchy. Deprivations are still a matter of fact in systems of stratification, and structural and historical discrimination and inequality persist as products of the social and legal history of the state and as by-products of stereotypes, prejudices, and internalized social myths. The confluence of these factors in law, politics, and society, even if not explicitly creating castes or estates through law, stabilizes exclusionary and marginalizing structures, obstructs transformative change, and undermines the adoption of robust distributive measures. In other words, different forms of oppression, as Young defines the term, subsist and manifest clearly and strongly in systems of stratification. However, the law moves from being a mechanism that manifestly legitimatizes oppression to gradually becoming—at least in discourse and as a potential—a tool that states, individuals, and collectivities can use to reverse structural and persistent inequality.

This chapter analysed how law addresses poverty, showing that different strategies, not all based on an equality-approach or even a human rights-based approach, have been adopted throughout history. How law has addressed poverty has changed throughout time and in different societies. Throughout history, poverty has been the object of criminal law, social and economic rights, and equality and non-discrimination law. This chapter argues that approaching law through equality has a significant added value. This approach may coexist with other human rights-based approaches, such as approaching poverty through socio-economic rights. Each tackles a different aspect of poverty and promotes responses that are not mutually exclusive but rather coexist and often support one another.

An equality approach is valuable for identifying the complexity of discriminatory practices that develop in a context of poverty. It allows for the identification of vulnerabilities and disadvantages that cause and derive from poverty, in a self-reinforcing cycle. If the identification of these vulnerabilities and disadvantages is partial and blurry, so are the responses provided through judicial protection. Therefore, considering these factors is key to an effective response to poverty, and it is made possible through the adoption of an equality approach.

An equality analysis unveils the multiple forms of oppression suffered by persons living in poverty, as well as intersectionalities that explain the manifestations of poverty in context. Furthermore, when bills of rights or human rights conventions do not safeguard economic, social, and cultural rights, equality becomes a primary vehicle for bringing poverty into the law and before the Judiciary. As Chapter 7 will discuss in more detail, this was one of the strategies used by the IACtHR to discuss poverty at a time when the Court did not consider Article 26 of the ACHR (on the progressive realization of socio-economic rights) as justiciable. In conclusion, the equality approach has added value when compared to the sole use of socio-economic rights to address poverty.

Yet, to say that poverty should be addressed through the lens of equality does not clarify how this takes place in practice. In the Inter-American System of Human Rights, poverty has been read by the IACtHR as a category that may be understood as falling within three protected grounds under Article 1(1) of the ACHR, namely: 'economic status', 'social origin', and 'other social condition'.[146] The discussion of poverty under the protected grounds of 'economic and social situation' also appears in the UN Committee on Economic, Social and Cultural Rights. In its General Comment 20, the Committee affirmed that a person must not suffer discrimination based on pertaining to an economic or social group or strata.[147] In addition to referring to economic and social groups as protected categories against discrimination, the Committee recognized that poverty and inequality are reinforcing phenomena: 'A person's social and economic situation when living in poverty or being homeless may result in pervasive discrimination, stigmatization and negative stereotyping.'[148] According to the Committee, this discrimination, stigmatization, and stereotyping can lead to 'refusal of, or unequal access to, the same quality of education and health care as others, as well as the denial of or unequal access to public places'.[149]

However, the examples of the IACtHR and the UN Committee on Economic, Social and Cultural Rights are not the rule. Various jurisdictions resist recognizing poverty as a suspect classification covered by discrimination law. In addition, resistance may also be found in applying the principle of equality as complementary to the socio-economic rights approach to poverty or as a principle from which social rights emanate. Overcoming these

[146] IACtHR, Judgment (Preliminary Objections, Merits, Reparations and Costs), *Workers of the Fireworks Factory in Santo Antônio de Jesus and their Families v Brazil*, 15 July 2020. Series C No 318, para 185.

[147] United Nations CESCR, 'General Comment No.20: Non-discrimination in economic, social and cultural rights (art.2, para.2 of the International Covenant on Economic, Social and Cultural Rights)', E/C12/GC/20, 2 July 2009, para 35.

[148] Ibid.

[149] Ibid.

obstacles requires a wider conceptualization of the right to equality as multi-dimensional, as explained in Chapter 2. In addition, it requires the development or implementation of strategies by courts to assess poverty as a matter of equality. Fredman and Atrey have identified some of these strategies in their respective studies on considering poverty in law as a matter of equality. These strategies will be discussed in Chapter 4.

4

Judicializing Poverty

The Four-Prong Model for a Legal Assessment of Poverty Through Equality

> *The other day, late at night, I heard a writer say he was perplexed by world hunger. Perplexed! I asked him to have the kindness, the Christian charity, to include there all types of hunger, including my own, which may be different from that of my brothers and sisters.*
>
> **—Conceição Evaristo (2016)[1]**

Freedom from want has not always been the object of judicial assessment and enforcement. As Chapter 3 showed, the early development of the welfare state in the twentieth century was still marked by resistance to judicial enforcement of social entitlements to sufficiency. Moyn observes that the constitutionalization of social rights unfolded remarkably against a backdrop of relative silence regarding their enforcement mechanisms.[2] In his words, '[a]ccorded by states as wise policies from above, social rights in between and after the world wars were not intended to provide a basis for ongoing agitation from below, and certainly not a basis for demands for enforcement (including judicial enforcement)'.[3]

Moyn identifies a shift after 1989, notably after the end of the Cold War, when judicial review practices expanded seeking enforcement of basic provisions in the distribution of goods.[4] While economic and social rights were never constitutionalized in some jurisdictions, and, in others, they were rather set as obligations of progressive realization or even directive principles, by the end of the twentieth century, there was a growing understanding

[1] Conceição Evaristo, *Olhos d'Água* (Pallas 2016), 'A gente combinamos de não morrer', p 108. Translation by the author.

[2] Samuel Moyn, *Not Enough: Human Rights in an Unequal World* (Harvard University Press 2018), p 57.

[3] Ibid, p 55. See pp 43–47.

[4] Ibid, pp 198–199.

Judging Poverty and Inequality in Brazil. Tainá Garcia Maia, Oxford University Press. © Tainá Garcia Maia 2026.
DOI: 10.1093/oso/9780198994022.003.0004

that human dignity required the immediate realization of a minimum core of rights.

This change was further exacerbated by the emergence of what Ran Hirschl calls the judicialization of politics and mega-politics.[5] Hirsch describes as 'judicialization of politics' the phenomenon in which judicial activity is expanded to matters relating to public policy, political controversies, and core moral predicaments.[6] He considers this potentially one of the most significant political phenomena for governments in the late twentieth and early twenty-first centuries.[7] Writing in 2008, Hirsch asserted that this phenomenon had only recently expanded beyond 'flashy rights issues' to encompass mega-politics, that is, 'matters of outright and utmost political significance that often define and divide whole polities'.[8]

Hirschl identifies the phenomenon of the judicialization of mega-politics in several areas, the most relevant for the present study being what he calls 'core executive prerogatives' and transitional or restorative justice.[9] Core executive prerogatives encompass economic and social policies, such as income distribution, poverty eradication, and basic subsistence rights. Hirschl notes that courts have generally not been particularly active in these areas, with some notable exceptions—among them, he cites Brazil. However, a turn towards the judicialization of core executive prerogatives occurred with the judicialization of politics and mega-politics. In turn, restorative justice encompasses affirmative action and other forms of guaranteeing rights to historically discriminated groups, such as providing land rights to indigenous groups and collective reparations.

In these and other spheres, courts emerged as bodies that exercise control over the actions and inactions of the state. Today, the compatibilization of sufficiency and equality has transcended the frontiers of politics and entered the jurisdiction of national, regional, and international courts. In this context, courts emerge as potential key players in matters that were formerly public policy questions, such as the implementation of sufficiency and redistributive claims, including anti-poverty policies.

This chapter analyses legal strategies to address poverty through the lens of equality. Section 4.1 introduces the models of Fredman and Atrey for the insertion of poverty in equality cases, which are based on the jurisdictions

[5] Ran Hirschl, 'The Judicialization of Mega-Politics and the Rise of Political Courts' (2008) 11 Annual Review of Political Science 93, p 2.
[6] Ibid.
[7] Ibid, p 2.
[8] Ibid.
[9] Ibid, pp 9–13.

of English-speaking countries with common law features. Based on these studies, section 4.2 presents an integrated model of legal strategies. This model will be used to evaluate the practice of the STF and the IACtHR in Part II of the book.

4.1 The models of Fredman and Atrey

In 2011, Fredman asked what possible role a constitutional right to equality or statutory anti-discrimination law could have in addressing poverty. Based on the experiences of Britain, the US, Canada, and South Africa, she identified three points of entry for the use of equality in addressing poverty: poverty as a protected group; equality as a means to challenge anti-poverty measures; and positive duties derived from the right to equality as a means to ameliorate inequalities.[10] Based on the analysis of legislation and, notably, court decisions in the abovementioned four jurisdictions, Fredman concluded that courts and legislatures remained largely reluctant to regard equality as the suitable arena for addressing distributive and polycentric issues linked to poverty.[11] She argued that attention should possibly be focused on what she calls 'fourth generation' equality rights or a 'proactive understanding of equality',[12] that is, the recognition of positive duties to address equality.

Seven years after the publication of Fredman's study, Atrey made a similar investigation by looking at the judicial responses from courts in Canada, South Africa, and India. She identified two ways in which courts have addressed poverty in intersectional cases. The first is through an analysis of discriminatory context, and the second conceives poverty as a matter of substantive equality. Atrey found that poverty remained 'largely unfamiliar to discrimination law', but that the two abovementioned strategies departed from the trend of reading poverty as a ground of discrimination and, therefore, revitalized efforts to address poverty discrimination.[13]

The approaches of Fredman and Atrey reveal similarities, notably between Fredman's identification of the third category of legal response (the positive duty to address equality) and Atrey's identification of the second strategy for addressing poverty in intersectional cases (poverty as a matter of substantive

[10] Sandra Fredman, 'The Potential and Limits of an Equal Rights Paradigm in Addressing Poverty' (2011a) 22 Stellenbosch Law Review 566.

[11] Ibid, p 589.

[12] Ibid, p 567.

[13] Shreya Atrey, 'The Intersectional Case of Poverty in Discrimination Law' (2018) 18 Human Rights Law Review 411, p 439.

equality). Furthermore, the two theories are arguably complementary, as Fredman's study provides a general framework beyond the analysis of intersectionalities, and Atrey brings the innovative contribution of identifying context as a legal strategy in intersectional cases. Considering these two factors, this chapter integrates the two theories and identifies a resulting four-prong model of legal strategies for courts to use when addressing poverty through equality. The four-prong model is composed of the following strategies: (i) poverty or economic status as a suspect category of discrimination; (ii) equality as a test of the inclusiveness of anti-poverty policies; (iii) poverty as a matter of discriminatory context; and (iv) positive obligations emanating from substantive equality. Each strategy will be introduced and critically analysed in terms of its potential and limitations as vehicles for addressing poverty through the litigation of equality cases.

4.2 The four-prong model

4.2.1 Poverty or economic status as a suspect classification

The law may grant individuals the right not to be discriminated against based on poverty. This could take place through equality clauses that expressly acknowledge poverty, socio-economic disadvantage, or economic condition as a protected ground against discrimination. Alternatively, this right may be enshrined through an open-ended equality clause if the latter is interpreted as including poverty as an analogous ground of discrimination.

The international level offers examples of different models of protection of economic vulnerability in equality and non-discrimination clauses. 'Social origin' is a suspect category of discrimination under Article 14 of the European Convention on Human Rights; Article 26 of the International Covenant on Civil and Political Rights (ICCPR); and common Article 2 of the ICCPR and the International Covenant on Economic, Social and Cultural Rights. In the Inter-American System of Human Rights, Article 1(1) of the ACHR expressly prohibits discrimination based on 'economic status' and 'social origin'.

The reference to 'economic status', 'social origin', or 'social and economic condition' appears to face less resistance than the inclusion of 'poverty' per se as a protected ground in equality clauses. On the one hand, poverty may be interpreted as being encompassed by these terms. On the other hand, interpreting poverty as falling within the scope of these grounds, instead of recognizing it as an independent ground, runs the risk of opening the door to litigation from non-protected groups that nonetheless fall within a suspect classification and seek to challenge poverty eradication policies. For example, affluent groups that do not benefit from anti-poverty measures could argue they are discriminated against based on socio-economic status. Given this risk, it has been proposed in literature that it would be more appropriate to adopt an asymmetric definition of these grounds, such as 'socio-economic disadvantage'.[14]

Looking at English-speaking domestic jurisdictions, Fredman qualified this strategy as the first point of entry for equality to address poverty. Yet her studies on Britain, Canada, the US, and South Africa showed that this approach had not been achieved in all four jurisdictions. The UK domestic anti-discrimination legislation adopts an equality guarantee with an exhaustive list of grounds, which does not include poverty or socio-economic disadvantage.[15] Still, socio-economic disadvantage was mentioned in the first section of the UK Equality Act (2010). According to the Act: 'An authority to which this section applies must, when making decisions of a strategic nature about how to exercise its functions, have due regard to the desirability of exercising them in a way that is designed to reduce the inequalities of outcome which result from socio-economic disadvantage.'[16] However, Fredman observes that it was made clear that this provision did not amount to an individual right to claim based on socio-economic disadvantage.[17] In November 2010, the then Home Secretary and Minister for Women and Equalities, Theresa May, described the socio-economic duty as a provision 'meant to force public authorities to take into account inequality of outcome when making decisions about their policies' and dismissed it as 'ridiculous' and 'simplistic'.[18] She argued that '[y]ou can't make people's lives better by simply passing a law saying that they should be made better' and announced that the government was 'scrapping the socio-economic duty for good'.[19] Nonetheless, the socio-economic duty was enacted in Scotland in 2018,[20] and in 2021 it commenced in Wales.[21]

[14] Fredman (2011a), *supra* note 10, p 584; see also Canadian Human Rights Act Review Panel, *Report of the Canadian Human Rights Act Review Panel* (2000).

[15] United Kingdom, 'Equality Act', 8 April 2010, Articles 4–12.

[16] Ibid, Section 1; Fredman (2011a), *supra* note 10 p 582.

[17] Fredman (2011a), *supra* note 10, p 582.

[18] gov.uk, 'Theresa May's equality strategy speech' (2010) <https://www.gov.uk/government/speeches/theresa-mays-equality-strategy-speech> accessed 18 March 2024.

[19] Ibid.

[20] Scottish Government, 'Fairer Scotland Duty: interim guidance for public bodies' (2018) <https://www.gov.scot/publications/fairer-scotland-duty-interim-guidance-public-bodies/pages/2/> accessed 18 March 2024.

[21] Welsh Government, 'Socio-economic Duty: an overview' (2020) <https://www.gov.wales/socio-economic-duty-overview> accessed 17 March 2017; Wales Centre for Public Policy, 'Implementing the Socio-economic Duty: learning from experience' (2021) <https://www.wcpp.org.uk/commentary/implementing-the-socio-economic-duty-learning-from-experience/> accessed 17 March 2024.

In the US jurisdiction, Fredman identifies resistance from the US Supreme Court against applying heightened judicial scrutiny over policies that discriminate against poor people.[22] In contrast, in Canada, three jurisdictions at the provincial level adopted 'social condition' as a prohibited ground of discrimination, and the remaining ones recognized narrower grounds (such as social origin, source of income, and receipt of public assistance) as protected grounds.[23] At the federal level, in 2000, the Canadian Human Rights Review Panel strongly recommended the inclusion of 'social condition' as a protected ground under the Canadian Human Rights Act.[24] The Panel argued that, like the other grounds of discrimination protected under the Act, poverty is immutable in the sense that it rests beyond the control of most poor people, at the very minimum, over considerable periods of their lives.[25] Furthermore, evidence shows that poverty can be inherited, as studies identify a correlation between parents' educational level and that of their child and indicate that children of poor parents are more likely to live in poverty.[26] The Panel also noted that poverty and low levels of education have been associated throughout history with patterns of disadvantage and reveal an interrelationship with other protected grounds, such as race, sex, and disability.[27] Therefore, it recommended the inclusion of this ground in the Canadian Human Rights Act, arguing that, '[a]t the very least, the addition of this ground would ensure there is a means to challenge stereotypes about the poor in the policies of private and public institutions'.[28] However, over twenty-five years after this proposition, the amendment has still not happened. This general scenario is further intensified by a resistance to engage in distributive issues, which Fredman identifies in the Canadian Supreme Court.[29]

Similarly, Fredman finds instances in the South African jurisdiction that indicate it may be considering the inclusion of grounds covering poverty in the equality clause.[30] In 2000, the Promotion of Equality and Prevention of Unfair Discrimination Act referred to socio-economic status as a directive principle and suggested that special consideration be given to its inclusion

[22] Fredman (2011a), *supra* note 10.
[23] Ibid.
[24] *Report of the Canadian Human Rights Act Review Panel*, *supra* note 14.
[25] Ibid, pp 112–113.
[26] Ibid, p 112.
[27] Ibid, pp 112–113.
[28] Ibid, p 113.
[29] Fredman (2011a), *supra* note 10, p 583.
[30] Ibid.

in the definition of prohibited grounds.[31] Yet, no such amendment has been adopted so far.[32]

In any case, one should note that, even if a jurisdiction recognizes economic status, social origin, poverty, or an analogous ground as a protected classification against discrimination, this strategy still faces significant limitations in responding to poverty. First, courts might be resistant to recognizing redistributive claims on these grounds. Considering that distributive harms are inherent to all conceptualizations of poverty or vulnerability to poverty, the inability to respond to redistributive claims and order redistributive remedies curtails the capacity of an equality approach to respond to poverty.

Second, courts might be more prone to recognizing discrimination based on these grounds when analysing a differentiation explicitly based on class. For example, if Brazil were to enact a prohibition today on voting by persons whose patrimony falls below a certain threshold, the case would easily fall under 'economic status' as a suspect category under Article 1(1) of the ACHR. Yet such a direct link between class and the impugned measure is not always—and not often—that straightforward. Discrimination based on poverty may take place through measures and omissions that are not based on class but, nonetheless, reveal a poverty dimension. For example, a measure may indirectly discriminate against individuals living in poverty or generate detrimental socio-economic effects on protected groups that are disproportionately represented among those living in poverty.

Finally, the potential impact of discrimination clauses that expressly recognize social origin and economic status as a suspect classification faces further obstacles when enshrined in treaties that only protect civil and political rights. When this is the case, a court will generally perceive its competence as limited to that category of rights. Accordingly, such a discrimination clause inside a treaty or bill of rights that essentially safeguards civil and political rights may be limited in its potential as an effective legal tool against poverty. If distributive inequalities are unlikely to be assessed, the impact of this approach is rather limited. Accordingly, recognizing economic status and/or social origin as prohibited grounds of discrimination is a valuable but insufficient strategy to respond to these challenges.

[31] South Africa, 'Promotion of Equality and Prevention of Unfair Discrimination Act', 2 February 2000, Article 34(1).

[32] In 2017, the Act was amended to include 'HIV/AIDS status' to the definition of 'prohibited grounds', as proposed in 2000, but not 'socio-economic status'. See ibid, Amended by Judicial Matters Amendment Act 8 of 2017.

4.2.2 Equality as a test of the scope and effect of anti-poverty measures

Equality can provide the lens through which anti-poverty measures are tested, an approach to which Fredman finds various jurisdictions have been 'reasonably open'.[33] This strategy is valuable for assessing compliance with equality in the creation and implementation of anti-poverty measures. Moreover, it allows for judicial scrutiny of anti-poverty measures in different dimensions.

Courts may use this approach to evaluate the extent to which anti-poverty measures are underinclusive. In jurisdictions resistant to imposing redistributive obligations on the legislature, courts might nonetheless feel comfortable with scrutinizing the inclusiveness of schemes already created and implemented in a state. For example, in *Chapman v the United Kingdom*, the European Court of Human Rights (ECtHR) found that Article 8 of the European Convention on Human Rights (right to respect for private and family life) did not imply a right to be provided with a home. In the words of the Court, '[w]hile it is clearly desirable that every human being have a place where he or she can live in dignity and which he or she can call home, there are unfortunately in the Contracting States many persons who have no home'.[34] The ECtHR concluded that '[w]hether the State provides funds to enable everyone to have a home is a matter for political not judicial decision'.[35] Similarly, in *Stec and others v the United Kingdom*, the ECtHR affirmed that states have the freedom to decide 'whether or not to have in place any form of social security scheme, or to choose the type or amount of benefits to provide under any such scheme'.[36] Nonetheless, the Court found that, if a state decides to create a benefit or pension scheme, it must do so in a manner compatible with the European Convention on Human Rights' prohibition against discrimination.[37] Under this understanding, states would be under no obligation to adopt positive redistributive measures, but once they do create a redistributive policy, it cannot be discriminatory.

In jurisdictions that adopt this reasoning, this second entry for addressing poverty through equality is a valuable tool for guaranteeing a minimum dialogue between poverty policies and equality guarantees. Through this

[33] Fredman (2011a), *supra* note 10, p 585.
[34] European Court of Human Rights (ECtHR), *Chapman v the United Kingdom*, App 27238/95, 18 January 2001, para 99.
[35] Ibid.
[36] ECtHR, *Stec and others v the United Kingdom*, Apps 65731/01 and 65900/01, 12 April 2006, para 53.
[37] Ibid.

approach, even the scope of anti-poverty policies may be modified if the policy excludes groups in violation of the right to equality. Alternatively, in jurisdictions reluctant to perceive courts as the adequate forum for determining the scope of public policies, the right to equality can be used for additional assessments of public policies without expanding their scope. Courts may rely on the principle of equality to analyse the effects of anti-poverty measures by assessing whether they reinforce social stigma against vulnerable groups or are based on a stereotyped understanding of those groups and their needs.[38] One example of such a stigma would be reinforcing a perception of women as financially dependent on men and the latter as the head of the family in economic matters.

4.2.3 Poverty as a matter of discriminatory context

A third strategy is assessing poverty as part of the context of the impugned violation of rights. Atrey argues that poverty can be considered a discriminatory context when assessing the disadvantages to which a group is subjected.[39] Through this method, social and legal context—such as poverty—is taken into consideration when identifying the disadvantage to which a group is subjected and its impact on the enjoyment of rights. Therefore, this method amplifies the object of the assessment of discrimination.

The context of violations of rights and its relationship with systemic and entrenched disadvantages and forms of domination was the object of study by Cathi Albertyn and Beth Goldblatt. Albertyn and Goldblatt echoed critical legal feminism's suggestion to adopt a substantive understanding of equality in which inequalities are not read as incidental byproducts of stereotypes or prejudice but rather as profoundly structural, entrenched in the very fabric of how society is organized.[40] Because systemic patterns of disadvantage are group-based, eradicating them requires examining the individual in the context of their group, therefore including the social and economic conditions in which the group is generally inserted.[41]

[38] Cf Fredman (2011a), *supra* note 10, pp 584–587.

[39] This section will also take into consideration Khaitan's recognition that economic disadvantage is a relevant factor in assessing group disadvantage. See Tarunabh Khaitan, *A Theory of Discrimination law* (Oxford University Press 2015), pp 51–56.

[40] Cathi Albertyn and Beth Goldblatt, 'Facing the Challenge of Transformation: Difficulties in the Development of an Indigenous Jurisprudence of Equality' (1998) 14 South African Journal on Human Right 248, p 252.

[41] See ibid.

This section analyses two ways courts may engage with poverty as context. The first was identified by Atrey in cases of intersectional discrimination. I add to this analysis an additional way of considering poverty as context, namely, identifying vulnerabilities. Arguably, when poverty is a vulnerability experienced by a protected group, there is a case of intersectionality. However, by dividing the contextual analysis of poverty into these two classifications, this section recognizes that courts may expressly engage with a contextual analysis of poverty without finding intersectional discrimination or even referring to the concept of intersectionality. As Part II of the book will explain, this has often taken place at the IACtHR.

In any case, be it through the recognition of the content and scope of intersectional discrimination or through the vulnerabilities approach, the consideration of a context of poverty in equality cases has significant potential. Quoting Atrey, '[t]he contextual approach allows a 360 degree view of the discrimination claim'.[42] Judges may cast a wide net in discrimination analysis by including context as a relevant factor for identifying the disadvantages or even identities at play in a discrimination claim.[43] This approach enables them to move beyond a rigid focus on predefined grounds and narrowly defined groups.[44]

This strategy contrasts significantly with reasonings that fixate on a single ground of discrimination and narrowly identify the groups and disadvantages associated with a discrimination claim, thereby excluding other circumstances and context from the analysis. Atrey argues that this approach appears to be particularly useful for tackling the concentration of poverty within protected groups,[45] an assertion that is confirmed by our empirical analysis in Part II.

4.2.3.1 Identifying disadvantages and identities in intersectional discrimination

The concept of intersectional discrimination has been the object of detailed and continuous analysis in scholarly work and is increasingly making its way into the work of courts. At the IACtHR, the concept was first applied in the 2015 case of *Gonzales Lluy and others v Ecuador*. The case concerned the discrimination suffered by Talía Gonzales Lluy, a female child living with HIV

[42] Atrey (2018), *supra* note 13, p 426.
[43] Ibid.
[44] Ibid.
[45] Ibid, p 428.

in poverty.[46] The IACtHR found that the discrimination experienced by Talía 'was caused not only by numerous factors, but also arose from a specific form of discrimination that resulted from the intersection of those factors; in other words, if one of those factors had not existed, the discrimination would have been different'.[47]

In his concurring opinion in the *Gonzales Lluy* case, Judge Ferrer Mac-Gregor highlighted the difference between intersectional and multiple or composite discrimination. Multiple discrimination is the distinction, exclusion, or restriction based on two or more factors.[48] When multiple discrimination is found, one must assess the interaction of the multiple factors, analysing whether they produce separate or simultaneous impacts.[49] If simultaneous, the case is one of intersectional discrimination.[50]

Judge Ferrer qualifies intersectional discrimination as a specific type of multiple discrimination. When it takes place, the factors of discrimination are analytically inseparable, as their interaction transforms the very experience of discrimination. This means that the experience of discrimination can no longer be 'disaggregated into different reasons'.[51] Furthermore, the consequences suffered by the victims of intersectional discrimination are different from those suffered by the victims of only one specific form of discrimination.[52] In the words of the Judge, '[n]one of the forms of discrimination assessed independently would explain the particularity and specificity of the harm suffered in the intersectional experience'.[53]

In cases of intersectionalities, an analysis of context becomes essential to assessing the manifestations of discrimination because it reveals the different and unique harm endured by the victim and the confluence of factors resulting in discrimination. When intersectional discrimination occurs, the resulting discrimination is not a mere sum of the various factors of discrimination. For example, the discrimination suffered by a trans black man is not simply discrimination based on gender identity, on the one hand, and discrimination

[46] See Concurring Opinion of Judge Eduardo Ferrer Mac-Gregor Poisot in IACtHR, Judgment (Preliminary Objections, Merits, Reparations and Costs), *Gonzales Lluy and others v Ecuador*, 1 September 2015. Series C No 298, para 6.

[47] *Gonzales Lluy and others v Equador* (2015), ibid, para 290.

[48] This definition, quoted by the Judge, can be found in: OAS, 'Inter-American Convention on Protecting the Human Rights of Older Persons', 15 July 2015, Article 2.

[49] Concurring opinion of Judge Eduardo Ferrer Mac-Gregor Poisot, in *Gonzales Lluy and others v Ecuador* (2015), *supra* note 46, para 9.

[50] Ibid, paras 10–11.

[51] Ibid, para 11.

[52] Ibid.

[53] Ibid, para 12.

based on race, on the other, each being a static and non-volatile factor that does not communicate with one another. Instead, the very content and scope of each will be affected and amplified by the other. In other words, complex forms of disadvantage and oppressions based on multiple factors (such as race, gender identity, age, and poverty) result in a product of discrimination that cannot be reduced to the mere sum of its parts.[54] As Kimberlé Crenshaw explains when looking specifically at race and gender, '[t]he intersection of racism and sexism factors into Black women's lives in ways that cannot be captured wholly by looking at the race or gender dimensions of those experiences separately'.[55]

Applying this theory to the context of poverty in a racially and socially stratified state, the gender-based discrimination that an upper-middle-class white woman will endure in Brazil is essentially different from the gender-based discrimination felt by a black woman living in poverty. First, the gender stereotypes applied to the former are different from those applied to the latter.[56] After all, the stereotypical perception of who a middle-class white woman should be and how she should act is different from the stereotypical expectations imposed on a low-income black woman, each case carrying its own detrimental effects. Second, the resources that are available for each to respond to gender-based discrimination are equally different. Accordingly, the structural and discriminatory barriers each of these two women face to realize their rights are different.

Considering a context of poverty is thus key to identifying and responding effectively to intersectional discrimination. Failure to consider poverty when it is one factor in a case of intersectionality implies that the judicial remedies provided will be partial, as they do not consider a factor of intersectional discrimination. In addition, they may reflect a miscomprehension of the manifestations of discrimination. For illustrative purposes, return to the example from the paragraph above. The very content and scope of the racism and gender discrimination suffered by the black woman living in poverty in Brazil are delimited and often exacerbated by the situation of poverty in which she lives. Therefore, failure to consider the context of poverty in the analysis of intersectional discrimination equates to a failure to identify the identities involved, the disadvantages suffered, the very content of discrimination, and, therefore, the required remedies.

[54] Cf Kimberlé Crenshaw, 'Mapping the Margins: Identity Politics, Intersectionality, and Violence against Women' (1991) 43 Stanford Law Review 1241; see Albertyn and Goldblatt (1998), *supra* note 40, p 253.

[55] Crenshaw (1991), *supra* note 54, p 1244.

[56] See Lélia Gonzalez, 'Racismo e Sexismo na Cultura Brasileira' in *Revista Ciências Sociais Hoje* (Anpocs 1984).

Shortcomings of an approach that disregards intersectionality were highlighted by well-known publicists, including Crenshaw, Flávia Biroli, and Ina Kerner. When discussing the experiences of discrimination of black women, Crenshaw wrote that '[t]he problem is not simply that both discourses [one focused on gender only and one focused on race only] fail women of color by not acknowledging the "additional" issue of race or of patriarchy but that *the discourses are often inadequate even to the discrete tasks of articulating the full dimensions of racism and sexism*'.[57] Because the very experience of racism and sexism is different for women of colour, antiracism and feminism as isolated discourses and grounds of political—and here I add, legal—analysis are limited, 'even on their own terms'.[58]

Similarly, Biroli and Miguel Luis Felipe explain that a person's social position is defined in the intersection of mechanisms of oppression.[59] When analysing the specific case of Brazil, they take note of socio-demographic data and find evidence that an individual's social position is produced by the interplay of gender, class, and race.[60] This coincides with what Patricia Hill Collins perceived as general contours of intersectionality, namely, 'race, class, gender, sexuality, ethnicity, nation, ability, and age operate not as unitary, mutually exclusive entities, but as reciprocally constructing phenomena that in turn shape complex social inequalities'.[61]

Intersectionality can and has been used by publicists and human rights organs as an 'analytical strategy', to quote Collins.[62] In this dimension, it provides lenses through which social practices, problems, and phenomena associated with social inequalities can be analysed. Through this analytical strategy, one can reframe discussions on the formation of identities, the issues of sameness and difference, and social power, among other concerns.

However, if a court is resistant to recognizing economic condition as a suspect category, or if it does not perceive a given case as one that differentiates based on this classification, it is unlikely that this factor of intersectionality will be considered. Accordingly, one could argue that, while the consideration of poverty as a factor of intersectionality is highly important in equality cases, in isolation it produces limited effects in jurisdictions that are resistant to recognizing discrimination based on poverty or economic status more generally.

57 Crenshaw (1991), *supra* note 54, p 1252. Italics added by the author.

58 Ibid.

59 Flávia Biroli and Luis Felipe Miguel, 'Gênero, raça, classe: opressões cruzadas e cconvergências na reprodução das desigualdades' (2015) 20 Mediações—Revista de Ciências Sociais 27.

60 Ibid, p 51.

61 Patricia Hill Collins, 'Intersectionality's Definitional Dilemmas' (2015) 41 Annual Review of Sociology 1, p 2.

62 Ibid, pp 11–15.

In any case, the next subsection will explain that a context of poverty becomes relevant for courts even if a given instrument does not include economic status and social origin as suspect classifications, or if a court is resistant to recognizing discrimination based on these grounds.

4.2.3.2 Recognizing vulnerabilities

Even if a tribunal is unwilling to recognize poverty, economic status, or social origin as a ground of discrimination, it may nonetheless take into consideration a context of poverty. When an individual lives in poverty, the context of poverty may be interpreted as a factor of vulnerability to the realization of human rights. Therefore, poverty may be valuable for recognizing that the context in which an individual lives increases their vulnerability to experiencing disadvantages and oppressions.

Poverty may affect an individual's vulnerability to oppressions and the extent to which these oppressions can be directed against a given group and impact them. Accordingly, the contextual analysis allows courts to assess the degree of a person's vulnerability by identifying the real-life conditions of the alleged victim and how those conditions—including poverty—reinforce disadvantage, harm, and oppression.[63] Through this approach, courts may assess the impact of the impugned measure by considering the vulnerabilities derived from the context of poverty of the victims (see section i. below). Alternatively, they may assess the context of poverty and the resulting vulnerabilities to identify an institutional obligation to take these vulnerabilities into account when designing and implementing policies and actions (see section ii. below).

i. Locating the impugned measure in context to assess its impact

The identification of vulnerabilities may guide a court's assessment of the impact of a measure on a protected group by considering the actual socio-economic circumstances in which the alleged victim lives. In other words, the contextual analysis may assist courts in locating the impugned act or omission of the state within real-life conditions and exploring how they cause or reinforce disadvantage, harm, and oppression.

One example of the use of this approach is the IACtHR's case of *Furlan and family v Argentina*, decided in 2012. This case concerned the lack of a timely response by the Argentinian judiciary to resolve a civil action against the State initiated by a child with disabilities, Sebastián Furlan, and his father. Sebastián

[63] Cf Albertyn and Goldblatt (1998), *supra* note 40, p 261.

was a child when he was involved in an accident on the premises of a building that belonged to the Army, in the vicinity of his own house. The accident occurred in an abandoned military training circuit, which, having been left unprotected, became a space used by children for playing games, practising sports, and relaxing.[64] As a result of the accident, Sebastián suffered serious injuries and now lives with disabilities.

The IACtHR recalled that minors and persons with disabilities must enjoy effective access to justice and due process of law on an equal footing with those who are not subject to the same disadvantages. However, the Court went beyond requiring equal treatment. It took into consideration 'the highly vulnerable situation of Sebastián Furlan, as a minor with a disability, living in a family with limited financial resources'.[65] Based on the recognition of this vulnerability, it found that the State 'was required to adopt all adequate and necessary measures to address such a situation'.[66] In the concrete case, this meant ensuring the promptness of civil proceedings, on which opportunities for rehabilitation depended. More specifically, the IACtHR concluded that Argentina failed to guarantee the intervention of the Juvenile Defender's Office or to pursue a differentiated application of the law regarding the enforcement of the domestic judgment. According to the Court, such measures, if applied, would have made it possible to mitigate the disadvantageous situation Sebastián Furlan faced.[67]

In this case, the contextual analysis, which included the consideration of the socio-economic condition of the victim and his family, allowed the IACtHR to assess the impact of the delayed judicial proceedings on Sebastián and on the exacerbation of his vulnerabilities. The IACtHR was particularly attentive to the legal consequences for the minor and the impact that the violation of his rights had on his ability to obtain adequate rehabilitation and health care, given his financial situation.

This contextual assessment resonates with Albertyn and Goldblatt's understanding of contextual analysis within a transformative equality jurisprudence. The authors propose that such an analysis involves four points. First, it involves the examination of the socio-economic conditions of the individuals and groups concerned. Second, it considers the impact of the impugned measure on the litigant, their group, and others who are not parties to the case but are nonetheless affected by the provision. This analysis requires assessing

[64] IACtHR, Judgment (Preliminary Objections, Merits, Reparations and Costs), *Furlan and family v Argentina*, 31 August 2012. Series C No 246, para 72.
[65] Ibid, para 269.
[66] Ibid.
[67] Ibid.

the impact of the impugned provision on social patterns and systematic disadvantage. Third, contextual analysis requires identifying intersectionalities in the nature of group disadvantages and the privileges of the relatively advantaged cognate groups. Lastly, it requires a full assessment of the historical context of the case.[68]

In the *Furlan* case, the IACtHR focused on the first and second steps of assessment in Albertyn and Goldblatt's conceptualization of contextual analysis. These two steps—assessment of the socio-economic conditions of the individuals and groups concerned and analysis of the impact of the impugned provision—give rise to the strategy of considering the socio-economic context of the alleged victim to assess the impact of the impugned measure, including possible inequalities. In turn, the third step identified by Albertyn and Goldblatt gives rise to the strategy identified in subsection 4.2.3.1 above, that is, promoting a contextual analysis for the identification of intersectional discrimination and its resulting disadvantages and oppressions.

Albertyn and Goldblatt argue that the contextual analysis affects the type of evidence and argument that must reach a tribunal. They find that statistical and sociological evidence, as well as socio-economic analysis, might be crucial.[69] Furthermore, they suggest that this approach poses greater challenges to judges in ensuring they can step outside their personal experiences and critically analyse situations that may be unfamiliar to them.[70] The use of statistical and sociological data is likely to be particularly relevant in the implementation of the strategy identified in subsection 4.2.3.1, that is, identifying disadvantages and identities in intersectional discrimination. In turn, the contextual assessment discussed in this section might prove more dependent on socio-economic analysis, as in the *Furlan* case.

ii. The institutional focus

A different understanding of vulnerability was proposed by Martha Albertson Fineman, who describes it as an inherent aspect of human existence. She emphasizes that vulnerability stems from our own embodiment, which inevitably exposes individuals to the possibility of varying degrees of harm, injury, and misfortune—ranging from minor events to severe disruptions—whether caused by accidents, deliberate actions, or other factors.[71] She explains that all

[68] Albertyn and Goldblatt (1998), *supra* note 40, p 261.
[69] Ibid.
[70] Ibid.
[71] Martha Albertson Fineman, 'The Vulnerable Subject: Anchoring Equality in the Human Condition' (2008) 20 Yale Journal of Law and Feminism 1, p 9.

individuals are subject to vulnerabilities to a certain extent. While they may attempt to mitigate the impact of the abovementioned events, they cannot eliminate the possibility of their occurrence. Vulnerabilities include events that are, ultimately, beyond human control.[72]

While no one is able to entirely eliminate vulnerabilities from their lives, the quality and quantity of resources individuals possess or command can influence how human vulnerability is experienced.[73] Therefore, this approach calls for an institutional focus by placing the individual in context and requiring institutional action. More specifically, it recognizes that society 'can and does mediate, compensate, and lessen our vulnerability through programs, institutions, and structures'.[74]

Fineman's vulnerability analysis finds its ultimate objective in the argument that vulnerabilities fall to a certain extent under the responsibility of the state, which must be responsive to them.[75] In her understanding, this structural focus brings a political advantage: it directs attention to institutions rather than individuals' behaviours, prompting an assessment of how institutions provide assets in ways that may unfairly favour certain individuals or groups, even if unintentionally.[76] The irrelevance of intent is therefore highlighted—what is relevant is whether institutions are structured to 'respond unequally to the reality of our shared vulnerability'.[77]

The institutional focus of the contextual approach centres on the duty of institutions to adopt positive measures to respond to vulnerabilities in context. This strategy is thus closely related to the one described in the next subsection, and it dialogues well with the concept of the transformative dimension of equality, discussed in Chapter 2.

4.2.4 Positive obligations emanating from substantive equality

Turning to the fourth method, poverty can be a matter of substantive equality. Here, equality assumes a 'remedial' purpose, and law becomes the tool through which a transformation in systemic forms of domination and oppression, as well as in the distribution of power and resources, may take place.

72 Ibid.
73 Ibid, p 10.
74 Ibid, p 10.
75 Ibid, p 13.
76 Ibid, p 13.
77 Ibid, p 18.

As Chapter 2 explained, Fredman identifies phases or 'generations' of equality laws (see section 2.2.3.1). The first phase required the dismantlement of formal legal impediments to the exercise of rights. Fredman includes in this category laws abolishing slavery, suffrage legislation, and norms granting women equal legal capacity in civil and family matters. One example is Britain's Equal Franchise Act of 1928, granting equal voting rights to women and men.[78] Subsequently, the second phase of the development of the principle of equality was the emergence of anti-discrimination legislation.[79] Under this category are statutory restrictions on discrimination in employment, education, and services, such as equal pay acts and sex or race discrimination acts.[80] One example is sex discrimination legislation in the European Community, such as Council Directive 76/207/EEC of 1976 on equal treatment of men and women in access to employment, vocational training and promotion, and working conditions.[81]

While important, these laws had a limited capacity to promote transformation in ingrained discriminatory structures. In this context, an expansion took place in the recognition of the prohibited grounds of discrimination and the spaces in which equality was to be guaranteed. Fredman identifies the inclusion of sexual orientation as a protected ground against discrimination as a development belonging to this phase, as well as the expansion of the application of anti-discrimination laws across all public functions.[82] One example is the European Union's Council Directive 2000/78/EC of 2000 on equal treatment in employment and occupation. The Directive recognizes that discrimination based on religion or belief, disability, age, or sexual orientation may undermine the objectives of the EC Treaty and accordingly shall be prohibited throughout the community, whether manifested as direct or indirect discrimination.[83] The expansion of anti-discrimination law can be understood as a separate phase or a continuation and evolution of the second phase.

Fredman argues that a sustained movement arose at the same time, shifting the overwhelming focus from negative prohibitions related to discrimination to positive duties to promote equality. Legislation imposing positive equality duties was expanding, and a growing focus on 'mainstreaming' emerged. In

[78] UK Parliament, '1928 Equal Franchise Act', Parliamentary Archives, HL/PO/PU/1/1928/18&19G5c12, 2 July 1928.
[79] Sandra Fredman, *Discrimination Law* (2nd edn, Oxford University Press 2011b), p 6.
[80] Ibid.
[81] Council of the European Communities, 'Council Directive 76/207/EEC on the implementation of the principle of equal treatment for men and women as regards access to employment, vocational training and promotion, and working conditions', 9 February 1976.
[82] Fredman (2011b), *supra* note 79, p 7.
[83] Council of the European Union, 'Council Directive 2000/78/EC establishing a general framework for equal treatment in employment and occupation', 27 November 2000.

the 2000s, there was a strong emphasis on gender mainstreaming in the EU, requiring decision-making bodies to assess the impact of all their decisions on gender equality, rather than treating it as a side concern.[84] Fredman calls these positive duties derived from equality the 'fourth generation' of equality rights.

In the 2011 edition of her book *Discrimination Law*, Fredman wrote that the move from negative to positive duties derived from equality was still in its infancy. Positive duties were, in her words, 'generally timid, focusing more on changes in procedure than progress in substance'.[85] Still, she highlighted that this development could provide a significant venue for the litigation of poverty cases through the right to equality. However, as Chapters 6 and 7 will explain, Fredman's finding of a generally timid expression of this new phase of equality law contrasts strongly with the practices of the STF and the IACtHR.

To understand the extent to which this development may impact the litigation of poverty cases, it is relevant to recall Fredman's multidimensional framework for assessing substantive equality, covering the redistributive, the recognition, the transformative, and the participative dimensions. The link between poverty and inequality in its redistributive dimension is clear: as a rule, every conceptualization of poverty is connected to a distributive harm, whether in terms of income or capabilities. In this context, courts may analyse the extent to which state omission to redistribute resources and opportunities violates their obligation to promote equality.

Yet applying equality to cases of poverty has a much broader scope than allowing for a distributive assessment. Considering equality in its transformative dimension allows courts to expand the concept of disadvantage beyond maldistribution of resources to encompass an analysis of the constraints derived from power structures that affect individuals based on their status. This dimension calls for the promotion of structural change as a means to address exclusions and other forms of oppression without requiring that individuals use their agency in a specific manner. The participative dimension of substantive equality allows courts to identify obstacles to social and/or political representation of the poor in society. Finally, the recognition dimension offers a tool for courts to identify and tackle stereotypes, stigma, non-physical violence, and forms of humiliation against groups living in poverty, thus allowing for the identification of an otherwise 'invisibilized' context of discrimination. All of these dimensions call for state action to protect recognition, participation, and, when appropriate, accommodation of difference, therefore promoting transformative equality.

[84] Fredman (2011b), *supra* note 79, p 7.
[85] Ibid, p 8.

This multifaceted understanding of equality leads to a similarly multifaceted analysis of the causes and consequences of poverty. When applying this framework, courts are provided with a valuable tool to analyse poverty beyond deprivation of income, including vulnerabilities in relation to empowerment, recognition, and social and political participation. Based on this multifaceted analysis, courts may call on states to adopt positive measures to reverse polycentric inequalities against persons living in poverty.

Even if a case is not initially portrayed as an equality case, a court's analysis of the justification for implementing a positive measure may nonetheless touch upon equality. After all, the identification of structural oppressions in a context of poverty justifies the invocation of the concept of equality and the consequent identification of a duty to act to reverse the oppressions related to socio-economic vulnerability.

This strategy can also be used for courts to identify an obligation for states to act towards tackling vulnerabilities of specific groups who are disproportionately represented among those living in poverty, including through affirmative action. Ultimately, through what Atrey qualifies as a human rights-based approach[86]—in contrast to a formalistic or technical approach to equality as simply treating likes alike—the very deprivation of rights that derives from (or even constitutes) poverty becomes a violation of equality, particularly when disadvantaged groups experience disproportionate harm.

4.3 Concluding remarks

Different strategies have been developed to accommodate poverty into the legal concept of equality. One strategy is to recognize economic condition, social class, and/or poverty as suspect classifications, that is, categories historically associated with marginalization, stigmatization, and oppression. While some of these categories (particularly economic condition and social origin) have been recognized in some jurisdictions as protected grounds against discrimination, the expansion of protected categories to cover poverty is still limited. In this context, other strategies become key to addressing poverty through the right to equality.

One alternative strategy is conducting an equality analysis of anti-poverty policies. When poverty is the object of public policy, courts may scrutinize these policies through the lens of the right to equality. Another strategy is

[86] Atrey (2018), *supra* note 13, p 437.

locating poverty not as the factor of differentiation but as a space in which certain groups—for example, groups defined by race, gender, sexual orientation, and gender identity—suffer disadvantages. In other words, poverty may be considered as context. This strategy may be applied to recognize the obligation of states to compensate for or reduce vulnerabilities, to assess the impact of a measure in the context of the vulnerabilities of the concrete case, or to identify and address intersectionality.

Intersectionality brings to light the shortcomings of an interpretation of equality that ignores the context of poverty when the latter is present. A mono-analytical approach to equality might consider that the discrimination suffered, for example, by a poor black man and a poor white gay man would be sufficiently addressed by the concepts of racism and homophobia, respectively. However, intersectionality, as an analytical strategy, denounces this perception as an illusion. Failing to consider the poverty dimension would represent a significant obstacle to identifying the scope of racism and homophobia and the disadvantages they represent to the specific victim situated at this intersection of vulnerabilities.

Finally, an additional strategy is interpreting the obligation of states to respond to poverty through the lens of positive duties that emanate from the right to substantive equality. This strategy appears to be particularly promising to address the root causes and effects of poverty, the perpetuation of poverty cycles and its disproportional impact on specific groups, and to promote transformative equality by tackling not only material and individual disadvantage but also oppressive structures and power relations.

PART II
EMPIRICAL ANALYSIS

5
The Evolution of Poverty in Brazil (1988–2023)

So we have regained our freedom. And we will have development. Yet social justice is lacking. This is Brazil's greatest challenge at the end of the century. This will be my government's number one goal. [. . .] I will govern for everyone. But if it is necessary to end the privileges of a few to bring justice to the vast majority of Brazilians, let there be no doubt: I will stand with the majority.

—Fernando Henrique Cardoso, Presidential Inaugural Address (1995)[1]

Brazil experienced the wealth of sugarcane mills and plantations in early colonial times, but it did not overcome hunger; it proclaimed its national independence and abolished slavery, but it did not overcome hunger; it discovered the wealth of gold deposits in Minas Gerais and coffee production in the Paraíba Valley, but it did not overcome hunger; it industrialized and built a notable and diversified productive sector, but it did not overcome hunger. This cannot continue this way.

As long as there is a Brazilian brother or sister living in hunger, we will have plenty of reason to cover ourselves with shame. Therefore, I have made a food security program called 'Fome Zero' one of my government's priorities. As I said in my first speech after the election, if, at the end of my term, all Brazilians have the possibility to have breakfast, lunch, and dinner, I will have fulfilled my life's mission. [. . .] This is a cause that can and should belong to everyone, without distinction of class, party, or ideology. In the face of the outcry of those who suffer the scourge of hunger, what must prevail is the ethical imperative of joining forces, capacities, and instruments to defend what is most sacred: human dignity.

—Luis Inácio Lula da Silva, Presidential Inaugural Address (2003)[2]

[1] Fernando Henrique Cardoso, *Inauguration Address: 1 January 1995* (1995). Translation by the author.
[2] Luis Inácio Lula da Silva, *Inauguration Address at the National Congress: 1 January 2003* (2003). Translation by the author.

Judging Poverty and Inequality in Brazil. Tainá Garcia Maia, Oxford University Press. © Tainá Garcia Maia 2026.
DOI: 10.1093/oso/9780198994022.003.0005

> *Twenty years ago, when I was elected president for the first time, alongside fellow vice-president José Alencar, I began my inaugural speech with the word 'change'. The change we sought was simply to concretize constitutional precepts. Starting with the right to a dignified life, without hunger, with access to employment, health care, and education. On that occasion, I said that my life's mission would be fulfilled when every Brazilian man and woman could eat three meals a day. Having to repeat this commitment today—given the rise of poverty and the return of hunger, which we had overcome—is the most serious symptom of the devastation that has been inflicted upon the country in recent years.*
>
> **—Luis Inácio Lula da Silva, Presidential Inaugural Address (2023)**[3]

Since the fall of the military dictatorship in Brazil, most of the nation's presidents have unfailingly echoed the imperative of poverty eradication in their inaugural addresses, underscoring its significance as an enduring challenge to the promotion of social justice and a primary objective of their governments. The prominence of the fight against poverty in political discourse underscores its enduring significance as both a persistent challenge and a central political concern in the country.

In 1988, as Brazil proclaimed its first democratic constitution after two decades of military rule, approximately 32 million people lived in extreme poverty.[4] By the end of the twentieth century, amid the stabilization of the Brazilian economy, this number had declined significantly, with approximately 25 million people living in extreme poverty.[5] Brazil's poverty rate was, at that time, virtually identical to the regional average in Latin America and the Caribbean.[6]

The beginning of the twenty-first century ushered in the expansion of antipoverty policies in the country and an unprecedented decline in its poverty rates, positioning Brazil as an internationally recognized paradigmatic case of poverty reduction.[7] Such was the magnitude of poverty reduction in the

[3] Luis Inácio Lula da Silva, *Inauguration Address at the National Congress: 1 January 2023* (2023). Translation by the author.

[4] Poverty & Inequality Platform, 'Poverty rate, % $2.15' (*World Bank*) <https://pip.worldbank.org/poverty-calculator> accessed 28 August 2025. For slightly lower figures applying a different poverty line in 1988 and the end of the twentieth century, see Ricardo Paes de Barros, Ricardo Henriques, and Rosane Mendonça, 'Desigualdade e Pobreza no Brasil: retrato de uma estabilidade inaceitável' (2000) 15 Revista Brasileira de Ciências Sociais 123, p 125, Table 1.

[5] Poverty & Inequality Platform, 'Poverty rate, % $2.15', *supra* note 4.

[6] Ibid.

[7] Deborah Wetzel, 'Bolsa Família: Brazil's Quiet Revolution' *Valor Econômico* (4 November 2013) <https://www.worldbank.org/en/news/opinion/2013/11/04/bolsa-familia-Brazil-quiet-revolution> accessed 6 May 2023; Jim Young Kim, 'Brazil's Contribution to a World Free of Poverty' *Valor Econômico*

country that, in March 2014, the World Bank published a feature story titled 'How to Reduce Poverty: A New Lesson from Brazil for the World?'.[8] Quoting the publication: 'If there is one thing Brazil does well, it is globalization. It made soccer and its soap operas global phenomena, transforming Brazil into a global brand. Now it's time for the country's poverty reduction model to have its day.'[9]

However, by the end of the second decade of the twenty-first century, indicators of monetary and multidimensional poverty in the country were ascending once more, regressing to levels surpassed over a decade prior. While, in 2014, the World Bank qualified Brazil as a success story of poverty reduction, by 2017 international headlines painted a starkly different picture, announcing the return of millions of individuals to poverty and hunger across the country.[10]

This chapter analyses the evolution of poverty levels in Brazil from 1988 to 2023, considering the public policies adopted by the Brazilian State and the country's political and economic context in points of inflection in poverty levels. Section 5.1 introduces the methodology for analysing the evolution of poverty in the country. Subsequently, section 5.2 examines the movements of regression and progression of monetary poverty in connection with public policies in Brazil from 1988 to 2023, and section 5.3 conducts the same analysis with regard to multidimensional poverty. Finally, section 5.4 discusses

(24 March 2014) Opinion <https://www.worldbank.org/en/news/opinion/2014/03/24/brazil-contribution-world-without-poverty> accessed 6 May 2023; Marianna Rios, '"Brazil has succeeded in overcoming extreme poverty", claims the MDS' (*World Without Poverty: Brazil Learning Initiative*, 2015) <https://wwp.org.br/en/brazil-has-succeeded-in-overcoming-extreme-poverty-claims-the-mds-based-on-the-national-household-sample-survey-2014/> accessed 6 May 2023; Annie Gasnier, 'Au Brésil, 12 millions de familles mangent grâce à une bourse' *Le Monde* (14 September 2010) <https://www.lemonde.fr/planete/article/2010/09/14/au-bresil-12-millions-de-familles-mangent-grace-a-une-bourse_1411106_3244.html> accessed 6 May 2023.

[8] World Bank, 'How to Reduce Poverty: A New Lesson from Brazil for the World?' (World Bank, 2014) <https://www.worldbank.org/en/news/feature/2014/03/22/mundo-sin-pobreza-leccion-brasil-mundo-bolsa-familia> accessed 6 May 2023.

[9] Ibid.

[10] Daniel Trielli, Peter Prengaman, and Sarah DiLorenzo, 'Millions return to poverty in Brazil as "boom" decade erodes' *Seattle Times* (22 October 2017) <https://www.seattletimes.com/business/millions-return-to-poverty-in-brazil-eroding-boom-decade/> accessed 13 February 2024; Sam Cowie, 'Brazil: Extreme poverty on the rise as elections loom' *Al Jazeera* (26 September 2018) <https://www.aljazeera.com/economy/2018/9/26/brazil-extreme-poverty-on-the-rise-as-elections-loom> accessed 13 February 2024; Ernesto Londoño and Flávia Milhorance, 'Ravaged by Covid, Brazil Faces a Hunger Epidemic' *The New York Times* (23 April 2021) <https://www.nytimes.com/2021/04/23/world/americas/covid-brazil-hunger.html> accessed 13 February 2024; Juan Royo Gual, 'Brazil vuelve a pasar hambre' *El Mundo* (20 June 2021) <https://www.elmundo.es/internacional/2021/06/20/60ce0267fc6c83b50d8b4650.html> accessed 13 February 2024; Bruno Meyerfeld, 'Au Brésil, « la faim est partout, et l'Etat nulle part »' *Le Monde* (29 September 2022) <https://www.lemonde.fr/economie/article/2022/09/29/au-bresil-le-retour-de-la-faim-legs-de-jair-bolsonaro_6143619_3234.html> accessed 13 February 2024.

the manifestations of intersectionalities in the persistence of poverty in Brazil.

5.1 Methodology

The assessment of the evolution of extreme and non-extreme monetary poverty in Brazil is based on data from the World Bank (using the 2017 PPP)[11] and the IBGE's Summary of Social Indicators (SIS). Subsidiary sources include the IBGE's Continuous National Household Sample Survey (PNADC) and reports from the Brazilian Ministry of Social Development and Fight Against Hunger. The SIS reports were used mostly for data from 2014 onwards, because of the limited availability of data on this object in the preceding reports. For analysing extreme poverty levels established under the PBF line from 1992 to 2013, the study uses data from the Secretariat of Evaluation and Information Management of the Ministry of Social Development and Fight Against Hunger (SAGI). Because the analysis of the evolution of poverty in Brazil ends in 2023, the poverty measurements based on World Bank standards did not use the updated 2025 poverty line values.

The analysis of multidimensional poverty derives from socio-economic indicators from the IBGE (including the IBGE's measurement of multidimensional poverty, which was introduced once, in the 2019 SIS), the World Bank's Multidimensional Poverty Measure, the Multidimensional Poverty Index, and relevant secondary sources. In light of the limited temporal coverage of these indexes, the chapter proposes a four-dimensional analysis of multidimensional poverty in Brazil, covering: (i) food security (measured by hunger levels and severe and moderate food insecurity); (ii) health and longevity (measured by life expectancy and child mortality); (iii) access to education (measured by illiteracy rate, school attendance, and access to university); and (iv) access to water, sanitation, and electricity (measured in relation to the household and the individual). The main sources for this four-prong analysis of multidimensional poverty were reports from the United Nations Food and Agriculture Organization (FAO) and the IBGE, particularly the IBGE's PNADC. This data is relevant as the IACtHR and particularly the STF have

[11] As the book's analysis of the evolution of poverty in Brazil ends in 2023, it does not apply the updated value of the IPL of June 2025. Rather, it applies the last update made in the period under analysis, namely: US$2.15 per day (2017 PPP) for the IPL measurements, $3.65 per day (2017 PPP) for the lower-middle-income countries poverty line, and $6.85 per day (2017 PPP) for the upper-middle-income poverty line.

made broad use of statistics on poverty levels, notably on multidimensional poverty disaggregated by race.

Finally, the research analyses the state of poverty through an intersectional perspective. In other words, it analyses how the abovementioned poverty dimensions have impacted certain groups of society differently. This analysis focuses on race, gender, and class, and its source was data from the IBGE, mainly the National Household Sample Survey (PNAD), PNADC, and SIS. Some of the data discussed in this chapter, particularly those presented in sections 5.3 and 5.4, has been referred to by the STF and the IACtHR in their respective assessments of equality in the context of poverty.

5.2 Monetary poverty

5.2.1 The 'Lost Decade'

In 1964, a military *coup d'etat* took place in Brazil, marking the beginning of a military dictatorship that would last until 1985, when a civil government assumed the presidency through an indirect election carried out by the National Congress. The redemocratization of the country took place amid what became known as the 'Lost Decade', a period of economic stagnation, high levels of inflation, and a rise in foreign debt.

In the 1980s, Brazil was going through an economic recession, rising inflation, and unemployment, and faced striking numbers of malnutrition in children. In the year Brazil's democratic constitution was proclaimed, 22.42% of its population lived in extreme poverty. In other words, approximately 30 million people lived under these conditions—a number that is significantly higher if one considers non-extreme poverty.

From 1986 to 1994, seven different economic plans were enacted by three different presidents, and Brazil changed its currency four times as part of economic strategies to control inflation. Inflation was only finally controlled in 1994, when the economic plan *Plano Real* was officially implemented during President Itamar Franco's government.

5.2.2 Economic stabilization and distributive policies following the *Plano Real*

The '*Plano Real*' successfully attained its biggest aim of combating hyperinflation in Brazil. These economic measures in the mid-1990s constituted an important step for the development of the Brazilian economy and its domestic market, contributing to the significant reduction in the levels of extreme poverty and monetary poverty in the country. According to Anna Peliano, the most significant programme for reducing hunger and poverty in the 1990s was the stabilization of the currency.[12] In the 1990s, 8.2 million Brazilians were lifted out of indigence, and 10.1 million people were lifted out of poverty.[13]

The person behind the *Plano Real* was the then Minister of Economy, Fernando Henrique Cardoso (FHC). In 1994, FHC was elected President of the Republic and re-elected in 1998, winning both times against the already famous Luiz Inácio 'Lula' da Silva. During Cardoso's government, important social programmes were created, including initiatives that aimed at providing a minimum level of income to citizens and combating hunger. Examples include the Food Basket Programme, the Programme for the Eradication of Child Labour, the School Grant, the Young Agent Programme, the Food Grant, and the Gas Grant Programme.[14]

In 1992, 23.29% of the Brazilian population lived in extreme poverty, according to the World Bank. By 1995, this number had fallen to 14.74%. This represents a 36.7% reduction in Brazil's headcount poverty ratio over three years. In the following years of the FHC government, the poverty ratio oscillated a little. The second mandate of FHC finalized in 2002, with a headcount poverty ratio of 11.74%.

5.2.3 The Labour Party ('PT') years: 2003–2015

In 2002, Lula was elected President of Brazil in a historical election, taking the Labour Party (PT) and an openly declared left-wing government to power for the first time since redemocratization. Lula took office in January 2003, in a public ceremony that had a historically high citizen attendance for Brazil, with official estimates varying from 70,000 to 200,000 persons in the crowd.

[12] Adriana Veiga Aranha (Org), *Fome Zero: Uma História Brasileira* (MDS, Vol I, 2010), p 38.

[13] Ibid.

[14] The oficial names of the programmes, in their original language, are: *Cesta Alimento* (the Food Basket Programme); *Programa de Erradicação do Trabalho Infantil* (the Programme for the Eradication of Child Labour); *Bolsa Escola* (the School Grant); *Programas Agente Jovem* (Young Agent Programme); *Bolsa Alimentação* (Food Grant); and *Programa Auxílio Gás* (Gas Grant Programme). Furthermore, the federal government authorized transfer of federal resources to municipalities to implement programmes of conditional cash transfer associated with socio-educational measures. See Brazil, 'Law No. 9,533', 10 December 1997.

The main objective of Lula's first mandate was the implementation of the Zero Hunger Programme.[15] On the first day of his mandate, Lula created the Extraordinary Ministry of Food Security and Fight Against Hunger (MESA), which was substituted on January 2004 by the Ministry of Social Development and Fight Against Hunger (MDS[16]). In October 2003, the Programme *Bolsa Família* (PBF) was created. Because of the centrality of the programme to the reduction of poverty in Brazil in the twenty-first century, the following paragraphs will present a brief overview of its history and content.

The PBF was established on 20 October 2003, through the unification of existing income transfer programmes that had been created during the FHC government. Clóvis Roberto Zimmermann argues that the unification was a great advance from a human rights perspective. It avoided fragmentation and made the programme more accessible. In his words, 'with the centralization, it became easier for a person to determine the state organ to which he or she should turn to in case of a request to enter the programme, a measure that is essential to facilitate access by the most vulnerable social groups'.[17] In addition, before the unification, the different programmes had been managed by different ministries, which often had to compete among themselves for resources. The unification reduced administrative costs, optimized state action, and created an intersectoral management of the resources, thus avoiding fragmentation.

This centralization was accompanied by a significant expansion of the anti-poverty agenda, as the *Bolsa Família* reached an unprecedented scale compared to its predecessors. When analysing the use of conditional cash transfer (CCT) programmes in Brazil, Anthony Hall identifies a sharp increase in expenditure on these programmes following the creation of the *Bolsa Família*. For comparison purposes, he finds that in the last year of the FHC administration, CCTs accounted for R$ 2.4 billion, representing approximately one-quarter of the social assistance budget for the poor in 2002. In the last year of Lula's first mandate, they had reached R$ 8.2 billion, comprising approximately 38% of the 2006 social assistance budget.[18] When assessed in relation

[15] In its original name, '*Programa Fome Zero*'. See Clóvis Roberto Zimmermann, 'Os Programas Sociais sob a Ótica dos Direitos Humanos: o caso do Bolsa Família do governo Lula no Brasil' (2006) SUR—International Journal on Human Rights 145, p 7; da Silva, *Inauguration Address at the National Congress: 1 January 2003*, *supra* note 2.

[16] The name changed to 'Ministry of Social and Agrarian Development' under Michel Temer's government, to 'Ministry of Citizenship' under the Bolsonaro government, and to 'Ministry of Social Development and Assistance, Family, and Fight against Hunger' in Lula's third non-consecutive mandate.

[17] Zimmermann (2006), *supra* note 15, p 151. Translation by the author.

[18] Anthony Hall, 'Brazil's Bolsa Família: A Double-Edged Sword?' (2008) 39 Development and Change 799, p 801.

to the total social budget and GDP, this meant that spending on CCTs rose from less than 1% to 2.9% of the total social budget from 2001 to 2006, and from 0.2% to 0.5% of GDP during Lula's first mandate.[19]

The *Bolsa Família* is based on three axes. The first is income complementation, that is, cash transfer[20] granted to families directly by the federal government. It aims to provide immediate poverty relief. The second axis is access to rights, which is represented by the conditionalities[21] connected to the programme. That is, receiving this income transfer depends on the fulfilment of certain conditions, including undergoing prenatal tests, nutritional assessments, and maintaining school attendance of 60–65% for children enrolled in primary education. The objective of the second component is to guarantee basic social rights through a compromise accepted by the beneficiary families. The existence of these conditionalities for the concretization of the income transfer aims to reinforce access to education, health, and social assistance.[22]

[19] Ibid, pp 801-802.

[20] Until 2021 (the year in which the *Bolsa Família* was extinguished under the Bolsonaro government), the benefits created under the programme comprised four components: (i) a basic benefit aimed at families living in extreme poverty, as defined by the government; (ii) a variable benefit (limited to five benefits per family, each valued at R$41.00), paid to families living in poverty or extreme poverty with pregnant women, nursing mothers, and children or teenagers up to 15 years old; (iii) a variable benefit (limited to two benefits per family, each valued at R$41.00), paid to families living in poverty or extreme poverty with teenagers aged 16 or 17; and (iv) a benefit for overcoming extreme poverty (limited to one per family), aimed at certain families that were already recipients of the *Bolsa Família* and that had children or teenagers aged 0–15. The target group of the latter component were families whose total household income, added to the value of any of the other three components of the *Bolsa Família*, equated to R$89.00 or less a month per capita. The basic benefit amounted to R$89.00; the variable benefit for pregnant women, children, and teenagers up to 15 years old could vary from R$41.00 to R$205.00; the variable benefit for teenagers of 16 and 17 years old varied from R$41.00 to R$96.00. The variable benefit for overcoming extreme poverty varied according to the number of family members and the household income. Because it is hard to predict the value of the variable benefit for overcoming extreme poverty *in abstracto*, only the first three benefits and their value in 2021 are considered here. Based on these standards, a family that received the PBF could be granted a monthly monetary amount ranging from R$89.00 to R$390.00 (values that in 2020 equated to US$17.11 and US$74.99, in exchange value). In 2023, in the third month of the third non-consecutive mandate of Lula after his electoral victory against Bolsonaro, the presidency instituted Provisional Measure No 1,164 (2023), reinstituting the *Bolsa Família*. For information on the updated values, see note 71.

[21] Until 2021, the conditionalities were the following: children aged 6–17 must be enrolled in school and attend at least 85% of classes (for those aged 6–15) or 75% (for those aged 16–17). Furthermore, children under 7 years old must take the vaccines recommended by the public health system and attend a doctor every six months for a medical check-up. Pregnant women must also agree to attend their medical consultations and get prenatal care. See Secretaria de Desenvolvimento Social, 'Condicionalidades do Programa Bolsa Família' (2020) <https://www.sedes.df.gov.br/condicionalidades-bolsa-familia/> accessed 11 October 2020. See also Brazil, 'Law No. 10,836', 9 January 2004, Article 3. Since March 2023, there are four conditionalities: (i) carrying out prenatal care; (ii) complying with the national immunization programme schedule; (iii) monitoring the nutritional status of children aged less than 7 years old; and (iv) minimum school attendance of 60% (for children aged 4–6) or 65% (for children aged 6–18 who have not completed primary education). See Brazil, 'Provisional Measure No. 1,164', 2 March 2023, Article 10; Brazil, 'Law No. 14,601', 19 June 2023, Article 10.

[22] In the understanding of Janine Berg, employment expert at the ILO Brasília Office: 'These conditions include keeping school-age children in school and complying with basic health care requirements, such as keeping the inoculation schedules for children, and attending medical appointments for pregnant women and nursing mothers. The object of the foregoing conditions is not to punish families but to lay responsibility jointly on beneficiaries and the public authorities, the latter being bound to identify the reasons for possible

Lastly, the third axis is articulation with other public policies. The programme can integrate with and articulate complementary social policies to reduce vulnerability and assist the development of families in need.[23]

In addition to CCTs, Brazil's anti-poverty strategy in the PT years encompassed food security programmes aimed at food production and distribution,[24] access to water,[25] and initiatives for the inclusion of marginalized groups (including affirmative action). These strategies will be discussed in detail in section 5.3, as they tackle directly multidimensional deprivations.

An additional factor explaining the evolution of poverty in Brazil during the PT government is the economic context in which Brazil found itself. Brazil's exports increased during Lula's government, and the State enjoyed a positive trade balance, in contrast to the situation the country faced at the end of the 1990s. The 2008 international crisis did not heavily impact Brazil at that time, and the Brazilian Central Bank announced that the State's foreign debt was smaller than its assets in 2008, which meant that, for the first time in its history, Brazil had assumed a net external creditor position. The diplomatic staff of Brazil expanded significantly, and the State tightened its political and economic ties with China, Africa, and the Mercosur.

The Brazilian economy thrived during that period, domestic consumption levels and social mobility increased, and jobs were created, particularly in the tertiary sector. This generally favourable economic context was met with a significative expansion of socio-economic public policies for the implementation of a social rights agenda.[26] In this context, studies indicate a decline in social stratification and a rise in occupational mobility.

In 2008, Marcelo Neri introduced the hypothesis that a new middle class (class 'C') had emerged in the country.[27] Although influential, the hypothesis

non-compliance with conditions and implement public policies to assist such families. The programme thus emphasizes the guarantee of the rights of persons.' See Janine Berg, *Brazil. Conditional transfers as response to the Crisis: the Bolsa Família Programme* (ILO Notes on the Crisis, 2009), p 3. A different analysis is presented by Fredman, who criticizes conditionalities in cash transfer programmes for their potential stigmatization effect and for assuming gender roles. See Sandra Fredman, 'Women and Poverty—A Human Rights Approach' (2016b) 24 African Journal of International and Comparative Law 494, pp 508–512.

[23] Ministério da Cidadania, 'O que é' <https://www.gov.br/cidadania/pt-br/acoes-e-programas/bolsa-familia/o-que-e> accessed 1 September 2021.

[24] For an example, see gov.br, 'Programa de Aquisição de Alimentos (PAA)' <https://www.gov.br/cidadania/pt-br/acoes-e-programas/inclusao-produtiva-rural/paa#:~:text=O%20Programa%20de%20Aquisição%20de,e%20incentivar%20a%20agricultura%20familiar> accessed 6 May 2023.

[25] For an example, see gov.br, 'Programa Cisternas' (2019) <https://www.gov.br/cidadania/pt-br/acoes-e-programas/inclusao-produtiva-rural/acesso-a-agua-1/programa-cisternas> accessed 6 May 2023.

[26] See Paulo de Martino Jannuzzi and Paula Montagner, 'Estado de bem-estar, políticas públicas e mobilidade social no Brasil' in Jorge Abrahão de Castro and Marcio Pochmann (eds), *Brasil: Estado de bem-estar social?: limites, possibilidades e desafios* (Fundação Perseu Abramo 2020).

[27] Marcelo Cortes Neri (Coord), *A Nova Classe Média* (FGV, 2008).

is contested by some publicists who discuss stratification theories, class, and status and argue that it was rather the lower classes of Brazil that experienced the greatest income gains during the PT years relative to their starting point. One such study was prepared by Adalberto Cardoso and Edmond Préteceille. The authors recognize that a significant increase in the number of members of the middle class took place between 2002 and 2014. However, 80% of the new jobs created in the formal labour market came from the commerce and services industry, and 50% were in companies with less than 100 employees. These jobs offered low pay and were unstable. In addition, the lower classes (called 'popular classes' by the authors) continued to be the majority in the country, even in the metropoles, comprising approximately 48.4% of the families in Brazil in 2014, while the middle class constituted only 12.2%.[28] Quoting the authors, '[f]or long we know that a factory worker that ceases to be poor does not, for that fact alone, stop being a factory worker to become a member of the middle class'.[29]

Therefore, Cardoso and Préteceille consider it an exaggeration to identify the emergence of a new middle class. Instead, they propose that Neri's 'C class'[30] did indeed acquire income and social mobility, but this was mostly the result of gains by employed members of families that were neither living in extreme poverty nor considered middle class. The authors conclude that the period from 2002 to 2014 provided improvements in the living conditions of the popular classes. This led to new and growing demands for health and education services, thereby increasing the need for qualified middle-class professionals providing these services.[31] In addition, this scenario created opportunities for ascendant social mobility *intra* and, above all, *inter*generational.[32]

The studies of Salata support the conclusions of Cardoso and Préteceille. Salata observes that, from 2002 to 2013, a policy of valorization of the minimum wage was implemented. Such a policy generally impacts more low-income workers.[33] Additionally, this period witnessed an increase in the levels of schooling in the population (see section 5.3.2.2), including for lower

[28] Adalberto Cardoso and Edmond Préteceille, 'Classes Médias no Brasil: Do que se Trata? Qual seu Tamanho? Como Vem Mudando?' (2017) 60 DADOS—Revista de Ciências Sociais 977, p 1010.

[29] Ibid, p 1008.

[30] The authors propose that the 'C class', which indeed expanded during the Lula governments, was not a 'new middle class'. Instead, they qualify it as a group formed by the lower and strictly middle class, as well as by families that are partly formed by members of the middle class and members of the 'popular classes'. See ibid, p 998.

[31] Ibid, p 1008.

[32] Ibid.

[33] André Salata, 'Distribuição de renda no Brasil entre 2002 e 2013: Redução das desigualdades entre classes?' (2018a) 53 Latin American Research Review 76, p 77.

classes, and a reduction in the levels of unemployment. Salata identifies the working class as the group with the highest proportional income gains.[34]

The aforementioned studies indicate an exaggerated optimism in Neri's qualification of the emergence of a new middle class as a result of the social changes in the first decade of the 2000s. Nonetheless, they consistently find improvements in the living conditions of the lower classes and point to significant modifications in social stratification.

In 2010, Dilma Rousseff was elected the successor of Lula, maintaining PT as the party leading the Executive in the federal government. In 2011, the federal government launched the plan 'Brazil Without Extreme Poverty'. The programme targeted individuals living in monetary poverty and was guided by three pillars: the guarantee of immediate income to families living in extreme poverty; access to public services (education, health, and citizenship); and productive inclusion, which meant increasing capacity and opportunities for work and income generation for families living in poverty in cities or the countryside.[35] In 2012, a law introduced a nationwide quota system for students from public schools (a group mainly composed of low-income youth) to access public universities (see section 5.3.2.2). In 2013 and 2015, equality in labour rights was guaranteed to maids, a group mainly composed of black women.[36]

It was during Rousseff's presidency that Brazil attained what was then a historically low number of persons living in extreme poverty and monetary poverty. Brazil's experience was such an interesting case that, in 2013, the International Policy Centre for Inclusive Growth, the Institute for Applied Economic Research (IPEA), the MDS, and the World Bank Group signed an interinstitutional partnership creating the Brazil Learning Initiative for a World without Poverty (WWP). The WWP disseminated material in several languages on the anti-poverty and social protection policies implemented by Brazil, fostering knowledge exchange and dialogue on good practices among policymakers.[37] At that time, Brazil's reputation as a successful agent in the

[34] André Salata, 'Ensino Superior no Brasil das últimas décadas: Redução nas desigualdades de acesso?' (2018b) 30 Tempo Social 219. Salata's research indicates that the highest proportional gains in income were those of the working class, with the middle class actually having the lowest proportional gains in income.

[35] gov.br, 'Brasil Sem Miséria' (2015) <https://www.gov.br/secretariadegoverno/pt-br/iniciativas/internacional/fsm/eixos/inclusao-social/brasil-sem-miseria> accessed 6 May 2023; see also Rômulo Paes-Sousa and Paulo de Martino Jannuzzi, 'Going Beyond the Eradication of Extreme Poverty: Debating the Sustainable Development Goals in Brazil' in Alberto D Cimadamore, Gabriele Koehler, and Thomas Pogge (eds), *Poverty and the Millennium Development Goals: A critical look forward* (Zed Books 2016).

[36] Brazil, 'Constitutional Amendment No. 72', PEC das Domésticas, 2 April 2013; Brazil, 'Complementary Law No. 150', Lei das Domésticas, 1 June 2015.

[37] WWP, 'What is WWP?' (*World Without Poverty. Brazil Learning Initiative*) <https://wwp.org.br/en/what-is-wwp/> accessed 1 September 2021

reduction of poverty and hunger was internationally recognized. In 2011, José Graziano da Silva, who had coordinated the design of the Zero Hunger Programme and had been Lula's Special Minister of Food Security and Fight against Hunger, was elected Director-General of the FAO.[38]

In 2014, Brazil was removed from the FAO Hunger Map. On 15 December 2015, the WWP announced calculations made by the MDS based on PNAD data from 2014, according to which only 2.5% of Brazil's population was living in extreme poverty. The WPP recalled that, '[a]t this rate, in World Bank terms, extreme poverty can be considered to have been eradicated in Brazil'.[39]

Jannuzzi and Montagner identify a meaningful change in social mobility rates during this period. Through the analysis of data from the PNADs on intragenerational social mobility, they find that Brazil returned, in 2014, to ascending mobility levels similar to the historically high rates of 1982, when social mobility rates were still positively impacted by the effects of the 'Economic Miracle' period[40] and the increase in rural-to-urban migration.[41] In the same year, Brazil reached reduced levels of downward mobility compared to those attained in the final years of the 1990s.[42] The authors also find that the rate of ascending intragenerational social mobility of black and brown men was historically high in 2014.[43]

Figure 5.1 shows that the poverty headcount ratio in Brazil decreased by 11.6 percentage points from 1992 to 2014 (from 13.6% to 2% of the population), if one applies the PBF line. The decrease is even steeper if one applies the IPL as published by the World Bank—a decrease of 19.96 percentage points, from 23.29% to 3.33%. The year 2014 marks a historical low in the poverty headcount ratio in Brazil (2% under the PBF line, and 3.3% under the IPL).

The evolution of monetary poverty (encompassing both extreme and non-extreme monetary poverty) follows a development similar to the one observed for extreme poverty. Figure 5.2 shows a sharp decrease in poverty from 2003 to 2014. Applying the PBF poverty line, the figure shows a decline of 19.6 percentage points between 2003 and 2014 (from 24.6% to 5%) and a total decrease of 26.4 percentage points between 1992 and 2014 (from

[38] FAO, 'José Graziano da Silva of Brazil elected FAO Director-General' (2011) <https://www.fao.org/news/story/pt/item/80713/icode/> accessed 6 May 2023.

[39] Rios, *supra* note 7.

[40] A period of significant economic growth in Brazil from 1968 to 1973, which was coined as the 'Economic Miracle'.

[41] Jannuzzi and Montagner (2020), *supra* note 26, pp 136–140.

[42] Ibid, pp 136–140.

[43] Ibid, pp 144–145.

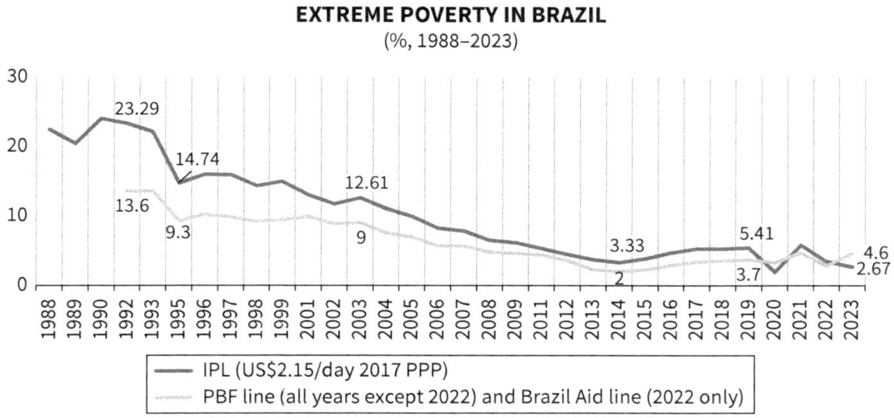

Fig 5.1 Extreme poverty levels in Brazil (1988–2023)

Source: Based on data from: Poverty & Inequality Platform/World Bank (for the IPL); SAGI 2014/MDS and SIS 2022–2024/IBGE (for the PBF and Brazil Aid Line).

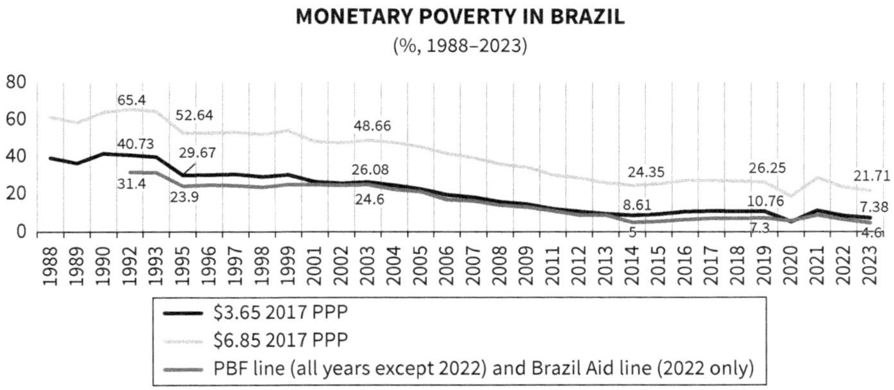

Fig 5.2 Monetary poverty in Brazil (1988–2023)

Source: Based on data from: Poverty & Inequality Platform/World Bank (for the World Bank lines); SAGI 2014/MDS and SIS 2022–2024/IBGE (for the PBF and Brazil Aid Line).

31.4% to 5%). This represents an 84% reduction in poverty levels from 1992 to 2014.

The World Bank's lines for higher-middle-income and lower-middle-income economies show a very similar decrease. From 1992 to 2014, there was a reduction of 78.9% of the population living on less than US$3.65 2017 PPP, and a reduction of 62.8% of those living on less than US$6.85 2017 PPP in the country.

The Zero Hunger Programme and, notably, the *Bolsa Família* have been considered the decisive drivers of the significant decrease of poverty in Brazil in the twenty-first century.[44] In March 2014, Dr Jim Yong Kim, President of the World Bank Group, wrote:

> When it comes to success stories, Brazil is an obvious champion. Between 2001 and 2011, extreme poverty more than halved—from 9.7 to 4.3 percent of the population. A total of 22 million people—more than the population of Angola or Romania—were lifted out of poverty. Moreover, in contrast to many middle income countries, inequality fell over the same period. These impressive achievements were due to more than just a growing economy and a dynamic labor market. They owe a lot to Brazil's pioneering design and implementation of innovative social programs, with *Bolsa Família* being the most prominent example.[45]

However, by the end of Rousseff's first mandate, Brazil had entered a political and economic crisis that culminated in the 2016 presidential impeachment, a decline in social indicators, and the rise of the extreme right in the country. Unemployment was rising, reaching 8.9% by the end of 2015.[46]

5.2.4 The aggravation of the political and economic crisis and the Covid-19 pandemic

In 2016 and 2017, during the administration of Michel Temer—Rousseff's former Vice President and her successor following her *impeachment*—the economic crisis was deepening. As an austerity measure, a constitutional amendment was approved in 2016, setting a ceiling on public spending for twenty years, including expenditures on health and education.[47] In 2017, Law No 13,429 was approved under the justification that a response to the economic crisis and the rising levels of unemployment was needed.[48] The law expanded opportunities for outsourcing and made labour guarantees more flexible.

In the first trimester of 2017, unemployment reached 13.9%, almost double the rate for the same period in 2014.[49] Cardoso and Préteceille show that a

[44] Cf Paulo de Martino Jannuzzi, Enrico Moreira Martignoni, and Baiena Feijolo Souto, 'Programa Bolsa Família e sua contribuição para redução da pobreza no Brasil' (2012) 4 Revista Brasileira de Monitoramento e Avaliação.

[45] Kim, *supra* note 7.

[46] IBGE, 'PNADC. Séries históricas: desemprego' <https://www.ibge.gov.br/estatisticas/sociais/trabalho/9173-pesquisa-nacional-por-amostra-de-domicilios-continua-trimestral.html?=&t=series-historicas&utm_source=landing&utm_medium=explica&utm_campaign=desemprego> accessed 22 September 2025.

[47] Brazil, 'Constitutional Amendment No. 95', 15 December 2016.

[48] Brazil, 'Law No. 13,429', 31 March 2017.

[49] IBGE, 'PNADC. Séries históricas: desemprego', *supra* note 46.

Fig 5.3 Unemployment levels in Brazil (2012–2023)
Source: Based on data from: PNADC Séries históricas/IBGE

considerable part of the employment that had been generated between 2002 and 2014 in the tertiary sector in companies of less than 100 workers appears to have been lost during the crisis.[50] By the end of the Temer presidency, unemployment stood at 11.7% (see Figure 5.3).[51]

In October 2018, Jair Bolsonaro was elected president, taking office in January 2019 in a public ceremony with a high citizen attendance of 115,000 persons according to official government estimates. His administration unfolded amid an increasingly deep political, social, and economic crisis in the State.

In his inaugural address, Bolsonaro placed a strong focus on the economic crisis, along with other key pillars of his presidential campaign, including the fight against corruption, family values, and public security. Addressing the National Congress, he qualified his mission as 'rebuilding our homeland, finally freeing it from the yoke of corruption, crime, economic irresponsibility, and ideological submission'.[52] Addressing the crowd, he listed the challenges he identified for his government: 'We have the great challenge of facing the effects of the economic crisis, record unemployment, the ideologization of our children, the distortion of human rights, and the deconstruction of the

[50] Cardoso and Préteceille (2017), *supra* note 28, p 1010.
[51] IBGE, 'PNADC. Séries históricas: desemprego', *supra* note 46.
[52] Jair Messias Bolsonaro, *Inauguration Address at the National Congress: 1 January 2019* (2019). Translation by the author.

family.'[53] The economic crisis was thus a central theme in the political discourse, alongside a deepening political crisis.

In 2019, extreme poverty was 1.85 times higher than the ratio in 2014, returning to levels similar to the one reached in 2011 and 2012 (see Figure 5.1). The situation was further exacerbated by the Covid-19 pandemic, notably as Brazil ranked among the countries most affected by the pandemic according to the World Bank.[54]

In April 2020, Law No 13,982 was promulgated aiming to mitigate the economic effects of the pandemic.[55] It created a temporary unconditional cash transfer to individuals fulfilling certain requirements of age and lack of formal employment whose household income was up to half the minimum wage per capita (the *Cadastro Único* line, as discussed in Chapter 2) or whose total household income was no higher than three minimum wages. The benefit was called *Auxílio Emergencial* ('Emergency Aid') and was initially instituted by law for a period of three months, with the possibility of prorogation during the Covid-19 emergency.[56] The National Congress approved the cash transfer of R$ 600,00 per month, a number three times higher than the one suggested by the presidency, according to the Congress,[57] and over three times the average *Bolsa Família* benefit calculated in 2020, according to the Chamber of Deputies.[58] The benefit was limited to two quotas per family, with each quota being claimed by a different adult in the same household or both quotas being claimed by a single mother.[59] The creation of the Emergency Aid in this initial configuration appears to correlate with the decline in the levels of extreme poverty in 2020 in Brazil (see Figures 5.1 and 5.2 above). Yet, by 2021, the headcount poverty rate was again on the rise.

[53] Jair Messias Bolsonaro, *Inauguration Address at the Presidential Palace: 1 January 2019* (2019). Translation by the author.

[54] World Bank, 'Impacts of COVID-19 in Brazil: Evidence on persons with disabilities during the pandemic' (*World Bank*, 2021) <https://www.worldbank.org/en/country/brazil/brief/impactos-da-covid19-no-brasil-evidencias-sobre-pessoas-com-deficiencia-durante-a-pandemia> accessed 7 May 2023.

[55] Brazil, 'Law No. 13,982', 2 April 2020.

[56] Ibid, Article 2.

[57] Elina Rodrigues Pozzebom, 'Aprovado pelo Congresso, auxílio emergencial deu dignidade a cidadãos durante a pandemia' *Agência Senado* (30 December 2020) <https://www12.senado.leg.br/noticias/materias/2020/12/30/aprovado-pelo-congresso-auxilio-emergencial-deu-dignidade-a-cidadaos-durante-a-pandemia> accessed 7 May 2023.

[58] Tiago Miranda, 'Proposta aumenta Bolsa Família em 50% durante pandemia' *Agência Câmara de Notícias* (20 April 2020) <https://www.camara.leg.br/noticias/655130-proposta-aumenta-bolsa-familia-em-50-durante-pandemia#:~:text=O%20benefício%20médio%20pago%20a,2%20milhões%20de%20famílias%20atendidas> accessed 7 May 2023. The Emergency Aid and the *Bolsa Família* were not cumulative. When it was more advantageous to the household, the Emergency Aid temporarily replaced the *Bolsa Família* benefit *ex officio*. See Law No. 13,982, *supra* note 55, Article 2, §2.

[59] Only in 2021, an amendment modified the language of the law, substituting the term 'single mothers' for 'single parent' and noting that such a qualification was independent of one's sex. See Brazil, 'Law No. 14,171', 10 June 2021; Law No 13,982 (2020), Article 2.

Five months after the promulgation of Law 13,982 (2020), the duration of Emergency Aid was extended until 31 December 2020. However, its value was halved (R$ 300,00 per month) while remaining limited to two quotas per family.[60] In March 2021, the Emergency Aid was extended for four months, and again for three extra months in August 2021, at R$ 250,00 per month and limited to one quota per family.[61] Single mothers were entitled to R$ 375,00 per month, and a family composed of just one person would receive R$ 150,00 per month.[62]

The pandemic resulted in over 600,000 confirmed Covid-19 deaths in Brazil from 2020 to December 2021. In addition to the loss of lives, it also significantly impacted the Brazilian economy. In 2021, the World Bank noted that Brazil's economy was recovering unevenly after experiencing a GDP decline of 4.1% in 2020, with several labour market indicators still lagging behind pre-pandemic levels.[63] It also highlighted the ongoing impact of the crisis on human rights and human capital, pointing to a decrease in children's participation in educational activities—from 99% before the pandemic to 89%—and the fact that only about 40% had resumed face-to-face classes.[64] It found that the pandemic hit the most individuals living in vulnerability, including persons with disabilities. More than 50% of households with members with disabilities reported being unable to cover their basic needs—a figure 25% higher than that of households without members with disabilities.[65]

On 24 September 2021, the Central Bank of Brazil reported that specialists estimated that inflation would reach 8.45% by the end of 2021.[66] In the first trimester of 2021, unemployment reached 14.7% (see Figure 5.3).[67] With the decline in intensity of the Covid-19 emergency, unemployment decreased, reaching 7.9% in the last trimester of the Bolsonaro administration (October–December 2022).[68] However, this decrease should be read with caution. As explained by the IBGE, 54% of the decrease in the levels of unemployment

[60] Brazil, 'Provisional Measure No. 1,000', 2 September 2020, Article 1.

[61] Brazil, 'Provisional Measure No. 1,039', 18 March 2021, Articles 1 and 2. See also gov.br, 'Prorrogado por mais três meses o pagamento do Auxílio Emergencial 2021' (2021) <https://www.gov.br/casacivil/pt-br/assuntos/noticias/2021/agosto/prorrogado-por-mais-tres-meses-o-pagamento-do-auxilio-emergencial-2021> accessed 7 May 2023.

[62] Provisional Measure No 1,039 (2021), Article 2, §§1 and 2.

[63] World Bank, 'Impacts of COVID-19 in Brazil: Evidence on persons with disabilities during the pandemic', *supra* note 54.

[64] Ibid.

[65] Ibid.

[66] Banco Central do Brasil, 'Focus: Relatório de Mercado' (*Banco Central*, 2021) <https://www.bcb.gov.br/content/focus/focus/R20210924.pdf> accessed 30 September 2021.

[67] IBGE, *Pesquisa Nacional por Amostra de Domicílios Contínua Segundo Trimestre de 2021 (abr.-jun.)* (Indicadores IBGE, 2021), Table 3.

[68] IBGE, 'PNADC. Séries históricas: desemprego', *supra* note 46.

identified in the third trimester of 2021 derived from the creation of occupations in the informal sector.[69] From the second trimester of 2020 to the fourth trimester of 2022, the number of individuals working in the informal sector rose significantly (from 30,700 to 38,554, which represents an increase of 25.6%).[70]

Despite the vulnerability of the jobs created during this period, the decline in unemployment, combined with the launch of the Brazil Aid Programme in November 2021, contributed to the decrease in poverty levels in Brazil in 2022.[71] The 'Brazil Aid' Programme (in Portuguese, *Auxílio Brasil*) was a conditional cash transfer programme formally established in August 2021–that is, three months before the expected end of the Emergency Aid–and launched in November that year. The programme was established through Provisional Measure No 1,061 (2021), which discontinued the PBF.

The cash transfer under the Brazil Aid was significantly higher than that provided through Emergency Aid in 2021, particularly after the creation of the so-called 'extraordinary benefit' under Brazil Aid in December 2021. The latter was initially scheduled to run from January to December 2022—the year of the presidential dispute—and guaranteed that all beneficiaries of the programme would receive a minimum of R$400.00.[72] Two months before the 2022 presidential elections, the National Congress approved a significant increase in the value of Brazil Aid to be granted for five months (from August to December 2022), guaranteeing a minimum cash transfer of R$600.00.[73]

5.2.5 The start of Lula's non-consecutive third mandate

After the end of the Bolsonaro government and the start of Lula's third mandate, the PBF, which had been discontinued in 2021 by former President

[69] Umberlândia Cabral and Caio Belandi, 'Desemprego recua para 12,6% no terceiro trimestre e atinge 13,5 milhões de pessoas' *Agência IBGE Notícias* (29 December 2021) <https://agenciadenoticias.ibge.gov.br/agencia-noticias/2012-agencia-de-noticias/noticias/32362-desemprego-recua-para-12-6-no-terceiro-trimestre-e-atinge-13-5-milhoes-de-pessoas> accessed 8 May 2023.

[70] IBGE, 'PNAD Contínua Painel' <https://painel.ibge.gov.br/pnadc/> accessed 6 May 2023.

[71] IBGE, *Síntese de Indicadores Sociais: Uma Análise das Condições de Vida da População Brasileira 2024* (Estudos & Pesquisas Informação demográfica e socioeconômica 2024), p 72.

[72] Brazil, 'Provisional Measure No. 1,076', 7 December 2021. This temporary benefit was made permanent in May 2022. See Brazil, 'Law No. 14,342', 18 May 2022, Article 1.

[73] Brazil, 'Constitutional Amendment No. 123', 14 July 2022, Art.5.I; Agência Senado, 'Congresso muda Auxílio Brasil no primeiro semestre e assegura benefício de R$ 600' *Senado Notícias* (15 July 2022) <https://www12.senado.leg.br/noticias/materias/2022/07/15/congresso-muda-auxilio-brasil-no-primeiro-semestre-e-assegura-beneficio-de-r-600> accessed 28 August 2025.

Bolsonaro, was reinstated, granting, as a minimum, R$600,00 to families entitled to the benefit.[74] Data from the IBGE show that Brazil reached a historical low in the percentage of the population living in extreme poverty as measured by the updated IPL in 2023.[75] When the PBF line is applied instead of the IPL, Figure 5.1 might suggest that an even lower rate was reached in 2022. However, such a conclusion would be oversimplified, as the PBF poverty line—since the reinstatement of the programme in 2023—is more than twice the value of the Brazil Aid line for extreme poverty in 2022 (see Figure 2.1).

According to the calculations of the IBGE, without the benefits of social programmes such as the *Bolsa Família* and the BPC, 11.2% of the Brazilian population would be living in extreme poverty as measured by the IPL.[76] A similar trend emerges in relation to monetary poverty as measured by the World Bank's poverty line for upper-middle-income countries (US$6.85 in 2017 PPP/day). According to IBGE calculations, 36.7% of Brazil's population lived on less than $6.85/day in 2021. In 2023, that number had fallen to 27.4%. Absent social benefits from anti-poverty public policies, however, it would have stood at 32.4%.[77] Together with a continuous decrease in unemployment levels,[78] cash transfer programmes in Brazil were fundamental to this outcome.[79]

[74] Since its reinstatement in 2023, the programme is composed of the following components: (i) the Citizenship Income Benefit (R$142,00 per member of the family); (ii) the Complementary Benefit, paid to families whose total Citizenship Income Benefit is less than R$600,00 per household (the value of the complementary benefit is the amount required to reach that monetary threshold); (iii) the Early Childhood Benefit, paid to families with children aged less than 7 (R$150,00 per child); and (iv) the Variable Family Benefit, paid to families with pregnant women, children aged 7–12 years old or teenagers aged 12–18 (the value of this variable benefit is R$50,00, to be calculated based on the number of family members falling in the abovementioned categories). This CCT is to be given to the head of the family as registered in the Cadastro Único, preferably to a woman. See Law No 14,601, *supra* note 21, Articles 7–8. In 2023, the federal government announced that 81.2% of the *Bolsa Família* benefits were provided to women. See gov.br, 'Mulheres são responsáveis familiares em 81% das concessões do Bolsa Família' (2023) <https://www.gov.br/planalto/pt-br/acompanhe-o-planalto/noticias/2023/03/mulheres-sao-responsaveis-familiares-em-81-das-concessoes-do-bolsa-familia> accessed 26 April 2023.

[75] IBGE, 'SIS 2024, Tabelas "Padrão de vida e distribuição de rendimentos"', Table 2.18 (Pobr_Geo) (2024) <https://www.ibge.gov.br/estatisticas/sociais/populacao/9221-sintese-de-indicadores-sociais.html?edicao=42003&t=resultados> accessed 3 September 2025; Luiz Bello, 'Em 2023, pobreza no país cai ao menor nível desde 2012' *Agência IBGE Notícias* (4 December 2024) <https://agenciadenoticias.ibge.gov.br/agencia-noticias/2012-agencia-de-noticias/noticias/42043-em-2023-pobreza-no-pais-cai-ao-menor-nivel-desde-2012> accessed 3 September 2025. According to the World Bank's calculation, Brazil's lowest poverty rate occurred in 2020 (see Figure 3 to visualize this divergence). This finding, however, contrasts with the IBGE's calculations based on both the IPL and the PBF line and appears contradictory given the country's hunger rates that year.

[76] IBGE, *SIS 2024*, *supra* note 71, p 55, Graphic 11.

[77] Ibid.

[78] IBGE, 'PNADC. Séries históricas: desemprego', *supra* note 46.

[79] See IBGE, *SIS 2024*, *supra* note 71, pp 54–55.

5.3 Multidimensional poverty

The public policies implemented in Brazil with an impact on poverty have not been restricted to cash transfer programmes. This section analyses the evolution of multidimensional poverty in Brazil, introducing data from the MPI and the World Bank's MPM for multidimensional poverty in Brazil (section 5.3.1), and a dashboard approach to multidimensional poverty (section 5.3.2).

5.3.1 Multidimensional poverty in indexes

The first MPI country briefing on Brazil was published in 2010, using data from 2003.[80] Subsequent reports on Brazil relied on data from 2006 (MPI reports from 2011 to 2015),[81] from 2014 (MPI reports from 2016 to 2017),[82] and, more recently, from the 2015 PNAD (from 2018 to the most recent MPI report published in 2024).[83] Using a scale of 0–1, where one represents the highest level of deprivation, the index showed that Brazil's score of multidimensional poverty was 0.039 in 2003, with 8.5% of the population living in multidimensional poverty, and an average intensity[84] of poverty of 46%.[85] The most recent MPI reports, based on data from 2015, show that Brazil's MPI score decreased to 0.016, with 3.8% of the population living in multidimensional poverty.[86] Yet, they reveal a great discrepancy between the country's urban and rural populations. While only 2% of the urban population lives in multidimensional poverty and 3.9% is vulnerable[87] to it, 14.2% of the rural population is poor under the MPI and 19% is vulnerable to poverty. The 2023 MPI further shows that health is the leading dimension contributing to

[80] OPHI, *Country Briefing: Brazil* (2010).

[81] OPHI, *Country Briefing: Brazil* (2011); OPHI, *OPHI Country Briefing Dec 2015: Brazil* (2015).

[82] OPHI, *Global MPI Country Briefing 2018: Brazil (Latin America and the Caribbean)* (2018); OPHI, *OPHI Country Briefing December 2016: Brazil* (2016); OPHI, *OPHI Country Briefing 2017: Brazil* (2017).

[83] OPHI, *Global MPI Country Briefing 2024: Brazil (Latin America and the Caribbean)* (2024).

[84] The average proportion of dimensions in which poor people are deprived. See *Country Briefing: Brazil* (2010), *supra* note 80, p 1.

[85] Ibid, p 1.

[86] UNDP, *Briefing note for countries on the 2024 Multidimensional Poverty Index: Brazil* (Unpacking deprivation bundles to reduce multidimensional poverty, 2024), p 2.

[87] For a person to be living in acute multidimensional poverty under the MPI, they must suffer deprivation in at least one-third of the weighted indicators. If deprivation occurs in half or more of the dimensions, a person will be considered as living in severe poverty. Persons deprived in 20 to 33% (ie one-fifth to one-third) of the indicators are considered vulnerable to poverty. See UNDP, 'MPI 2024 FAQS' <https://hdr.undp.org/mpi-2024-faqs> accessed 18 March 2026.

multidimensional poverty in Brazil (49.8%), followed by standard of living (27.3%), and, lastly, education (22.9%).[88]

The World Bank's measurement of multidimensional poverty in Brazil is based on more recent data than the MPI. The MPM historical data relies on the PNADCs from 2011, 2016–2019, and 2022–2023.[89] In 2011, 6.3% of the Brazilian population lived in multidimensional poverty. The multidimensional poverty headcount ratio fell below 6% in 2016, returned to that level or slightly higher from 2017 to 2019, before declining again to approximately 4% from 2022 onwards.[90] The temporary rise in the MPM is explained by the increase in monetary poverty, as all other indicators either consistently improved or remained the same in the period covered by the index. In 2023, the indicator in which the largest percentage of the population in Brazil faced deprivation was sanitation (32.1%, down from 36.5% in 2016), followed by educational attainment (13.4%, down from 22.1% in 2011), monetary poverty, and drinking water (1.2%, down from 2.0 in 2016).[91]

However, these measurements suffer from significant limitations. First, both indexes were created very recently and allow for a limited comparative assessment of the evolution of multidimensional poverty in Brazil in the period analysed in this chapter.[92] Second, the most recent MPI reports are based on the 2015 PNAD. While 2015 marks the resumption of increased levels of monetary poverty in the country, the starting point of that increase is still historically low (see Figures 5.1 and 5.2). The levels of monetary poverty in Brazil were still significantly low, and much lower than in 2021, after the deepening of the country's economic, political, and sanitary crisis before and during the Covid-19 pandemic. Similarly, the historical MPM data on Brazil is restricted to 2017 and 2019, then jumping ahead to 2022 and 2023, therefore missing

[88] UNDP, *Briefing note for countries on the 2024 Multidimensional Poverty Index: Brazil*, *supra* note 86, p 2.

[89] World Bank, 'Historical MPM data', MPM-Historical-Data-AM2024-Final <https://documents.worldbank.org/en/publication/documents-reports/documentdetail/099109206232539968?> accessed 29 August 2025. Last update: April 2024; World Bank, 'Individuals in households deprived in each indicator, 120 economies, circa year 2021 (2018-2024)', <https://documents1.worldbank.org/curated/en/099001206232524312/pdf/IDU-194bdd26-98c5-48f5-921c-3225b66a5716.pdf> accessed 29 August 2025. Last update: June 2025.

[90] World Bank, 'Historical MPM data', *supra* note 89; 'Individuals in households deprived in each indicator, 120 economies, circa year 2021 (2018-2024)', *supra* note 89.

[91] 'Individuals in households deprived in each indicator, 120 economies, circa year 2021 (2018-2024)', *supra* note 89; 'Historical MPM data', *supra* note 89.

[92] Furthermore, in the case of the MPI, the OPHI advises users against conducting comparisons of the 2021 MPI with the index published in previous years, due to changes in the methodology. Any comparison, the OPHI warns, should account for these changes. The OPHI itself conducts analyses to allow comparability—the 'Changes over Time' series. However, there is yet no Changes Over Time Country Briefing for Brazil.

the impact of the Covid-19 crisis and the deepening of the political and socio-economic crisis in the State.

Given these limitations, this book proposes a dashboard approach to multidimensional poverty focusing on four dimensions: (i) food security (measured by hunger levels and severe and moderate food insecurity); (ii) health and longevity (measured by life expectancy and child mortality); (iii) access to education (measured by illiteracy rate, school attendance, and access to university); and (iv) access to water, sanitation, and electricity (measured in relation to the household and the individual). The main sources were reports from the IBGE, particularly the PNADC, and data from the FAO.

These dimensions were selected for three main reasons: the particularities of Brazil and the object of the flagship anti-poverty policies carried out by the Brazilian government in the last two decades; data availability under the PNADC for the period under analysis; and commonalities between indexes of multidimensional poverty and national analyses of multidimensional poverty. Other dimensions and indicators could also have been included in the dashboard (eg access to the Internet, access to medication, and access to prompt medical consultation). The choice of the four dimensions and their respective indicators does not intend to diminish the importance of other dimensions. The very choice of following a dashboard approach aims to be non-exclusive and non-hierarchical with respect to the dimensions.

5.3.2 A dashboard approach

5.3.2.1 Hunger

In 1974, the National Survey of Family Expenditure (ENDEF) revealed that one in every two children in Brazil suffered from some degree of undernourishment. Subsequently, during the 'Lost Decade', the rural sector underwent a modernization process, but small-scale farming and family agriculture faced obstacles. This had a negative effect on food production for the domestic market, further impacting the already grim scenario identified in the ENDEF. In this context, the price of basic food parcels was rising.[93]

This food crisis would had to be addressed in the redemocratization period. However, in the 1980s, Brazil suffered from a serious inflation crisis, which only reached an end during the Itamar Franco mandate (1992–1995),

[93] Cf IPEA, 'Diálogos com Anna Peliano—A Fome tem Pressa: Reflexões sobre o Enfrentamento da Fome no Brasil' (2021) <https://www.youtube.com/watch?v=CS5jZXXWt2I&t=19696s> accessed 3 November 2021.

as explained in the previous section. According to Anna Peliano, at the beginning of the 1990s, that is, just before Itamar Franco's government, 'the setting was one of scorched earth'.[94]

During the Itamar Franco government, important changes took place not only in the economy through the *Plano Real* and the resulting success in controlling inflation (see section 5.2) but also in public policy against hunger. In 1993, through an initiative headed by IPEA and the sociologist Herbert José de Sousa, known as Betinho, Brazil's Hunger Map was published.[95] The Map revealed that 32 million people lived in hunger in the country, which, at the time, was equivalent to saying that the whole population of Argentina lived in such conditions in Brazil.[96] The publication of the Hunger Map gained significant attention in the Brazilian media, mobilized civil society, and led to the introduction of a series of public policies, many of which were decentralized and integrated other levels of the federation beyond the federal state. The National Plan on the Fight against Hunger and Extreme Poverty was inaugurated, as was the Citizenship Action against Hunger and Extreme Poverty and for Life. In 1993, the National Council on Food and Nutritional Security (CONSEA) was created.[97]

After Itamar Franco, FHC assumed the presidency and created a series of social programmes, including the Food Basket Programme and the Food Grant, as discussed in section 5.2. These and other programmes were unified under the Lula government, leading to the creation of the *Bolsa Família*. The latter played an important role in significantly reducing hunger levels in Brazil. In a report from 2013, FAO reported a decrease of 54.3% in the proportion of undernourished people in Brazil from 1990–1992 to 2011–2013 (more specifically, from 15 to 6.9% of the population).[98] In 2014, during the mandate of Dilma Rousseff, Brazil left the FAO World Hunger Map, meaning that less than 5% of its population was living in hunger.[99]

[94] *Fome Zero: Uma História Brasileira*, *supra* note 12, p 32.

[95] IPEA explains that it had already developed the technical study that became known as the Hunger Map. Betinho transformed this technical study into a political instrument, which guided public policy in the State. Besides mapping poverty, the Hunger Map mapped agriculture in the country and presented suggestions to tackle the food crisis. See IPEA, 'Diálogos com Anna Peliano, *supra* note 93.

[96] Anna Maria T M Peliano (Coord), *O Mapa da Fome: Subsídios à Formulação de uma Política de Segurança Alimentar* (Documento de Política No 14, IPEA, 1993), p 5.

[97] *Fome Zero: Uma História Brasileira*, *supra* note 12, p 36.

[98] FAO, WFP, IFAD, *The State of Food Insecurity in the World 2013. The multiple dimensions of food security* (2013), p 45, Table A1.1.

[99] The Hunger Map was based on the Prevalence of Undernourishment (PoU) indicator. The PoU measures the likelihood that a person in a population has insufficient dietary energy. It does not measure the full extent of malnutrition or account for hunger across different population groups. It is an indicator for 'capturing the extent of chronic food deprivation', to quote FAO. See ibid. Today, FAO prepares two types of hunger maps: one tracking undernourishment and another tracking food insecurity. In the Hunger

However, by 2018, hunger was again on the rise in the country. In 2018, severe food insecurity[100] returned to levels similar to those attained around 2009.[101] Research from Rede PENSSAN shows an even grimmer picture, indicating that, in 2017–2018, Brazil had already returned to 2004 levels in terms of households living with food security (approximately 60% of the total households in the country).[102] The situation became more severe during the Covid-19 pandemic. From September to December 2020, less than half the households in the country lived in food security, and 9% of the households living with food insecurity faced hunger.[103]

In August 2021, President Bolsonaro announced the creation of the Brazil Aid and *Alimenta Brasil* ('Nourish Brazil') programmes, thereby extinguishing and replacing the *Bolsa Família* by the end of 2021 (see section 5.2.4).[104] Another significant change in the field of food security was the formal extinction of the CONSEA in the first month of the Bolsonaro government.[105] Both the *Bolsa Família* and the CONSEA were reinstated in 2023, after the disputed 2022 presidential elections, approximately two months after the beginning of Lula's third non-consecutive mandate.[106]

In the mid-2010s, FAO modified its methodology for monitoring hunger and food insecurity, tracking undernourishment on a three-year average and the prevalence of moderate or severe food insecurity in the population.

Map focusing on undernourishment, a country is classified as off the Hunger Map when the prevalence of undernourishment falls below 2.5% of its population over a three-year average. See FAO, 'Hunger map' <https://www.fao.org/interactive/hunger-map/en/> accessed 29 August 2025.

[100] Under the IBGE's nomenclature, severe food insecurity occurs when there is a quantitative reduction of food for adults and children in a household. In this scenario, the family might experience the most acute form of food insecurity: hunger.

[101] Coordenação de Trabalho e Rendimento IBGE, *Pesquisa de orçamentos familiares 2017-2018: análise da segurança alimentar no Brasil* (2020).

[102] Rede PENSSAN, *Inquérito nacional sobre insegurança alimentar no contexto da pandemia da Covid-19 no Brasil (Versão Resumida)* (2021), p 2.

[103] Ibid.

[104] Brazil, 'Provisional Measure No. 1,061', 9 August 2021. The provisional measure was converted into Law No 14,284. See Brazil, 'Law No, 14,284', 29 December 2021.

[105] The extinction of the CONSEA became concrete in September 2019. The CONSEA was created in 1993 and lasted one year. In 2003, it was re-established. The CONSEA functioned as an advisory organ for the Presidency of the Republic, integrating the National System of Food and Nutritional Security (SISAN) from 2003 to 2019. It was formed by representatives of civil society (two-thirds of its composition) and representatives of the government (one-third). According to the Brazilian government, the Council served as 'an institutional space for democratic oversight and society's participation in the formulation, monitoring, and evaluation of public policies of food and nutritional security, with the aim of promoting the progressive realization of the human right to adequate food, in collaboration with the other components of SISAN'. Among other responsibilities, it was the Council's role to propose to the Interministerial Chamber of Food and Nutritional Security (CAISAN) 'the priorities and guidelines of the public policies on the field and of the National Plan of Food and Nutritional Security, based on the deliberations of the National Conferences of Food and Nutritional Security'. See Conselho Nacional de Segurança Alimentar e Nutricional, 'O que é o Consea?' (2017) <http://www4.planalto.gov.br/consea/acesso-a-informacao/institucional/o-que-e-o-consea> accessed 11 October 2021.

[106] See notes 21 and 74 *supra* for information on the new structure of the *Bolsa Família* since March 2023.

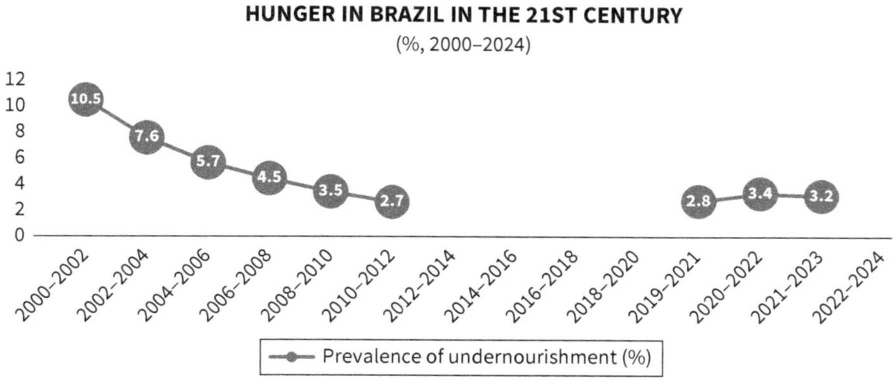

Fig 5.4 Undernourishment in Brazil (2000–2024)
Source: Based on data from: FAOSTAT 2025/FAO[a]
[a] The gap in the graphic appears whenever the rate of undernourishment falls below 2.5%, at which point a country is considered to have left the FAO World Hunger Map under FAO's current methodology.

Figure 5.4 shows the percentage of the Brazilian population living in undernourishment in the twenty-first century, based on the recalculated values under this revised methodology. The figure only shows data for the periods in which Brazil appeared in the Hunger Map. Under FAO's current criteria, a state is removed from the Hunger Map when fewer than 2.5% of its population is living in undernourishment. According to FAO, in 2024, Brazil once again left the Hunger Map.[107]

5.3.2.2 Education

Moving to the education dimension, data from the IBGE shows a significant change in the levels of education deprivation in the first two decades of the twenty-first century. The illiteracy rates of the Brazilian population aged 15 or over declined by approximately 40% from 2005 to 2019 (from 11.1% to 6.6%),[108] reaching 5.4% in 2023.[109] While the rate among the older

[107] FAO, 'Hunger map', *supra* note 99; gov.br, 'Brasil sai do Mapa da Fome da ONU: conquista histórica reflete políticas públicas eficazes' (2025) <https://www.gov.br/mds/pt-br/noticias-e-conteudos/desenvolvimento-social/noticias-desenvolvimento-social/brasil-sai-do-mapa-da-fome-da-onu-conquista-historica-reflete-politicas-publicas-eficazes> accessed 22 September 2025.

[108] IBGE, 'PNAD Séries históricas' <https://www.ibge.gov.br/estatisticas/multidominio/condicoes-de-vida-desigualdade-e-pobreza/9127-pesquisa-nacional-por-amostra-de-domicilios.html?=&t=series-historicas> accessed 9 September 2021; IBGE, *Síntese de Indicadores Sociais: Uma Análise das Condições de Vida da População Brasileira 2016* (Estudos & Pesquisas Informação demográfica e socioeconômica, 2016), p 58, Figure 4.2.

[109] IBGE, *PNAD Contínua Educação 2023* (Pesquisa Nacional por Amostra de Domicílios Contínua, 2024), p 2.

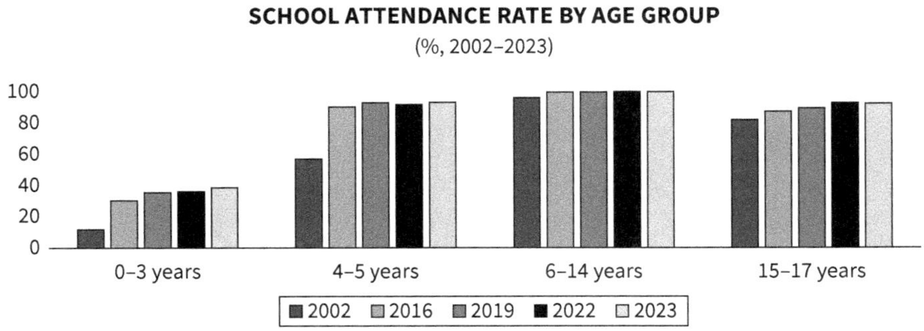

Fig 5.5 School attendance in Brazil (2002–2023)
Source: Based on data from: SIS 2013/IBGE and PNADC Educação 2022–2023/IBGE

population[110] remained considerably higher than the national average in 2019, it had almost halved over that period (from 33.7% to 18%).[111] In 2023, the illiteracy rate in the older population was 15.4%.[112]

Access to elementary and middle school, high school, and university also increased considerably. Since 2016, access to elementary and middle school has been almost universal in Brazil, and the tendency is that the same will take place for high school in the upcoming years. School attendance—that is, the percentage of persons studying—increased for all age groups, compared to the levels attained in 2002 (see Figure 5.5). Furthermore, while the percentage of individuals aged 18–24 attending or having completed higher education is still low (see Figure 5.6), the last two decades show progress.

From 1994 to 2019, there was a significant increase in the number of enrolments in higher education institutions. In 1995, 1.3 million persons aged 18–24 were enrolled in a higher education institution. In 2005, this number had gone up to 3.4 million individuals and, in 2015, to 5.1 million.[113] This change occurs in the context of increased investments in the democratization of access to education and in the expansion of higher education in Brazil from the mid-1990s onwards, particularly from 2005 to 2015.[114] In 2002, 29.2%

[110] From 2005 to 2015, the oldest age-group covered by this analysis in the PNAD was 65 years old or older. From 2016 to 2019, it became 60 years old or more. The difference in age-groups is due to the adoption of different methods for measuring illiteracy across time.

[111] IBGE, 'PNAD Séries históricas', *supra* note 108; SIS 2016, *supra* note 107, p 58, Figure 4.2.

[112] IBGE, *PNADC Educação* 2023, *supra* note 109, p 2.

[113] Salata (2018a), *supra* note 34.

[114] The expansion of higher education institutions was particularly notable in the private sector. Salata shows that, in 2014, Brazil had 2,070 private institutions of higher education, accounting for 4,664,542 enrolments in presential Bachelor courses. In comparison, in the same year, there were 298 public institutions of higher education, in which 1,821,621 students were enrolled in presential Bachelor courses. See ibid, p 226.

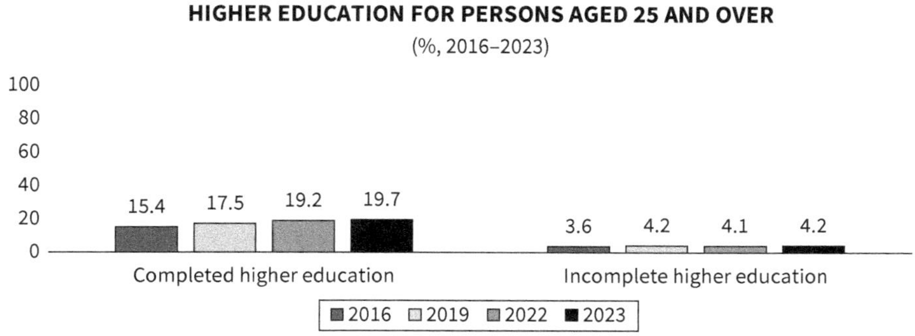

Fig 5.6 Higher education for persons aged 25 or over in Brazil (2016–2023)
Source: Based on data from: *PNADC Educação* 2023/IBGE

of students aged 18–24 years were studying at university level. By 2013, that number had increased to 55%.[115] Furthermore, the median number of years of study for a person aged 25 years or over in Brazil has also increased significantly: in 2001, it was six years; in 2023, 9.9 years.[116]

A series of events in the late 1990s and in the 2000s explain these developments, including: an increase in the number of universities—both private and public ones, but particularly the former; the creation of government programmes for scholarships and loans at low-interest rates to low-income students; the creation of affirmative action measures; higher rates of high school attendance and completion; and, arguably, income generation for low-income families. After decades of stagnation, higher education started to expand during the FHC's government (1994–2002). This expansion was accompanied by the creation and implementation of the Student Financing Fund for Higher Education (FIES) in 1999, a governmental programme still in force that grants loans at low-interest rates to low-income students enrolled in private universities. In 2005, the programme PROUNI was created by Law No 11,096, providing full and partial scholarships to students in private universities who graduated from a public high school and whose family income fell below a certain threshold (up to 1.5 minimum wages for full scholarships, and up to 3 minimum wages for partial scholarships). Furthermore, in the first decade of

[115] IBGE, *Síntese de Indicadores Sociais: Uma Análise das Condições de Vida da População Brasileira 2014* (Estudos & Pesquisas Informação demográfica e socioeconômica 2014), p 109, Figure 3.8; IBGE, *Síntese de Indicadores Sociais: Uma Análise das Condições de Vida da População Brasileira 2013* (Estudos & Pesquisas Informação demográfica e socioeconômica 2013), p 125, Figure 3.6.

[116] IBGE, *Síntese de Indicadores Sociais: Uma Análise das Condições de Vida da População Brasileira 2012* (Estudos & Pesquisas Informação demográfica e socioeconômica 2012), p 128, Table 3.9; IBGE, *PNADC Educação* 2023, *supra* note 109, p 1.

the 2000s, public universities started instituting quota systems for admission based on the type of school of origin (to the benefit of students coming from public schools), race and ethnicity (to the benefit of black, brown, and indigenous groups), and for persons with disabilities.

Initially, the quotas were an initiative of certain universities. However, a nationwide obligation for public universities to adopt affirmative action arose at the end of Rousseff's first mandate.[117] This took place through Law No 12,711 (2012), which reserved 50% of vacancies in federal public universities for students who had completed their entire high school education in public schools. Out of those reserved places, at least half were to be allocated to low-income students whose family income was equal to or less than one minimum wage *per capita*. Furthermore, the vacancies referred to in the statute were to be allocated so as to ensure representation of black, brown, and indigenous students, as well as students with disabilities, in each course, in a proportion at least equal to their representation in the population of the respective state in which the university is located.[118] Subsequently, Law No 12,990 (2014) reserved to black and brown people 20% of the vacancies offered in public examinations for positions as public servants in the federal public administration.[119] Some of these measures were impugned before the STF, but the Court found them to be a tool for the promotion of equality, as Chapter 6 will explain.

The measures mentioned above appear to correlate with a significant increase in the number of black and brown students aged 18–24 years old in higher education. Based on the PNAD, Tereza Campello identified an increase from 400,000 to 1.6 million black and brown university students in 2002 and 2015, respectively. This represents an increase of 268% in thirteen years.[120]

5.3.2.3 Life expectancy and child mortality

Vera Schattan P Coelho and Marcelo F Dias studied the evolution of health and inequality in Brazil from 1980 to 2010. In 1980, the life expectancy of a Brazilian was 62.2 years, and child mortality was 69.1 per 1,000 live births. In

[117] Succeeding Lula in 2011, Dilma Rousseff selected as the official slogan of her first mandate 'Brazil—a Country without Misery'. The slogan of her second mandate (initiated in 2015 and finalized in 2016, was 'Brazil—a nation that Educates').

[118] Brazil, 'Law No. 12,711', 29 August 2012, Articles 1 and 3. See also Brazil, 'Decree No. 7,824', 11 October 2012, Article 2, I and II.

[119] Brazil, 'Law No. 12,990', 9 June 2014. In 2025, the statute was revoked and replaced by Law No 15,142, which increased the quota to 30% for a ten-year period, after which the affirmative action programme is to be revised. See Brazil, 'Law No. 15,142', 3 June 2025.

[120] Tereza Campello (ed), *Faces da Desigualdade no Brasil: Um olhar sobre os que ficam para trás* (CLACSO, FLACSO, agenda igualdade 2017), p 49.

2010, this number had changed to 73.9 years and 17.2 deaths per 1,000 live births, respectively.[121] This represented an increase of 11.7 years in 30 years, which is higher than the average increase in Latin American countries and countries of medium and low income in the same period. In 2023, child mortality was 12.62 per 1,000 live births.[122]

From 1980 to 2010, child mortality was reduced by 77%, placing Brazil among the emerging countries that most reduced child mortality during this period, even surpassing China, India, and South Africa.[123] This period also witnessed a reduction in the disparities between Brazil's five regions (North, Northeast, Centre-West, Southeast, and South) in relation to child mortality and life expectancy.[124] In 2019, child mortality in the country was 11.9 per 1000 inhabitants, which is 5.3 points lower than it was in 2010, and life expectancy was 76.6 (2.7 years more than in 2010).[125] In 2021, life expectancy decreased to 72.8 years amid the Covid-19 pandemic, but in 2022 it was on the rise again, reaching 75.5 years.[126] In 2023, life expectancy is Brazil was 76.4 years.[127]

5.3.2.4 Access to water, sanitation, and electricity

Progress has also been reached in access to water, sanitation, and electricity. In 2001, 87.31% of the households in Brazil had access to water supply and indoor plumbing, 92.35% had access to sewage treatment—with or without a sewerage—and 96% had access to electricity. By 2015, all these indicators had improved, reaching 95.64%, 98.07%, and 99.71%, respectively.[128]

While these numbers indicate important progress in providing infrastructure to Brazilians households, they still do not reveal quasi-universal access to electricity, water, and sewage, since they measure household rather than

[121] IBGE, *Tábua completa de mortalidade para o Brasil—2019: Breve análise da evolução da mortalidade no Brasil* (2020).

[122] IBGE, 'Taxa de mortalidade infantil' <https://cidades.ibge.gov.br/brasil/pesquisa/39/30279> accessed 29 August 2025.

[123] Vera Schattan P Dias Coelho and Marcelo F Dias, 'Saúde e desigualdade no Brasil' in Marta Arretche (ed), Trajetórias das desigualdades Como o Brasil mudou nos últimos cinquenta anos (Editora UNESP 2015), p 255.

[124] Ibid, pp 257–258.

[125] Estatísticas Sociais, 'Em 2019, expectativa de vida era de 76,6 anos' *Agência IBGE Notícias* (26 November 2020) <https://agenciadenoticias.ibge.gov.br/agencia-sala-de-imprensa/2013-agencia-de-noticias/releases/29502-em-2019-expectativa-de-vida-era-de-76-6-anos> accessed 7 May 2023.

[126] Agência IBGE Notícias, 'Em 2022, expectativa de vida era de 75,5 anos' (IBGE, 2023) <https://agenciadenoticias.ibge.gov.br/agencia-sala-de-imprensa/2013-agencia-de-noticias/releases/38455-em-2022-expectativa-de-vida-era-de-75-5-anos> accessed 15 February 2024.

[127] IBGE, 'Tábuas Completas de Mortalidade', BRASIL: Tábua Completa de Mortalidade—Ambos os Sexos—2023 (2023) <https://www.ibge.gov.br/estatisticas/sociais/populacao/9126-tabuas-completas-de-mortalidade.html> accessed 29 August 2025.

[128] IBGE, 'PNAD Séries históricas', *supra* note 108.

individual access to basic infrastructure. As poorer families in Brazil generally have more people living in the same house, an analysis based on the headcount ratio rather than households reveals a much less optimistic picture, which should not be overlooked. In 2023, only 67.9% of the population had access to sewage disposal through a sewerage or a stormwater drainage system, 85.3% had access to water mains, and 92% enjoyed direct or indirect garbage collection.[129]

5.3.2.5 Conclusion

When measured across these four dimensions, multidimensional poverty declined in Brazil in the twenty-first century. However, with the rise in monetary poverty in the country from 2015 to 2021 and the dismantling of well-established programmes and institutions promoting food security, the hunger dimension saw a recent and meaningful retrocession. The increase in monetary poverty also created risks of setbacks in the education dimension. After all, when monetary poverty is on the rise, the costs of choosing education over work also increase. This risk of retrocession was further exacerbated by the Covid-19 pandemic: as identified by the World Bank, that period witnessed a reduction in the participation of children in education. Nonetheless, from 2022 onwards, monetary poverty decreased in the country, and school attendance levels increased in most age groups between 0 and 24 years old. In 2024, Brazil once again left the FAO Hunger Map.

While the analysis conducted in section 5.2 and 5.3 was colour- and gender-blind, the manifestations of poverty in Brazil are not. In an isolated analysis, the IBGE developed a dashboard approach to multidimensional poverty, introduced in the 2019 SIS and covering access to education, social protection, adequate housing, basic sanitation, and the Internet.[130] This analysis

[129] IBGE, *SIS 2024*, *supra* note 71, p 63, Figure 16.

[130] IBGE, *Síntese de Indicadores Sociais: Uma Análise das Condições de Vida da População Brasileira 2019* (Estudos & Pesquisas Informação demográfica e socioeconômica, 2019), pp 71–75. In the IBGE's conceptualization of multidimensional poverty, deprivation on the educational dimension is found when a child aged 6–14 is not attending school, when a person aged 15 or older is illiterate, or when a person aged 16 or older has not completed basic education. Deprivation in social protection is found when two conditions are simultaneously met: first, the household does not include a member aged 14 or older who contributes to social security or who is retired; and (ii) the household has an income per capita lower than half of the minimum wage, and no household member receives a wage from other sources (including social programmes). Deprivation in housing is found when either: (i) the household does not have a bathroom for their exclusive use; (ii) the external walls of a house are built with non-durable materials; (iii) the average number of inhabitants of the house is three persons per room used as a bedroom; or (iv) the household spends more than 30% of their family income on rent. Deprivation in basic sanitation is found when the household does not have simultaneous access to three services of sanitation, namely: direct or indirect garbage collection, mains water supply, and sewage disposal through sewerage, a stormwater drainage system, or a septic tank (in Portuguese, 'Esgotamento sanitário por rede coletora, pluvial ou fossa ligada à rede'). Finally, deprivation related to the Internet is found when a household does not have access to the Internet.

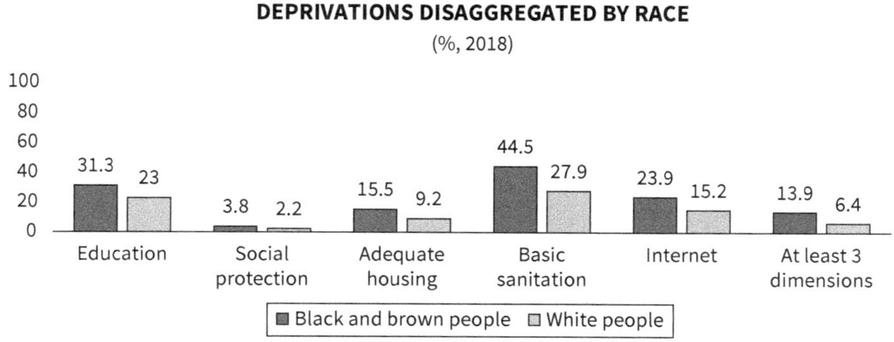

Fig 5.7 Share of the population living with deprivations disaggregated by race in Brazil (2018)

Source: Based on data from: SIS 2019/IBGE

revealed intersectionalities in the persistence of multidimensional poverty in the country, notably with regards to race, class, and residency.

In the residency dimension, the report shows that the North and the Northeast of Brazil were the regions with the highest incidence of poverty in three or more dimensions simultaneously (23.3% in the North, and 19.2% in the Northeast, compared to 8.4% in the Central-West, 7.4% in the South, and 4% in the Southeast). In relation to racial differences, black and brown men and women experienced a higher proportion of deprivations in all the dimensions when compared to white men and women (see Figure 5.7).[131]

The report also shows differences based on occupation. For example, in 2018, a little over half of domestic workers faced deprivation in education (50.7%), compared to only 5.2% of public servants and members of the military.[132] In addition, there was a clear distinction in levels of deprivation based on whether an employee engaged in formal or informal work. Only 2.3% of the employees in formal work were deprived in at least three dimensions, while 13.2% of the employees in informal work lived under these conditions.[133]

In spite of the perpetuation of these significant gaps and high levels of deprivation of vulnerable groups, Tereza Campello, who was Rousseff's Minister of Social Development and Fight Against Hunger in both of her mandates, observes that the reduction of monetary poverty in Brazil from 2002 to 2015 walked hand in hand with the reduction in inequalities (including racial inequality) in access to rights, services, and goods.[134] Based on data from the

[131] Ibid.
[132] Ibid.
[133] Ibid.
[134] Campello (2017), *supra* note 120, p 70.

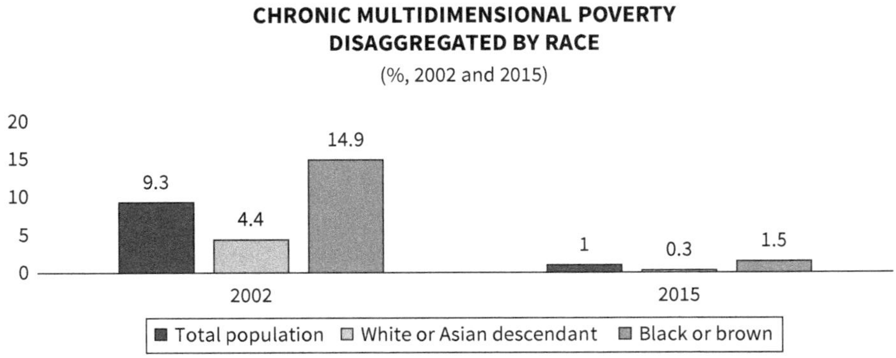

Fig 5.8 Share of the population living in multidimensional poverty in Brazil disaggregated by race (2002 and 2015 comparison)

Source: Based on data from: Campello (2017), considering the World Bank's methodology for calculating multidimensional poverty and using data from PNAD/IBGE

2002–2015 PNADs, Campello finds a reduction in multidimensional poverty during this period, which also resulted in a reduction in racial inequality (see Figure 5.8 for an analysis of chronic multidimensional poverty disaggregated by race).[135]

In conclusion, multidimensional poverty is experienced differently by different groups. The same holds true for monetary poverty. The manifestations of intersectionalities in the changes of poverty levels and the perpetuation of poverty in Brazil will be analysed in more detail in section 5.4.

5.4 A matter of class, colour, or gender?

The phenomenon of poverty, be it monetary or multidimensional, does not affect all groups equally. Some groups are particularly vulnerable to poverty in Brazil and are disproportionately represented among those living in monetary and multidimensional poverty. This section discusses the impact of poverty by applying intersectionality as an analytical strategy.

The discussion on inequalities and poverty could be conducted with a focus on a myriad of groups, including lesbian, gay, bisexual, transgender, intersex, and queer communities, indigenous peoples, and persons with disabilities, among others. Without negating the importance of studying the impact of poverty on these groups, this subsection focuses on class, race, and gender.

[135] Figure 10 shows the racial classifications as presented and grouped by Campello based on IBGE categories. See ibid, p 71.

This choice is explained by two main factors. First, the particularities of the phenomenon of poverty in Brazil, a postcolonial and patriarchal country, with very high rates of income inequality, which was the last State in the Americas to abolish slavery and the State that received the highest number of enslaved Africans in the continent. Second, the accessibility of the data discussed throughout this chapter disaggregated by race, class, and gender.

In 2023, women still earned, an average, 79% of men's earnings.[136] This difference in salary takes place despite women aged 25 years or older having more years of study, on average, than men of the same age group.[137] The racial gap is even more pronounced: the black and brown population earned only 58.9% of the income of the white population.[138]

According to the IBGE, black and brown persons comprised 51.1% of the Brazilian population in 2009 and 56.5% in 2023.[139] Yet in 2009, 66.2% of the houses in the *favelas* were headed by black women or men, and 67% of the homeless population was black or brown.[140] In the 2020s, this pattern of inequality at the intersection of race and class persisted: although black and brown people constituted just over half of the labour force in 2021 (55.2%), they accounted for almost two-thirds of those living in unemployment, 74.8% of the lowest income decile, and only 28.2% of the highest income decile.[141] In 2023, 70% of those living in poverty and extreme poverty were black or brown.[142]

In 2015, 71.2% of black and brown women and 68.9% of black and brown men lived in extreme poverty, poverty, or vulnerability.[143] In comparison, 46.5% of white women and 46.2% of white men lived in the same conditions in that year.[144] In 2019, the IBGE found that, in terms of income, white men were the group with the greatest comparative advantages in an analysis disaggregated by race and gender. Next came white women, followed by black and

[136] IBGE, *SIS 2024*, *supra* note 71, p 20.
[137] IBGE, *PNADC Educação* 2023, *supra* note 109, p 4.
[138] IBGE, *SIS 2024*, *supra* note 71, p 20.
[139] IBGE, *PNAD 2009* (Pesquisa Nacional por Amostra de Domicílios, 2009), Table 1.2; IBGE, *PNAD Contínua: Características gerais dos domicílios e dos moradores 2023* (Pesquisa Nacional por Amostra de Domicílios 2024), p 13.
[140] IPEA, *Políticas sociais: acompanhamento e análise* (2014), p 96.
[141] IBGE, *Desigualdades Sociais por Cor ou Raça no Brasil* (Estudos e Pesquisas Informação Demográfica e Socioeconômica, 2022), pp 2 and 5.
[142] IBGE, *SIS 2024*, *supra* note 71, p 57.
[143] IPEA considered, in 2009, that 'those whose *per capita* household income was less than R$67.00 were considered extremely poor; those whose income was between R$67.00 and R$134.00 were considered poor; if the income was higher than R$134.00 and less than R$465.00 (the minimum wage on that year), they were considered vulnerable; and, finally, those who had a [family income *per* capita] higher than or equal to the 2009 minimum wage were not poor'. Translation by the author. See IPEA and others, *Retrato das Desigualdades de raça e gênero* (2014), p 35.
[144] Ibid, Tables 10.10a2 and 10.10a3.

brown men. Black and brown women appeared last, receiving only 44.4% of the income of white men in Brazil in 2019.[145]

Intersectional discrimination can also be perceived through the comparison of occupations disaggregated by race. Most black and brown public servants occupy positions of lower qualification, prestige, and remuneration compared to white public servants with the same level of education. According to 2012 data from the Integrated System of Human Resources Management (SIAPE), catalogued by IPEA, black and brown people represented only 5.9% of diplomats, 15% of lawyers from the Office of the Attorney General, and 19.5% of public defenders. In less-valued careers in public service, such as technical support, they accounted for almost 40% of public servants.[146]

Racial inequalities are also significant in education, one of the dimensions of multidimensional poverty analysed in the previous section. In 2023, the illiteracy rate of black and brown persons aged 15 or older was more than double that of white persons (7.1% and 3.2%, respectively).[147] The gap was significantly bigger with regard to persons aged 60 or older (22.7% and 8.6%, respectively).[148] In addition, while the white population aged 25 or older had, on average, 10.8 years of study, the black and brown population had only 9.2 years.[149]

As explained earlier in this chapter, the number of higher education institutions in Brazil and the number of students enrolled in them both expanded throughout the twenty-first century. This increase benefited white, black, and brown youth, but significant inequalities persisted. In 2001, 39.6% of the students aged between 18 and 24 were attending a higher education institution (the other 60.4% were studying at a lower educational level). By 2011, that percentage had increased to 65.7%. The change is proportionately more pronounced in the black and brown population, considering their low starting point (from 10.2% in 2001 to 35.8% in 2011).[150] While these numbers show the impact of policies for social inclusion in racial inequalities (see Figure 5.8), they also show that the vast majority of black and brown students aged 18–24 years old were behind in their education (45.2% were still attending high school in 2011, and 11.8% were attending basic school).[151] The gap is even

[145] IBGE, *Desigualdades Sociais por Cor ou Raça no Brasil* (Estudos e Pesquisas informação Demográfica e Socioeconômica 2019), p 3.

[146] Tatiana Dias Silva and Josenilton Marques da Silva, *Nota Técnica. Reserva de vagas para negros em concursos públicos: uma análise a partir do Projeto de Lei 6.738/2013* (IPEA, 2014), p 9.

[147] IBGE, *PNADC Educação* 2023, *supra* note 109, p 2.

[148] Ibid.

[149] Ibid, p 4.

[150] IBGE, *SIS 2012, supra* note 116, p 116, Figure 3.4.

[151] Ibid.

clearer when looking more broadly at the youth aged 18–24 years (whether students or not) disaggregated by race. In 2023, 29.5% of white youth aged 18–24 were enrolled in university and 6.5% had already obtained a bachelor's degree, whereas only 16.4% of black and brown youth in the same age group were undertaking a bachelor's programme and 2.9% had a bachelor's degree.[152]

Turning to health, while 38.8% of the white population had health or dental insurance in 2019, only 21.4% of the black population had such insurance.[153] In addition, the life of black and brown male youth is more often cut short by incidents of violence than that of white youth. For every 100,000 young black and brown men, 185 died as a result of violence in 2019, in comparison to 63.5 white young men for every 100,000.[154]

This section concludes with a discussion of class. One could argue that a poverty analysis disaggregated by class states the obvious, since poverty, by definition, implies a clear distinction between economic groups. However, as Chapter 2 explained, poverty is not only monetary but also multidimensional. A premise of the welfare state is the universality of a certain level of welfare, including health and education. In theory, lacking income does not automatically or necessarily equate to lagging significantly behind in terms of health and education, among other indicators. Therefore, persons belonging to a lower class do not necessarily live in multidimensional poverty. Second, class is not defined exclusively based on income. This book adopts Erik Olin Wright's definition of class as groups formed through the unequal distribution of labour power, means of production, organization, and skills.[155] It also acknowledges Pierre Bourdieu's contribution to the study of classes by recognizing class as a social collectivity, each with a *habitus* and distinct relative positions in society. These positions are defined based on the distribution of forms of capital (be it economic, cultural, social, or symbolic), which grant power to a group in its relations with others.[156]

The IBGE analysed school attendance rate disaggregated by race, residency (rural or urban), and household income per capita. Looking at data from 2019, the Institute identified that the biggest inequality resided in disaggregation by income. In relation to persons aged 18–24, the proportion of individuals from

[152] IBGE, *PNADC Educação 2023*, *supra* note 109, p 9.

[153] IBGE, Ministério da Economia and Ministério da Saúde, *Pesquisa Nacional de Saúde 2019: Informações sobre domicílios, acesso e utilização dos serviços de saúde. Brasil, Grandes Regiões e Unidades da Federação* (2020), p 30.

[154] Desigualdades Sociais por Cor ou Raça no Brasil (2019), *supra* note 145.

[155] Erik Olin Wright, 'A General Framework for the Analysis of Class Structure' in David B Grusky (ed), *Social Stratification: Class, Race, and Gender in Sociological Perspective* (4th edn, Routledge 1984).

[156] See Edison Ricardo Bertoncelo, 'O espaço das classes sociais no Brasil' (2016) 28 Tempo Social 73.

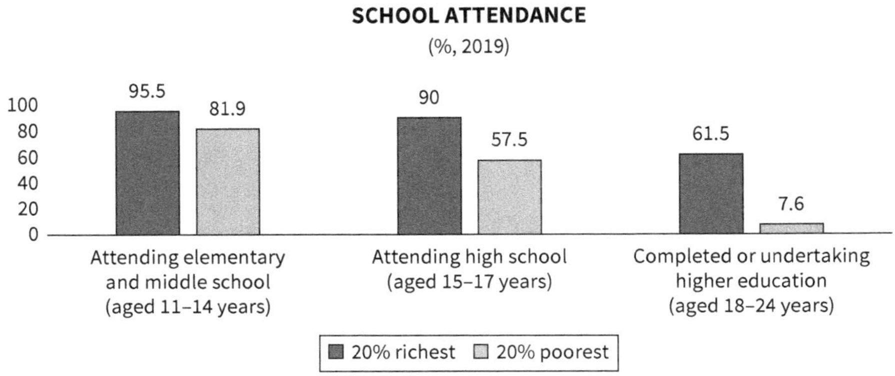

Fig 5.9 School attendance in Brazil (2019)
Source: Based on data from: SIS 2020/IBGE

the first quintile (ie the 20% poorest) attending or having finished higher education was eight times lower than that of the richest quintile of the population (7.6% versus 61.5%). A gap based on income is present in every level of education (see Figure 11).

The data from the IBGE suggests that the disparities in school attendance are greater across income groups than across racial groups.[157] Class is also a key reason for students to drop out of high school. In 2023, the most frequent self-declared motive for persons aged 14–29 to drop out of school was the need to work.[158] In this context, it becomes particularly important to analyse the proportion of students that are behind in their grade level (ie those who are enrolled in a grade below the one in which they would have been enrolled had they not dropped out of school or experienced grade repetition), disaggregated by family income. The IBGE made such an analysis based on family income covering students aged 13–16 attending elementary or middle school. In 2013, students among the 20% poorest in terms of family income had a rate of age-grade distortion 3.3 times higher than students from the 20% richest families. The gap between the two groups had been bigger at the beginning of the twenty-first century (the rate of age-grade distortion of the 20% poorest was then 4.3 times higher than that of the 20% richest). Although the rate of

[157] IBGE, *Síntese de Indicadores Sociais: Uma Análise das Condições de Vida da População Brasileira 2020* (Estudos & Pesquisas Informação demográfica e socioeconômica 2020), p 64, pp 90–91. 90.4% of the white population aged 11–14 attended elementary and middle school, compared to 85.8% of the black and brown population; 79.6% of the white population aged 15–17 attended high school, compared to 66.7% of the black and brown population; and 35.7% of the white population aged 18–24 attended or completed high education, compared to 18.9% of the black and brown population.

[158] IBGE, *SIS 2024*, *supra* note 71, p 79. In the case of women, the need to work, together with pregnancy and domestic work or domestic care responsibilities, is the main reason why women and girls aged 15–29 drop out of school and do not return.

age-grade distortion of the 20% poorest is still high, a reduction took place from 2004 to 2013: 67.8% of the students in the first quintile aged 13–16 were behind in their studies in 2004; by 2013, that number had dropped to 54%.[159]

Salata conducted a comparative analysis in Brazil on the chances that children of parents from certain occupational groups had to undertake higher education. He found that, in 1995, a child of a white-collar worker was thirty-five times more likely to access higher education than a child of a non-qualified manual worker. In 2015, the advantage was still significant but had notably decreased: the likelihood of accessing higher education was ten times higher for a child of a worker from the service class. Subsequently, Salata reduced his analysis to cover only children who had completed high school. The gap between the two groups reduced but remained significant: in 1995, children of parents belonging to the service class were twelve times more likely to access higher education than children of non-qualified manual workers. By 2015, that number had fallen to eight times the likelihood.[160]

In the realm of health, differences based on income are also manifest. According to a study conducted in 2019 by the IBGE together with the Ministries of Health and Economy, 75.7% of persons whose household income per capita was higher than five minimum wages had a dentist appointment that year, compared to only 36% of persons whose household income per capita was smaller than one quarter of the minimum wage.[161] A significant difference between the two groups can also be noted with regard to the percentage of persons who had visited a doctor in that year (89.6% and 67.6%, respectively) and the percentage of persons having received all the medical drugs prescribed to them in their last medical visit (94.9% and 78.6%, respectively).[162]

Finally, it is relevant to observe the differences in access to basic sanitation. In relation to the Brazilian population as a whole, the rate of access to waste collection, water supply, and sanitation treatment with a sewerage or stormwater drainage system in 2023 was: 92%, 85.3%, and 67.9%, respectively. If restricted to the population living with less than US$6.85 at 2017 PPP a day, the numbers change to: 83.7%, 77.4%, and 52.4%, respectively. If restricted to the population living with less than US$2.15 at 2017 PPP a day, the difference is even more striking: 76.8%, 74.4%, and 48.4%, respectively.[163]

[159] IBGE, *SIS 2014*, *supra* note 115, p 106, Figure 3.6. In comparison, the age-grade distortion rate of the fifth quintile showed almost no change in that period (from 16.9% to 16.2%).

[160] Salata (2018a) *supra* note 34, pp 233–237.

[161] IBGE, *PNS 2019*, *supra* note 153, pp 42–43, Figure 25.

[162] Ibid, p 47, Figure 32.

[163] IBGE, *SIS 2024*, *supra* note 71, p 63, Figure 16.

5.5 Conclusions: manifestations of inequalities in poverty in Brazil

The analysis of poverty levels in Brazil from 1988 to 2023 shows that considerable changes have taken place. The specific numbers of the poverty ratio throughout this period vary depending on the methodology applied to measure poverty (see Chapter 2). Even when the same poverty line is being measured, the methods used in the measurement may vary and accordingly lead to different results. For example, even though the World Bank explains that it uses data from the IBGE's PNAD and PNADC to measure the headcount poverty ratio in Brazil,[164] the figures provided by the Bank are significantly lower than those presented by the IBGE's SIS, which is also based on the PNADC (see Figure 5.10). Differences in values are also observed depending on whether the calculations are based on deflated or nominal figures.

Nonetheless, despite the methodological differences in those calculations, all the measurements indicate the same pattern: from 1992 to 2014, Brazil went through a striking reduction in its headcount poverty ratio and in multidimensional poverty, as measured in sections 5.2 and 5.3. From 2015 to 2021, extreme poverty and monetary poverty increased once more. By 2019, the poverty headcount ratio in Brazil, measured by the World Bank's IPL and by the PBF line, was similar to the levels in 2011 and 2012.

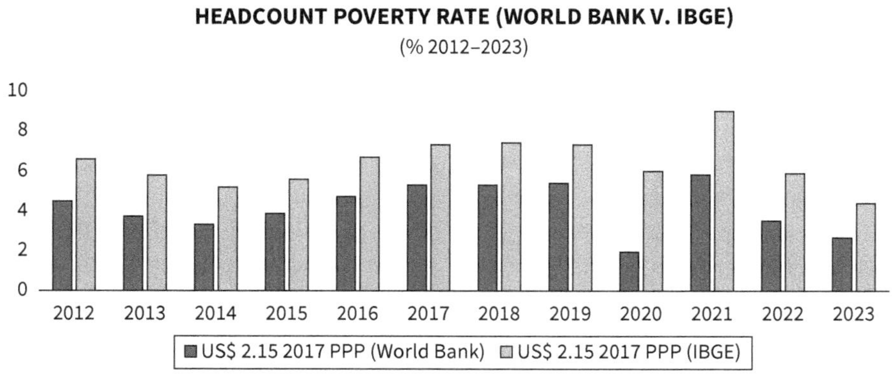

Fig 5.10 Headcount poverty rate (World Bank versus IBGE, 2012–2023)
Source: Based on data from: Poverty & Inequality Platform/World Bank and SIS 2024/IBGE

[164] World Bank, 'Brazil. Survey Information' <https://pip.worldbank.org/country-details/BRA?pathName=Poverty%20Calculator&pathLink=%2Fpoverty-calculator> accessed 3 September 2025.

An increase in the levels of deprivations from the end of the 2010s to 2022 can also be identified in the multidimensional analysis of poverty. In 2018, hunger was on the rise, further exacerbated by the pandemic. The other elements of multidimensional poverty studied in section 5.3 did not evidence retrocession, with the exception of life expectancy (yet this specific retrocession is mostly associated with the effects of the Covid-19 pandemic, and a return to higher levels of life expectancy was already taking place in 2022). Furthermore, if monetary poverty were to continue rising in the country, an increase in deprivation in the education dimension would likely follow. In stratification theories that follow the rational action theory, education is associated with costs.[165] There is a cost involved in the choice to send a child to school and in the choice made by a member of the youth to pursue a college degree instead of joining the workforce full time. These costs go beyond a semester fee or enrolment payment, particularly as Brazil has public schools and public universities. They refer to income that is not gained when a member of the youth pursues an education instead of working, assisting with household duties, or helping their parents with manual labour. When hunger, extreme poverty, and monetary poverty rise, the costs of education also increase, particularly the costs of higher education.

In 2020, there was a decrease in the headcount poverty ratio, which is likely associated with the original configuration of the Emergency Aid benefit. Poverty and extreme poverty levels rose again in 2021, before decreasing in 2022 and falling further in 2023. According to the IBGE's calculations, Brazil's headcount poverty rate reached a historical low in 2023, as measured by both the IPL and the World Bank's upper-middle-income poverty line.[166] Sustaining this low level of extreme poverty and achieving further reductions in monetary poverty across racial and regional groups will be critical to preventing retrocessions in multidimensional poverty in the country.

While this analysis of the evolution of general poverty levels in Brazil is important, it is rather limited in its explanatory potential. It ignores inter-group differences and relevant interconnections between poverty and inequality. Not every group is similarly vulnerable to poverty or to the same intensity of multidimensional poverty. Section 5.4 highlighted differences in income in Brazil based on gender. With regard to race, it found significant distinctions of income, occupation, education, housing, and health. With regard to class differences, it found distinctions in the level of deprivation in the dimensions

[165] See Salata (2018a) *supra* note 34.
[166] IBGE, 'SIS 2024, Tabelas "Padrão de vida e distribuição de rendimentos"', *supra* note 75.

of education, health, and housing. While progress has been achieved in the last two decades, poverty in Brazil is still shaped by intersectional inequalities.

The flagship of Brazil's anti-poverty policy aiming at the reduction of monetary and extreme poverty has been CCTs. Yet CCTs did not work in isolation. Brazil's anti-poverty strategy has encompassed programmes of food security and access to water, services, and goods for marginalized groups, including affirmative action measures. These multidimensional strategies, often guided by absolute lines based on income to define their target groups, can broadly be classified as distributive measures with a purpose beyond income distribution, aiming at the reduction of multidimensional poverty. Some of these measures were specifically designed acknowledging past disadvantages (such as the quota system for admission to public universities and to positions in the public sector). In addition, some distributive measures, such as the *Bolsa Família*, included conditionalities, while others, such as the BPC, did not.

By providing an overview of the evolution of poverty in Brazil, this chapter introduced the factual context in which the practices of the STF and the IACtHR, in cases where Brazil is the respondent state, are situated. The next two chapters will introduce the results of the empirical study of the jurisprudence of these two courts with jurisdiction over the acts and omissions of the Brazilian State. The STF is the highest court in Brazil with primary responsibility for ensuring compliance with the Constitution. The latter protects the right to equality and non-discrimination and sets the eradication of poverty as a fundamental objective of the Brazilian State. In turn, the IACtHR is the regional human rights court with jurisdiction over Brazil's actions and inactions since 1998.[167]

[167] Inter-American Commission on Human Rights, 'B-32: American Convention on Human Rights "Pact of San José, Costa Rica"' <https://www.cidh.oas.org/basicos/english/Basic4.Amer.Conv.Ratif.htm> accessed 6 May 2023.

6

Equality and Poverty in the STF

The 1988 Constitution of the Federative Republic of Brazil (CF/88) was promulgated on 5 October 1988, after over two decades of military dictatorship in the country. Justice Cármen Lúcia explains that the Constitution was born out of the profound crisis that deeply shook Brazilian society. Within this crisis was a context of social, economic, and regional inequalities that entangled Brazilian politics.[1] Unsurprisingly, social justice, poverty eradication, and equality and non-discrimination were granted a central space in the constitutional text.

The Constitution brings forth the understanding that, in a context in which social democracy and social justice were absent, the law would be the means to attain these aims.[2] In spite of disputes during the drafting of the 1988 Constitution—which are likely inherent to processes of transitional justice and constitution-making—Flávia Danielle Lima observes that there was consensus in certain areas, one being fundamental rights. Lima argues that this consensus derived 'from the need to overcome the former political regime and from the Constituents' commitment to meet this expectation'.[3]

The focus on fundamental rights and social justice is clear in the Preamble of the 1988 Constitution:

> We, the representatives of the Brazilian People, convened in the National Constituent Assembly to institute a democratic state destined to ensure the exercise of social and individual rights, liberty, security, well-being, development, equality and justice as supreme values of a fraternal, pluralist and unprejudiced society, founded on social harmony and committed, in the domestic and international orders, to the peaceful solution of disputes, promulgate, under the protection of God, the following CONSTITUTION OF THE FEDERATIVE REPUBLIC OF BRAZIL.[4]

[1] Cármen Lúcia Antunes Rocha, 'Ação afirmativa: O conteúdo democrático do princípio da igualdade jurídica' (1996) 33 Revista de Informação Legislativa 283, p 288.
[2] Ibid, p 288.
[3] Flávia Danielle Santiago Lima, 'Revisitando os pressupostos da juristocracia à brasileira: mobilização judicial na Assembleia Constituinte e o fortalecimento do Supremo Tribunal Federal' (2018) 63 Revista da Faculdade de Direito UFPR 145, p 156. Translation by the author.
[4] Brazil, 'Constitution of the Federative Republic of Brazil of 1988', 5 October 1988.

Judging Poverty and Inequality in Brazil. Tainá Garcia Maia, Oxford University Press.
DOI: 10.1093/oso/9780198994022.003.0006

This chapter analyses empirically the jurisprudence of the STF on poverty and equality. Section 6.1 opens the investigation by explaining how the Brazilian Constitution addresses equality and poverty. Next, section 6.2 explains the methodology of the empirical study, and section 6.3 presents and analyses its main results. The patterns identified in the STF's decision-making process are summarized in section 6.4.

6.1 Legal framework: poverty and inequality in the 1988 Constitution of Brazil

The first four of the 250 Articles of the CF/88 list the fundamental principles that guide the Republic and its organization. Article 1 sets human dignity and citizenship as two of the five pillars of the democratic rule of law. Article 3 sets forth four fundamental objectives of the Republic, three of which relate directly to social justice and equality. More specifically, Article 3.I, III, and IV sets as a fundamental objective of the State 'to build a free, just and solidary society', to eradicate poverty and marginalization and reduce social and regional inequalities, and to promote the well-being of all 'without prejudice based on origin, race, sex, colour, age or any other forms of discrimination'.[5]

Immediately after the list of fundamental principles comes Chapter I on Collective and Individual Rights and Duties. Chapter I is composed of a single provision (Article 5), which reads: 'Everyone is equal before the law, without distinction of any nature, so as to guarantee to Brazilians and foreigners residing in the country the inviolability of the right to life, to freedom, to equality, to safety and property'.[6] The drafting history of this provision reveals that the Article had originally been conceived as a non-discrimination clause with no open-ended expression. In the original formulation: 'no one shall be harmed or privileged on the grounds of race, sex, colour, civil status, age, rural or urban work, religious belief, sexual orientation, political or philosophical conviction, mental or physical disabilities, or social condition'.[7] There was space for reading poverty as a suspect criterion of discrimination in the original proposition, falling under the expression 'social condition'. This proposal was later changed to omit the reference to sexual orientation as a protected group and to replace the single reference to 'social condition' for 'any particularity

[5] Ibid, Article 3.I –3.IV.
[6] Ibid, Article 5. Translation by the author.
[7] Câmara dos Deputados, *A construção do artigo 5º da Constituição de 1988* (Obras Comemorativas, Edições Câmara 2013), 'FASE A—Anteprojeto do Relator', p 27. Translation by the author.

or social condition'.[8] Subsequently, this proposal was also modified and gave rise to Article 5 as it stands in the constitutional text, that is, a general equality clause.

Open-textured equality clauses grant the Judiciary discretion in determining when a classification is prohibited. Accordingly, in Brazilian domestic jurisdiction, it is for judges—and notably the STF as the primary interpreter of the Constitution—to determine whether a collectivity is a protected group under the constitutional protection of equality and non-discrimination.

The general equality guarantee of Article 5 applies to civil, political, and social rights.[9] The latter category of rights is protected under Chapter II of the Constitution (Articles 6–11), which safeguards, among others, 'health, nutrition, labour, housing, transport, leisure, security, social security, protection of motherhood and childhood and assistance to the destitute'.[10] The right to a minimum is guaranteed to a certain extent in this chapter, as it safeguards, among other rights, the right to a national minimum wage 'capable of meeting a worker's basic living needs and those of his or her family for housing, nourishment, education, health, leisure, clothing, hygiene, transportation, and social security, with periodic adjustments to maintain its purchasing power'.[11]

The general equality guarantee of Article 5 is complemented in the CF/88 by specific equality provisions referring to equality in the context of a specific right and, generally, one specific protected group. These specific equality provisions can be classified under three types of clauses. The first covers formal equality, generally with reference to a specific protected group. For example, Article 226 of the Constitution determines that the rights and duties in a marital relationship are to be exercised equally by women and men. It also protects the family, be it constituted under marriage or cohabitation, with one or two parents.[12] Article 227, §6, determines that children born out of wedlock and adopted children have the same rights and qualifications as those born of married parents. Another example is Article 7, XXXII, which prohibits

[8] Ibid, 'FASE C—Anteprojeto do Relator', p 28. Translation by the author.

[9] Article 5 of the CF/88 prescribes that 'everyone is equal before the law, without distinction of any nature [...] in the following terms'. The term 'following terms' refers to seventy-eight items of the provision (Article 5.I–5.LXXVIII), most of which protect civil and political rights. Social rights are the object of a separate chapter of the Constitution protecting social rights (Chapter II, on 'Social Rights'). Despite this formal division, it is common practice at the STF to refer to the general equality clause not only in relation to civil and political rights but also in relation to social and economic rights. For examples, see: STF, Judgment, *ADPF 186/DF*, 26 April 2012. Justice rapporteur: Ricardo Lewandowski; STF, Judgment, *ADC 41/DF*, 08 June 2017. Justice rapporteur: Roberto Barroso.

[10] CF/88, *supra* note 4, Article 6.

[11] Ibid, Article 7, IV.

[12] See ibid, Article 226, §§3–5.

distinctions on the enjoyment of labour rights based on whether a worker performs manual, technical, or intellectual work.

The second type of specific equality clauses prescribes positive measures[13] for protected groups. One example is Article 37, VIII, according to which the State shall institute quotas for persons with disabilities in admission to public employment.[14] Quotas based on disabilities are the only ones constitutionally required. Quota systems based on race and economic condition have been prescribed by infra-constitutional law. Another example is Article 203, V, which sets as one of the objectives of social assistance the guarantee of a minimum monthly benefit for persons with disability and older persons who do not have the means to guarantee their own subsistence and who do not have a family who is able to do so.

Finally, the third and last type of specific equality provisions are clauses that reiterate the application of the principle of equality in state functions (eg health care, education, and tax law). For example, Article 170 refers to equality as a guiding principle of the economic order. The economic order shall be conducted in light of its aim of ensuring a dignified existence for all, in consonance with the precept of social justice and with due observance of the principle of reduction of regional and social inequalities.[15] Article 227, §1, II, sets the duty of the State to implement social assistance programmes aimed at the social integration of persons with disabilities, tackling structural challenges faced by this group and eliminating all forms of discrimination against them. Article 196 recognizes health as a duty of the State and a right of all, which should be ensured through socio-economic policies that guarantee universal and equalitarian access to health. Articles 205 and 206, I and IV, determine, respectively, that education is a right of all, and it must be ensured based on equality of conditions for access to and attendance in school, with free education being granted in official institutions.

The third type of specific clauses directly impacts the legal treatment of poverty. By granting free and equalitarian access to basic public services, such as health care and education, the Constitution directly tackles, through its equality provisions, the exclusions that compose multidimensional poverty. Furthermore, these provisions require not only redistributive measures for the individual but also accommodation of different needs through structural

[13] For the purposes of this study, the terms 'positive measure' and 'affirmative action' will be used interchangeably.

[14] CF/88, *supra* note 4, Article 37, VIII, reads: 'the law will reserve a percentage of the positions and public employments to persons with disabilities, and it will define the criteria for their admission'. Translation by the author.

[15] Ibid, Article 170, *caput* and VII.

change (eg the abovementioned Article 227, §1, II). The establishment of legal duties related to poverty through equality can also be found in Article 23, X, which determines that the Union, the Federal District, the Counties, and the Municipalities have joint powers to 'combat the causes of poverty and the factors of marginalization, promoting the social integration of the underprivileged sectors'.[16]

6.2 Methodology of the empirical analysis

6.2.1 Case selection

6.2.1.1 Equality jurisprudence

The mapping of the equality jurisprudence of the STF covers collegiate decisions published between October 1988 and 29 October 2020. It encompasses legal actions for abstract review (ADI, ADC, ADO, and ADPF) and concrete review (extraordinary appeals, ordinary appeals, extradition actions, *habeas corpus*, injunction and writ of *mandamus*, among others) dealing with equality in substance. It is largely composed of final judgments, but it also includes injunctions that discuss equality and non-discrimination in the merits.

Practical considerations explain the choice not to include monocratic decisions in the study. First, the large number of monocratic decisions would prevent a comprehensive analysis of the STF's equality jurisprudence beyond prominent cases. Second, the study of collegiate decisions is sufficient to grasp the main characteristics of the equality jurisprudence and reflect judicial patterns in the Court's decision-making. After all, monocratic decisions are adopted by the STF in most requests for preliminary injunctions—in which case the decision may later be reviewed by the Court in a collegiate decision—and in matters that have already been defined in the Court's prevailing jurisprudence.

By applying these criteria, approximately 730 cases were studied. The results were manually filtered to include only decisions discussing the content and scope of the right to equality and non-discrimination or an alleged violation of this right. As a result, the investigation identified 267 relevant decisions. In seven of these, the STF found it lacked competence to make a ruling on the merits. This means that the Court has made a ruling addressing the principle of equality and non-discrimination in 260 cases.

[16] Ibid, Article 23, X.

Out of the 260 equality cases, 10% concerned distinctions based on economic status or included an analysis of poverty or vulnerability to monetary or multidimensional poverty. Yet only seventeen cases addressed poverty specifically in connection with a finding of equality/inequality. These seventeen cases were the object of a quantitative analysis aimed at identifying patterns in the Court's assessment of poverty through the right to equality. The STF's wider equality jurisprudence was considered only in the qualitative analysis, mostly for the purposes of identifying the Court's conceptualization of equality and poverty.

In the STF, a Justice is assigned to act as the '*relator*', a term that can be translated as *rapporteur*. The *rapporteur* is the Justice assigned to prepare the syllabus of the judgment and draft the decision reached by the majority (the '*acórdão*'). The latter is composed of very few paragraphs or, in some cases, even one single paragraph, which aims to summarize whether the Court found a law to be unconstitutional or, in cases of concrete review, whether it reached a finding in favour of the applicant. Therefore, the *acórdão* offers little help in determining the reasoning and tools the majority used to reach its decision. However, in 88.5% of the equality cases included in the study, the *acórdão* stated that the majority's decision was made 'under the terms of the *rapporteur*' or the syllabus largely repeated the words and the main arguments of the *rapporteur*. A similar rate is found when restricting the universe of cases to equality disputes addressing poverty (88.2% of these decisions were adopted 'under the terms of the *rapporteur*'). Accordingly, the qualitative and quantitative analysis of these cases was based on the vote of the *rapporteur*.[17] In the remaining cases, the votes of all Justices forming the majority opinion were read, and the research identified the common grounds reached by the Justices and determined whether they expressed the wish to follow the vote of the *rapporteur*. Using this method, the study aimed to bring forth results that represent the joint decision reached by the Court.

For the purposes of the qualitative analysis only, the votes of the Justices other than the *rapporteur* were studied even in cases adopted 'under the terms of the *rapporteur*'. The qualitative analysis also considers interviews conducted

[17] The analysis of the vote of the *rapporteur* as representative of the vote of the majority was the method adopted in publications from the Supreme Court itself for the analysis of the Court's decisions. See Supremo Tribunal Federal, *Convenção Americana sobre Direitos Humanos: Anotada com a jurisprudência do Supremo Tribunal Federal e da Corte Interamericana de Direitos Humanos* (2nd edn, STF, Secretaria de Altos Estudos, Pesquisas e Gestão da Informação 2022), p 8. See also Danilo dos Santos Almeida and André Martins Bogossian, '"Nos Termos do Voto do Relator": considerações acerca da fundamentação coletiva nos acórdãos so STF' (2016) 2 Revista Estudos Institucionais 263.

with Justices of the STF. The semi-structured interview guide is available in the data repository of the University of Münster.[18]

6.2.1.2 Poverty outside equality cases

To account for alternative judicial strategies to address poverty that do not include the right to equality, the study included a subsidiary search in the Court's database using the search word 'poverty'. The book focuses on the judicial strategies courts employ to address poverty within their equality jurisprudence. Given this object, the analysis of case law addressing poverty outside equality cases is merely subsidiary, intended to account for the possibility that courts may engage in a limited manner with poverty in their equality jurisprudence because poverty is rather assessed through other legal rights (such as social and economic rights).

To account for this possibility, a search was conducted in the STF's database using the word 'poverty' with filters. First, the search was restricted to the same temporal limit as the research on the Court's equality jurisprudence. Second, the results were restricted to collegiate decisions adopted by the whole bench. By applying these criteria, approximately forty-one cases were studied, nine of which were relevant to the object of the study, as they discussed deprivations derived from poverty or a context of poverty and reached a decision that tackled this object.

Cases falling outside the temporal scope of the research but considered prominent or paradigmatic (eg by marking jurisprudential changes or reaffirming a previously implicit jurisprudential understanding) were not included in the quantitative analysis so as not to generate biased results. They were only considered in the qualitative analysis. A notable example is the STF's decision in MI 7.300 (2021).

6.2.2 Coding and content analysis

The analysis of the judicial strategies each court uses to accommodate poverty in their equality case law is guided by the four-prong classification of judicial strategies introduced in Chapter 4. Recall that this classification covers the

[18] <https://data-management.uni-muenster.de/datastore> accessed 18 August 2025. The interview guide and research plan were submitted to the National Research Ethics Commission (CONEP) of the National Health Council of the Ministry of Health of Brazil, which approved the interview under ethical parameters. All eleven Justices currently sitting in the Supreme Court were invited to participate in the study. Interviews were conducted with two Justices of the STF that accepted the invitation. The results of these interviews are used in the qualitative analysis only.

following categories of judicial strategies: (i) poverty or economic status as a suspect category of discrimination; (ii) equality as a test of the inclusiveness of anti-poverty policies; (iii) poverty as a matter of discriminatory context; and (iv) positive obligations emanating from substantive equality.

Furthermore, to analyse the responsiveness of these strategies to multidimensional exclusions, the study assesses which dimension(s) of equality (redistributive, recognition, participative, and transformative), if any, has been applied by the STF in identifying and tackling exclusions arising in relation to poverty. Testing the dimensions of equality addressed by courts in their treatment of poverty allows the investigation to determine whether any dimension has been neglected in relation to poverty, and whether any strategy is more predominant in capturing the multidimensional manifestations of inequalities in the context of poverty. This assessment allows the study to test two hypotheses. First, that the dominant narrative in legal scholarship on the (under)development of equality as a tool to address multidimensional exclusions and oppressions derived from poverty is not applicable to the jurisdictions of the STF and the IACtHR. Second, that a fundamental added value of an equality approach to poverty resides in its ability to capture multidimensional forms of oppression, compared to an approach focused exclusively on socio-economic rights.

Cases were classified as covering the redistributive dimension of equality when the finding of discrimination referred to a distributive harm related to poverty or when the ordered remedy was a redistributive reparation as a measure for the promotion of equality. Cases were classified as addressing the recognition dimension when the assessment of inequalities involved the analysis of misrecognition related to poverty as an inequality, or when the court recognized the promotion of recognition as a remedy for these injustices. When the assessment of inequalities related to obstacles to social and/or political participation, the case fell under the participative dimension. For the purposes of this research, decisions in which the courts assessed obstacles to participation in education or access to high-level positions as barriers to full inclusion in society were considered to fall under this classification. Finally, cases were classified as addressing the transformative dimension when the judgment found that the state should accommodate differences (including needs arising from different identities) to promote substantive equality. This latter classification was also applied to cases in which the court, considering power hierarchies and other structural obstacles to equality endured by marginalized groups, called for the modification of institutions through structural change rather than expecting the marginalized groups to use their agency in one specific manner. The participative and transformative dimensions were considered 'accessory dimensions'; that is, the investigation did not treat them as autonomous but instead dimensions that accompany and give more precision to the redistributive and recognition dimensions, as explained in Chapter 2.

The code books used in the analysis of the equality case law concerning poverty and the wider equality jurisprudence of the two courts can be found in the data repository of the University of Münster.[19] The code book prepared for identifying the dimensions of equality applied in each jurisdiction is based on the four-dimensional model of substantive equality.

6.3 Empirical results

This section presents the results of the empirical analysis of the STF's jurisprudence on equality and poverty. Sections 6.3.1 and 6.3.2 identify the concept(s) of poverty and equality, respectively, adopted by the STF in its jurisprudence. By elucidating the conceptual underpinnings adopted by the Court, the section aims to establish a foundation for the subsequent analysis of the judicial strategies employed to address poverty through the prism of equality. Section 6.3.3 delves into the examination of the judicial strategies applied by the STF to tackle poverty through equality. This analysis identifies these strategies and assesses their responsiveness to the multidimensional exclusions and inequalities associated with poverty in Brazil.

6.3.1 Conceptualization of poverty

The STF has applied the concepts of monetary and multidimensional poverty in its equality case law. In addition, it has relied on the concept of economic vulnerability, which includes poverty but has a wider scope. One example of the STF's application of the monetary conceptualization of poverty is *RE 587.970* (2017), where the Court decided whether foreigners residing in Brazil were entitled to social assistance.[20] The case was brought before the STF by the National Institute of Social Security, which appealed against a decision of a lower court granting the right to social assistance to a foreign woman living below the BPC poverty line and residing for more than fifty-four years in Brazil. In the judgment, the STF analysed the inclusiveness of the

[19] <https://data-management.uni-muenster.de/datastore> accessed 18 August 2025.
[20] STF, Judgment, *RE 587.970/SP*, 20 April 2017. Justice rapporteur: Marco Aurélio.

BPC benefit with regard to the delimitation of its beneficiaries, considering the Constitution's aim of guaranteeing an existential minimum.

Monetary deprivation was also the focus of *ADI 3.330* (2012), a case concerning the constitutionality of the state programme PROUNI. As Chapter 5 explained, PROUNI provides scholarships for some categories of students to conduct their university studies in private institutions.[21] The beneficiaries are students who attended high school entirely in a public school or as scholarship-holders in a private school. For full funding, the programme aims at students whose family income is up to 1.5 minimal wage per capita. For a partial scholarship, the programme aims at students whose family income is up to 3 minimum wages per capita. In a vote adopted by the majority of the bench, the Justice *rapporteur*, Ayres Britto, found the PROUNI to be constitutional. He recalled that the CF/88 sets as a fundamental objective of the Republic the eradication of poverty and marginalization and the reduction of social and regional inequalities. It also determines that combating the causes of poverty and the factors of marginalization in a manner that promotes the social integration of the underprivileged sectors of society is within the shared competence of the Union, the states, the Federal District, and the Municipalities. Having referred to the constitutional framework, Justice Britto discussed the manifestations of poverty in the country in a context of inequalities. He found that poverty not only affects certain groups in a disproportional manner but also causes exclusion and marginalization. In this context, positive measures are a tool for realizing their right to equality.[22]

In the same case, Justice Joaquim Barbosa wrote a vote agreeing with the conclusion of the *rapporteur* but bringing forth in his reasons an analysis of poverty beyond the limits of a strictly monetary assessment and including the root causes of poverty in his analysis. Justice Barbosa argued that chronic poverty is the result of lack of educational opportunities, which impacts social mobility.[23] This process characterizes what he called 'cumulative cycles of competitive disadvantage', constituting a 'socio-economic blockage confining millions of Brazilians to live eternally in poverty'.[24] In this context, the impugned positive measure would merely be a 'mild attempt of mitigating this cruel situation'.[25] Justice Barbosa's vote expresses a multifaceted understanding of poverty, according to which the monetary dimension is one

[21] STF, Judgment, *ADI 3.330/DF*, 03 May 2012. Justice rapporteur: Ayres Britto.
[22] Ibid, paras 30–40.
[23] Vote of Justice Joaquim Barbosa in ibid, p 43. Translation by the author.
[24] Ibid. Translation by the author.
[25] Ibid. Translation by the author.

element reinforced by other dimensions—such as educational deprivations—that perpetuate a cycle of chronic poverty.

The extrapolation of the limits set by a monetary conceptualization of poverty is present in further cases. One example is *RE 567.985* (2013), in which the STF recognized shortcomings derived from reading poverty thresholds as absolute measurements for identifying poverty. This case concerned the rules regulating access to the BPC, which, as Chapter 2 explained, is a benefit of social assistance given to older persons and persons with disabilities living below a certain monetary line (less than one quarter of the minimum wage, according to the LOAS). This criterion for eligibility was further specified in the 2003 Elder Law Statute, which determines that, if the BPC is already provided to a member of a family, the monetary value of the benefit will not be included in the calculation of family income to determine whether another member of the same family is entitled to it. The object of the dispute before the STF was whether other social benefits received by a family member should be similarly disregarded in this calculation.

The Justice originally assigned to serve as the *rapporteur* of the case was Justice Marco Aurélio. He asserted that concrete situations might indicate that an older person or a person with disabilities is in need of the BPC even if that person has an income slightly higher than the one quarter of the minimum wage threshold. The Justice found in the very case he was analysing a clear illustration of his argument. One of the parties was a member of a family composed of an older couple[26] and a son with disabilities. While one of the older persons received an income equal to the minimum wage, their son was a person with disabilities in need of expensive treatment. Therefore, in the concrete case, the monetary threshold adopted by the legislator was insufficient to define extreme poverty.[27] In addition, Justice Marco Aurélio noted that, for a period, the poverty threshold set as one quarter of the minimum wage had been below the World Bank poverty line. However, at the time of the judgment, due to an update in the value of the minimum wage, the BPC poverty line had become higher than the IPL. Considering that this domestically defined threshold had become significantly higher than internationally adopted parameters for measuring monetary poverty, the Justice concluded that situations in which the domestic parameter was insufficient to capture poverty were exceptional.[28] This was one of the reasons that motivated him not to consider the impugned provision unconstitutional. Rather, he found

[26] The book preferred this term in relation to 'elderly couple', to avoid potentially stigmatizing language.
[27] STF, Judgment, *RE 567.985/MT*, 18 April 2013. Justice rapporteur: Gilmar Mendes, pp 15–17.
[28] Ibid, p 21.

that the monetary threshold set in that provision was not absolute and could be evaluated on a case-by-case basis.

While the majority of the bench agreed with Justice Marco Aurélio that the monetary threshold set under the LOAS could be insufficient to capture all situations of deprivation that merited access to the BPC, they did not agree that the provision should not be found unconstitutional. In a vote adopted by the majority, Justice Gilmar Mendes took note of the different definitions of poverty brought forth by the legislature (eg the *Bolsa Família* poverty line). He found that, since the adoption of the LOAS, factual (political, economic, and social) and juridical changes (eg the creation of other monetary thresholds for accessing additional social assistance benefits) had taken place. These changes should be read as granting flexibility to the absolute and exclusively monetary threshold established under the LOAS for defining extreme poverty.[29] He concluded that the definition of misery, guided only by the objective monetary definition of poverty, could not serve as a sufficient parameter to identify all situations of need that merited access to the BPC.[30] The majority of the bench agreed with Justice's conclusion and declared the law partially unconstitutional. Justice Mendes also argued for setting a deadline for the National Congress to solve this omission,[31] but the majority of the bench did not approve this suggestion.

In conclusion, while the STF has not used the term 'multidimensional poverty' in its equality jurisprudence, the Court's Justices have considered other dimensions beyond income when identifying the incidence of poverty among vulnerable groups. Notably, statistics on education, employment, and living conditions have been key, particularly in disputes concerning affirmative action. Another example is *ADPF 186* (2012), taken to the STF by the Democrats Party. The Democrats Party argued that establishing an ethnic-racial quota system at the University of Brasília (UnB) violated a series of constitutional norms. The quota system, instituted with a pre-defined duration of ten years, reserved 20% of the available study places at UnB for black students. It also reserved a small number of places for indigenous students for the same duration of time. Finally, it provided scholarships to black or indigenous students based on their economic status and gave these groups priority access to student accommodation. The plaintiff alleged that, while certain positive measures would be legal (eg those with a gender perspective), racial quotas should not be permissible. First, because no one was discriminated against in Brazil

[29] Ibid, pp 1–2. See also p 28.
[30] Ibid, pp 26–29.
[31] Ibid, p 28.

because they were black. Second, because such a measure created a racial conscience, in violation of the principle of equality, and generated inverse racism against white poor people while favouring the black middle class.[32]

In a vote adopted unanimously by the bench, the Justice *rapporteur*, Ricardo Lewandowski, made significant use of data from the IBGE to identify social hierarchies and exclusion based on race. Having noted the percentage of black and brown people in the population, the Justice compared data from 1999 and 2009, disaggregated by race and related to education, employment, and single parenthood.[33] IBGE data was also considered in the vote of Justice Luiz Fux in the same case, notably data on income, child mortality, illiteracy rates, and access to basic sanitation and health services. This data was taken as evidence that 'poverty has a colour' in Brazil.[34] While it is unclear whether Justice Fux read this data as unveiling elements of poverty or as consequences of monetary poverty, he analysed elements that objectively constitute multidimensional poverty in order to identify a context of vulnerability. Quoting the Justice, the disproportional presence of black and brown persons among those living in poverty was evidence of the reduced perspectives for this racial group to access 'the most basic opportunities for their development'.[35]

The consideration of statistical data on elements of multidimensional poverty to identify a situation of exclusion and inequality in Brazil was also central to *ADC 41* (2017).[36] This case concerned the challenge to Law No 12,990/2014, which reserved to black and brown people 20% of the vacancies offered in any public examination for positions in the direct or indirect federal public administration, as long as the examination was intended to fill three or more vacant positions. In a vote adopted unanimously, the Justice *rapporteur*, Roberto Barroso, identified a situation of institutionalized racism in Brazilian society, as evidenced by statistical data from the IBGE. He recalled the percentage of black and brown persons in the country in 2010 and their overrepresentation among those living in monetary poverty and experiencing deprivations in housing, health, education, and labour.

Finally, the jurisprudence of the STF includes cases in which the Court did not discuss poverty per se but rather economic vulnerability. One such example is *ADI 4.868* (2020), a case concerning affirmative action for admission in public universities in the Federal District.[37] The case concerned the

[32] *ADPF 186/DF* (2012), *supra* note 9.
[33] Ibid, pp 68–69.
[34] Vote of Justice Luiz Fux in ibid, p 105. Translation by the author.
[35] Ibid, p 126. Translation by the author.
[36] *ADC 41/DF* (2017), *supra* note 9.
[37] STF, Judgment, *ADI 4.868/DF*, 27 March 2020. Justice rapporteur: Gilmar Mendes.

challenge to the quota system that guaranteed 40% of the available places in public universities and faculties in the region to students who had completed both middle and high school entirely in a public school of the Federal District. While the applicant impugned only the differentiation based on the location of the school (the Federal District versus the other states in the federation), the STF nevertheless discussed the constitutionality of affirmative action based on socio-economic parameters. In a vote adopted by the majority of the Court, the Justice *rapporteur*, Gilmar Mendes, noted that university education in Brazil has always been characterized as a destination for the upper and middle classes. In this context, affirmative action based on socio-economic parameters is a public policy aimed at the social inclusion of lower classes.[38] Justice Mendes's analysis focused on classes, therefore concentrating on economic differences and vulnerability as the causes of deprivations of rights.

6.3.2 Conceptualization of equality

6.3.2.1 Substantive versus formal equality

The STF consistently reads into the CF/88 a protection of both formal and substantive equality.[39] This bipartite classification of equality was further developed in 2017, in a vote adopted unanimously by the bench. In ADC 41 (2017), concerning the quota system for positions in the public sector, the *rapporteur*, Justice Barroso, explained that the CF/88 safeguards three dimensions of equality: formal equality, substantive equality, and equality as recognition. The first dimension, formal equality, implies protection against the creation of privileges and discriminatory treatment and is safeguarded under Article 5, *caput*, of the CF/88. The second dimension refers to 'redistribution of power, wealth, and social well-being'.[40] It is safeguarded under Article 3, I and III of the Constitution, which sets the objectives of the Republic, including 'to build a free, just and solidary society' and 'to eradicate poverty and marginalization, and to reduce social and regional inequalities'.[41] Finally, equality as recognition means 'respect for minorities, their identity and their differences, be they racial, religious, sexual or any other'.[42] It is protected as an objective of the

[38] Ibid, pp 6–9.

[39] STF, Judgment, *ADI 2.144/DF*, 02 June 2016. Justice rapporteur: Teori Zavascki, pp 5–6; STF, Judgment, *ADI 1.276-2/SP*, 29 August 2002. Justice rapporteur: Ellen Gracie; STF, Judgment, *ADC 19/DF*, 09 February 2001. Justice rapporteur: Marco Aurélio; *ADPF 186/DF* (2012), *supra* note 9.

[40] *ADC 41/DF* (2017), *supra* note 9.

[41] CF/88, *supra* note 4, Article 3, I and III. Translation by the author.

[42] *ADC 41/DF* (2017), *supra* note 9, para 21. Translation by the author.

Republic, under Article 3, IV ('to promote the good of all, without prejudices of origin, race, sex, colour, age and any other forms of discrimination) and in the prohibition of racism (Article 5, XLII).

What Justice Barroso called 'substantive equality' appears to encompass the redistributive and transformative dimension of substantive equality. The Justice himself used the term 'redistributive' when referring to this dimension, applying it interchangeably with the term 'substantive' equality.[43] Furthermore, the constitutional provisions he indicated as integrating this dimension refer to structural changes, thereby relating to the transformative aim of substantive equality. In summary, substantive equality functions as an umbrella term encompassing the redistributive, transformative, and recognition dimensions mentioned by Barroso. The Justice's description of the dimensions of equality coincides with what has been described by publicists as the multiple dimensions of equality.[44]

In his vote, Justice Barroso discussed maldistribution and misrepresentation as oppressions located in the fabric of society and institutions, and as hindrances to the participatory dimension of equality. In addition, he analysed the distributive and the recognition dimensions of equality through the lens of intersectionality. The passage below is an eloquent illustration of the Justice's considerations of intersectionality when analysing redistributive injustices:

> [...] the poverty borne by blacks [...] is not equal to the poverty borne by whites. In fact, the unequal access to economic resources by the Afro-descendant population is not limited to the socio-economic aspect; it also has a strong racial component. As Nancy Fraser noted, 'race' organizes structural divisions between subaltern and non-subaltern paid employment, on the one hand, and between exploitable and 'superfluous' labour power, on the other', so that 'the economic structure generates racially-specific forms of maldistribution'. That is why blacks and browns still find it very difficult to assume the highest and most relevant social, economic, and political positions in the country: race represents a glass ceiling for their rise in the social pyramid. It is also due to this factor that, as Adriana Cruz pointed out, defending the adoption of universal redistribution policies alone, which are not sensitive to the racial element, is not equivalent to a 'zero point': 'ignoring the existence of inequalities and discrimination based on the racial factor implies an equally racialized form of social relationship [...], as it ensures the maintenance of an imbalanced structure.[45]

[43] Ibid.
[44] See Chapter 2.
[45] *ADC 41/DF* (2017), *supra* note 9, paras 48–49. Translation by the author.

This conceptualization of equality as substantive equality with manifestations in multiple dimensions can be identified throughout the equality jurisprudence of the STF, even when the Court did not explicitly refer by name to these dimensions. The STF has a *jurisprudence constante* that treats substantive equality as a central concept in equality cases, calling for positive measures, structural transformation, and the promotion of recognition.[46] Consider *RE 500.171-7* (2008) for illustrative purposes, a case in which the STF was asked to decide whether public universities could charge semester fees. In a vote adopted by the majority of the bench, the Justice *rapporteur*, Ricardo Lewandowski, recalled the teachings of Dalmo de Abreu Dallari refuting a conceptualization of equality as merely formal. In a passage quoted by the Justice, Dallari qualifies such a conceptualization as a 'hypocritical formalism' that disguises *de facto* inequalities.[47] Justice Lewandowski also referred to the teachings of Fábio Konder Comparato explaining that a different conceptualization of equality emerges when one considers the aim of achieving distributive justice. The resulting conceptualization is one that requires action from the state to promote social justice.[48]

Applying this reasoning to the concrete case, Justice Lewandowski found that public universities could not create economic barriers to students' access to education. This conclusion was not affected by the argument that the registration fee was arguably low. It was also not affected by the universities' argument that the impugned fees were intended to fund subsidies for underprivileged students. Because registration is an essential formality for one to access education at university level and considering that the State must proactively address social issues and guarantee rights, including the right to education, Justice Lewandowski concluded that public universities could not charge semester fees.

The abovementioned judgments discussed distributive justice by recognizing the need for affirmative action to respond to the maldistribution of material resources and by reading affirmative action as an emanation of the principle of equality in access to the right to education. The distributive dimension of equality was also addressed in *ADPF 186* (2012) on the constitutionality of the ethnic-racial quota system at UnB. In his vote as the

[46] For illustrative purposes, see: *ADPF 186/DF* (2012), *supra* note 9; STF, Judgment, *ADI 5.617/DF*, 15 March 2018. Justice rapporteur: Edson Fachin; STF, Judgment, *RE 1.058.333/PR*, 21 November 2018. Justice rapporteur: Luiz Fux; STF, Judgment, *RE 494.601/RS*, 09 August 2019. Justice rapporteur: Edson Fachin; STF, Judgment, *ADI 5.543/DF*, 11 May 2020. Justice rapporteur: Edson Fachin.

[47] STF, Judgment, *RE 500.171-7/GO*, 13 August 2008. Justice rapporteur: Ricardo Lewandowski, p 1024. Translation by the author.

[48] Ibid, pp 1024–1027.

rapporteur, Justice Lewandowski discussed equality as distribution first. He recalled John Rawl's theory of distributive justice and asserted that it is through the latter that isonomy is transformed into equality of opportunity, especially in relation to equitable participation in social rights.[49] In his words, overcoming *de facto* inequalities requires 'determined and consistent state intervention' concerning redistributive resources and opportunities to benefit the collectivity.[50] Furthermore, applying the principle of equality through the lens of distributive justice involves considering the relative position of social groups in relation to one another. This 'technique of distribution of justice', as Justice Lewandowski calls it, 'ultimately aims at promoting social inclusion for excluded or marginalized groups, especially groups who were historically compelled to live in the outskirts of society'.[51]

Subsequently, Justice Lewandowski addressed equality as recognition. He explained that centuries of slavery, repression, and prejudice built a 'depreciative perception of race in relation to traditionally subjugated groups'.[52] He argued that the repetition of social exclusion through the centuries leads to the perpetuation of a conscience of inferiority and conformity with the lack of perspective, thereby 'throwing [...] younger generations in the path of no-return towards social marginalization'.[53] In this context, he argued that the importance of affirmative action extends beyond its distributive purpose to encompass a symbolic role in the recognition and valorization of ethnic and cultural groups.[54]

The recognition dimension was also addressed in *ADI 3.330* (2012), concerning the scholarships programme PROUNI. When analysing the programme's constitutionality, the Justice *rapporteur*, Ayres Britto, observed that economically underprivileged individuals suffered inequalities. However, the Justice was not only referring to distributive inequalities but also to a form of oppression that is entrenched in culture and internalized by citizens, thereby manifesting in social relations. In his words, when inequality becomes 'widespread and lasts long enough to become a cultural trace of society, that is, when it becomes a characteristic of fundamental social relations or a true *praxis*, those segments of society perceived as inferior experience a disturbing feeling of low self-esteem'.[55]

[49] *ADPF 186/DF* (2012), *supra* note 9, p 52.
[50] Ibid. Translation by the author.
[51] Ibid, p 8. Translation by the author.
[52] Ibid, p 66. Translation by the author.
[53] Ibid, p 74. Translation by the author.
[54] Ibid, pp 72–74.
[55] *ADI 3.330/DF* (2012), *supra* note 21, p 25, para 31.

In conclusion, the analysis of the STF's equality jurisprudence reveals the adoption of a multidimensional understanding of equality. The latter encompasses the redistribution of material resources; the transformation of structures that perpetuate discrimination and historical power dynamics; the recognition of each person without stereotypes, stigma, or pressure for assimilation; and equal opportunity for participation in social, cultural, and political life. As Chapters 2 and 3 explained, this multidimensional conceptualization of substantive equality is expected to open space for the legal assessment of poverty through the lens of equality in judicial practice.

6.3.2.2 The relevance of affirmative action

When conceptualizing the constitutional right to equality as substantive equality, the STF has required state action to change historical and structural manifestations of inequality. In addition, the Court has been active in upholding the constitutionality of affirmative action. Out of the 260 equality cases decided by the STF from October 1988 to October 2020, forty-one concerned affirmative action. In 87.8% of these forty-one cases, the STF either reaffirmed or expanded the content and scope of the affirmative action measure. These numbers are even more striking when the analysis is restricted to affirmative action based on economic status, in which case the rate goes up to 100%.

Against this background, the strategy of tackling poverty as a matter of positive obligations is expected to be particularly evident in the STF's jurisprudence. This hypothesis is further strengthened by considering the Court's jurisprudence on quota systems. For the purpose of a more detailed analysis of the STF's jurisprudence on affirmative action, this study adopts the categorization of affirmative action proposed by Khaitan as facilitative and distributive measures. Khaitan classifies affirmative action based on the tools employed, the latter being divided into two categories: distributive (eg quota systems) and facilitative (eg reporting requirements). When distributive, the measure promotes an immediate distribution of benefits (politically, socio-culturally, or materially) by distributing the benefit itself.[56] In turn, facilitative measures promote a 'remote' or indirect distribution by creating a facilitative environment where the targeted benefits are more likely to ensue.[57] Affirmative action may concern tangible benefits (eg a job) or expressive ones (eg encouragement to apply for a job).[58] Finally, a distributive measure may be classified as strong or weak. In the former, group membership is the predominant factor

[56] Tarunabh Khaitan, *A theory of discrimination law* (Oxford University Press 2015), p 218.
[57] Ibid, p 218.
[58] Ibid, p 218.

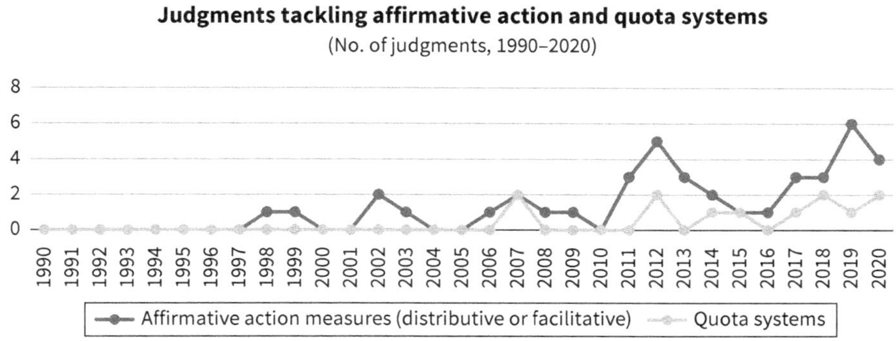

Fig 6.1 Judgments on affirmative action measures and quota systems (STF, 1988–2020)
Note: Figure 6.1 starts in 1990 because this is the year of the first decision concerning the right to equality and non-discrimination included in the study.[a]
[a]The source is my empirical research.

in distribution, whereas it plays a more limited role in the latter.[59] The paradigm example of strong distributive measures is quota systems.[60] Therefore, the analysis of judicial practice in cases with this object may be particularly descriptive of the limits of distributive justice in a jurisdiction.

By reducing the scope of the analysis only to cases involving quota systems, the study finds that, in eleven of the twelve cases concerning these measures, the STF either reaffirmed or expanded their content and scope. In only one case did the Court find that the scope of the impugned quota system should be reduced for it to be proportional.[61] More than half of the quota cases are related to persons with disabilities (58%). The second most preponderant protected group is race (25%), followed by economic status, gender, and residency (8% each).

The Court's active role in upholding the constitutionality of distributive and facilitative affirmative action is a recent development in the STF's equality jurisprudence. While the first case of the STF on affirmative action was decided in 1998, its first decision on distributive affirmative action measures dates from 2007. Most judgments on distributive or facilitative affirmative action have been issued since 2002, particularly from 2010 onwards (see Figure 6.1).

Chapter 5 explained that affirmative action played an important role as a public policy for eradicating extreme poverty and reducing monetary and

[59] Ibid, p 219.
[60] Ibid.
[61] STF, Judgment, *MS 26.310-5/DF*, 20 September 2007. Justice rapporteur: Marco Aurélio. Justice rapporteur: Marco Aurélio. The case concerned the application of quotas to persons with disabilities in a public examination with only two places for a position in the public administration.

multidimensional poverty in Brazil, notably in the first fifteen years of the twenty-first century. Unsurprisingly, this period coincides with the expansion of judgments on affirmative action at the STF.

6.3.3 Judicial strategies for accommodating poverty in equality cases

Having explained the STF's conceptualization of poverty (both monetary and multidimensional) and equality (strongly based on substantive equality and applied in practice through redistribution, recognition, participation, and transformation), the chapter will now analyse the judicial strategies employed by the STF to address poverty through the right to equality. From October 2020 to October 2020, the STF reached seventeen decisions addressing poverty in connection with an equality claim.[62] These decisions are the object of the quantitative analysis conducted in this section. The Court's broader equality jurisprudence (260 collegiate decisions) is considered only in the qualitative analysis in order to clarify the STF's interpretation of equality, poverty, and economic vulnerability and the implementation of these concepts in law.

Of the seventeen cases in the sample, thirteen concerned the positive obligation of the State to protect or fulfil the right to substantive equality (76.5% of the total number of cases). The second and third most frequently used strategies by the STF were addressing poverty as a suspect classification and discussing poverty as context (ten and seven cases, respectively, equivalent to 58.8% and 41.2% of the total sample). The Court discussed the inclusiveness of anti-poverty measures in only three cases (17.6% of the sample).

In some decisions, the STF concomitantly used two or more of these strategies. For example, positive obligations and context have often been used simultaneously, as the analysis of poverty as context provides arguments for assessing the constitutionality of positive obligations. In turn, positive obligations were interpreted as necessary means for fulfilling the right to equality considering a factual situation of persistent and historical inequalities. Context was analysed in 46.2% of the decisions of the STF concerning Brazil's positive obligations to address poverty derived from the right to equality and in 54.5% of the cases concerning affirmative action.

[62] See Chapter 1 for the methods used to identify this universe of cases and the limitations of those methods.

6.3.3.1 Suspect classification

Because Article 5 of the CF/88 is a general equality clause, it does not establish suspect classifications or protected groups. Nevertheless, the empirical analysis of the STF's equality jurisprudence shows that the Court has recognized certain grounds as suspect. In *ADI 3.330* (2012), concerning the PROUNI programme, the Justice *rapporteur*, Ayres Britto, recalled that the CF/88 does not list which factors of differentiation are permissible but provides indications on the prohibited ones.[63] The Justice recalled that Article 3, IV, of the CF/88 sets as a fundamental objective of the Republic the promotion of the well-being of all without prejudice on the grounds of 'origin, race, sex, colour, age and any other forms of discrimination'. He concluded that these grounds could not be used as factors of differentiation for determining a person's social value or character. They are mere accidental factors that do not reveal the essence of individuals.[64] The Justice found that the same reasoning must be applied to historical and cultural factors, such as socio-economic status.[65]

A similar reasoning was adopted by the Justice *rapporteur*, Justice Luiz Fux, in a vote adopted by the majority in *RE 898.450* (2016). This case concerned the disqualification of a candidate from a public examination for the position of soldier in the military police of the State of São Paulo because the candidate in question had a tattoo on his left leg.[66] Justice Fux explained that an element of differentiation (or '*discrimen*' factor) could not rely on traits that are intrinsic to a person. Characteristics such as sex, residence, age, and race cannot justify the application of a targeted norm against these groups unless those characteristics are directly related to the *raison d'être* of the differentiation.[67] While, in the concrete case, the impugned differentiation was not based on a prohibited ground of discrimination, there was no logical correlation between the factor of *discrimen* (a tattoo on the left leg) and the difference of treatment (selecting candidates that are competent to perform the duties required by the position).[68]

In addition, the STF has recognized specific collectivities as being subject to historical and pervasive discrimination and, as such, constituting protected groups. As a direct consequence of this recognition, it has called for equality not only in a negative but also a positive dimension, meaning that the State has a duty to promote *de facto* equality in favour of these groups. One example is

[63] *ADI 3.330/DF* (2012), *supra* note 21, p 28, para 37.
[64] Ibid.
[65] Ibid, paras 38–39.
[66] STF, Judgment, *RE 898.450/SP*, 17 August 2016. Justice rapporteur: Luiz Fux.
[67] Ibid, pp 25–26.
[68] Ibid, pp 27–45.

provided by *Pet 3.388* (2009), a case on the demarcation and registration of indigenous land in the state of Roraima. In a vote adopted by the majority, the Justice *rapporteur*, Ayres Britto, asserted that the CF/88 introduced a new type of equality into Brazilian constitutional law, called 'civic-moral equality'.[69] The right-holders of the latter are 'minorities who have been historically subjected to comparative disadvantages in relation to other social groups, because of ignominious prejudice and sometimes the most reprehensive collective impulse of cruelty'.[70] In the Justice's understanding, the promulgation of the CF/88 marked the beginning of a 'compensatory constitutional era', in which these historical and cumulative disadvantages are compensated by affirmative action aimed at social inclusion and integration.[71] This reasoning acknowledged protected groups as beneficiaries of affirmative action, in the application of the equality provisions of Brazilian constitutional law. A similar understanding is present in *ADI 4.424* (2012), concerning special criminal procedures in cases of violence against women. In a vote adopted by the majority, the Justice *rapporteur*, Marco Aurélio, recognized a 'constitutional conscience' in present-day constitutionalism in Brazil. This constitutional conscience legitimizes 'positive discriminations aimed at responding to the peculiarities of less favoured groups and compensating *de facto* inequalities, which derive from the crystallization of prejudice in culture'.[72] The right-holders of these measures are the collectivities this chapter calls 'protected groups'.

In addition, a direct reference to the term 'suspect' classification is found in the vote of the *rapporteur* in *ADPF 291* (2015), adopted by the Court's majority. This case concerned the challenge to Article 235 of the Military Criminal Code, entitled 'Pederasty or other libidinous act'. The provision prohibited libidinous acts carried out by a member of the military in a military premise, whether 'homosexual or not', to quote the regulation. The provision was impugned by the Prosecutor General, who challenged the constitutionality of the language used, specifically the terms 'pederasty' and 'homosexual or not'. The Justice *rapporteur*, Roberto Barroso, found that sexual orientation 'refers to an existential freedom and relates to a traditionally discriminated minority' and that 'its use as a ground of discrimination is, as a general rule, prohibited'.[73] The Justice explained that this criterion is considered 'suspect'

[69] STF, Judgment, *Pet. 3.388/RR*, 19 March 2009. Justice rapporteur: Ayres Britto, p 285, para 72. Translation by the author.

[70] Ibid. Translation by the author.

[71] Ibid.

[72] STF, Judgment, *ADI 4.424/DF*, 09 February 2012. Justice rapporteur: Marco Aurélio, p 13. Translation by the author.

[73] STF, Judgment, *ADPF 291/DF*, 28 October 2015. Justice rapporteur: Roberto Barroso, p 34, para 53. Translation by the author.

and is only legitimate if it passes a strict scrutiny test.[74] Justice Barroso referred to teachings of publicists discussing the equality jurisprudence of the US Supreme Court and the use of the strict scrutiny test in that jurisdiction to assess measures instituting detrimental differentiations based on suspect classifications.[75]

The STF has recognized a series of grounds as the object of historical discrimination and marginalization. Examples include sex and gender, race, sexual orientation, persons with disabilities, age, residence, and origin, among other factors. As this chapter explained, the first draft of what became Article 5 of the CF/88 prohibited discrimination based on a series of grounds, one of which was social condition.[76] Although Article 5 was ultimately adopted as a general equality clause, the practice of the STF indicates that socio-economic condition remains a 'suspect' or protected classification in the Court's assessment of equality claims. First, the Justices have repeatedly recognized socio-economic inequality as a fundamental cause of social exclusion in Brazil.[77] Against this background, the Supreme Court has consistently upheld that substantive equality is realized by the institution of affirmative action measures in favour of marginalized groups, including measures based on economic status (see section 6.3.3.4 below).

Finally, the analysis shows that the identification of 'suspect classifications' in the Supreme Court's equality jurisprudence is not a mere detail for its equality assessment. Cases involving 'suspect' classifications have a higher success rate, meaning that equality claims concerning suspect classifications have more often resulted in a finding of violation of equality and non-discrimination compared to cases not involving suspect classifications (see Table 6.1).

By reading the numbers above in Table 6.1 in isolation, one might be surprised by the comparatively low success rate of cases involving socio-economic status, gender/sex, race, and disability. However, the high number of non-violations of distinctions based on these categories should not be interpreted as an indicator of lenient behaviour by the STF towards restrictive measures on the rights of women, black and brown persons, persons with disabilities, and individuals living in socio-economic vulnerability. On the contrary, the central factor that explains this rate is the Court's *jurisprudence constante* of upholding the constitutionality of positive measures to the

[74] Ibid, p 34, para 53.
[75] Ibid, pp 33–34, para 52.
[76] Deputados (2013), 'FASE A—Anteprojeto do Relator', *supra* note 7, p 27.
[77] See Antunes Rocha (1996), *supra* note 1. For illustrative purposes, see *RE 1.058.333/PR* (2018), *supra* note 46, pp 25–26; *ADI 3.330/DF (2012)*, *supra* note 21, pp 25 and 43.

Table 6.1 Success rate disaggregated by the criterion of distinction (STF, 1988–2020)

Criterion	Violation	No violation	Total	Success rate (%)
Not suspect	81	89	170	47.6
Sexual orientation	9	0	9	100
Gender/sex	8	22	30	26.7
Race/ethnic origin	0	5	5	0
Socio-economic status	6	5	11	54.5
Disability	8	5	13	61.5
Age	8	3	11	72.7
Residency	8	2	10	80
National origin	4	4	8	50
Gender identity	3	0	3	100
Marriage	2	0	2	100
Religion	0	2	2	0
Total	137	137	274	

Note: the column 'total' cites a number (274) that is slightly higher than the total number of cases (260) because some cases refer to multiple classifications (eg cases of intersectionality).

Source: Author's empirical research.

benefit of these protected groups. In all five cases concerning race, in 77% of the cases concerning disabilities, and in 40% of the cases on sex/gender, the cases of non-violation were decisions in which the STF upheld the constitutionality of an impugned positive measure.[78] Similarly, three of the five cases of non-violation concerning socio-economic status were decisions in which the STF upheld the constitutionality of a positive measure in favour of an economically vulnerable group.[79] In addition, one of the remaining two cases of non-violation concerning economic status referred to a decision of the STF upholding the constitutionality of a measure restricting the privileges of affluent groups in accessing public services.[80]

[78] With regard to sex/gender, an additional factor explaining the low success rate is the numerous disputes included in the sample on whether a male widower of a female public servant had the right to a survivor's pension. Until very recently, the STF repeatedly upheld that excluding men from the right to survivors' pensions in the case of death of their female partner did not violate the right to equality. It was only in October 2020 that the Court found that any application of different criteria for widows and widowers for accessing survivor's pension to be unconstitutional. Until that date, a significant number of the decisions of non-violation concerning sex/gender related to this dispute. See STF, Judgment, *RE 659.424/RS*, 13 October 2020. Justice rapporteur: Celso de Mello.

[79] For the purposes of this study, measures instituting social assistance benefits to persons living in poverty were considered facilitative positive measures. Two of the three cases involving positive measures on the grounds of economic status concerned social assistance benefits to persons living in poverty.

[80] In *RE 581.488* (2015), the STF found that the determination from a lower instance court prohibiting the creation of what became known as 'class differences' under the Brazilian Unified System of Health (SUS) was a measure consistent with the principle of equality. The system of 'class differences' allowed patients to receive special treatment (eg being granted differentiated accommodation in a public hospital

Having analysed the consequences of the recognition of economic status as a suspect classification,[81] this section will now identify patterns in the decision-making process of the STF in cases concerning this ground of differentiation. The empirical research reveals four main characteristics of the Court's case law concerning differentiations based on economic status. First, the focus of the STF has been on economic vulnerability, a concept that is wider than monetary poverty. The abovementioned *ADI 3.330* (2012)[82] and *RE 500.171-7* (2001)[83] are examples of cases concerning economic status in

or being treated by a specific doctor) if they supplemented (on their own or through their private insurance) the costs of health services covered by the State. Based on the principle of equality and its application to the right to health, the STF found that public health cannot differentiate based on economic status. In other words, the Brazilian public health system, aiming at equality, could not allow different possibilities of health care based on the economic capacity of the patient, especially when it is the State who provides the treatment. Quoting the Justice *rapporteur*, *Dias* Toffoli, 'it is not conceivable that a system that calls itself egalitarian allows for the creation of castes within it'. See STF, Judgment, *RE 581.488/RS*, 03 December 2015. Justice rapporteur: Dias Toffoli, pp 17–22.

[81] Disregarding positive measures and disputes concerning a widower's right to survivor's pension (see *supra* note 78), the success rate of cases involving suspect classifications is 73.4%, in comparison with a success rate of 47.6% in cases not involving a suspect classification. One factor explaining the higher success rate of cases involving suspect classification is the application of different levels of scrutiny. The analysis indicates that the equality doctrine of the STF is composed of five steps: (i) the '*discrimen*' step (which requires that the factor of differentiation be: general and objective; sufficient to show that the parties differ from each other to a degree that justifies some level of differentiation in the treatment applied to them; and that it relates to a characteristic of the person, thing, or situation affected by the measure); (ii) the causal link/logical correlation step (which requires a logical correlation between the factor of differentiation and the resulting difference in treatment—for example, because police officers have to be physically active to fulfil their duties, an endurance fitness test can be applied in selection processes); (iii) legitimate aim; (iv) consonance with constitutionally protected interests; and (v) proportionality test (adequacy, necessity, and proportionality in the strict sense). With one single exception (*ADPF 291* (2015)), the STF does not explicitly refer to different tiers of scrutiny. However, the analysis of its equality jurisprudence shows that its practice might not be completely 'tierless'. The STF has more often assessed whether a measure pursues a legitimate aim and is proportional when the impugned measure refers to a suspect classification. Furthermore, in cases of violation, the number of discrimination claims involving a suspect classification that failed the proportionality test is more than double the claims not involving a suspect classification that failed the same test (41.8% versus 18.5%). The same applies to the test of legitimate aim (22.4% versus 6.2%). In constrast, the application of the logical correlation test remains high regardless of whether a case involves a suspect classification (73.9% and 60.4% for cases with and without a suspect classification, respectively). In conclusion, the analysis of the equality jurisprudence of the STF indicates that there are differences in the degree to which the equality test is applied by the STF in cases with a suspect classification—with the test of proportionality and the legitimate aim step becoming more preponderant in such cases. This difference in the level of scrutiny appears to be one explaining factor for the higher success rate of cases involving suspect classifications. Therefore, considering socio-economic status as a suspect classification is not a mere detail for the assessment of equality claims. As expected, the empirical analysis confirms a high rate of application of the legitimate aim and proportionality requirements in cases involving differentiation based on socio-economic status (60% and 50% of these cases include an assessment of the legitimate aim requirement and the proportionality test, respectively).

[82] This case concerns the scholarship programme PROUNI. The object of the dispute was the positive measure instituted to the benefit of low-income students, defined as those whose family income was not superior to 1.5 minimum wages per capita for a full scholarship or 3 minimum wages for a partial one (a group that includes, but is not limited to, persons living below Brazil's national lines of absolute poverty or the IPL).

[83] In this case, the STF was asked to determine whether it was constitutional for public universities to charge a semester fee. The Court found that the State cannot establish obstacles that would exclude underprivileged students (a category that covers students living in poverty but is wider than absolute poverty, as defined by the domestic poverty lines and the IPL).

which the scope of the case encompassed poverty but was not limited to it. Their focus transcended the limits of monetary poverty to concentrate on economic vulnerability and its interconnections with deprivations of fundamental rights. This wider focus covers persons living in poverty and 'popular classes',[84] that is, low-middle classes that are above the line of monetary poverty but often remain vulnerable to the latter and to multidimensional poverty.

Monetary poverty alone has been analysed as the factor of *discrimen* in only two collegiate decisions published by the STF from October 1988 to December 2020. The first is *RE 567.985* (2013), concerning the right of a family composed of an older couple and a son with disabilities to receive the BPC benefit, even though, formally, they did not qualify for the benefit based on the absolute BPC poverty line.[85] The second is *RE 587.970* (2017), concerning the right of a foreign elderly woman residing in Brazil for over five decades and living below the BPC poverty line to receive this social benefit.[86] The object of these two cases was the inclusiveness of anti-poverty policies. This indicates that such disputes remain the primary context in which the STF discusses poverty alone (instead of the wider concept of economic vulnerability) as a suspect classification.

Second, the analysis shows that the overwhelming majority of the disputes decided by the STF in the period under analysis concern an asymmetric definition of socio-economic status. In other words, the analysis of the STF has focused on socio-economic disadvantage. Inequality to the detriment of affluent individuals was found in only one case concerning a differentiation based on economic status. This case was *HC 95.009-4* (2008), concerning whether it was constitutional to use the privileged economic status of an individual accused of a crime as grounds for maintaining pre-trial detention.[87]

Third, the consideration of economic status as a suspect classification has contributed to the consideration of poverty in equality cases mainly in disputes in which the Court is called upon to revise a public policy already implemented by the State, be it a positive measure or a restrictive decision that aims at limiting privileges of affluent groups. Claims for the recognition of a duty of the State to revise a universalist policy because of its impact on the

[84] The book adopts the nomenclature used in Adalberto Cardoso and Edmond Préteceille, 'Classes Médias no Brasil: Do que se Trata? Qual seu Tamanho? Como Vem Mudando?' (2017) 60 DADOS—Revista de Ciências Sociais 977.

[85] *RE 567.985/MT* (2013), *supra* note 27.

[86] *RE 587.970/SP* (2017), *supra* note 20.

[87] STF, Judgment, *HC 94.009-4/SP*, 6 November 2008. Justice rapporteur: Eros Grau. However, the Justice rapporteur, whose vote was adopted by the majority of the bench, did not apply the tests of legitimate aim and proportionality in the equality assessment. This leaves open the question of whether a differentiation based on economic status to the detriment of the better-off could still be considered a differentiation based on a suspect classification in the jurisprudence of the STF (see *supra* note 81).

poor appear to face more resistance when the suspect classification is poverty alone.[88] In cases in which poverty or economic vulnerability is the factor of differentiation on its own, transformative claims might be unlikely to succeed.

In any case, the interpretation of economic status as a suspect classification in the case law of the STF opens venues for considering poverty in equality cases. However, this is still under development, and the leading cases in which the STF addressed poverty through equality have not been cases in which poverty was the suspect classification, but rather cases concerning other protected groups in which economic status was a factor of vulnerability that disproportionately affected the group in question. As the next sections will show, it has been the strategies of addressing poverty as context and, particularly, addressing the positive dimension of the right to equality that have served as the STF's primary tools for tackling poverty in equality cases.

6.3.3.2 Inclusiveness and impact of anti-poverty measures

The second strategy for addressing poverty as a matter of equality occurs when equality provides the lens through which anti-poverty measures are tested. This strategy has seldom been applied at the STF. This should not be read as indicating resistance by the Court to assess the inclusiveness of anti-poverty measures. Rather, it appears to relate to the small number of cases taken to the Court with this specific object.

The analysis shows that this strategy has not been the primary avenue for considering poverty in the STF's equality jurisprudence. As a rule, the Court has relied on it to address distributive claims. One example of a case with this object is the abovementioned *RE 587.970* (2013), concerning the right of foreigners living below the BPC line of poverty to receive the BPC benefit.[89] While the case has already been discussed in the previous sections, the following paragraphs will discuss additional aspects of the Justice *rapporteur*'s reasoning when analysing the inclusiveness of this distributive measure. In a vote adopted unanimously, Justice Marco Aurélio recalled the objectives of the law that created the BPC (the 'LOAS') and Article 203, V, of the CF/88 (which determines that one of the aims of social assistance is to guarantee a minimum monthly benefit for persons with disability and older persons who do not have the means to guarantee their subsistence or a family that is able to do so). Both provisions aim to protect those who are incapable of guaranteeing their own subsistence, in convergence with the principles of human dignity, social solidarity, poverty eradication, and assistance to those in need.

[88] See STF, Judgment, *ADPF 541/DF*, 26 September 2018. Justice rapporteur: Roberto Barroso.
[89] Ibid, pp 6–7.

These elements, the Justice argued, should serve as guides for interpreting the right to social assistance as safeguarded in the Constitution.[90]

Justice Marco Aurélio recalled the teachings of his colleague Justice Roberto Barroso, according to whom the concept of human dignity is composed of three elements: first, the intrinsic value of the human person; second, autonomy; and third, communitarian value. Justice Aurélio applied the autonomy perspective to the specific issue under discussion.[91] In his words, '[f]or a person to be capable of mobilizing his or her own reason in the search for building an ideal of a good life—which, in the end, motivates us to exist—it is fundamental that minimum material conditions be provided to him or her'.[92] He argued that '[t]he elimination of acute poverty emerges as a precondition for the construction of a truly democratic society, political stability, and development of the country as a whole'.[93]

Additionally, Justice Marco Aurélio noted a connection between dignity, juridical protection of a person based on the human condition, and the 'recognition of the realm of material protection that is essential for the construction of individuality and self-determination'.[94] Based on this, he found that the State must provide 'essential benefits for a person to have, simply, capacity to survive'.[95] Access to such essential goods is a subjective right of a public nature and constitutes the 'existential minimum'.[96]

However, economic constraints were cited as a limiting factor to fulfilling the right of all under the jurisdiction of the Brazilian State to the existential minimum. Therefore, Justice Marco Aurélio assessed whether there was a limit to what the State could do considering the limited economic resources. The claim was that, due to such a limit, assisting foreigners would reduce the ability of the State to provide public services to its nationals.[97]

The Justice found this argument to be inadmissible. He concluded that there was no condition of equality between persons who were incapable of providing for their own subsistence and other members of society. Hence, the former was prioritized as the object of state actions. Furthermore, no technical evidence was provided to the Court to show the financial impossibility of guaranteeing this right to foreigners or to prove the alleged impact on the public treasury. Additionally, it could be presumed that not many foreigners

[90] Ibid, p 9.
[91] Ibid, pp 10–11.
[92] Ibid, p 11. Translation by the author.
[93] Ibid.
[94] Ibid, p 12.
[95] Ibid. Translation by the author.
[96] Ibid. Translation by the author.
[97] Ibid, p 14.

residing in Brazil found themselves unable to provide for their own subsistence.[98] However, when making this argument, Justice Marco Aurélio highlighted that the LOAS referred to specific groups in situations of vulnerability (older persons and persons with disabilities). He interpreted this as a manifestation of the 'strict nature' of this benefit of social assistance.[99] By restricting the law to the abovementioned groups, Justice Aurélio argued, the LOAS required 'lack of capacity [by the individual living in poverty] to search for a solution to this situation [of poverty], as a consequence of special individual circumstances'.[100] In this passage, the reasoning of the Justice addresses the progressiveness of the socio-economic obligations of the state while also introducing traces of an agency approach to poverty. The passage suggests, to some extent, that people could be regarded as responsible for not finding ways to lift themselves out of poverty. Such reasoning is seldom upheld by a Justice *rapporteur* in equality cases in which poverty is discussed. Notably, in cases that reveal intersectionalities (particularly between race and socio-economic status), the bench tends to adopt a structural approach to poverty by recognizing that power structures often beyond the control of the individual produce constraints that tend to perpetuate cycles of poverty.

The inclusiveness of anti-poverty measures was also the object of *RE 567.985* (2013), concerning the monetary threshold for accessing the LOAS benefit,[101] and *ACO 3.359 MC-Ref*.[102] The latter involves a dispute on the volume of cuts in the Programme *Bolsa Família* (PBF) during the Covid-19 pandemic, which were concentrated in the Northeast region of the State (representing 61% of the total cuts). The dispute also involved a regional disparity in the grant of new registrations under the PBF (only 3% of the new benefits were granted to residents of the Northeast region of Brazil, and 75% to the South and Southeast regions of the State).[103] This disparity occurred even though Brazil's South and Southeast regions are two of the richest regions in the country, and the Northeast region is one of the poorest in terms of GDP per capita. The Justice *rapporteur*, Marco Aurélio, found that this disparity pointed to a discriminatory posture of retaliation by the Bolsonaro administration that impacted citizens, particularly those in greatest need.[104] By a unanimous decision, the STF granted the injunction by first suspending the cuts in the PBF while the state

[98] Ibid, pp 14–15.
[99] Ibid, p 14.
[100] Ibid. Translation by the author.
[101] *RE 567.985/MT* (2013), *supra* note 27.
[102] STF, Judgment, *ACO 3.359 MC-Ref/DF*, 05 August 2020. Justice rapporteur: Marco Aurélio.
[103] Ibid, pp 7–8.
[104] Ibid, pp 9–10.

of public calamity derived from the Covid-19 pandemic persisted. Second, it required the federal government to provide data justifying the concentration of the *Bolsa Família* benefit cuts in the Northeast Region. Lastly, it determined that equal treatment should be provided to all beneficiaries of the programme in all states of the federation.[105]

6.3.3.3 The contextual approach

The two approaches discussed above have been central for the STF to tackle cases in which it is called upon to analyse differentiations based on economic status or measures impacting persons living in economic vulnerability. In contrast, the third strategy (the contextual approach) has been central to cases in which the factor of differentiation is not economic status but other protected groups. This strategy has been applied in cases of intersectional discrimination and in cases in which the STF identifies that discrimination based on a specific ground (eg race or gender) produces multidimensional exclusions, including socio-economic vulnerability and poverty.

Addressing poverty as context in equality cases has been a fundamental tool in the STF's equality jurisprudence for addressing historical and structural disadvantages, including monetary and multidimensional poverty to which certain groups are subjected. This strategy has been applied in cases concerning the following classifications: race, gender, disabilities, and indigenous communities.[106]

When this approach is applied, the STF often considers statistical data and sociological studies clarifying the context that leads to the specific disadvantages under judicial scrutiny. One example is *ADI 2.649-6* (2008), a case concerning the constitutionality of a measure exempting persons with disabilities from costs in interstate collective transport.[107] When assessing the constitutionality of this positive measure, the Justice *rapporteur*, Cármen Lúcia, considered the challenges faced by persons with disabilities in achieving full societal integration. Her analysis incorporated the distributive and participative dimensions of equality. She highlighted that, according to data from the UN, 10% of the world's population lived with some kind of disability, and 80% of this population lived in developing countries.[108] She stressed that the highest levels of marginalization or exclusion of persons with disabilities

[105] Ibid, pp 2–3.
[106] In addition, the STF has used it in one case without a suspect classification, which concerned differences in maternity leave based on whether the child was adopted or biological.
[107] STF, Judgment, *ADI 2.649-6/DF*, 08 May 2008. Justice rapporteur: Carmen Lúcia.
[108] The term 'developing countries' is used because it is used in the vote.

were found among those living in economic deprivation.[109] Furthermore, she found that not only do persons with disabilities living in economic vulnerability face greater exclusion, but that many disabilities also disproportionately affect those living in poverty.[110] It was in light of this context that the impugned measure had been adopted in Brazil.[111] Justice Cármen Lúcia concluded that the impugned positive measure was constitutional, as it realizes the principle of equality by providing equality of rights and opportunities to persons with disabilities and fostering the reduction of social inequalities.[112]

Poverty was also taken into consideration as context in *RE 778.889* (2016), a case concerning differences in the duration of maternity leave based on whether the child was biological or adopted.[113] In a vote adopted by the majority, the Justice *rapporteur*, Roberto Barroso, found it unconstitutional to distinguish between adoptive and biological children in the delimitation of the duration of maternity leave. He also found that determining the duration of leave based on the adopted child's age was unconstitutional. This conclusion was reached based on a series of arguments, one of which related to poverty as context. Justice Barroso drew attention to a study conducted by IPEA showing that poverty was still the major motive for children to be taken into foster care.[114] He concluded that the State had a 'moral debt' to adopted children, 'either as a result of policies to fight poverty that it did not carry out or because of inadequate public policies that aggravated the problems of a poor childhood with institutionalization'.[115] In his understanding, '[t]he task that the State did not carry out is assumed by the adoptive family'.[116] In this context, '[t]he least the Government can do for these families and these children is to provide them with adequate conditions to adapt and overcome [these deprivations and traumas]'.[117] Instead of making adoption harder by limiting rights, the State must provide incentives for adoption. Equal access to maternity leave not only promotes such an incentive but also constitutes an important measure, as maternity leave assumes an indispensable role in fostering bonds of affection and care between the members of the recently established family.[118]

[109] *ADI 2.649-6/DF* (2008), *supra* note 107, p 40, para 8.
[110] Ibid, p 49, para 22.
[111] Ibid, p 40, para 9.
[112] Ibid, pp 49–51, para 22.
[113] STF, Judgment, *RE 778.889/PE*, 10 March 2016. Justice rapporteur: Roberto Barroso.
[114] Ibid, p 38, *supra* note 43.
[115] Ibid, pp 37–38, para 54. Translation by the author.
[116] Ibid. Translation by the author.
[117] Ibid. Translation by the author.
[118] Ibid, pp 34–38, paras 44–54.

The abovementioned cases discussed monetary poverty or economic vulnerability to poverty as context. In addition, the equality jurisprudence of the STF also provides examples of the analysis of multidimensional poverty as context, notably with regard to the dimensions of education, housing, and health. One example is *ADPF 186* (2012), concerning the ethnic-racial quota system at the UnB. When analysing the constitutionality of the quota system, the Justice *rapporteur*, Justice Lewandowski, recalled the teachings of Thomas Skidmore. Skidmore asserted that the darker the skin of a Brazilian, the higher the probability that the person is located at the lower end of the socio-economic scale in relation to every indicator—income, occupation, and education. In a passage quoted by the Justice, Skidmore explained that, even though Brazil did not institutionalize a biracial society after abolishing slavery (in contrast to the United States of America), discrimination persisted in the country in a complex fashion. The myth of a 'racial democracy', he argued, dominated the Brazilian elite and led to a refusal to recognize that race is, indeed, a barrier to social and economic ascension.[119] Justice Lewandowski found that Skidmore's theoretical analysis was confirmed by an assessment of statistical data from the IBGE. First, the Justice identified the proportion of black and brown people among the total population in Brazil. Next, he analysed the proportion of this racial group experiencing deprivations in the enjoyment of the right to education compared to the proportion of white persons experiencing these deprivations. He conducted this analysis by comparing IBGE data from 1999 and 2009, a strategy that allowed him to determine the persistency of racial gaps and assess the degree of deprivations in the fulfilment of rights based on race.[120] In addition to data relating to the degree of educational deprivations, the Justice also analysed statistical data showing additional forms of vulnerability, for example by noting the proportion of employers within each racial group, as well as the proportion of mothers in each of these racial groups who were raising their minor children without a father.[121]

It was also based on the contextual analysis that Justice Lewandowski assessed the constitutionality of the quota system as a measure situated within a context of material and symbolic disadvantages. He recalled the history of slavery and the perpetuation of varied forms of deprivations based on race, as identified by qualitative studies and statistical data.[122] Therefore, his analysis of context went beyond deprivation in the dimension of education. It included

[119] *ADPF 186/DF* (2012), *supra* note 9, p 68.
[120] Ibid, pp 68–71.
[121] Ibid.
[122] Ibid, pp 66–75.

monetary deprivation (evidenced by the reference to income in the decision), hierarchies of power (evidenced by the reference to the proportion of individuals occupying the position of employers in each racial group), and the perpetuation of derogatory perceptions of race contributing to social exclusion and vulnerability.

The consideration of data on socio-economic exclusion based on race provided context to the Justice's assessment of the underrepresentation of black and brown people in public universities. It allowed the Justice to identify a series of disadvantages that culminated in multidimensional poverty, were caused by racial inequalities, and reinforced these inequalities. In other words, this approach allowed the identification of disadvantages beyond educational deprivations that caused and reinforced the latter. For these reasons, the consideration of context became central to the analysis of the constitutionality of the impugned positive measure. In conclusion, the contextual approach proved central for the finding that the impugned racial quota system at UnB was constitutional as a measure for realizing substantive equality.

The consideration of multidimensional poverty as context is even clearer in *ADC 41* (2017), concerning the institution of a race-based quota system for access to positions in the public service.[123] Just as Justice Lewandowski did in *ADPF 186* (2012), the Justice *rapporteur* in *ADC 41* (2017), Justice Barroso, considered data on educational stratification disaggregated by race. In addition, he considered statistical data from the IBGE revealing the predominance of black and brown population among those living on the streets and among heads of families in the *favelas*.[124] Data from the IBGE also indicated the predominance of the black and brown population among those living in serious deprivation in the dimensions of health (eg racial gap in life expectancy), income, and monetary poverty (eg, although 50.7% of the population in 2010 was black or brown, this racial group represented 72% of the 10% poorest; in addition, the black and brown population earned on average 55% less income than the white population, and the salary gap subsisted even when comparing workers with the same level of education).[125] Finally, Justice Barroso considered data concerning segregation, marginalization, and different forms of oppression (eg he looked at the rate of homicide of black and brown persons and the rate of incarceration disaggregated by race and occupational stratification).[126] Based on this statistical analysis, he concluded that there was

[123] *ADC 41/DF* (2017), *supra* note 9.
[124] Ibid, p 43, para 28.
[125] Ibid, pp 41–46.
[126] Ibid.

sufficient evidence of structural and institutional racism in Brazil.[127] These inequalities were understood as an issue of redistribution and a condition associated with the perpetuation of symbols and cultural domination that deny recognition to black and brown persons.

The discussion of redistribution that guided *ADC 41* (2017) went beyond equality of opportunities and material resources to cover the redistribution of power and the reframing of symbols related to a historically oppressed group. In this vote adopted unanimously by the bench, Justice Barroso recognized the historical origins of racial discrimination, explaining structural racism as a mark of slavery and of the omissions of the state at the time of the abolishment of slavery.[128] He also identified multiple manifestations of racial oppression today, reading them in connection to the obligation of the State to promote structural change through positive measures.

By considering the context of multidimensional poverty in *ADC 41* (2017), Justice Barroso went beyond a discussion of distributive justice (intrinsic to cases concerning affirmative action) and incorporated a multidimensional assessment of substantive equality. This assessment covered the recognition dimension by discussing the quota system as a measure with the potential to break down cycles of reproduction of symbols that exclude and stigmatize the black and brown population[129] and as a measure producing a positive effect on the self-esteem and self-recognition of this group.[130] In addition, the Justice addressed the participative and transformative dimensions of substantive equality. Participative, because he asserted that the quota system could be justified as a measure promoting pluralism, representativeness, and diversity in public administration, as well as intra- and inter-generational social integration—therefore, going beyond social mobility as an exclusively distributive matter.[131] Transformative, because the measure aimed to transform structures of domination and racism through structural change. The Justice argued that, by adopting the impugned quota system, public examinations were adopting additional criteria to the selection process, such as diversity and plurality, and acknowledging their value to the public administration.[132] This recognition of the potentializing effect of representativeness was based on the understanding that 'public servants reflect, to some extent, their life stories, social experiences, values, and background in their work'.[133] A more

[127] Ibid, pp 46–47, paras 34–35.
[128] Ibid, p 41, para 25.
[129] Ibid, p 51, para 44.
[130] Ibid, pp 51–52, para 45.
[131] Ibid, pp 49–52, paras 39, 41, and 46.
[132] Ibid, pp 54–55, para 52; pp 56–57, para 56.
[133] Ibid, pp 56–57, para 56. Translation by the author.

plural composition allows state institutions at all levels and in all government branches 'to become more capable of acting in defence of the interests of all groups and segments of the population, therefore becoming more democratic'.[134]

In conclusion, the analysis of poverty (monetary and/or multidimensional) as context has allowed the STF to surpass the limits of distributive equality, even in cases concerning distributive measures such as quota systems. This approach has been used in a way that overcomes a focus on material goods in the Court's decision-making to include an analysis of hierarchies, power relations, and social symbols. The consideration of poverty as context has also allowed the STF to consider powerlessness as a form of oppression that derives from and simultaneously perpetuates social exclusion and marginalization. Therefore, this analysis provides lenses that unveil multidimensional vulnerabilities disproportionately affecting protected groups.

To engage with this strategy, statistical and sociological evidence has played an important role in the STF's delimitation of the context of poverty and forms of discrimination. This confirms the suggestion of Albertyn and Goldblatt, according to whom such data, studies, and socio-economic analysis are crucial for a contextual approach.[135]

6.3.3.4 Positive obligations

The chapter will now turn to the last strategy in our four-prong classification. Out of the seventeen equality cases in which the STF addressed poverty, thirteen concerned positive obligations (76% of the sample). These cases include disputes in which the STF analysed positive measures that have been implemented (eg cases concerning the constitutionality of quota systems) or should have been implemented by the State to protect and fulfil the right to equality (ie cases in which Brazil was providing the same treatment to two parties without taking into consideration past disadvantages and the need for accommodating differences). This category includes cases concerning the State's duty to actively promote equality, whether or not the means chosen to achieve this aim were strong distributive measures of affirmative action.

The recognition of the positive dimension of the right to equality is consolidated in the equality jurisprudence of the STF. Throughout its case law, the Court has consistently upheld that realizing the principle of equality often

[134] Ibid, p 57, para 56. Translation by the author.

[135] Cathi Albertyn and Beth Goldblatt, 'Facing the Challenge of Transformation: Difficulties in the Development of an Indigenous Jurisprudence of Equality' (1998) 14 South African Journal on Human Rights 248, p 261.

requires the State to take concrete action.[136] In other words, it is insufficient for the State to refrain from interfering with equality—it must also adopt measures to protect and fulfil the full realization of this principle.

The conceptualization of equality as 'positive equality' has been interpreted by Justice Marco Aurélio as enshrined in the very text of the CF/88. Justice Aurélio explains the incorporation of a positive model of equality as an outcome connected with the aim of the CF/88 of promoting social transformation, including the eradication of poverty (which he qualifies as a form of discrimination). In his words:

> I can assert, with no fear of being mistaken, that static, merely negative equality, in which discrimination is prohibited, has given way to effective, dynamic equality [in Brazilian constitutionalism], since the verbs 'build', 'guarantee', 'eradicate' and 'promote' [present in Article 3 of the CF/88] imply per se a change of perspective by denoting 'action'.
>
> This system of constitutional principles must be understood as a turning point. The stance ought to be, above all, affirmative. And it is necessary that this, too, be the position adopted by our legislators. After all, what is the purpose of the above-mentioned articles of the Federal Constitution, if not social transformation with the objective of eradicating poverty - which is one form of discrimination - and aiming, above all, at the well-being of every person and not only those born in golden cradles?[137]

The understanding that Brazilian constitutionalism has overcome the model of negative equality is also present in *ADPF 186* (2012). In his vote as the *rapporteur*, Justice Lewandowski affirmed that, when applied in isolation, formal equality may widen differences between individuals and, therefore, contribute to the perpetuation of *de facto* inequalities.[138]

Given the centrality of the positive dimension of equality to the STF's conceptualization of this principle, it comes as no surprise that the Court's jurisprudence includes a high number of decisions addressing the duty of the State to act towards promoting equality. This duty may be realized through the adoption of strong distributive positive measures or through other means of promoting individualized and structural change aimed at reducing institutional barriers and power structures that perpetuate marginalization and

[136] Cf *ADPF 186/DF* (2012), *supra* note 9, p 163.

[137] Marco Aurélio Mello, 'Óptica constitucional: a igualdade e as ações afirmativas' (2001) 17 Revista do Tribunal Regional do Trabalho da 15ª Região 156, p 159. Original text in Portuguese.

[138] *ADPF 186/DF* (2012), *supra* note 9, p 66.

exclusion. The State is duty-bound to compensate for flaws of distributive justice and forms of discrimination ingrained in society's culture that lead to conscious and unconscious reproduction of prejudice.[139] In other words, the State assumes a proactive role in promoting social justice by pursuing equality as redistribution and recognition, encompassing the aims of redistribution, recognition, participation, and transformation.

The repercussions of positive measures on the dimension of recognition were eloquently explained in Justice Luiz Fux's vote in *ADPF 186* (2012). Inspired by the writings of Nancy Fraser, Daniel Sarmento, Daniela Ikawa, and Flávia Piovesan, Justice Fux explained that neutral policies (such as race-blind public policies) are insufficient to combat the disparities revealed in the analysis of human development indices. The Justice argued that the insufficiency of race-blind policies for promoting equality is explained by the fact that racial injustice operates not only in the realm of distribution but also in the dimension of recognition, both culturally and symbolically.[140] He explained the recognition dimension of racial injustices in Brazil as relating to the way historically discriminated racial groups are perceived in their social context, their collective identity, and their self-esteem.[141]

The positive dimension of equality requires that the State promotes distributive justice while also going beyond it by fostering symbols that recognize the value of diversity and equal dignity.[142] The State must also foster the participation of marginalized groups in social and political life and decision-making, as well as promote structural change in a way that breaks the perpetuation of persistent structural discrimination. In *ADC 41* (2017), the Justice *rapporteur*, Roberto Barroso, considered that a strong distributive positive measure might promote the redistribution of opportunities while simultaneously impacting a group's self-esteem, positive identity, and interpersonal recognition. As a result, it increases representativeness in institutions, making the latter more plural and capable of producing decisions that are more inclusive and responsive to the different needs of a plural population.[143]

The analysis of the STF's equality jurisprudence shows that distributive claims are likely to succeed in the STF in cases in which the Court is called

[139] Ibid. p 67.

[140] Vote of Justice Luiz Fux in ibid, p 108.

[141] Ibid, p 108.

[142] Justice Lewandowski also quoted Nancy Fraser in her analysis of the increasing discussion of social justice in connection to revindications for recognition and redistribution. See *ADPF 186/DF* (2012), *supra* note 9, pp 72–73.

[143] *ADC 41/DF* (2017), *supra* note 9, pp 47–58.

upon to scrutinize the content and scope of public policies created by the State. Furthermore, the STF has generally upheld the constitutionality of positive measures, including strong distributive measures such as quota systems, and, in some cases, it has even expanded their scope. One example is *RE 567.985* (2013), in which the STF promoted a flexibilization of the monetary threshold of absolute poverty used to identify the right-holders of the BPC benefit.[144] However, these cases concern state policies that had already been implemented by the government and were brought before the Court to revise their content and scope.

In contrast, the STF seems more reluctant to accept transformative claims concerning a chronic state of poverty in Brazil when they are disconnected from the concrete implementation of a specific public policy.[145] Justice Gilmar Mendes upheld a similar understanding in the interview conducted for this research. The Justice affirmed that it would not be reasonable for a petitioner to ask the STF to remedy a situation of generalized poverty in Brazil, considering that it would be inefficient to address this situation through the Court.[146] He explained that the fight against poverty, including the eradication of hunger, does not take place through the Judiciary, but through public policies.[147] Justice Mendes concluded by explaining that the Judiciary revises the implementation of these public policies and acts in a 'corrective way', that is, correcting or remedying discrimination and revising the criteria adopted by public policies.[148] Similarly, in his interview, Justice Fachin highlighted the link between poverty eradication and appropriate public policies. In his words:

> The eradication of poverty is a fundamental objective of the Federative Republic of Brazil, and, as such, it must be tackled through appropriate public policies. It is a truism to say that public policies, in the rule of law, are made viable through the law. [. . .] There is no other way to make it possible. The issue would entail further reflection if, by 'Law', we were talking about courts. In this case, the dilemmas are more complex. As a rule, the implementation of public policies must be the responsibility of the Government and must reflect political agreements reached by the majority.[149]

[144] *RE 567.985/MT* (2013), *supra* note 27.
[145] See *ADPF 541/DF* (2018), *supra* note 88, concerning the cancellation of electoral registration cards.
[146] Interview with Justice Gilmar Mendes, 12:43–13:05.
[147] Ibid, 13:05–13:49.
[148] Ibid, 13:49–14:09.
[149] Interview with Justice Edson Fachin, question 8, p 5. Translation by the author.

6.3.3.5 Poverty outside of equality cases

Beyond equality cases, poverty was the object of ten full bench decisions published in the period under analysis and one leading case decided in April 2021. Important tools for the STF to address poverty outside of equality claims were economic, social, and cultural rights and the concept of *untermassverbot*,[150] the latter inspired by the German constitutional jurisprudence. These tools were sufficient to capture the distributive dimension that is often present in claims concerning poverty.

Despite the sufficiency of the social rights approach in grasping distributive injustices, individual votes published in four cases added a brief assessment of serious deprivations of rights in connection with considerations relating to substantive equality. This assessment allowed some of the Justices to discuss poverty beyond the distributive dimension that was the focus of the dispute. One example is *MI 7,300* (2021), in which a citizen asked the STF to rule on the omission of the federal State in the last seventeen years to adopt the necessary measures for implementing Law 10.834/2004.[151] This law recognized the right of every Brazilian, as well as every foreigner residing in Brazil for at least five years, to a universal basic income. Although the law established a universal and unconditional benefit, it permitted the State to implement it gradually, giving priority to those most in need.

This dispute was taken to the STF due to the State's inaction in implementing the universal basic income. While the case will be discussed in more detail in Chapter 8, this section will anticipate that one of the Justices engaged with notions of substantive equality, allowing him to take the discussion beyond the frontiers of distributive justice.

The Justice *rapporteur*, Gilmar Mendes, analysed the controversy through the lenses of the principle of *untermassverbot*, the constitutional right to social assistance, and the constitutional recognition that one of the fundamental objectives of the State is the eradication of poverty. While the vote of the *rapporteur*, adopted by the majority, essentially focused on distributive justice, Justice Marco Aurélio, who had originally been assigned as the *rapporteur* of the case, analysed the condition of poverty and the failure of the State to act through the perspective of participation. He explained that those who live below a social or existential minimum—understood as the level of income that is indispensable for the enjoyment of fundamental rights and political

[150] Understood by the STF as the prohibition of deficient protection derived from the principle of proportionality.

[151] STF, Judgment, *MI 7.300/DF*, 27 April 2021. Justice rapporteur: Gilmar Mendes.

engagement—live in subhuman conditions and are deprived of their full status as citizens. Citizenship and democracy, Justice Aurélio argued, encompass a basic level of access to resources that guarantees a dignified condition of life and impacts participation in the public sphere, where individuals should engage in deliberations as equals.[152] In the Justice's understanding, poverty and deprivations on access to food, school, and health constitute barriers to political participation. In his words, '[one cannot] conclude that the destitute have the same opportunities to take part in decision-making, the latter understood as the process of formation of the popular will, on equal conditions with the rest of society'.[153] The universal basic income, he argued, was an 'effective instrument to mitigate socio-economic vulnerabilities, assisting the reduction of vulnerabilities of those living in poverty'.[154]

Another example is *ADI 3.446* (2019), concerning the constitutionality of legal provisions that prohibited the detention of minors except in cases of *flagrante delicto* or the execution of an arrest warrant.[155] The prohibition derived from the enactment of the Statute of the Child and Adolescent (ECA) in the 1990s, which restructured the legal treatment of minors in Brazil. As a result of the ECA, minors living in poverty or living on the streets could no longer be detained based only on their socio-economic vulnerability. In other words, detention would not be the means to resolve children's social vulnerability. The STF resolved the dispute by analysing the rights of the child and the impact of detention on minors. Acting as the Justice *rapporteur*, Justice Gilmar Mendes considered the high number of children living in monetary and/or multidimensional poverty (considering the dimensions of housing, education, water, and sanitation, as well as information on and protection against child labour).[156] He recalled that the National Council on the Rights of the Child and the Youth found poverty to be one of the factors explaining the persistence of homelessness in the lives of children.[157] The Justice stressed that, despite the legal provisions protecting the rights of the child, numerous children still face deprivations of the most basic rights safeguarded by domestic and international norms. This situation of deprivation, violation of rights, and vulnerability would be intensified if their freedom of movement was curtailed through detention.[158] The Justice concluded that the prohibition of detention

[152] Vote of Justice Marco Aurélio in ibid, p 9.
[153] Ibid, pp 9–10.
[154] Ibid, p 11.
[155] STF, Judgment, *ADI 3.446/DF*, 08 August 2019. Justice rapporteur: Gilmar Mendes.
[156] Ibid, pp 14–15.
[157] Ibid.
[158] Ibid, pp 15, 18, and 19.

of minors except in the hypothesis of *flagrante delicto* or the execution of an arrest warrant was a measure in accordance with the rights of the child and the right to freedom from arbitrary detention.

While the vote of Justice Mendes was adopted unanimously by the bench, some Justices addressed notions of substantive equality in their individual reasoning. Justice Alexandre de Moraes adopted the same understanding as the *rapporteur* and explained that a different understanding would equate to the criminalization of poverty.[159] Justice Lewandowski took note of the abyssal inequality of income and opportunities in Brazil and found that being rich or poor defined the future of children across a myriad of dimensions. He stressed the need to transform this social injustice and explained that the detention of street children did not contribute to changing this situation. On the contrary, it was detrimental to the development of minors.[160] Justice Lewandowski concluded that the detention of street children constituted discrimination based on socio-economic condition and was a deleterious juridical solution to an eminently social problem.[161] By analysing the disadvantages faced by street children because of their age and socio-economic condition, Justice Lewandowski addressed the need to correct cycles of disadvantage and noted that detention would exacerbate those cycles. Furthermore, his vote highlights the need to apply laws and public policies in a transformative manner, promoting structural change. In its analysis of the civil and socio-economic rights of minors, it includes an assessment of equality in terms of distributive disadvantages and briefly touches on the potentially transformative role of law in responding to the structural oppressions and vulnerabilities experienced by these children.

Finally, in *ADPF 324* and *RE 958.252*, both from 2018, the STF was called to analyse restrictions on outsourcing derived from the jurisprudence of labour courts.[162] In both cases, it reached a majority of 7–4 votes when finding that outsourcing did not cause, by itself, precarious working conditions. Rather, the abusive nature of its implementation led to these violations. Therefore, the Court decided that outsourcing any activity is, in principle, legal. Furthermore, it held that outsourcing did not constitute a labour relationship between the contracting party and the employees of the outsourced

[159] Vote of Justice Alexandre de Moraes in ibid, p 48. On law as a means of criminalization of poverty, see Chapter 3.

[160] Vote of Justice Ricardo Lewandowski in *ADI 3.446/DF* (2019), *supra* note 155, p 33.

[161] Ibid, p 37.

[162] STF, Judgment, *ADPF 324/DF*, 30 August 2018. Justice rapporteur: Roberto Barroso; *RE 1.058.333/PR* (2018), *supra* note 46.

party. However, the contracting party remained responsible for verifying the idoneous character of the outsourcing party and its economic capacity. It also remained subsidiarily liable for the outsourcing party's non-compliance with labour standards and social security obligations.

The majority decision in *ADPF 324* (2018) was adopted 'in the terms of the vote of the *rapporteur*', Roberto Barroso, who developed a legal reasoning strongly based on the existence of a cause-and-effect relationship between the legal institute of outsourcing and precarious work relations with reduced wages. Four Justices disagreed with the majority's conclusion, and some of them explicitly discussed the impact of outsourcing in *de facto* inequalities. Justice Rosa Weber argued that there was a *de facto* inequality between employers and employees, considering that the closure of an employment relationship represented 'a risk of poverty and exclusion' to the worker.[163] In this context, formal equality between such economically distinct parties 'would be equivalent to making the employee a hostage of the will of his employer'.[164] Justice Weber argued that outsourcing is a complex phenomenon which requires a substantive, and not merely formal, assessment.[165] Therefore, she referred to statistical data and sociological studies on distributive injustices related to outsourcing and the reduction of collective organization of outsourced workers (which is arguably an analysis linked to the participative dimension of equality).[166] Considering this data, she concluded that social indicators prevented a legal analysis of outsourcing from being guided by abstractions derived from a formal conceptualisation. Instead, 'the concrete reality [...] calls for a closer look at the phenomenon and its use in [Brazil]'.[167]

Similarly, in his dissenting vote, Justice Marco Aurélio noted the *de facto* differences between workers and employers, expressly referring to economic inequality and its aggravation in the context of labour surplus and scarcity of jobs.[168] He highlighted the impact of outsourcing on the collective organization of workers and on workers' power in negotiation. He also noted the risk, identified in scholarly work, of outsourcing transforming into a 'mere vehicle of discrimination and degradation of the value of the workforce'.[169]

163 Vote of Justice Rosa Weber in *ADPF 324/DF* (2018), *supra* note 162, p 241. Translation by the author.
164 Ibid, p 242. Translation by the author.
165 Ibid, p 243.
166 Ibid, pp 243-250.
167 Ibid, p 254. Translation by the author.
168 Vote of Justice Marco Aurélio in ibid, p 329.
169 Ibid, p 326. Translation by the author.

6.4 Conclusion: identified patterns

The STF employs the four strategies outlined in Chapter 4 to address poverty as a matter of equality. The analysis of its equality jurisprudence reveals that the Court recognizes economic vulnerability as a protected characteristic requiring positive action from the State. It also scrutinizes the inclusiveness of anti-poverty measures through the right to equality, determining the expansion of their content and scope when finding inequality in the design or implementation of these policies. Moreover, the Court addresses poverty as context in cases concerning protected groups, notably racial groups, and identifies positive obligations derived from the right to equality to address this context when it disproportionately affects historically vulnerable groups.

In disputes where the challenged measure differentiated on the basis of economic condition, distributive claims often succeeded, and the distributive dimension of equality was predominant in the Court's analysis. The distributive dimension of equality was likewise preponderant when the Court applied an equality assessment to analyse the content and scope of anti-poverty measures. A much more nuanced result is found in the Court's application of the third and fourth strategies (the contextual approach to poverty and the consideration of positive equality). These two approaches appear to have the most potential in this jurisdiction for uncovering poverty-related multidimensional inequalities.

These findings potentialize the relevance of equality as a tool for addressing poverty judicially. Distributive harms inherently underlie all conceptualizations of poverty, as they materialize as exclusions from the enjoyment of resources and goods, including income and capabilities. Therefore, tackling distributive injustices and addressing claims for distributive remedies are necessary elements of a judicial response capable of breaking cycles of poverty sustainably. Given that the STF's application of the equality approach has been capable of addressing maldistribution in relation to poverty, equality emerges as an important tool in this jurisdiction for responding to the perpetuation of poverty cycles in its distributive dimension.

However, a comprehensive response to poverty must not only include but also go beyond redistribution, as poverty not only relates to maldistribution of resources and goods. Poverty can also be rooted in misrecognition and reinforce it. In addition, remedying poverty may require a structural approach to this socio-economic phenomenon, calling for structural change and, when adequate, accommodation of difference. This polycentric analysis of

Table 6.2 Dimensions of equality disaggregated by judicial strategy (STF, 1988–2020)

	Distributive equality	Equality as recognition	Participative equality	Transformative equality	Total number of cases
Suspect classification	10	1	3	1	10
Inclusiveness of anti-poverty measures	3	-	-	1	3
Context	7	3	5	4	7
Positive obligations	13	4	7	5	13

Source: Author's empirical research.

inequalities derived from or related to poverty is found in the STF's application of the contextual approach and particularly in the Court's consideration of the positive dimension of equality.

The vast majority of the equality cases in which the STF addressed poverty concerned positive obligations (see Table 6.2). In cases concerning the State's duty to act, the Court, more often than not, went beyond the scope of distributive justice. The single focus on distributive equality occurred in only 38.5% of the decisions with this object. The numbers are even more striking in cases concerning affirmative action: participative equality, transformative equality, and equality as recognition were addressed in 63.6%, 45.5%, and 36.4% of these cases, respectively.

As the book's Introductory chapter anticipated when discussing this study's hypotheses, distributive justice proved to be an important focus of the STF's analysis of the constitutionality of affirmative action measures, even more so in cases concerning strong distributive affirmative action (such as quota systems). However, it was an unexpected result to find that the STF has applied the other dimensions of substantive equality when assessing the justification of positive measures.

When distributive justice is the sole focus of the STF's assessment, the discussion of poverty through the lens of equality can, to a considerable degree, be interchangeable with an approach to poverty based on socio-economic rights. The analysis of poverty cases outside the Court's equality jurisprudence shows that the STF has been able to address poverty in distributive claims by relying exclusively on the progressive obligation of the State to protect and fulfil socio-economic rights. However, an equality assessment has the added value of transcending the limits of redistributive assessments (see Table 6.2).

Additionally, it allows the STF to address intersectionalities as an analytical strategy for understanding the manifestations of poverty and their impact on protected groups. This empirical finding confirms the assumption put forward in Chapter 3 with regard to the added value of an equality approach to poverty compared with the socio-economic approach.[170]

In conclusion, social rights have provided a sufficient venue for the STF to address distributive harms by bringing distributive injustices to the Court's scrutiny and requiring redistributive remedies. On the other hand, the equality approach has allowed the Court to assess redistributive harms through the lens of intersectionality and to surpass the limits of distributive justice when analysing the manifestations of oppressions related to poverty. By addressing poverty through equality, the STF unveils otherwise invisibilized forms of inequality related to poverty and is in a better position to respond effectively to it.

[170] See Chapter 3, section 3.4.

7
Equality and Poverty in the IACtHR

From 7 to 22 November 1969, the Inter-American Specialized Conference on Human Rights convened in San José, Costa Rica. Nineteen states participated, including Brazil.[1] As a result of the Conference, the ACHR, also known as the Pact of San José, was adopted on 22 November of that same year.

Brazil's history with the ACHR thus begins with the Convention's very conception, drafting, and adoption. However, while the Brazilian State was part of the process of adopting the ACHR, its ratification of the Convention would take longer. Only twelve states[2] signed the Pact on the very day it was adopted. For the other states in the region, the signing and subsequent ratification of the treaty would take almost a decade. For Brazil, the ratification only took place on 7 September 1992.

Armin von Bogdandy asserts that, at the time of the adoption of the ACHR, it was hardly imaginable that the treaty would become a pillar for transformative constitutionalism in the region; in other words, it was hardly conceivable the Convention would become a catalyst for the promotion of social change and a key means for addressing core structural challenges in Latin America.[3] In the 1960s and 1970s, a significant portion of Latin American countries, including much of the South Cone, was ruled by authoritarian regimes led by military dictators or a military junta. It was only around the end of the 1970s to the beginning of the 1990s—a period that marked the fall of the military dictatorship regimes in the Southern Cone—that the number of ratifications of the ACHR expanded rapidly.

With the fall of the authoritarian regimes and the gradual transition to democracy in the region, the promotion of rights gained widespread support in Latin American constitutionalism.[4] Bogdandy observes that, inspired by

[1] The participating states were: Argentina; Brazil; Chile; Colombia; Costa Rica; the Dominican Republic; Ecuador; El Salvador; the United States of America; Guatemala; Honduras; Mexico; Nicaragua; Panama; Paraguay; Peru; Trinidad and Tobago; Uruguay; and Venezuela. See OAS, 'Conferencia Especializada Interamericana sobre Derechos Humanos', Actas y documentos, 7–22 November 1969.

[2] Chile, Colombia, Costa Rica, Ecuador, El Salvador, Guatemala, Honduras, Nicaragua, Panama, Paraguay, Uruguay, and Venezuela.

[3] Armin von Bogdandy, 'The Mandate of the Inter-American System: Transformative Constitutionalism by a Common Law of Human Rights' in IACtHR (ed), *Dialogue Between Regional Human Rights Courts* (IACtHR 2020), p 65.

[4] Ibid, p 65.

Judging Poverty and Inequality in Brazil. Tainá Garcia Maia, Oxford University Press.
DOI: 10.1093/oso/9780198994022.003.0007

the maxim '*Nunca más*' (which translates to 'never again'), most constitutions in the region adopted extensive and progressive catalogues of human rights and granted a special place for international human rights in their domestic order.[5] Amid this context, the IACtHR became a strong promoter of human rights protection in the region through its interpretation of the American Convention, addressing structural challenges such as violence, failure of institutions to respond to human rights violations or vulnerabilities, and—particularly relevant to this chapter—social exclusion and marginalization.[6]

This chapter presents the empirical analysis of the IACtHR's jurisprudence on poverty and equality. Section 7.1 explains how equality and poverty are addressed in the text of the ACHR. Section 7.2 outlines the methodology employed in the empirical study. Section 7.3 presents and analyses the main findings. Finally, section 7.4 summarizes the patterns identified in the Court's jurisprudence.

7.1 Legal framework: the American Convention on Human Rights

The right to equality and non-discrimination is safeguarded under Articles 1(1) and 24 of the ACHR. Article 1(1) establishes the obligation of States Parties to respect and guarantee the rights safeguarded therein 'without any discrimination for reasons of race, color, sex, language, religion, political or other opinion, national or social origin, economic status, birth, or any other social condition'.[7] It is a non-discrimination clause with an open-ended expression ('any other social condition') indicating a non-exhaustive list of protected grounds and, accordingly, a semi-constrained judicial discretion to extend the list, shaped by the existing enumerated grounds.

In turn, Article 24 is a general equality clause. It states that '[a]ll persons are equal before the law' and, '[c]onsequently, they are entitled, without discrimination, to equal protection of the law'.[8] Although Article 24 does not refer to protected grounds of discrimination, the IACtHR has interpreted this provision as referring to the same protected groups recognized in Article 1(1) and in the Court's jurisprudence.[9]

[5] Ibid, pp 65–66.
[6] Cf Ibid, pp 69–70.
[7] Organization of American States (OAS), 'American Convention on Human Rights, "Pact of San Jose"', 22 November 1969, Article 1(1).
[8] Ibid, Article 24.
[9] IACtHR, Judgment (Preliminary Objection, Merits, Reparations and Costs), *Flor Freire v Ecuador*, 31 August 2016. Series C No 315, paras 114–124.

The IACtHR has consistently highlighted that these two provisions should not be confused with one another. In its words: 'if a State discriminates in the respect and guarantee of a Convention-based right, it would be failing to comply with the obligation established in Article 1(1) and the substantive right in question'.[10] If, however, 'the discrimination relates to an unequal protection of the domestic law or its application, the fact must be analyzed in light of Article 24 of the American Convention'.[11] Despite this apparently clear-cut division between the applicability of Articles 1(1) and Article 24, the IACtHR has at times recognized the simultaneous violation of the two provisions, without specifying which specific act violated each of them.[12]

Clarification of the reasons for the simultaneous application of Articles 1(1) and 24 came in the 2018 case of *VRP, VPC and others v Nicaragua*. The latter concerned the international responsibility of Nicaragua for the failure to act with due diligence in the case of sexual violation perpetrated by a non-state agent against his 8-year-old daughter, VRP (the victim's pseudonym). The IACtHR decided to analyse the inequality claims in light of both Articles 1(1) and 24 'every time the arguments are centred on the issue related to the failure [of the state] to adopt specific and enhanced positive action to guarantee conventional rights, based on sex and gender, as well as the condition of the victim as a person in development'.[13] This judgment indicates that an analysis of state inaction to comply with the positive obligations emanating from the principle of equality gives rise to the simultaneous application of the two provisions. While the application of this reasoning has not always been uniform,[14] this doctrinal development is expected to lead to more consistency in future disputes.

[10] IACtHR, Judgment (Preliminary Objections, Merits, Reparations and Costs), *Afro-Descendant Communities Displaced from the Cacarica River Basin (Operation Genesis) v Colombia*, 20 November 2013. Series C No 270, para 333.

[11] Ibid.

[12] Cf IACtHR, Judgment (Preliminary Objections, Merits, Reparations and Costs), *Gonzales Lluy and others v Ecuador*, 1 September 2015. Series C No 298, para 199; IACtHR, Judgment (Preliminary Objections, Merits, Reparations and Costs), *Gutiérrez Hernández and others v Guatemala*, 24 August 2017. Series C No 339, para 185.

[13] IACtHR, Judgment (Preliminary Objections, Merits, Reparations and Costs), *VRP, VPC* et al *v Nicaragua*, 8 March 2018. Series C No 350, para 289.

[14] For example, around nine months after the *VRP* case, the Court published its judgment on *IV v Bolivia*, where it did not rule on a violation of Article 24 of the ACHR, even though the case related to the alleged failure of Bolivia to adopt positive measures to guarantee conventional rights. While this may be attributed to the failure of the Commission to allege a violation of Article 24, it is important to recall that the Court has consistently upheld its competence to analyse the alleged facts in light of other Articles than those explicitly mentioned in the claims of the Inter-American Commission on Human Rights and of the representatives, based on the *iura novit curia* principle. See also Rafael Nieto Navia, 'La aplicación del principio Jura Novit Curia por los órganos del sistema interamericano de derechos humanos' in Ernesto J Rey Caro and María Cristina Rodríguez de Taborda (eds), *Estudios de Derecho International en homenaje a la dra Zlata Drnas de Clément* (Advocatus 2014); IACtHR, Judgment (Preliminary Objections, Merits, Reparations and Costs), *IV v Bolivia*, 30 November 2016. Series C No 329.

Article 1(1) expressly prohibits discrimination based on 'economic status' and 'social origin'. The *travaux préparatoires* of the ACHR do not provide much guidance with regard to the reasons for differentiating between 'economic status' and 'social origin', and the issue has not been clarified in the equality jurisprudence of the IACtHR either. In this context, guidance may be sought from similarly phrased human rights instruments. As mentioned in Chapter 4, the term 'social origin' is present in other instruments of international human rights law, including the ICCPR. The Covenant served as inspiration for the drafting of the equality provisions of the ACHR and could be a valuable source for unveiling the content and scope of the term. However, neither the ICCPR nor the Human Rights Committee defines 'social origin' explicitly. Yet such a conceptual discussion can be found in the work of the Committee on Economic, Social and Cultural Rights (CESCR).

In General Comment 20, the CESCR affirmed that social origin refers to 'a person's inherited social status'.[15] It can be linked to property, birth, and economic and social status. Property is understood broadly by the Committee as including 'real property (e.g. land ownership or tenure) and personal property (e.g. intellectual property, goods and chattels, and income), or the lack of it'.[16] Birth encompasses differentiations such as castes, children born out of wedlock, children born of stateless parents, adopted children, and members of families that have these characteristics.[17] Economic and social status refers to persons living in poverty, homeless people, and other strata in society.[18]

General Comment 20 points to a conceptualization of social origin as having a broader scope than economic status. It transcends a focus on purely economic statuses and includes the categories of birth and social status. At the same time, this concept acquires limited coverage, as it refers to an 'inherited' status. In any case, it is clear that both 'social origin' and 'economic status' refer, to different degrees, to class and status. As Manfred Nowak explains, '[t]he distinguishing qualities of birth, property and social origin relate to the prohibition of discrimination on the basis of *status* or *class*'.[19] This means that membership to a social class or to groups enjoying different levels of status in society cannot justify privileged or disadvantaged treatment.[20]

[15] United Nations CESCR, 'General Comment No.20: Non-discrimination in economic, social and cultural rights (art.2, para.2 of the International Covenant on Economic, Social and Cultural Rights)', E/C12/GC/20, 2 July 2009, para 24.

[16] Ibid, para 25.

[17] Ibid, para 26.

[18] See ibid, para 35.

[19] Manfred Nowak, *UN Covenant on Civil and Political Rights. CCPR Commentary* (2nd edn, NP Engel Publishers 2005), p 56.

[20] Ibid.

In conclusion, by referring to both social origin and economic status, the ACHR recognizes protected grounds covering status and class. Therefore, it sets a legal basis for providing protection against discrimination to social groups whose vulnerabilities emerge from a lack of wealth, including situations of monetary poverty, as well as to marginalized groups who are subject to relations of domination and misrecognition that facilitate or exacerbate monetary or multidimensional poverty.

Having determined that poverty is covered by the protected grounds of Article 1(1), it is now necessary to analyse the spaces in which the right to equality is applied under the text of the ACHR. In other words, it is necessary to determine the scope of this provision. Article 1(1) sets an obligation for states to act in accordance with the principle of equality in relation to all rights safeguarded in the ACHR. The Convention contains eighty-two articles, twenty-two of which safeguard civil and political rights and one of which establishes the obligation of states to adopt measures to progressively achieve the full realization of social, economic, and cultural rights (Article 26 of the ACHR).

In 2017, the IACtHR found that Article 26 was justiciable. This evolution can be linked to the influence of Judge Ferrer Mac-Gregor, who was elected to the IACtHR in 2012 and served as the Court's President from 2018 to 2019. As Ferrer himself explains in his concurring opinion in *Lagos del Campo v Peru*, he had defended the justiciability of Article 26 since his first case as a Judge of the Court, in 2013.[21] However, it was only in 2017, with *Lagos del Campo v Peru*, that this understanding was upheld by the majority of the bench.

One persistent objector to this change in the IACtHR's jurisprudence is Judge Antonio Sierra Porto, President of the Court from 2014 to 2015. In his partially dissenting opinion in *Lagos del Campo*, Judge Sierra Porto criticized what he qualified as a 'dynamic of '*vis expansiva*' of state responsibility', detached from the text of the ACHR and intrinsically dependent on the alleged power of the Court to modify the catalogue of human rights at the Inter-American System of Human Rights in each case.[22] The dissenting Judge affirmed that the Court's recognition of the justiciability of Article 26 fails to

[21] IACtHR, Concurring Opinion of Judge Eduardo Ferrer Mac-Gregor Poisot in IACtHR, Judgment (Preliminary Exceptions, Merits, Reparations and Costs), *Lagos del Campo v Peru*, 31 August 2017. Series C No 340, para 3. The case in question was *Suaréz Peralta v Ecuador*. See Concurring Opinion of Judge Eduardo Ferrer Mac-Gregor Poisot in IACtHR, Judgment (Preliminary Exceptions, Merits, Reparations and Costs), *Suárez Peralta v Ecuador*, 21 May 2013. Series C No 261.

[22] Concurring Opinion of Judge Humberto Antonio Sierra Porto in *Lagos del Campo v Peru* (2017), *supra* note 21, para 13.

meet a threshold of predictability and thus hinders states from preventing or internally repairing possible violations of the ACHR.[23] He also criticized the majority's understanding as one that contradicts the San Salvador Protocol, which safeguards social, economic, and cultural rights and determines, rather restrictively, that only trade union rights and the right to education would fall within the competence of the IACtHR, and only in relation to the States Parties to the Protocol.[24]

The justiciability of Article 26 has been maintained by the majority of the IACtHR since 2017. This means that, from that year onwards, the Court has considered itself competent to find violations of a wide range of socio-economic rights. In other words, it has considered that the ACHR establishes for states a justiciable obligation to guarantee those rights.

Article 26 determines that states are under the obligation to adopt measures, especially those involving economic and technical dimensions, with the aim of achieving progressively 'the full realization of the rights implicit in the economic, social, educational, scientific, and cultural standards set forth in the Charter of the Organization of American States as amended by the Protocol of Buenos Aires'.[25] Therefore, the ACHR does not include a list of socio-economic rights linked to freedom from want. However, it makes a cross-reference to the standards established in the OAS Charter.

Article 2(g) of the OAS Charter proclaims the eradication of extreme poverty as an essential purpose of the organization, recognizing that extreme poverty 'constitutes an obstacle to the full democratic development of the peoples of the hemisphere'.[26] The elimination of extreme poverty is also set in Article 3(f) of the Charter as a principle reaffirmed by the American States and recognized as 'an essential part of the promotion and consolidation of representative democracy' and 'the common and shared responsibility of the American States'.[27] Furthermore, social justice and social security are safeguarded in Article 3(j) as 'bases of lasting peace'.[28] In addition, Article 34 of the Charter establishes an agreement among Member States that 'equality of opportunity, the elimination of extreme poverty, equitable distribution of wealth and income and the full participation of their peoples in decisions relating to their own development are, among others, basic objectives of

[23] Ibid.
[24] Ibid, paras 16–20.
[25] 'American Convention on Human Rights', "Pact of San Jose", *supra* note 7, Article 26.
[26] OAS, 'Charter of the Organization of American States', 30 April 1948, amended by the Protocol of Buenos Aires of 27 February 1967, Article 2(g).
[27] Ibid, Article 3(f).
[28] Ibid, Article 3(j).

integral development'.[29] To achieve these aims, the provision recalls that states agree to 'devote their utmost efforts' to accomplish basic goals, including a 'substantial and self-sustained increase of per capita national product', equitable distribution of the national income, equitable taxation, equitable and efficient land-tenure systems, fair wages, employment opportunities, and acceptable working conditions for all.[30] The provision also lists the attainment of standards that are directly linked to the concept of multidimensional poverty as basic goals, including: '[r]apid eradication of illiteracy and expansion of educational opportunities for all', '[p]rotection of man's potential through the extension and application of modern medical science', proper nutrition, and adequate housing.[31] Finally, Article 45(a) determines that '[a]ll human beings, without distinction as to race, sex, nationality, creed, or social condition, have a right to material well-being and to their spiritual development, under circumstances of liberty, dignity, equality of opportunity, and economic security'.[32]

It is interesting to note that, despite the references to the eradication of poverty in the OAS Charter, social condition or status is not a protected ground of discrimination in the text of the Charter, in contrast to the text of Article 1(1) of the ACHR. Article 3(l) of the Charter reaffirms the proclamation of the fundamental rights of the individuals by American States 'without distinction as to race, nationality, creed, or sex' only.[33] In any case, because poverty is covered under the protected grounds of Article 1(1) of the ACHR, reading the latter together with Article 26 of the ACHR and accordingly in light of the provisions of the OAS Charter means that states are under the obligation to respect, protect, and guarantee a broad range of socio-economic rights in accordance with the principle of equality. Therefore, they are under the obligation to act towards the progressive full realization of social and economic rights while taking into consideration the specific needs of vulnerable groups, including those living in poverty, as required by the positive dimension of the right to equality. However, this conclusion depends upon the continuance of the IACtHR's interpretation of Article 26 as being justiciable.

[29] Ibid, Article 3(j).
[30] Ibid, Article 34 (a)–(g).
[31] Ibid, (h)–(k).
[32] Ibid, Article 45(a).
[33] Ibid, Article 3(l).

7.2 Methodology of the empirical analysis

7.2.1 Case selection

7.2.1.1 Equality jurisprudence

The analysis covers judgments and advisory opinions on equality published by the IACtHR from its creation in 1979 to the end of December 2020. In total, seventy-one relevant cases and nine advisory opinions were found. In eighteen of the seventy-one cases, the IACtHR did not reach a decision on the merits of the equality claim, either because it chose not to pronounce itself on the claim or because it relied on the principle of equality and non-discrimination only as an interpretative tool, rather than reaching a decision on the merits of an alleged violation of that principle. The IACtHR thus reached a decision on the merits of an alleged violation to the principle of equality and non-discrimination in fifty-three cases.

Among these fifty-three cases, 30.2% addressed distinctions based on economic status or included an analysis of poverty or vulnerability to monetary or multidimensional poverty. In some of them, the Court referred to poverty as a vulnerability only, without explicitly linking this vulnerability to the assessment of compliance with the right to equality. Poverty was only explicitly integrated into the equality assessment and linked to a finding of compliance with or breach of the principle of equality in ten contentious cases. These ten cases were the object of the quantitative analysis. The Court's wider equality jurisprudence, as well as the contentious cases and advisory opinions in which poverty was discussed as context without being directly related to an equality claim, were considered only for the purposes of the qualitative analysis conducted throughout this section.

7.2.1.2 Poverty outside equality cases

To account for the use of alternative strategies outside an equality-based approach for addressing poverty in the IACtHR, the study mapped and analysed poverty cases falling outside the Court's equality jurisprudence. For this purpose, it conducted a search on the Court's database *Thesaurus* using the word 'poverty'. In addition, cases were added to the sample based on cross-referencing in the judgments of the IACtHR and separate votes of the Court's judges in equality cases concerning poverty.[34] Taken together, this method allowed for the identification of six relevant cases.

[34] Footnote 201 in the *Fireworks Factory* case and the separate opinion of Judge Eduardo Ferrer Mac-Gregor in the case of *Hacienda Brasil Verde Workers v Brazil* were valuable sources for the identification of additional cases addressing poverty outside equality claims.

7.2.2 Coding and content analysis

This chapter employs the same coding and content analysis methods as those used in Chapter 6, which are described in detail in section 6.2. It utilizes the four-prong classification of judicial strategies for addressing poverty as a matter of equality, covering: (i) poverty or economic status as a suspect category of discrimination; (ii) equality as a test of the inclusiveness of anti-poverty policies; (iii) poverty as a matter of discriminatory context; and (iv) positive obligations emanating from substantive equality. To evaluate the extent to which each of these strategies, as applied by the IACtHR, has been responsive to multidimensional exclusions, the chapter examines which dimension(s) of equality—redistributive, recognition, participative, and transformative—the Court has applied when resorting to each of the aforementioned judicial strategies.

7.3 Empirical results

7.3.1 Conceptualization of poverty

As early as 1990, monetary poverty was at the centre of an advisory opinion submitted to the IACtHR. Specifically, in the advisory opinion *Exceptions to the exhaustion of domestic remedies* (OC-11/90), the Court was called to clarify, among other issues, whether the requirement of exhaustion of domestic remedies applied to indigents whose economic condition made them unable to access judicial remedies.[35] The Court recalled that Article 1(1) imposed a positive duty on states to take all necessary measures to ensure human rights and to remove existing impediments to their realization.[36] Applying this reasoning to the object of the advisory opinion, it found that, when an individual is prevented from accessing legal remedies due to an inability to pay for legal counsel or the costs of the procedure, that person is being discriminated against on the basis of their economic status.[37] If a state fails to adopt the necessary measures to guarantee the right of equal protection

[35] IACtHR, Advisory Opinion, *Exceptions to the exhaustion of domestic remedies (Art. 46(1), 46(2)(a) and 46(2)(b) American Convention on Human Rights, OC-11/90*, 10 September 1990. Series A No 11, 10 September 1990.

[36] Ibid, para 34.

[37] Ibid, para 22.

before the law (such as providing legal counsel), the victim can take the case directly to the Inter-American System of Human Rights.[38]

From that Advisory Opinion onwards, the IACtHR has analysed compliance with the right to equality in connection with situations of monetary poverty (including extreme poverty) and economic vulnerability. Throughout its equality jurisprudence, it refers explicitly to the concept of extreme poverty,[39] a term that, when introduced without further specification, generally refers to the IPL.

When the word 'poverty' appears in the IACtHR's equality jurisprudence, the Court does not specify whether it refers to monetary or multidimensional poverty. However, the context in which this word is inserted refers, as a rule, to an analysis of income and economic vulnerability. While this points to an overwhelming focus on the monetary dimension of equality, a judgment published by the IACtHR in 2020 indicates that a 'dashboard analysis' of deprivations also informs the Court's assessment of poverty. This took place in the case of *Workers of the Fireworks Factory in Santo Antônio de Jesus and their Families v Brazil*, concerning an explosion in a fireworks factory that killed approximately sixty persons in the state of Bahia in Brazil. When analysing the context of poverty and structural marginalization of the victims of the explosion, the IACtHR examined data from the IBGE concerning the monthly per capita income of the population in the municipality where the explosion took place and the percentage of the local population living below the BPC poverty line[40] and the extreme poverty line.[41] However, the Court's analysis also extended beyond income and economic maldistribution. The Court referred to statistical data from the IBGE concerning deprivations in the dimension of education. Immediately after noting the levels of deprivation in income and education, it recalled that Brazil had acknowledged the existence of great poverty in the municipality where the explosion occurred and that it had recognized the link between poverty and the spread of work in clandestine factories in the region.[42] While the joint analysis of monetary poverty and

[38] Ibid, para 31.

[39] See IACtHR, Judgment (Preliminary Objections, Merits, Reparations and Costs), *Hacienda Brasil Verde Workers v Brasil*, 20 October 2016. Series C No 318; IACtHR, Advisory Opinion, *The Environment and Human Rights (State obligations in relation to the environment in the context of the protection and guarantee of the rights to life and to personal integrity—interpretation and scope of Articles 4(1) and 5(1) of the American Convention on Human Rights), OC-23/2017*, 15 November 2017. Series A No 23; IACtHR, Judgment (Preliminary Objections, Merits, Reparations and Costs), *Workers of the Fireworks Factory in Santo Antônio de Jesus and their Families v Brazil*, 15 July 2020. Series C No 318.

[40] One quarter of the minimum wage (see Chapter 2). The Court also noted the proportion of individuals living on less than half the minimum wage.

[41] Without further specification, references to extreme poverty generally refer to the IPL (see Chapter 2).

[42] *Workers of the Fireworks Factory in Santo Antônio de Jesus and their Families v Brazil* (2020), *supra* note 39, paras 59–60.

deprivations in the education dimension had already occurred in an earlier case against Brazil (*Hacienda Brasil Verde Workers v Brazil*),[43] it was in the *Fireworks Factory* case that the IACtHR more clearly integrated this assessment as a component of poverty.

In any case, even when the Court analyses poverty as a serious deprivation of income or economic vulnerability, it also takes into consideration the context of multidimensional vulnerabilities of victims living in economic vulnerability. One example is the 2012 case of *Furlan and family v Argentina*.[44] This case concerned the failure of the Argentinian Judiciary to resolve in a timely matter a judicial dispute between the State and a child who had suffered an accident on the premises of a building belonging to the Army and, as a result of the accident, lived with disabilities. The IACtHR noted that the child and his family had scarce financial resources, which impacted the child's ability to access medical treatment. Given this context, the IACtHR found that the State was under a duty to ensure the promptness of judicial proceedings, as the child's rehabilitation depended on the timeliness of the proceedings and their execution.[45] Therefore, the Court addressed economic vulnerability while, at the same time, recognizing the differentiated impact of income deprivation for a child with disabilities. It thus discussed economic vulnerability in context, taking into consideration the specific vulnerabilities of Sebastián Furlan.

7.3.2 Conceptualization of equality

OC-11/90 shows that, from its inception, the IACtHR has adopted a conceptualization of the principle of equality and non-discrimination that transcends formal equality. In the advisory opinion *Exceptions to the exhaustion of domestic remedies*, the IACtHR held that, under Article 1(1) of the ACHR, the State Parties are under an obligation to create the necessary structures for guaranteeing human rights. It explained that the term 'to ensure', present in Article 1(1), means taking 'all necessary measures to remove any impediments which might exist that would prevent individuals from enjoying the rights the Convention guarantees'.[46] Simply put, this provision imposes a positive obligation on the parties to the ACHR.[47]

[43] *Hacienda Brasil Verde Workers v Brasil* (2016), *supra* note 39.
[44] IACtHR, Judgment (Preliminary Objections, Merits, Reparations and Costs), *Furlan and family v Argentina*, 31 August 2012. Series C No 246, para 269.
[45] Ibid.
[46] *OC-11/90*, *supra* note 35, para 34.
[47] See ibid, para 22.

In the 2003 advisory opinion on the *Juridical Condition and Rights of Undocumented Migrants* (OC-18/03), the IACtHR explained that there is an 'inseparable connection' between the principle of equality and non-discrimination[48] and the obligation to respect and guarantee human rights[49]—in other words, negative and positive human rights obligations. It also affirmed that the interpretation of the principle of equality must bear in mind the 'continuing development of international law'.[50] In addition, it found that the principle of equality and non-discrimination was a basic principle of international law,[51] an obligation *erga omnes*[52] and a peremptory norm with *jus cogens* character.[53]

Throughout its jurisprudence, the IACtHR recognized that an obligation to ensure substantive equality (or, in the words of the Court in the *Fireworks Factory* case, 'material equality') emanates from the equality provisions of the ACHR.[54] The relevance of the positive dimension of equality at the IACtHR can be observed empirically. Among the fifty-three contentious cases in which the Court reached a decision on the merits of an alleged violation of the right to equality and non-discrimination, 41.5% extended beyond the negative dimension of this right.

For illustrative purposes, consider once more the case of *Furlan and family v Argentina* (2012). In the judgment, the IACtHR explained that the right to equality before the law and non-discrimination comprises two concepts. The first is a negative concept related to the prohibition of arbitrary differentiation. The second is an affirmative concept related to an obligation to act, or, quoting the Court, 'the obligation [. . .] to create real equal conditions towards groups who have been historically excluded or who are exposed to a greater risk of being discriminated'.[55]

Similarly, in the *Fireworks Factory* case, the IACtHR explained that two dimensions emanate from the principle of equality enshrined in Article 24 of the ACHR. The formal dimension safeguards equality before the law, while the material or substantive dimension requires 'the adoption of positive measures of promotion in favor of groups that have historically been discriminated

[48] The Court recognized equality and non-discrimination as two connected concepts that are difficult to separate from one another.
[49] IACtHR, Advisory Opinion, *Juridical Condition and Rights of Undocumented Migrants, OC-18/03*, 17 September 2003. Series A No 18, para 85.
[50] Ibid, para 120.
[51] Ibid, para 86.
[52] Ibid, para 109.
[53] Ibid, para 110.
[54] Cf *Workers of the Fireworks Factory in Santo Antônio de Jesus and their Families v Brazil* (2020), *supra* note 39, para 199.
[55] *Furlan and family v Argentina* (2012), *supra* note 44, para 267.

against or marginalized due to the factors referred to in Article 1(1) of the American Convention'.[56] The IACtHR explained that the substantive dimension of equality implies an obligation to adopt measures that ensure equality is real and effective or, in other words, 'to correct existing inequalities, to promote the inclusion and participation of historically marginalized groups, and to guarantee to disadvantaged individuals or groups the effective enjoyment of their rights and, in short, to provide individuals with the real possibility of achieving material equality'.[57] In conclusion, equality implies that states have an obligation to actively combat instances of exclusion and marginalization.[58] Likewise, in *Expelled Dominicans and Haitians v Dominican Republic*, the IACtHR explained that the principle of equality and non-discrimination establishes for states an obligation to 'combat discriminatory practices at all their levels, especially in public entities and [...] adopt the necessary affirmative measures to ensure that everyone is truly equal before the law'.[59]

Those examples show the application of the distributive and the participative dimensions of equality in the Court's assessment of compliance with the duties derived from substantive equality. Distributive, by requiring states to take measures, including affirmative measures as may be necessary, to correct past disadvantage and distributive harms in the access to resources and opportunities for the realization of rights (eg by providing legal counsel). Participative, by requiring states to promote the inclusion and participation of historically marginalized groups. For example, in the 2015 case of *Gonzales Lluy and others v Ecuador*, the IACtHR was called upon to analyse the impact of the actions and omissions of Ecuador on the rights of Talía Gabriela Gonzales Lluy, a child who at the age of 3 was contaminated with HIV during a blood transfusion performed at a private health clinic.[60] The IACtHR held that the right to protection against discrimination included the situation of persons with HIV, as this condition implied physical effects on the individual, as well as economic, social, and other barriers affecting a person's development and participation in society.[61]

In addition, the Court has consistently included the recognition dimension in its analysis of compliance with the obligations derived from Articles 1(1) and 24 of the ACHR. One example is the case of *IV v Bolivia*, concerning a

[56] *Workers of the Fireworks Factory in Santo Antônio de Jesus and their Families v Brazil* (2020), *supra* note 39, para 199.
[57] Ibid.
[58] Ibid.
[59] IACtHR, Judgment (Preliminary Objections, Merits, Reparations and Costs), *Expelled Dominicans and Haitians v Dominican Republic*, 28 August 2014. Series C No 282, para 264.
[60] *Gonzales Lluy and others v Ecuador* (2015), *supra* note 12, para 255.
[61] Ibid, para 255.

tubal ligation performed in 'IV' (the victim's pseudonym) without her consent following a caesarean.[62] The Court found that the power imbalance between doctor and patient was exacerbated, first, by the unequal power relations that have historically characterized the relations between men and women and, secondly, by gender stereotypes that reinforce the position of women as dependent and subordinated.[63] It found that, when applied in the space of health, gender stereotypes may result in distinctions, exclusions, or restrictions that undermine or nullify the recognition, enjoyment, or exercise of human rights, including the sexual and reproductive rights of women.[64] In particular, it can have an 'impact on and affect a woman's access to information on sexual and reproductive health, as well as the way in which her consent is obtained'.[65]

While the case of *IV v Bolivia* addressed misrecognition harms derived from the relations between private parties, the Court's assessment of the recognition dimension in its equality jurisprudence has generally referred to the application of stereotypes by state agents and institutions and their impact on the enjoyment of human rights. One example is the 2014 judgment in *Norín Catríman v Chile*, concerning the selective implementation of the Chilean anti-terrorist legislation against members of the Mapuche Indigenous people based on negative stereotypes that associated members of this community with terrorism.[66]

The analysis of the application of stereotypes by public authorities as an act of discrimination has been consistently present in cases of gender-based violence before the IACtHR. One example is the 2017 case of *Gutiérrez Hernández and others v Guatemala*, concerning the disappearance of Mayra Angelina Gutiérrez Hernández.[67] The Court explained that stereotypes distort reality and lead to decisions being made based on myths and preconceptions instead of facts. In addition, the omission of states to act with due diligence in the protection of rights and in relation to the use of detrimental stereotypes promotes impunity, distrust in the Judiciary, and sends a message of acceptance and tolerance of violence against women. In the words of the Court, it constitutes, 'in itself, discrimination against women in the access to justice'.[68]

[62] *IV v Bolivia* (2016), *supra* note 14.
[63] Ibid, para 186.
[64] Ibid, para 187.
[65] Ibid.
[66] IACtHR, Judgment (Merits, Reparations, and Costs), *Norín Catrimán et al (Leaders, Members and Activist of the Mapuche Indigenous People) v Chile*, 29 May 2014. Series C No 279, para 223.
[67] *Gutiérrez Hernández and others v Guatemala* (2017), *supra* note 12. See also *Gonzales Lluy and others v Ecuador* (2015), *supra* note 12, paras 159 and 200; and IACtHR, Judgment (Preliminary Objections, Merits, Reparations and Costs), *Espinoza Gonzáles and others v Peru*, 20 November 2014. Series C No 468, para 288.
[68] *Gutiérrez Hernández and others v Guatemala* (2017), *supra* note 67, para 176. See also *Gonzales Lluy and others v Ecuador* (2015), *supra* note 67.

Lastly, the Court's assessment of equality includes a transformative dimension, first, by requiring states to accommodate differences with the aim of enabling parity of participation and equal conditions for the enjoyment of human rights. For example, in *Tiu Tojín v Guatemala* (2008), the IACtHR found that persons belonging to the Maya Indigenous community faced obstacles in travelling to the domestic courts in Guatemala and in obtaining translation for judicial procedures.[69] In light of this context, it held that, pursuant to the principle of non-discrimination, states must guarantee that members of Indigenous communities can access justice. For this purpose, 'it is necessary that the States grant an effective protection taking into account their specific features, economic and social characteristics, as well as their special situation of vulnerability, their common law, values, uses and customs'.[70] In the concrete case, this duty required Guatemala to ensure that the members of the Maya Indigenous community could understand the legal proceedings (eg by offering them interpreters) and to guarantee, 'as far as possible, that the victims of the present case do not have to make excessive or exaggerated efforts to access the centers for the administration of justice in charge of the investigation of the present case'.[71]

Second, the Court's assessment of equality includes a transformative dimension by requiring states to promote structural change, therefore surpassing the limits of an analysis concerning the immediate maldistribution or misrecognition at issue in the equality claim. This obligation to promote structural change takes place within a context that recognizes the role of structures and institutions in perpetuating the vulnerabilization of protected groups and sustaining cycles of inequality. Perhaps the most notable example of this application of the transformative dimension in the equality assessment related to poverty is the *Fireworks Factory* case, as will be explained in detail in the next section.

7.3.3 Judicial strategies for accommodating poverty in equality cases

Judge Ferrer explains that poverty or economic status has been the object of analysis in the case law of the IACtHR in three different ways. First, the Court

[69] IACtHR, Judgment (Merits, Reparations, and Costs), *Tiu Tojín v Guatemala*, 26 November 2008. Series C No 190.
[70] Ibid, para 96.
[71] Ibid, para 100.

has analysed poverty and economic status in association with what the Judge calls 'traditionally identified vulnerable groups (children, women, indigenous peoples, people with disabilities, migrants, etc.)'[72] Second, the Court has analysed poverty and economic status not only as contextual elements increasing the vulnerability of a group but as grounds of the intersectional discrimination identified by the Court. Finally, it has analysed poverty or economic status in isolation as independent grounds requiring special protection.[73]

All three forms of assessment of poverty and economic status have been applied by the IACtHR in its equality case law. In the first modality, the Court generally assessed poverty through the contextual approach, often without making clear considerations as to how the identification of a context of poverty impacted its finding of inequality and without express recognition of intersectional discrimination. In the second and third modalities, a context of poverty is expressly discussed in the assessment of the equality claim. In addition, modalities two and three are frequently applied in cases concerning the positive obligations derived from the right to equality, and often in cases where poverty is assessed as an element of economic status—thus constituting a 'second-degree' suspect classification, as section 7.3.3.1 will explain.

From its creation in 1979 to the end of December 2020, the IACtHR published ten judgments addressing poverty in connection with an equality claim. These decisions are the object of this section's quantitative study. The IACtHR's broader equality jurisprudence is considered only in the qualitative analysis of the Court's interpretation of equality, poverty, and vulnerability.

Out of the ten cases that compose the sample, seven concerned the positive obligation of the state to protect or fulfil the right to substantive equality, seven addressed poverty or socio-economic status as protected grounds, and the same number of cases addressed poverty as context. No cases discussed the inclusiveness of anti-poverty measures. In most decisions, two or more of these strategies were used simultaneously.

7.3.3.1 Suspect classification

Article 1(1) of the ACHR recognizes 'economic status' and 'social origin' as prohibited grounds of discrimination. The inclusion of these two grounds under this provision allows for the consideration of poverty as a 'second-degree' suspect classification, that is, a category covered by the 'umbrella'

[72] Separate opinion of Judge Eduardo Ferrer Mac-Gregor Ferrer in *Workers of the Fireworks Factory in Santo Antônio de Jesus and their Families v Brazil (2020)*, *supra* note 39, para 55.
[73] Ibid.

classifications of 'economic status' and 'social origin'. The analysis of poverty as a ground of discrimination is further facilitated by Article 1(1) being drafted as a semi-open non-discrimination clause, that is, it lists prohibited grounds of discrimination while also including an open-ended expression ('other social condition'). The latter reveals the non-exhaustive nature of the list of prohibited grounds and allows the Court to include additional categories under the scope of the provision.

Until 2016, the IACtHR had consistently considered poverty and economic vulnerability as factors of vulnerability that intersected with and aggravated other vulnerabilities, such as disability and age. The focus of the Court's analysis was on vulnerabilities and the discrimination resulting from their confluence.[74] Yet, in 2016, the Court analysed poverty in isolation.

In the 2016 case *Hacienda Brasil Verde Workers v Brazil*, one of the objects of the Court's equality assessment was structural discrimination based on poverty.[75] The case concerned the rights of eighty-five rescued workers who had been subject to forced labour and debt servitude in Brazil. The IACtHR identified that the workers were originally from the poorest regions in the country, they had lived in a situation of poverty, and were either illiterate or had little or no educations. Considering this context, the IACtHR found that the workers had suffered discrimination based on economic status.[76] It found that Brazil had not taken into consideration the vulnerability of the eighty-five workers, 'grounded on the discrimination based on economic status to which they were subjected'.[77] Accordingly, the State violated the victims' right against slavery and involuntary servitude in relation to Article 1(1) of the ACHR.

In his separate opinion in the case, Judge Ferrer Mac-Gregor explained that this decision marked the first instance in which the Court had identified 'poverty as a component of the prohibition against discrimination based on "economic position"' in an isolated manner, that is, without reference to other suspect criteria.[78] He reiterated the Court's conclusion in his own separate opinion and clarified that poverty, including its manifestation as a multidimensional phenomenon, falls under the grounds of 'economic status', 'social origin', and even 'any other social condition' under Article 1(1) of the ACHR:

[74] See, eg, *Furlan and family v Argentina* (2012), *supra* note 44; IACtHR, Judgment (Preliminary Objections, Merits, Reparations and Costs), *Artavia Murillo et al (In Vitro Fertilization) v Costa Rica*, 28 November 2012. Series C No 257; *Gonzales Lluy and others v Ecuador* (2015), *supra* note 12.

[75] *Hacienda Brasil Verde Workers v Brasil* (2016), *supra* note 39, para 340.

[76] Ibid, paras 339–341.

[77] Ibid, para 341.

[78] Separate opinion of Judge Eduardo Ferrer Mac-Gregor Poisot in ibid, para 44.

> 49. In this regard, the Inter-American Court—as the judgment reveals—has ruled that everyone in a situation of vulnerability merits special protection owing to the special obligations that the States must meet to satisfy the general obligation to respect and to ensure human rights. The Inter-American Court has recalled that it is not sufficient that States abstain from violating rights; rather, it is essential that they adopt positive measures, determined in function of the particular needs for protection of the subject of law, due to his personal situation or to the specific situation in which he finds himself, such as that of extreme poverty or marginalization.
>
> 50. Thus, poverty forms part of the content of the prohibition to discriminate based on the economic status of a person or group of persons. In addition, poverty, since it is a multidimensional phenomenon, may be approached based on different grounds for protection in light of Article 1(1) of the American Convention, such as economic status, social origin or any other social condition, and the protection of these categories of protection can be provided separately, or in a multiple or intersectional manner, according to the specific case.[79]

Judge Ferrer explained that economic condition as a prohibited ground of discrimination refers to structural situations that deprive a segment of the population of the general conditions necessary for a decent and autonomous life, including 'access to and enjoyment of the most basic social services'.[80] This definition of economic condition appears to be narrower than the one adopted by the IACtHR. The Court's equality jurisprudence does not evidence a reduction of the scope of economic condition as a protected ground to merely structural situations involving the denial of basic needs. For example, in the case of *Artavia Murillo et al ('In Vitro Fertilization') v Costa Rica*, the IACtHR found that, by instituting in practice a general prohibition on *in vitro* fertilization, Costa Rica imposed a disproportionate impact on infertile couples who did not have the financial resources to undergo the procedure abroad.[81] This case is an example of a dispute in which the Court recognized the existence of discrimination (indirect, in this specific dispute) based on economic status without linking that discrimination to structural situations that prevented a decent and autonomous life. Therefore, considering the Court's equality jurisprudence, Judge Ferrer's definition of economic condition as a ground of discrimination connected to structural situations that 'prevent a person from developing a decent life' should not be read as a strict delimitation of this suspect classification. Rather, an interpretation in consonance

[79] Ibid, paras 49–50.
[80] Ibid, para 54.
[81] *Artavia Murillo et al (In Vitro Fertilization) v Costa Rica (2012), supra* note 74, paras 303 and 314.

with the Court's equality case law leads to the conclusion that the Judge provided a definition of economic status in a context of structural poverty and indicated the multiplicity of spaces in which this form of inequality may be found—such as 'housing, education, health, recreation, public services, social security and culture'.[82] This interpretation of the Judge's declaration is strengthened by the fact that the references used in this excerpt of his vote referred to poverty.[83]

In this separate opinion, Judge Ferrer also clarified that poverty often intersects with other factors of discrimination. In the specific case of slavery, he noted that, 'generally, normally or almost always', the victims of slavery are poor persons who have been historically discriminated against 'as a result of their race, sex and/or origin'.[84] When this happens, the case involves multiple/compounded or intersectional discrimination. Furthermore, the Judge clarified that acknowledging the relevance and frequency of the cases of multiple or intersectional discrimination does not exclude the recognition of the vulnerability of persons who do not fall under multiple protected categories but are nonetheless poor, marginalized, or excluded.[85]

In the 2016 judgment in *Hacienda Brasil Verde Workers v Brasil*, Judge Ferrer identified a point of inflection in the Court's jurisprudence concerning poverty. He interpreted the Court's pre-2016 case law as engaging with poverty 'tangentially or as an aggravating factor of the context in the different cases in which the IACtHR had ruled'.[86] In contrast, from the *Hacienda Brasil Verde Workers* case onwards, he identified a tendency to examine poverty through the lens of intersectionality or as an element in itself of accessibility of social rights.[87]

Almost four years after the *Hacienda Brasil Verde Workers* case, the IACtHR published its judgment on another leading case concerning poverty. This was the *Fireworks Factory* case. In this judgment, the IACtHR availed itself of the opportunity to analyse the extent to which poverty could be considered a special category of protection against discrimination under Article 1(1) of the ACHR. It concluded that there was no obstacle to considering it a prohibited ground of discrimination under the ACHR. First, because the list of protected grounds of Article 1(1) was merely illustrative. Second, because 'poverty

[82] Separate opinion of Judge Eduardo Ferrer Mac-Gregor Poisot in *Hacienda Brasil Verde Workers v Brasil* (2016), *supra* note 39, para 54.
[83] Ibid, para 54, footnote 82.
[84] Ibid, para 53.
[85] Ibid, para 55.
[86] Separate opinion of Judge Eduardo Ferrer Mac-Gregor Poisot in *Workers of the Fireworks Factory in Santo Antônio de Jesus and their Families v Brazil* (2020), *supra* note 39, para 60.
[87] Ibid.

may well be understood to fall within the category of "economic status" to which the Article expressly refers, or in relation to other categories of protection such as "social origin" or "any other social condition", in view of its multidimensional nature'.[88] While this extract could be interpreted as indicating that the Court would not interpret poverty as an autonomous ground under Article 1(1) but rather falling under the aforementioned categories of economic status or social origin, the Court referred explicitly to discrimination based on the victim's poverty status throughout the decision.[89]

In any case, be it as an autonomous ground of discrimination or as a status encompassed by the category 'economic status' or 'social origin', poverty has been addressed as a suspect classification in the equality jurisprudence of the IACtHR. This has a direct impact on the Court's application of its equality test. First, cases with a suspect classification are subject to higher scrutiny with regards to compliance with the principle of equality and non-discrimination. Every time an unequal treatment is motivated by one of the prohibited categories of discrimination under Article 1(1) of the ACHR, the IACtHR applies a presumption of discriminatory treatment and inverts the burden of proof in favour of the alleged victim.[90] For the presumption of discrimination to take place, the Court does not look for discriminatory intent nor requires proof that the impugned decision has been 'fundamentally and solely' based on the protected personal characteristics shared by the marginalized group.[91] It suffices that the suspect classification has been considered, either explicitly or implicitly, in the adoption of a specific decision.[92] The Court's analysis is thus centred on the objective reasons (and not subjective or interior motivations) for adopting a difference in treatment.[93]

[88] *Workers of the Fireworks Factory in Santo Antônio de Jesus and their Families v Brazil* (2020), *supra* note 39, para 185.

[89] Ibid, paras 190 and 200. Poverty was once again recognized as a factor of discrimination in a more recent case, outside the book's temporal cut for quantitative analysis, relating to indirect intersectional discrimination: IACtHR, Judgment (Preliminary Objections, Merits, Reparations and Costs), *Manuela and others v El Salvador*, 02 November 2021. Series C No 441.

[90] In cases concerning a suspect classification, the IACtHR examines the state's justification to verify whether the impugned measure: (i) is legitimate and pursues an imperative aim; (ii) responds to real and proven risks; and (iii) is proportional (adequate and effectively conducive to the pursued aim; necessary and proportionate in the strict sense). If the case does not concern a suspect classification, the Court applies a more flexible assessment of the state's justification: it assesses whether the state acted arbitrarily, meaning that the measure was not based on rational and objective reasons. No presumption of discrimination applies, and there is no inversion in the burden of proof. See, eg, IACtHR, Judgment (Merits, Reparations, and Costs), *Atala Riffo and daughters v Chile*, 24 February 2012. Series C No 239, para 124; *IV v Bolivia* (2016), *supra* note 14, para 240.

[91] *Atala Riffo and daughters v Chile*, *supra* note 90, para 94.

[92] Ibid.

[93] The suspect classification can refer to the victim's (actual or perceived) traits or, in the case of children, those of their parents. See ibid; *Flor Freire v Ecuador* (2016), *supra* note 9, para 120.

Table 7.1 Success rate disaggregated by the criterion of distinction (IACtHR, 1979–2020)

Criterion	Violation	No violation	Total	Success rate (%)
Not suspect	4	10	14	28.6
Gender/sex	16	0	16	100
Race/ethnic origin	12	1	13	92.3
Economic status	8	0	8	100
Sexual orientation/gender expression	5	1	6	83.3
Age	4	0	4	100
Migratory status	4	0	4	100
Language	3	0	3	100
Disability	2	0	2	100
National origin	2	1	3	66.7
HIV and other medical condition	2	0	2	100
Political opinion	2	2	4	50
Refugee status	1	0	1	100
Total	65	15	80	

Note: the column 'total' cites a number (80) that is higher than the total number of cases (53).This is explained by the fact that some cases involved multiple classifications (eg cases of intersectionality) or multiple claims.

Second, cases with a suspect classification have a significantly higher success rate when compared to those not involving a suspect classification. Note that, in Table 7.1, cases concerning economic status have a 100% success rate.

When the IACtHR addressed poverty or economic vulnerability as a suspect classification, distributive claims were often the object of the dispute. These claims have generally been successful, with notable examples being the two leading cases of the IACtHR's equality jurisprudence addressing poverty (the *Hacienda Brasil Verde Workers* case and the *Fireworks Factory* case, both against Brazil). In addition, more often than not, the distributive dimension has not been analysed in isolation by the IACtHR. For example, in the two abovementioned leading cases, redistributive injustices were considered in connection with structural discrimination and as requiring structural change, thereby engaging the transformative dimension of equality.

7.3.3.2 The contextual approach

The consideration of poverty as context has been a fundamental strategy through which the IACtHR has addressed poverty in equality cases. This strategy has rarely been used by the Court in isolation and generally accompanies the assessment of the positive duties derived from substantive equality.

One example of the consideration of poverty as context is the *Furlan* case, in which the Court recalled the 'direct and significant' link between disabilities, on the one hand, and poverty and social exclusion, on the other.[94] Another example is the case of the *Expelled Dominicans and Haitians v Dominican Republic* (2014), in which the context of poverty informed the Court's assessment of the vulnerabilities of persons of Haitian origin in the Dominican Republic. The case concerned the arbitrary detention and expulsion of Haitian and Dominicans of Haitian origin from the territory of the Dominican Republic without due process of law. When analysing the facts, the IACtHR observed that there was a context of abuse and discrimination against persons of Haitian descent at the time of the alleged violations. In its words, 'a situation existed in the Dominican Republic in which Haitians and persons born in Dominican territory of Haitian descent, who were usually undocumented and living in poverty, frequently suffered abuse or discrimination, including from the authorities, which exacerbated their situation of vulnerability'.[95] The Court dedicated a complete session of its decision to the assessment of the socio-economic situation of Haitians and persons of Haitian descendancy in the Dominican Republic.[96] It noted, among other data, the levels of poverty and extreme poverty of this population as identified by the World Bank. It also observed data from the Inter-American Commission on Human Rights (IACommHR) according to which poverty affected this group disproportionately and was related to the obstacles faced by them to access identity documents.[97] This intersectionality between poverty, ethnicity, and origin guided the Court's assessment of the vulnerabilities experienced by the victims of the concrete case.[98]

It is important to distinguish between two modalities of the IACtHR's consideration of poverty as context. The first is the identification of elements that integrate the personal context of the alleged victim (eg the individual condition of poverty in *Furlan*). This modality informs the victim's special vulnerabilities. It is then the duty of the state to refrain from exacerbating these vulnerabilities and to take active steps towards reversing the oppressions derived from their stigmatization. The second modality is the identification of a general context in which the alleged human rights violations are inserted in the concrete case. The identification of a general context demarcates the facts

[94] *Furlan and family v Argentina* (2012), *supra* note 44, para 201; cf IACtHR, Judgment (Merits, Reparations, and Costs), *Ximenes-Lopes v Brazil*, 4 July 2006. Series C No 149, para 104.
[95] *Expelled Dominicans and Haitians v. Dominican Republic* (2014), *supra* note 59, para 171.
[96] Ibid, paras 155–158.
[97] Ibid, para 156.
[98] For a concrete example, see ibid, paras 194–195.

of the dispute within the framework of the particular conditions in which they transpired.[99] The Court explains that identifying the context in which the facts occur allows for their characterization 'as part of a systematic pattern of human rights violations, as a practice applied or tolerated by the State, or as part of massive, and systematic or generalized attacks on some sector of the population'.[100]

Context is a relevant element in the IACtHR's examination of the evidence, in its identification of the scope of the positive obligations of the state derived from substantive equality, and in its determination of reparations. If the state is or should have been aware at the time of the facts of a systemic context of violations that impacts a specific group, it becomes bound by an *enhanced* or *stricter* duty of due diligence.[101]

The identification of a context of poverty and structural marginalization was central to the *Fireworks Factory* case. In this case, the IACtHR recalled that, since the years of slavery, the region in which the explosion took place had been home to a large population of Afro-descendants, 'owing, in part, to the fact that in the sixteenth century it received a large number of slaves brought in to work in agriculture, especially on the cane sugar plantations and in tobacco farming'.[102] After the abolition of slavery in Brazil, formerly enslaved individuals and their descendants still faced several barriers to exercising citizenship, including severe obstacles to their rights to housing and property and entry into the labour market (see Chapter 3).[103] Many of those individuals remained in bonded labour in the region and faced significant constraints to find formal employment.[104] Quoting the Court, for years the formerly enslaved population 'only found employment in the informal sector where the use of unqualified labor predominated, and this has kept a large part of the population in conditions of poverty'.[105]

Having recalled the historical roots of social exclusion and vulnerability in the region, the IACtHR referred to data from the Atlas on Human Development in Brazil published two years after the explosion. This data

[99] *Gonzales Lluy and others v Ecuador* (2015), *supra* note 12, para 43.

[100] Ibid.

[101] Context has had a particularly preeminent position in cases concerning gender-based violence. For an example, see IACtHR, Judgment (Preliminary Objections, Merits, Reparations and Costs), *Véliz Franco et al v Guatemala*, 19 May 2014. Series C No 277. For the legal consequences of the absence of context in the Court's assessment, see *Gutiérrez Hernández et al v Guatemala*, para 139. On the topic of poverty, see *Workers of the Fireworks Factory in Santo Antônio de Jesus and their Families v Brazil* (2020), *supra* note 39.

[102] *Workers of the Fireworks Factory in Santo Antônio de Jesus and their Families v Brazil* (2020), ibid, para 57.

[103] Ibid.

[104] Ibid.

[105] Ibid, para 58.

revealed a situation of social vulnerability in the municipality of Santo Antônio de Jesus, where the explosion occurred. At that time, 65% of the population was vulnerable to poverty, 25.5% of the children lived in extreme poverty, and 58% of the individuals over 18 years of age who were employed were found in precarious informal work.[106] The Court also took into consideration the present-day situation of the municipality. Based on data from the IBGE published in 2010, it found that 76.5% of the population of the municipality identified themselves as Afro-descendants, 42.18% of the population received half of the minimum wage (the *Cadastro Único* poverty line, as Chapter 2 explained) and 16.40% received one quarter of the minimum wage (the BPC poverty line). Furthermore, 13.30% of the population aged between 15 and 24 did not study or work, and 38.9% of the persons older than 18 had not completed primary school and were engaged in informal work, such as the production of fireworks.[107] Having noted this data, the IACtHR recalled that Brazil itself had acknowledged before the IACommHR that there was great poverty in the municipality and, as a result, families would work in clandestine factories.[108]

The context of poverty experienced by the victims and their families was taken into consideration in the Court's assessment of state compliance with the right to equality. The Court observed that the absence of compensation for eighteen years after the explosion had taken place produced a significant impact on the victims and their families, 'because they lived in a context of poverty and discrimination, as a result of which they did not have sufficient financial resources to cover the expenses of the required medical and psychological treatment, and even the care needed to treat the different injuries suffered in the explosion by the survivors'.[109] In addition, the Court went beyond an analysis of the individual context of poverty of the victims and their families to discuss the general context of poverty and structural discrimination in the municipality. The analysis of the general context was pivotal to its conclusions concerning the scope of the positive duties of the State to act in due diligence before the explosion. It found that Brazil had 'failed to take any measure that could be assessed by the Court as a way of addressing or seeking to reverse the situation of structural poverty and marginalization of the fireworks factory workers based on the factors of discrimination that coalesced in this case'.[110]

[106] Ibid, para 60.
[107] Ibid, para 59.
[108] Ibid.
[109] Ibid, para 240.
[110] Ibid, para 200.

7.3.3.3 Positive obligations

In 1999, the IACommHR was called upon to analyse the compatibility of affirmative action measures as a means of promoting political participation of women, on the one hand, and the principle of equality and non-discrimination, on the other. The Commission found that affirmative measures were, in principle, fully in compliance with the principle of equality and non-discrimination and could well be necessary to achieve substantive equality of opportunity.[111] It was based on this understanding that, in 1998, the Commission recommended to the OAS member states that they 'continue and expand measures to encourage participation by women in decision-making in the public sphere, including positive measures'.[112]

In 2019, the IACommHR defined affirmative actions as measures 'adopted to guarantee, on an equal footing, the enjoyment or exercise of one or more basic human rights and freedoms of persons or groups that need it, as long as said measures do not entail upholding separate rights for distinct groups and are not perpetuated after achieving their goals'.[113] The Commission held that these measures aim at mitigating and eliminating the causes of discrimination against vulnerable groups and at the 'complete and equitable enjoyment of basic human rights and freedoms for groups in situations of vulnerability and/or historical discrimination'.[114] It highlighted the need for the adoption of these measures and recommended that states 'draw up public policies that make it possible to prevent structural situations of discrimination'.[115]

The IACtHR has not yet been called upon to settle a dispute concerning a contested distributive measure of affirmative action.[116] However, it has

[111] Inter-American Commission on Human Rights (IACommHR), 'Considerations regarding the compatibility of affirmative action measures designed to promote the political participation of women with the principles of equality and non-discrimination', 1999.

[112] IACommHR, 'Report of the Inter-American Commission on Human Rights on the Status of Women in the Americas', OEA/SerL/V/II100 Doc 17, 13 October 1998, Section V C, para 1.

[113] Ibid, para 63.

[114] IACommHR, 'Compendium: Equality and non-discrimination. Inter-American Standards', OEA/SerL/V/II171 Doc 31, 12 February 2019, p 70, paras 63–64.

[115] Ibid, para 65.

[116] The words 'affirmative action' are used by the Court in 2021 in the case *Maya Kaqchikel Indigenous Peoples of Sumpango et al v Guatemala*. The case concerns the failure of the state to promote the right to freedom of expression and cultural rights of four Indigenous communities in Guatemala, including through affirmative action. The Court found that Guatemala had an obligation to guarantee substantive equality to Indigenous communities in the establishment and use of their own means of communication and in their access to radio frequencies, compared to groups with financial resources that have the material conditions to compete for the acquisition of radio frequencies. By failing to adopt measures of affirmative action, Guatemala maintained a system that indirectly discriminated against Indigenous people, who, in their majority, live in a structural situation of poverty. This represented a *de facto* hindrance to the exercise of freedom of expression by these groups. IACtHR, Judgment (Merits, Reparations, and Costs), *Maya Kaqchikel Indigenous Peoples of Sumpango et al v Guatemala*, 6 October 2021. Series C No 440, paras 132–156.

actively addressed the positive obligation of states to protect and fulfil the right to equality and non-discrimination. The empirical analysis of the Court's equality jurisprudence shows that almost half of the equality cases decided from the Court's creation to the end of December 2020 discuss states' positive obligations in relation to the right to equality and non-discrimination (41.5% of the sample). From its inception, the Court has recognized that positive obligations derive from Articles 1(1) and 24 of the ACHR, an understanding now consolidated in the Court's jurisprudence.

The positive dimension of equality was the central object of two leading cases concerning poverty, both of which had Brazil as the respondent state. In *Hacienda Brasil Verde Workers*, the allegations presented before the Court were, first, that the facts occurred in a context in which thousands of workers were annually subjected to slavery in the federated state where the farm was located. Second, that, even though the Brazilian authorities had received complaints on behalf of the workers of the farm since 1989, Brazil had failed to adopt reasonable measures to prevent and respond to these human rights violations. The IACommHR claimed that the facts of the case evidenced '*de facto* discrimination against a group of persons who has been marginalized in the enjoyment of their rights'.[117] The representatives, in turn, argued that this group of persons, distinguished by their origin, ethnicity, race, and economic position, was subject to structural discrimination. They noted that the majority of the victims of the case were 'poor men, between 17 and 40 years old, afro-descendants […] who came from extremely poor states such as Piauí, where they lived in conditions of extreme poverty and vulnerability'.[118] The representatives argued that this situation amounted to structural discrimination.[119]

The IACtHR recalled its *dictum* according to which states are under an obligation 'to adopt positive measures to revert or modify any discriminatory situations in their societies that prejudice a specific group of people'.[120] This obligation 'entails the special duty of protection that the State must exercise with regard to acts and practices of third parties who, with its tolerance or acquiescence, create, maintain or promote discriminatory situations'.[121]

[117] *Hacienda Brasil Verde Workers v Brasil* (2016), *supra* note 39, para 216.
[118] Ibid, para 226.
[119] Ibid.
[120] Ibid, para 336. For examples of the use of this *dictum*, see *OC-18/03*, *supra* note 49, para 104; IACtHR, Judgment (Merits, Reparations, and Costs), *Xákmok Kásek Indigenous Community v Paraguay*, 24 August 2010. Series C No 214, para 271; *Véliz Franco et al v Guatemala* (2014), *supra* note 101, para 206; *Espinoza Gonzáles and others v Peru* (2014), *supra* note 67, para 220; IACtHR, Judgment (Preliminary Objections, Merits, Reparations and Costs), *Duque v Colombia*, 26 February 2016. Series C No 310, para 92.
[121] *Hacienda Brasil Verde Workers v Brasil* (2016), *supra* note 39, para 336.

In addition, the Court held that anyone living in a situation of vulnerability is entitled to 'special protection'.[122] The latter implies the adoption of positive measures, determined in light of the individual's special protection needs, whether based on their personal condition (eg disabilities) or the specific situation in which they are situated (eg extreme poverty or marginalization).[123] Failure to adopt specific measures addressing 'the particular situation of victimization that reveals the vulnerability of a universe of individualized persons' in a context of structural discrimination implies that international responsibility is incurred by the state.[124]

In the concrete case against Brazil, the IACtHR considered, in its equality analysis, the context of monetary poverty of the victims, their significative deprivations in the dimension of education, and their origin from the country's poorest regions, which have lower levels of human development and limited employment opportunities. These conditions placed the workers in a situation of vulnerability, making them more susceptible to being misled and recruited through false promises and deception.[125] The Court observed that this situation of imminent risk had historical roots and had been known by the State at least since 1995, when the federal government expressly acknowledged that forced labour existed in the country.[126] The Court also noted that several reports of the International Labour Organization (ILO) and the Brazilian Ministry of Labour recognized that extreme poverty leads a person to accept the working conditions offered to them and the risks attached to these offers. The Court quoted the ILO, according to which poverty (understood as deprivation of income and deprivations in the fulfilment of the most basic human needs) is the main cause of modern slavery.[127] Considering this context, the IACtHR concluded that Brazil had failed to take into account the vulnerability of the victims of forced slavery in the *Brasil Verde* Farm, who were discriminated against based on their economic condition.[128] More specifically, it found that Brazil was responsible for the violation of freedom from slavery 'in relation to Article 1(1) of this instrument, that occurred in the context of a situation of historical structural discrimination based on the economic status of the 85 workers identified in [. . .] this judgment'.[129]

[122] Ibid, para 337.
[123] Ibid.
[124] Ibid, para 338.
[125] Ibid, para 339.
[126] Ibid.
[127] International Labour Organization; ILO Office in Brazil, *Combatendo o Trabalho Escravo Contemporâneo: o exemplo do Brasil* (2010), pp 111–113 *apud* ibid, para 340.
[128] *Hacienda Brasil Verde Workers v Brasil* (2016), *supra* note 39, para 341.
[129] Ibid, para 343.

The discussion of state responsibility for failure to address vulnerabilities, including the perpetuation of a situation of poverty, was expanded in the separate opinion of Judge Ferrer. The Judge identified a link between situations of structural discrimination and the need for states to adopt positive measures. In his understanding, certain violations are not isolated facts but manifestations of specific and institutional contexts of denial of human rights.[130] Applying this discussion to poverty, the Judge recognized that international law did not provide an explicit definition of 'structural poverty' as a form of discrimination. Nonetheless, the work of special rapporteurs on extreme poverty has allowed for the identification of persons living in such conditions.[131] Based on the UN Guiding Principles on Extreme Poverty and Human Rights, Judge Ferrer explained that extreme poverty is created, enabled, and perpetuated by actions and inactions of the state and other agents. Gaps in public policy generate a situation of perpetuation of intergenerational poverty. Poverty is further entrenched by structural and systemic inequalities, including social, political, economic, and cultural dimensions.[132]

Judge Ferrer noted that the *Hacienda Brasil Verde Workers* case was the first in which the IACtHR had explicitly found a state to be internationally responsible for perpetuating a situation of historical and structural exclusion.[133] In addition, he argued for a distinction between 'positive equalization measures' and 'positive equalization actions'.[134] The latter is general in scope and aims to compensate for group inequality. One example would be general actions taken by Brazil to combat slave labour. In turn, 'positive equalization measures' are individualized measures tailored to a specific situation, and they must be implemented once states are able to identify the specific segment of a group that is vulnerable to a violation. One example would be measures focusing on a specific geographic area that is particularly vulnerable to forced labour recruitment. The analysis of whether a state fulfilled its obligation to apply positive equalization actions and measures involves an assessment of sufficiency and effectiveness.[135] Judge Ferrer concluded that 'the

[130] Separate opinion of Judge Eduardo Ferrer Mac-Gregor Poisot in ibid, para 56.
[131] Ibid, para 68.
[132] Ibid.
[133] Ibid, para 84. In contrast, Judge Vio Grossi disagreed with the conclusion of Judge Ferrer and argued that the Court's Judgment did not recognize state responsibility for the perpetuation of 'structural discrimination', notwithstanding the reference to the term 'historical structural discrimination' in the fourth operative paragraph of the Judgment. Judge Vio Grossi argued that the Court's finding of international responsibility 'relates only to the special situation of the said workers and not to the "historical structural discrimination" that existed at the time of the facts of the case. However, this constitutes the context in which those facts took place and, consequently and to a certain extent, explains them, even though it does not justify them'. Cf Concurring Opinion of Judge Eduardo Vio Grossi in ibid, para 4.
[134] Separate opinion of Judge Eduardo Ferrer Mac-Gregor Poisot in ibid, paras 92–93.
[135] Ibid, paras 93 and 96.

ineffectiveness, incapacity and deficient implementation of general actions to prevent discrimination within a State may produce and perpetuate, for years, the existence of discrimination towards certain disadvantaged groups'.[136]

The discussion of the positive obligations of states to effectively address poverty was developed further in the *Fireworks Factory* case. When analysing whether Brazil had fulfilled its positive obligations to ensure material equality to marginalized groups in a situation of structural poverty, the IACtHR did not explicitly assess the positive equalization actions adopted by Brazil to respond to the situation of poverty in the region.[137] It analysed statistical data from the IBGE revealing significant deprivations in access to education, sufficient income to live free from monetary poverty, and formal work. Its analysis did not include data on the reduction of poverty levels or the poverty gaps in Brazil.[138] Instead, the Court considered statistical data to determine whether structural poverty could be identified in the municipality of Santo Antônio de Jesus at the time of the events and still at the time of the judgment.

Because the data used by the IACtHR to identify the special vulnerabilities of the victims came from the IBGE, that is, Brazil's own agency, the Court concluded that Brazil was aware of the victims' situation of heightened vulnerability.[139] While observing that the State had argued that it had introduced a series of public policies and an effective legal framework to reduce inequalities, the Court found that the situation of structural discrimination in the region had not changed.[140] In addition, it found that, by allowing the fireworks factory 'to locate and operate in an area in which a substantial part of the population was vulnerable, the State had an enhanced obligation to oversee the operating conditions of the factory and to ensure that real measures were taken to protect the life and health of the workers and to guarantee their right to material equality'.[141] Quoting the Court:

[136] Ibid, para 96.

[137] *Workers of the Fireworks Factory in Santo Antônio de Jesus and their Families v Brazil* (2020), *supra* note 39, paras 188–190 and 197–199. The *Bolsa Família* programme and its coverage in the municipality were mentioned in the Judgment only in reference to the State's response to the allegation of violation of the right to equality and non-discrimination. See ibid, para 146.

[138] While an analysis of the measures taken by Brazil after the explosion would not have impacted the Court's finding of state responsibility, the Court may take into consideration the fact that a state has adopted measures after a violation of human rights as an indication that the violation is not continuous or that the state is taking steps in the right direction to address a situation of vulnerability. This analysis may also impact the type of collective reparations that is ordered by the Court in light of the present-day deficiencies in state action.

[139] *Workers of the Fireworks Factory in Santo Antônio de Jesus and their Families v Brazil* (2020), *supra* note 39, para 201.

[140] Ibid, para 201.

[141] Ibid, para 202.

> In sum, the Court finds that the situation of poverty of the presumed victims, added to the intersectional factors of discrimination described above that exacerbated the condition of vulnerability: (i) facilitated the installation and operation of a factory dedicated to a particularly dangerous activity, without any oversight of the hazardous activity or the occupational health and safety conditions by the State, and (ii) led the presumed victims to accept work that jeopardized their life and integrity and that of their underage children. In addition, (iii) the State failed to take measures to ensure material equality in the right to work for a group of women who were marginalized and faced discriminated [*sic*]. This situation signifies that, in this case, the State failed to ensure the right to just and favorable conditions of work, without discrimination, as well as the right to equality established in Articles 24 and 26, in relation to Article 1(1) of the Convention.[142]

The reasoning of the Court indicates that its assessment of whether Brazil had complied with its positive duties derived from substantive equality incorporated the requirement of effectiveness.[143] The consideration of a threshold of effectiveness is also present in the separate opinion of Judge Ferrer in the case. The Judge noted the argument that Brazil had adopted an effective legal framework to reduce inequalities and had implemented several public policies towards this aim.[144] Nonetheless, he found that the State had failed to prove the effectiveness of these measures—more specifically, the State had not demonstrated that the situation of structural discrimination faced by the women working in the manufacture of fireworks had changed. Furthermore, he considered that there was a lack of concrete measures (such as promoting formal employment in the region) allowing these women to enjoy the real content of the right to just and favourable working conditions.[145] Therefore, this context evidenced 'ineffectiveness, insufficiency or absence of measures, norms, actions or policies in favor of structurally marginalized groups', falling under Article 24 of the ACHR.[146]

The consideration of effectiveness as a threshold for compliance with the positive duties derived from substantive equality amplifies to a significant degree the range of distributive harm that the IACtHR can identify in cases concerning poverty. Furthermore, for poverty to be effectively reduced in every

[142] Ibid, para 203.

[143] A similar recognition of the persistence of (monetary and multidimensional) poverty as an indication of structural discrimination is found in a more recent case: *Maya Kaqchikel Indigenous Peoples of Sumpango et al v Guatemala*, *supra* note 116, para 139.

[144] Separate opinion of Judge Eduardo Ferrer Mac-Gregor Poisot in ibid, para 112.

[145] Ibid, paras 112–112.

[146] Ibid, para 114.

region of the state requires structural change and consideration of the different vulnerabilities affecting specific segments of the population. Therefore, the analysis of the implementation of these measures touches upon the transformative dimension of the equality assessment, transposing the focus from the individual victims to collective harms and, to a certain degree, from agents to institutions.

7.3.3.4 Reparations

The last strategy identified in the jurisprudence of the IACtHR for addressing poverty through the lens of equality is the consideration of poverty in the determination of reparations. The consideration of poverty for the purposes of determining the reparations owed to the victims of discrimination can take place when the impugned differentiation is based on economic status specifically, as well as in cases in which poverty is an additional factor of vulnerability culminating in intersectional disadvantages and vulnerabilities. In order words, the consideration of poverty in the determination of forms of reparation can derive from the application of intersectionality as a critical praxis.

Patricia Hill Collins explains intersectionality as a broad-based knowledge project with three interdependent sets of concern. These are: (i) intersectionality as a field of study; (ii) intersectionality as an analytical strategy; and (iii) intersectionality as critical praxis.[147] Lawyers and, here I argue, judges of domestic and regional courts are practitioners who address intersectionality not as a theoretical concept to be mastered or analysed but as a possible praxis. For these groups, intersectionality is a critical praxis to be applied in social justice work.[148] One area in which it can be used in practice is in the pleadings for, and the issuance of, orders of reparations.[149]

The reparations asked by the victims and ordered by a court can take into consideration the context of poverty and its links to structural discrimination. When victims suffer discrimination related to a general context of systemic poverty, this can be considered by a court when determining collective reparations. The case of the *Firework Factory* offers an example of the institution of reparations taking into consideration a collective dimension in the context of structural poverty. The IACtHR noted that Brazil had argued that it had implemented a series of public policies, such as the *Bolsa Família*, over the

[147] Patricia Hill Collins, 'Intersectionality's Definitional Dilemmas' (2015) 41 Annual Review of Sociology 1, p 3.
[148] Ibid, p 16.
[149] See ibid, p 16

past decades. While expressing its appreciation for the efforts of the State, the IACtHR asserted that the evidence provided by Brazil was insufficient to show a significant impact of the public policies adopted from the time of the factory explosion until the Court's judgment in July 2020 on the individuals that still worked manufacturing fireworks in the municipality of Santo Antônio de Jesus. Having concluded that the situation of vulnerability of the population of the municipality had not changed significantly, the IACtHR ordered Brazil to design and execute a socio-economic development programme specifically designed for the population of Santo Antônio de Jesus, within two years of the notification of the judgment and in coordination with the victims and their representatives. The Court also listed specific focus areas for the design of the programme, including measures to address the lack of employment for vulnerable groups and school dropout. In addition, it required the State to produce reports on the implementation of this programme and the implementation and application of the National Guidelines on Business and Human Rights, especially in relation to specific topics, such as the inclusion and non-discrimination of vulnerable groups.[150]

Also in cases of individual rather than collective reparations, poverty can be a relevant factor in determining reparations when the impact of the impugned discrimination is exacerbated by the individual context of the victim's poverty. For example, in the *Furlan* case, the IACtHR took into consideration the impact that the delay in domestic proceedings had on the child's opportunities for rehabilitation. It ordered the State to provide free and immediate medical, psychological, and psychiatric treatment to the victims, including free medication.[151]

As these examples show, the consideration of poverty and other factors of intersectionality for the purposes of reparations can change the range and content of the reparatory measures to be ordered. Taking these elements of intersectionality into consideration is relevant for realizing the objective of compensating and, when possible, reversing the damage suffered by the victim. After all, to compensate for the damage suffered by a victim of discrimination, a court must first identify the harm suffered. In cases of intersectionality, identifying discrimination requires identifying the multiple factors that conflate with one another. Accordingly, for a measure of reparation to be able to compensate for and/or reverse the harm suffered in a case of intersectional discrimination, it must be established considering the multiple

[150] *Workers of the Fireworks Factory in Santo Antônio de Jesus and their Families v Brazil* (2020), *supra* note 39, paras 289–291.
[151] *Furlan and family v Argentina* (2012), *supra* note 44, para 284.

dimensions of the discrimination and oppression suffered (see Chapter 2) and the context of multiple vulnerabilities in which they took place. In this context, Young's analysis of the multiple dimensions of oppression and Fredman's recognition of the multiple aims of substantive equality become valuable for tribunals to rule cases inserted in a context of poverty and, when appropriate, to order collective reparations with the aim of promoting structural change.

7.3.3.5 Poverty outside of equality cases

Outside of its equality jurisprudence, the IACtHR addressed poverty in six contentious cases from the Court's creation until the end of 2020.[152] The first was *'Juvenile Reeducation Institute' v Paraguay* (2004), when the Court asserted that, in determining reparations, it should take into consideration the fact that the child victims of the impugned violations were very poor.[153] In two cases, the IACtHR analysed poverty as a product of the impugned acts of the state that violated other human rights.[154] For example, in *Mapiripán Massacre v Colombia*, it found that poverty was a consequence of the attacks perpetrated in Mapiripán and the resulting situation of internal displacement.[155] In two cases, it explained that violations of some rights (such as the right to property) produce a particular impact on people living in poverty. Accordingly, quoting the Court in *Santo Domingo Massacre v Colombia*, 'States must take into account that groups of people who live in poverty face an increased degree of harm to their rights, precisely due to their situation of greater vulnerability'.[156] Finally, in the remaining case, the Court found that every person in a situation of vulnerability is entitled to special protection.[157] Without explicitly discussing equality, it held that persons living in adverse circumstances, such as extreme poverty, face a higher risk of living with disabilities. Therefore, it concluded that states must take positive measures to address this situation of vulnerability.[158]

[152] IACtHR, Judgment (Preliminary Objections, Merits, Reparations and Costs), *'Juvenile Reeducation Institute' v Paraguay*, 2 September 2004. Series C No 112; IACtHR, Judgment (Preliminary Objections, Merits, Reparations and Costs), *Moiwana Community v Suriname*, 15 June 2005. Series C No 145; IACtHR, Judgment (Merits, Reparations and Costs), *Mapiripán Massacre v Colombia*, 15 September 2005. Series C No 134; *Ximenes-Lopes v Brazil* (2006), *supra* note 94; IACtHR, Judgment (Preliminary Objections, Merits and Reparations), *Santo Domingo Massacre v Colombia*, 30 November 2012. Series No 259; and IACtHR, Judgment (Merits and Reparations), *Uzcátegui et al v Venezuela*, 3 September 2012. Series C No 249.

[153] *'Juvenile Reeducation Institute' v Paraguay* (2004), *supra* note 152, para 262.

[154] *Moiwana Community v Suriname (2005)*, *supra* note 152; *Mapiripán Massacre v Colombia* (2005), *supra* note 152.

[155] *Mapiripán Massacre v Colombia* (2005), ibid, paras 180–186.

[156] *Santo Domingo Massacre v Colombia* (2012), *supra* note 152, para 273; see also *Uzcátegui et al v Venezuela* (2012), *supra* note 152, paras 204 and 206.

[157] *Ximenes-Lopes v Brazil* (2006), *supra* note 94, para 103.

[158] Ibid, para 104.

7.4 Conclusion: identified patterns

The IACtHR has engaged with poverty as a vulnerability to the fulfilment of human rights. Particularly in its pre-2016 jurisdiction, the Court had not always been clear as to how this recognition of vulnerability impacted its finding of discrimination in the concrete case. However, more recent judgments have explicitly recognized poverty as a factor of intersectional discrimination and even as an independent ground requiring measures of special protection. Notably, positive obligations have been central to the Court's equality jurisprudence addressing poverty.

Today, poverty is explicitly recognized by the IACtHR as a factor of vulnerability covered by the protected ground 'economic condition' and protected against discrimination. The Court has often assessed poverty as a contextual element—at times directly linked to the equality claim and to manifestations of exclusion, and other times as a general context in which the case as a whole and all the alleged human rights violations were inserted.

The analysis of the IACtHR's jurisprudence confirms the suggestion put forward by Fredman thirteen years ago on the potential of 'fourth generation' equality rights for addressing poverty. By recognizing the positive dimension of equality as an integral element of this right, the IACtHR brings to its jurisdiction actions and inactions of the State Parties to address disadvantage and status inequality. Through this approach, it addresses distributive and polycentric harms arising in relation to poverty.

The multiple dimensions of equality have been considered by the Court in its application of all the strategies identified in Chapter 4, except for the analysis of the inclusiveness of anti-poverty measures, as no case with that object has yet reached the IACtHR.[159] Notably, all cases concerning positive obligations in a context of poverty recognized distributive inequalities. Yet it was when poverty was assessed as a suspect classification, either as a component of socio-economic condition or a factor of intersectional discrimination, that the IACtHR assessed equality the most in its multiple dimensions (see Table 7.2).

These results demonstrate that poverty has been integrated into the IACtHR's equality jurisprudence through multiple strategies, all of them capable of capturing multidimensional inequalities in relation to poverty.

[159] The Court's analysis in *Fireworks Factory* was centred around the perpetuation of poverty in the municipality, rather than an assessment of the content and scope of the anti-poverty policies implemented by Brazil.

Table 7.2 Dimensions of equality disaggregated by judicial strategy (IACtHR, 1979–2020)

	Distributive equality	Equality as recognition	Participative equality	Transformative equality	Total number of cases
Suspect classification	5	2	1	3	7
Context	7	-	1	3	7
Positive obligations	7	-	1	3	7

Furthermore, they indicate that the Court's interpretation of the right to equality in relation to poverty has contributed to its consideration of multiple dimensions of oppressions related to or derived from poverty. In comparison, the Court's consideration of poverty as a vulnerability outside equality cases has generally focused on distributive harm and therefore has tended to adopt a largely monocentric focus.

8
A Comparative Analysis and Paths Forward

Hope is like a road in the country; there was never a road, but when many people walk on it, the road comes into existence.

—Lu Xun, 'The Epigrams of Lusin'[1]

Law is not always transformative or emancipatory.[2] It can reinforce patterns of dominance and legitimize the status quo to the detriment of historically vulnerable collectivities. Similarly, courts are not always agents for the promotion of social change. They can resist evolutive interpretations of the law and refrain from adopting decisions that could be perceived as activist. Despite this duality between domination and emancipation in the role and functioning of the law, scholars increasingly associate contemporary Latin American constitutionalism with a transformative project.

Ferraz finds in Latin America one of the highest concentrations—if not the highest—of constitutional provisions emphasizing substantive equality.[3] Similarly, Botero and Brinks observe that the region experienced a wave of democratization in the late twentieth century, during which human rights discourse gained prominence and formal rights were significantly expanded within domestic legal systems.[4] According to Diego Werneck Arguelhes, transformative constitutions are now widespread across the region and tend

[1] Lu Xun, 'The Epigrams of Lusin' in Lin Yutang (ed), *The Wisdom of China* (Michael Joseph 1944).

[2] See Michael McCann, 'Law and Social Movements: Contemporary Perspectives' (2006) 2 Annual Review of Law and Social Science 17, p 35. In McCann's words: 'Legal institutions and norms tend to be Janus-faced, at once securing the status quo of hierarchical power while sometimes providing limited opportunities for episodic challenges to and transformations in that reigning order [...]. How law matters depends on the complex, often changing dynamics of the context in which struggles occur'.

[3] Octávio Luiz Motta Ferraz, 'Substantive Equality in law and Reality' in Conrado Hübner Mendes, Roberto Gargarella, and Sebastián Guidi (eds), *The Oxford Handbook of Constitutional Law in Latin America* (Oxford University Press 2022), p 709.

[4] Daniel Brinks and Sandra Botero, 'Inequality and the Rule of Law: Ineffective Rights in Latin American Democracies' in Daniel Brinks, Marcelo Leiras, and Scott Mainwaring (eds), *Reflections on Uneven Democracies: The Legacy of Guillermo O'Donnell* (Johns Hopkins University Press 2014), p 218.

Judging Poverty and Inequality in Brazil. Tainá Garcia Maia, Oxford University Press. © Tainá Garcia Maia 2026.
DOI: 10.1093/oso/9780198994022.003.0008

to share a common normative vision.[5] Yet these same scholars underscore a persistent gap between the ambitious promises of these constitutional frameworks and their actual capacity to address entrenched issues, including structural inequality.

Persistent and structural challenges—such as high inequality, chronic poverty, and the concentration of economic and political power—persist in the region, despite the transformative ambitions of constitutions and domestic and regional courts in Latin America. The expansion of rights, the consolidation of transformative constitutionalism as a *habitus* of constitutional judges, and even courts' self-understanding as guardians of rights and active promoters of change appear insufficient, on their own, to promote the promised social changes and egalitarian transformation.

Historical and persistent obstacles to the equal realization of rights, including freedom from want and from the multidimensional deprivations related to poverty, require legal, social, and political action. Expanding rights, whether through the codification of norms or their evolutive interpretation by the interpreters of the law, offers a partial response to a far more complex set of issues.

First, the mere existence of rights does not necessarily translate into their realization, as vulnerable groups, including those living in monetary and multidimensional poverty, face unequal opportunities to secure the fulfilment of those legal promises and to have their interests, needs, and perspectives represented in the processes through which law is created, interpreted, and applied. In other words, the ability of different social groups to effectively utilize formal legal rights and navigate the litigation process varies, reflecting broader social hierarchies. Different groups hold varying degrees of power in ensuring their interests, needs, and desires are represented in the processes of codification and interpretation of the law, and they face unequal opportunities to bring their claims before courts. As Ferraz aptly observes, 'there is a clear social gradient in how successfully groups are able to benefit from the formal rights of the legal system'.[6]

Second, even when courts adopt transformative language, they may be incapable—or, as Arguelhes argues, unwilling—to ensure the effective implementation of their rulings. Arguelhes emphasizes the importance of distinguishing between what a court says (including the use of strong statements

[5] Diego Werneck Arguelhes, 'Transformative Constitutionalism: A View from Brazil' in Philipp Dann, Michael Riegner, and Maxim Bönnemann (eds), *The Global South and Comparative Constitutional Law* (Oxford University Press 2020), p 169.

[6] Ferraz (2022), *supra* note 3, p 716.

and rhetoric that evokes transformative aspirations) and what it actually does. Practices such as the absence of monitoring mechanisms and the strategic avoidance of confrontation with other branches—particularly in cases involving state omissions in the protection and promotion of rights—often result in a disconnect between judicial discourse and judicial action.[7] Arguelhes identifies the lack of monitoring mechanisms as a significant obstacle to achieving tangible social transformation, highlighting the need for courts to coordinate effectively with other branches of government and engage relevant stakeholders.[8] In his view, transformative constitutionalism requires more than a transformative constitutional text: it demands active engagement by legal professionals and political authorities in shaping policies and legal arguments that align with the transformative objectives articulated in constitutional provisions and other legal instruments.[9]

Third, while courts play a crucial role in protecting and guaranteeing the realization of rights of disadvantaged and marginalized groups, they are not enough on their own. The importance—but insufficiency—of courts alone in promoting social change in the face of persistent and structural social problems, such as high inequality and, here I add, chronic poverty, has being the object of analysis by Ferraz. He underscores the relationship between the promotion of transformative change and the need to confront enduring barriers to social justice. In his words, '[d]eep and comprehensive transformation can only be achieved through the removal of [these] structural obstacles […] which seems a task much more suited to politics than law and courts'.[10]

This is not to say that courts cannot or do not contribute to the promotion of social change and to confronting barriers to social justice, such as high inequality and structural poverty. On the contrary, this study has identified that the STF and the IACtHR have made important contributions to unveiling and addressing the persistent interconnections between poverty and inequality in Brazil. The equality case law of the two courts addressing poverty legitimized and even expanded positive measures benefiting individuals living in poverty or in socio-economic vulnerability, as well as groups disproportionately and historically represented among those living in such conditions. Yet, these judicial contributions have not occurred in isolation; rather, they have unfolded within the broader context of the development of state policies addressing poverty in multiple dimensions—albeit with a strong emphasis on

[7] Werneck Arguelhes (2020), *supra* note 5, pp 181–183.
[8] Ibid, pp 182–183.
[9] Ibid, p 169.
[10] Ferraz (2022), *supra* note 3, p 717.

distributive remedies, as discussed in Chapter 5. Conversely, the social policies examined in that chapter and their substantial impact on poverty eradication in Brazil did not arise in a legal vacuum. They were supported by—and, in some cases, even modified and expanded through—litigation, as Chapters 6 and 7 explained.

Section 8.1 analyses the impact of the STF's and the IACtHR's equality jurisprudence concerning poverty and economic vulnerability on poverty eradication in Brazil. Having studied the decisions of the two courts in the preceding two chapters, the book now turns to an analysis of the implementation of these decisions and their impact on public policies in the country. It finds that the STF has mostly acted as a subsidiary policymaker, confirming and, at times, expanding distributive measures with an impact on individuals and groups living in poverty and economic vulnerability. In turn, the IACtHR has explicitly recognized failure to reverse chronic poverty affecting vulnerable communities as a violation in itself of the right to equality. As collective reparations, it has ordered the adoption of specific positive measures to effectively reverse this scenario. Section 8.2 juxtaposes the jurisprudential practices of the two courts in accommodating poverty within the framework of equality. Lastly, Section 8.3 outlines suggestions for these jurisdictions to navigate the complexities of poverty adjudication.

8.1 Judicial contributions to a socio-political challenge

8.1.1 Policy review in the STF: confirming and expanding distributive measures

Our study finds two key contributions of the STF to poverty reduction in Brazil. First, the Court has played a central role in confirming the constitutionality of positive measures, including strong distributive measures of affirmative action, in favour of historically discriminated groups disproportionality represented among those living in monetary and multidimensional poverty. Second, the Court has expanded the scope of anti-poverty public policies, notably cash transfer programmes—for example, by including foreigners residing in Brazil among the individuals entitled to cash transfer programmes and by adding caveats to the absolute poverty line used to determine which individuals are entitled to receiving the BPC. In adjudicating these disputes concerning positive measures to the benefit of economically vulnerable groups, including cash transfer programmes and quota systems for accessing education and public employment, the right to equality was central to the Court's legal analysis.

Through *ADPF 186* (2012) and *ADC 41* (2017), the STF confirmed the constitutionality of quota systems both for admission in higher education and for positions in the federal public administration. These strong distributive measures have played an important role in Brazil's efforts to increase the number of black and brown students in higher education and in public positions, with direct effects on multidimensional—and arguably monetary—poverty. More specifically, the quota system in public universities has been associated with an increase of 1.2 million black and brown university students aged 18–24 between 2002 and 2015.[11] This expansion enhances access to education, providing a distributive remedy to multidimensional poverty. It also impacts social stratification in the labour market and in education, addressing the marginalization of the black and brown population and their disproportionate concentration in positions with lower salaries and status.

The STF's impact on educational stratification and its interconnections with poverty in Brazil also derives from *ADI 3.330* (2012), which confirmed the constitutionality of the PROUNI. The PROUNI grants scholarships at private universities to students who graduated from public high schools and whose family income falls below a certain threshold of economic vulnerability. These measures of affirmative action—the continuation of which, after being challenged before the STF, depended on the Court's confirmation of their constitutionality—played an important role, together with CCTs, in responding to monetary and multidimensional poverty in the country.

Decisions of the STF that merely confirm the constitutionality of existing distributive measures of affirmative action generally pose little difficulty in their implementation. The situation is trickier when the Court expands the content and scope of a positive measure, including anti-poverty public policies. For example, through *RE 567.985* (2013) and *RE 587.970* (2017), the STF expanded the scope of beneficiaries of the BPC, a benefit of social assistance granted to older persons and persons with disabilities whose household income per capita is below the monetary poverty line of one quarter of the minimum wage. The implementation of the Programme *Bolsa Família* (PBF), Brazil's flagship anti-poverty policy, has also come under the tribunal's scrutiny. In *ACO 3.359 MC-Ref* (2020), the STF examined cuts to the programme made during the Covid-19 pandemic and their concentration

[11] Tereza Campello (ed), *Faces da Desigualdade no Brasil: Um olhar sobre os que ficam para trás* (CLACSO, FLACSO, agenda igualdade 2017), p 49.

in the Northeast region of the country. By unanimous decision, it suspended the cuts for the duration of the state of public calamity caused by the pandemic and required the federal government to justify their regional concentration.

The implementation of the STF's rulings expanding the content, scope, and delivery of cash transfer programmes depends on state actors outside the Court. One central actor in this process is the MDS. Information provided by the Ministry for the purposes of this research indicates that the Court's determinations were largely incorporated into the administration of cash transfer programmes. According to the Ministry, 34,451 foreigners currently receive the BPC, of whom 6,883 are persons with disabilities and 27,568 are older persons.[12] With respect to the PBF, the MDS confirmed the suspension of cuts for the duration of the Covid-19 pandemic.[13] It also reported that it has taken action to implement the STF's final judgment on *ACO 3.359*.[14] Notably, since July 2024, the Ministry has introduced high-precision estimates of poverty and vulnerability to poverty at the municipal level. This procedure was developed by IPEA in cooperation with the Ministry and draws on data from the PNADC, the national census, and the *Cadastro Único*. The new tool improves the focus of the programme by prioritizing municipalities with lower coverage and highlighting areas that require better coverage and registration management. In the words of the Ministry, the updated estimates allow it to 'reprioritize the allocation of new benefits to municipalities where the programme has not yet reached all eligible families (those with lower coverage rates) and indicates the areas that need to enhance their oversight of the procedures adopted to manage the [*Bolsa Família*] benefit and registration processes'.[15]

Despite these modifications in Brazil's cash transfer programmes impelled by judicial decisions, implementation of the STF's equality jurisprudence concerning poverty remains imperfect. The Court's decision concerning the flexibilization of the monetary line of extreme poverty for accessing the BPC, dated from 2013, has not yet being implemented. While the National Congress amended the LOAS twice to incorporate the decision from the Supreme Court,[16] the relativization of the BPC line requires specific regulation

[12] Ministry of Social Development and Fight Against Hunger, *Pedido de Acesso à Informação 71003.011320/2025-70* (2025). The Ministry's response was based on data from 10 March 2025.

[13] Ibid.

[14] The decidion from 2020 to which this paragraph referred earlier was a preliminary injunction. The final judgment was delivered by the Court in 2023. See STF, Judgment, *ACO 3.359/DF*, 25 April 2023. Justice rapporteur: Alexandre de Moraes.

[15] Ibid. Translation by the author.

[16] Article 20 §§11 and 11-A allows for the expansion of the family income threshold for accessing the BPC from one quarter to half of the minimum wage per capita through the consideration of other

and a decree for its implementation.[17] However, no such decree has yet been issued.[18]

Poverty is not the only subject area in which the STF has confirmed or expanded positive obligations derived from equality. The Court's wider equality case law reveals an extensive jurisprudence on positive measures,[19] and, in some cases, the creation of new positive obligations for the State derived from the right to equality.[20] In contrast, the creation of new positive measures does not occur in the STF's jurisprudence addressing poverty. In the realm of poverty, its jurisprudence is centred on revising the content and scope of measures already created by the legislature or the executive and on overseeing their application. The STF's most prominent role in poverty adjudication, therefore, lies in revising these policies—particularly positive measures—assessing their constitutionality, and, when appropriate, expanding their scope to cover a wider group of right-holders.

Through its equality case law concerning poverty, the STF often works as a 'subsidiary policymaker', revising the content and scope of anti-poverty policies and positive measures rather than taking action on its own. This conclusion derives from our empirical study and is further supported by the results of the interviews with Justices Mendes and Fachin, who stressed that the primary space for poverty eradication lies in public policies. On the one hand, the essentially subsidiary character of the STF as a policymaker in the field of poverty alleviation points to nuanced expectations of the role and capacity of the tribunal to promote transformative social change on its own. On the other hand, as the decisions of the STF addressing poverty as a matter of equality generally confirm or revise existing public policies (be they anti-poverty policies or positive measures for the promotion of equality to historically marginalized groups), their implementation is arguably facilitated when compared to the implementation challenges faced by courts acting as primary drivers in policymaking.

evidentiary elements of poverty and vulnerability. Article 20-B specifies the meaning of 'other evidentiary elements [of poverty and vulnerability]' and lists three elements that shall be considered: the degree of disability; dependency on others for basic daily activities; and the impact of medical expenses—including costs for health treatments, special foods, diapers, and medications that are not covered by the State—provided these are necessary for health. See Brazil, 'Law No. 8,742', Organic Law of Social Assistance (LOAS), 7 December 1993, Articles 20 §§11 and 11-A and 20-B.

17 Ibid, Article 20 §11, Article 20-B §1; Brazil, 'Law No. 14,176', 22 June 2021, Article 6, single paragraph.

18 *Pedido de Acesso à Informação 71003.011320/2025-70*, *supra* note 12.

19 Tainá Garcia Maia, 'Brazil' in Niels Petersen (ed), *Equality's Guardians: How Courts Conceptualize Equal Protection and Non-Discrimination Guarantees* (Oxford University Press 2025), pp 178–179.

20 For example, in *ADO 26* (2019), the STF found that the state had a duty to criminalize homophobia and transphobia based on the right to equality. See STF, Judgment, *ADO 26/DF*, 13 June 2019. Justice rapporteur: Celso de Mello.

8.1.2 The IACtHR's creation of new positive measures: bringing vulnerability to the centre

The equality case law of the IACtHR addressing poverty has a different scope and faces different implementation challenges compared to that of the STF. Even though the IACtHR has analysed poverty both as a vulnerability and as the main object of its equality assessment in cases against the Brazilian State, it has not examined in depth the content and scope of CCTs or the distributive measures of affirmative action implemented in Brazil. Instead, focusing on an interpretation of effectiveness that requires concrete changes in poverty levels not only nationally but also at the municipal level, the IACtHR has required Brazil to create and implement additional measures and action plans for reversing structural poverty.

The IACtHR has placed great weight on data showing the persistence of poverty nationally and locally. It has ruled that failure to adopt positive measures that are sufficient to reverse chronic poverty violates the right to equality under Article 24 of the ACHR.[21] Effectiveness appears to be the keyword in its assessment, even to the detriment of progressive realization. Hence, the IACtHR subjects the effectiveness of poverty eradication measures to judicial scrutiny to a degree that differs from the STF. Through this approach, it has created new positive obligations for Brazil in relation to the perpetuation of poverty in historically marginalized communities, the *Fireworks* case being the most notable example.

In the *Fireworks Factory* case, the IACtHR required Brazil, among other measures of reparation, to 'design and execute a socio-economic development program, in consultation with the victims and their next of kin, in order to facilitate the insertion of those working in the manufacture of fireworks into other labor markets and to enable the creation of other economic alternatives'.[22] It further specified the scope of the required development programme, which must focus on the lack of employment opportunities, 'especially for young people over 16 years of age and Afro-descendant women living in poverty'.[23] Professional and vocational training courses enabling workers to access different labour markets, such as commerce, agriculture, and data processing, as well as other relevant economic sectors in the region, must be created.

[21] IACtHR, Judgment (Preliminary Objections, Merits, Reparations and Costs), *Workers of the Fireworks Factory in Santo Antônio de Jesus and their Families v Brazil*, 15 July 2020. Series C No 318.

[22] Ibid, para 318.18.

[23] Ibid, para 289.

Furthermore, the programme must design initiatives to prevent school drop-outs caused by child labour. Lastly, it must include awareness campaigns concerning human rights and the risks associated with fireworks production.[24]

Implementation of the IACtHR's orders is ongoing. While the Court gave Brazil a deadline of two years following the notification of the judgment for it to design and execute the abovementioned socio-economic development programme,[25] the latter is still under development. Brazil has placed on the government of the federated state of Bahia the responsibility to lead the efforts in creating and implementing a socio-economic development programme in the municipality in which the explosion of the fireworks factory occurred.[26] The plan is being developed by an intersectoral and interinstitutional working group. Meetings have been organized with members of the federal, state, and municipal public administration; members of the Brazilian judiciary; members of the Public Prosecutor's Office; and civil society.[27] According to the government of Bahia, the plan will include, among other initiatives, 'education and professional training programs for youth and adults, access to credit lines for rural workers and entrepreneurs, and investments in technology, connectivity, agriculture, rural production, and food security'.[28]

While the development of the plan is still ongoing, Brazil has informed the Court that it has already implemented several initiatives to facilitate the integration of workers in markets other than fireworks production.[29] Among other initiatives led by the municipal and federal government are workshops to train rural women in producing regional foods, online courses on female entrepreneurship and financial education, and the creation of spaces equipped with state-of-the-art technology for youth training. The State has also declared that it has taken action to combat child labour and to raise awareness on labour rights and the risks involved in fireworks production. In its words, '[t]hese actions aimed to meet the requirements of the [IACtHR's] ruling and promote the social and economic inclusion of the local population'.[30]

[24] Ibid.

[25] Ibid.

[26] Ministry of Human Rights and Citizenship of Brazil, *Pedido de Informação nº 00105.001332/2025-08 (4786717)* (2025); Brazil, *Corte IDH. Caso Empregados da Fábrica de Fogos de Santo Antônio de Jesus e seus familiares vs. Brasil. Relatório de cumprimento* (2023), p 14.

[27] *Pedido de Informação nº 00105.001332/2025-08 (4786717), supra* note 26.

[28] ba.gov.br, 'Governo da Bahia apresenta avanços na reparação às vítimas e familiares da explosão da fábrica de fogos em Santo Antônio de Jesus' (2024) <https://www.ba.gov.br/justica/noticias/2024-08/17672/governo-da-bahia-apresenta-avancos-na-reparacao-vitimas-e-familiares-da> accessed 20 March 2025. Translation by the author.

[29] Brazil, *Corte IDH. Caso Empregados da Fábrica de Fogos de Santo Antônio de Jesus e seus familiares vs. Brasil. Relatório de cumprimento, supra* note 26, p 14.

[30] Ibid. Translation by the author.

Because the Court's analysis of poverty in the *Fireworks Factory* case was strongly focused on effectiveness within the affected municipality, the expected direct impacts of the implementation of its orders will also be limited regionally. Furthermore, as the Court's assessment did not include an examination of the content and scope of existing anti-poverty public policies in the country, its orders did not discuss Brazil's CCTs and instead required the creation of a new development plan. As no such development plan has yet been created, the impact of this judgment cannot at present be determined.

Nonetheless, the IACtHR's potential impact on poverty alleviation in Brazil extends beyond what can be measured by mere compliance. Through its judgments addressing poverty and socio-economic vulnerability in Brazil, the IACtHR has brought vulnerability, in its multiple dimensions, to the centre of the analysis of state obligations to respect, protect, and promote equality. Notably, it has interpreted failure to reverse historical situations of chronic poverty that affects marginalized communities in the country as a violation of the right to equality. If adopted by domestic courts in Brazil, this understanding would expand the space for the judicialization of poverty and multidimensional vulnerabilities resulting from chronic poverty, positioning the courts not only as subsidiary policymakers but also as primary agents with oversight over failure of the state to effectively reverse structural inequality and chronic poverty.

An illustrative example of how judicial impact can extend beyond formal compliance is the *Hacienda Brasil Verde Workers* case—the first judgment in which the IACtHR addressed poverty in Brazil. In its ruling, the Court did not order Brazil to adopt new positive measures to reverse or mitigate the collective socio-economic vulnerabilities of the groups to which the victims belonged. Nevertheless, when asked for the purposes of this study whether any measures had been adopted in light of that judgment—particularly regarding public policies aimed at reducing the heightened risk of forced labour among socio-economically vulnerable groups—the Brazilian Ministry of Human Rights reported that a new national plan for the eradication of slave labour is currently being developed.[31] This will be the first update in sixteen years.[32] Although this initiative is not a direct consequence of the Court's judgment and does not find in it its main impetus, the Ministry's answer can be read as an indication of the IACtHR's influence on Brazil's policymaking and institutional responses to vulnerabilities (including socio-economic ones).

[31] *Pedido de Informação nº 00105.001332/2025-08 (4786717)*, *supra* note 26.

[32] Ibid; Ministry of Human Rights and Citizenship of Brazil, 'Novo Plano Nacional de Erradicação do Trabalho Escravo está em fase de elaboração, após 16 anos sem atualização' (2025) <https://www.gov.br/mdh/pt-br/assuntos/noticias/2025/janeiro/novo-plano-nacional-de-erradicacao-do-trabalho-escravo-esta-em-fase-de-elaboracao-apos-16-anos-sem-atualizacao> accessed 29 March 2025.

8.2 Judicial tools for bringing equality to the poverty equation: a comparative analysis

The chapter now undertakes a comparative assessment of the tools employed by each court that have enabled them to make the contributions to poverty eradication and alleviation in Brazil identified earlier. Both the STF and the IACtHR have acknowledged inequality as a root cause of chronic poverty affecting historically marginalized groups in Brazil. Notably, both jurisdictions have highlighted the interconnections between the persistence of poverty and the perpetuation of racial inequality in Brazil. In identifying the racial aspect of poverty, the two courts have often addressed poverty as context and reaffirmed the State's obligation to promote equal rights through positive measures. Yet, their approaches differ when poverty is analysed in isolation as the main object of the equality assessment.

Section 8.2.1 identifies the key points of contact between the approaches of the two courts. Next, section 8.2.2 discusses their main differences. Drawing on this comparative analysis and on the courts' impact on poverty eradication and alleviation in Brazil, Section 8.3 proposes recommendations to enhance their capacity to respond to poverty and its links to inequality.

8.2.1 Shared practices: the role of substantive and positive equality in poverty adjudication

The texts of the CF/88 and the ACHR articulate different models of equality protection. The Brazilian Constitution's codification of equality finds its pillar in the general equality clause of Article 5. In turn, the ACHR safeguards this right through both a general equality clause and a non-discrimination clause containing a non-exhaustive list of protected groups. Despite the differences between the models of equality protection adopted in the drafting of each of these instruments, the conceptualization of equality in the jurisprudence of the STF and the IACtHR has been virtually identical. Both courts adopt a substantive conceptualization of equality, from which they derive positive obligations for the state to adopt measures protecting and promoting equality in its various dimensions. This conceptualization of equality directly impacts the spaces for addressing poverty in equality and non-discrimination law.

Through this approach, the two courts have actively addressed distributive claims derived from the right to equality in a context of poverty. This result contrasts significantly with Fredman's findings in her 2011 study on British, US, Canadian, and South African jurisdictions. While Fredman argued for the potential of equality in the field of poverty, she found that there was still a strong reluctance to view equality as generating social rights. She concluded that the right to equality had not yet been sufficiently developed to directly tackle distributive inequalities.[33] This finding is not reflected in our empirical results. In the case law of the STF and the IACtHR, the assessment (and success) of distributive claims is predominant in equality cases related to poverty.

Notwithstanding the predominance of the distributive dimension in their assessment of poverty, the two tribunals have explicitly recognized the implications of poverty in equality as participation, recognition, and transformation, particularly in relation to the persistence of poverty among historically vulnerable groups. The call for structural change to accommodate the specific needs of individuals living in poverty has focused on positive measures that accommodate poverty-related vulnerabilities and increase these individuals' opportunities for recognition and participation in society.

The STF and the IACtHR have an extensive jurisprudence on positive measures to respond to persistent exclusion, marginalization, and stigmatization, including the historical subjugation of specific social groups to monetary and multidimensional poverty. A significant portion of their equality case law on poverty concerns positive obligations, a result that is even more accentuated in the jurisprudence of the STF. By interpreting the right to equality together with socio-economic guarantees, the STF and the IACtHR have addressed distributive inequalities as a direct emanation of the right to equality in its positive dimension. In the jurisprudence of the IACtHR, the interpretation of equality as substantive equality has resulted in the recognition of a positive obligation for states to effectively act towards reversing structural poverty and marginalization that make vulnerable not only social and economic rights but also civil and political rights of individuals living in poverty (eg the right to life in the *Fireworks Factory* case).

Our analysis shows that positive measures are highly relevant for the judicialization of poverty in the two courts. However, this is not the only legal pathway used in the two jurisdictions for addressing poverty through the lens of equality. In the IACtHR, an important strategy for poverty judicialization is to address it as a protected ground. The most notable example is the *Fireworks case*, in which the IACtHR recognized the poor as a protected group whose right to substantive equality must be respected, protected, and fulfilled,

[33] Sandra Fredman, 'The Potential and Limits of an Equal Rights Paradigm in Addressing Poverty' (2011a) 22 Stellenbosch Law Review 566.

including through effective positive measures. Based on this framework, the IACtHR held Brazil accountable for failing to effectively reverse chronic poverty and address its disproportionate effects on the Afro-descendant community in a Brazilian municipality.

A possible explanation for the accommodation of poverty as a matter of the right to equality in these two jurisdictions may be found in the space granted to the eradication of poverty in their legal texts. Overcoming poverty is set as a fundamental objective of the Republic of Brazil in the Constitution and an essential purpose of the OAS under the OAS Charter. Article 3.III of the CF/88 sets eradicating poverty and marginalization and reducing social and regional inequalities as fundamental objectives of the Republic. Therefore, both the eradication of poverty and the reduction of inequalities (as distributive harm and misrecognition) receive constitutional protection as pillars of the State and fundamental aims. In the Inter-American System, eradicating poverty is considered an essential purpose of the OAS under Article 2(g) of the OAS Charter. The OAS Charter qualifies poverty as an obstacle to full democratic development and, accordingly, its eradication as an essential part of promoting and consolidating representative democracy. The Charter also protects social justice as a basis for lasting peace.

It can be argued that these instruments open the door for the potential judicialization of an otherwise political matter by including the eradication of poverty in their legal texts connected to justiciable provisions. Addressing poverty and marginalization becomes not only a duty of political agents but also a legal obligation to which a subjective right corresponds. This expands the space for courts to exercise judicial scrutiny over the state's actions and inactions in fulfilling its duty to promote social justice and poverty eradication.

However, this is not in itself an explanation for the assessment of poverty on multiple equality fronts. An additional explanation for this pattern can be found in the influence of transformative constitutionalism in these jurisdictions. Since 1990 in the case of the IACtHR[34] and at least since 2002 for the STF,[35] these two courts have explicitly interpreted equality as substantive equality, which entails positive duties for the state. Furthermore, both courts have exercised judicial scrutiny over state action and inaction, calling on the

[34] IACtHR, Advisory Opinion, *Exceptions to the exhaustion of domestic remedies (Art. 46(1), 46(2)(a) and 46(2)(b) American Convention on Human Rights, OC-11/90*, 10 September 1990. Series A No 11.

[35] STF, Judgment, *ADI 1.276-2/SP*, 29 August 2002. Justice rapporteur: Ellen Gracie. Before 2002, even if not explicitly using the term to 'substantive equality', the STF had already recognized the constitutionality of measures of affirmative action. Early examples within the temporal scope of this research are *RE 218.461-3 AgR* (1998) and *ADI 1.946-5* (1999). See STF, Judgment, *RE 218.461-3 AgR/SP*, 4 August 1998. Justice rapporteur: Sydney Sanches; STF, Judgment, *ADI 1.946-5/DF*, 29 April 1999. Justice rapporteur: Sydney Sanches.

legislature or public administration, as appropriate, to adopt concrete measures to reverse situations of *de facto* and structural inequalities. Almost half of the equality jurisprudence of the IACtHR concerns positive obligations derived from the equality clauses of the ACHR. Similarly, the STF has consistently adopted the understanding that the right to equality must be interpreted and implemented to respond to *de facto* inequalities. Therefore, positive measures are seen not as exceptions to the principle of equality but rather its very realization. This conceptualization directly impacts the strategies adopted by the two courts for addressing poverty.

This conceptualization of equality and its impact on the interpretation of positive obligations in relation to poverty may be a by-product of the influence of transformative constitutionalism in Latin America. Manuel José Cepeda Espinosa, former Justice at the Colombian Constitutional Court (2001–2009), uses the expression 'responsive law' to refer to the interpretation of law aimed at promoting transformative impact and substantive justice.[36] To trace the intellectual foundations of this concept within Colombian constitutional law, Cepeda draws on the work of Philip Selznick and Philip Nonet, who advanced this notion in contrast to a formalist conception of law.[37] While a formalistic understanding of the law views the latter as essentially autonomous from politics, the model of responsive law is result-oriented: it envisions a legal system that responds to institutional challenges and promotes transformation.[38] The framing of law as responsive has been referred to by different terms in legal scholarship. Von Bogdandy and René Urueña use the term 'transformative constitutionalism'. Transformative constitutionalism is guided, among other aims, by the interpretive objective of transforming realities. Law and courts become two central pathways for solving structural social problems.

Urueña and von Bogdandy identify in the case law of the IACtHR a transformative thrust in relation to structures of violence, weak institutions, and exclusion—the latter being particularly relevant to this book's analysis.[39] Looking at the IACtHR's jurisprudence on amnesty laws, its understanding and protection of victims of human rights violations, and its jurisprudence on women's rights, the authors argue that the Court has embraced an

[36] Manuel José Cepeda Espinosa, 'Responsive Constitutionalism' (2019) 15 Annual Review of Law and Social Science 21.

[37] See Philippe Nonet and Philip Selznick, *Law & Society in Transition: Toward Responsive Law* (2nd edn, Routledge 2017).

[38] Cepeda Espinosa (2019), *supra* note 36. On the link between constitutional law and politics, see also Gilmar Mendes, 'As cortes constitucionais e sua condição de policy-maker: análise jurisprudencial da atuação do Supremo Tribunal Federal' in Tribunal Constitucional (ed), *Estudos em homenagem ao Conselheiro Presidente Joaquim de Sousa Ribeiro*, vol II (Almedina 2019), pp 684–691.

[39] Armin von Bogdandy and René Urueña, 'International Transformative Constitutionalism in Latin America' (2020) 114 American Journal of International Law 403, p 407.

interpretative approach that, at its core, endeavours to foster profound social change.[40] The results of our empirical analysis of the Court's equality case law concerning poverty point to a similar conclusion, with notable examples being the *Hacienda Brasil Verde Workers* case and the *Fireworks Factory* case.

Both the STF and the IACtHR have repeatedly recognized the legal obligation of the state to adopt concrete measures for responding to the challenges of structural and historical discrimination, so that the law promotes a structural transformation. This objective guides the very interpretation of the law. In *ADI 3.330*, concerning the scholarship programme PROUNI, the Justice *rapporteur*, Ayres Britto, stressed the importance of law as an instrument for promoting positive equality and transforming social unbalances.[41] When faced with pervasive factual inequalities, the law may institute juridical inequalities through positive measures benefiting disadvantaged groups in order to counterbalance the weight of those factual inequalities. Justice Britto explained positive measures as a logical requirement for breaking down relations of dominance in the political, social, economic, and cultural realm and, accordingly, 'setting society in the axis of a widespread horizontality'.[42] He argued that it is hardly surprising that the law might confer advantages to offset prior and persistent factual disadvantages, since it typically operates by drawing distinctions.[43] The Justice concluded that 'law exists to impose a compensatory inequality when faced with an inequality that disturbs harmony and social balance consistently'.[44] In other words, law serves 'as an instrument for social rebalancing'.[45]

The transformative or responsive dimension of constitutional law was the object of analysis by Justice Marco Aurélio in his vote in *ADPF 186* concerning the institution of a racial quota system in UnB. Justice Aurélio explained that the drafters of the 1988 Constitution were aware that equality had been safeguarded throughout Brazil's constitutional history in a formal, rather than transformative, manner. The 1988 Constitution, also known as the Citizen Constitution, changed this scenario. Equality was no longer guaranteed in a static, essentially negative manner. Instead, law would safeguard 'effective' or 'dynamic' equality, thereby requiring action. According to the Justice, by making use of verbs that call for action—such as 'build', 'guarantee', 'eradicate', and 'promote'—Article 3 of the 1988 Constitution sought

[40] Ibid, p 413.
[41] STF, Judgment, *ADI 3.330/DF*, 03 May 2012. Justice rapporteur: Ayres Britto, pp 25–26, paras 31–33.
[42] Ibid, p 26, para 33. Translation by the author.
[43] Ibid, p 27, para 34. Translation by the author.
[44] Ibid. Translation by the author.
[45] Ibid. Translation by the author.

to effect social transformation. The adoption of this language shows that it is not sufficient to simply refrain from discriminating. An affirmative attitude is needed for equal opportunities to be made feasible.[46] Justice Aurélio concluded that affirmative action was necessary for redressing the historical debt owed to vulnerable groups in Brazil and for promoting equality. He asserted that 'over the years, State neutrality has proven to be a huge failure'. Therefore, he argued for the urgent implementation of a 'program for the underprivileged' capable of 'taking boys and girls off the streets' and 'promoting education'.[47]

Unsurprisingly, the transformative role of constitutional law was also discussed by the STF's bench in another leading case concerning affirmative action, *ADC 41* (2017). Like Justice Marco Aurélio in the aforementioned vote, Justice Cármen Lúcia identified in the words of Article 3 of the CF/88 an obligation for the State to adopt 'an active conduct' towards implementing the fundamental principles listed in that provision.[48] The Justice recalled her own writings in an article published in 1996, in which she had read in Article 3 of the CF/88 the determination that law would be an instrument through which an authentically democratic republic would be concretized. It was under this precept that Article 3 spelled out the fundamental objectives of the Republic of building a new society guided by the constitutional pillars of the promotion of equality and the eradication of poverty, which, in the understanding of Justice Cármen Lúcia, is one of the most significant sources of discrimination and prejudice in the State.[49]

Justice Fachin upheld a similar understanding in the interview conducted for this study. He argued that, in Brazilian constitutionalism, the key to understanding the role of law in the eradication of poverty lies in what he calls the 'double memory' of the CF/88.[50] On the one hand, the CF/88 is committed to 'overcoming the past, to the end of the dictatorship, and to the restoration of democracy with public spaces open to popular participation, via representation or direct action'.[51] On the other hand, it rests on 'the commitment to the future, with the transformation of a social, economic, and cultural scenario marked by injustice, inequality, and discrimination'.[52] He explained that

[46] Vote of Justice Luiz Fux in STF, Judgment, *ADPF 186/DF*, 26 April 2012. Rapporteur: Ricardo Lewandowski, pp 210–213.

[47] Ibid, p 215. Translation by the author.

[48] *ADC 41/DF (2017)*, p 171. Translation by the author.

[49] Ibid, pp 171–173. See Cármen Lúcia Antunes Rocha, 'Ação afirmativa: O conteúdo democrático do princípio da igualdade jurídica' (1996) 33 Revista de Informação Legislativa 283, pp 289–290.

[50] Interview with Justice Edson Fachin, question 8, p 5. Translation by the author.

[51] Ibid.

[52] Ibid.

'[t]his memorial has the nature of a binding norm, and every judge in Brazil is a magistrate of the Constitution'.[53]

The influence of transformative constitutionalism on the equality jurisprudence of the STF and the IACtHR helps explain the relative openness of both courts to addressing poverty through the lens of equality, including distributive equality. Whether these courts have effectively and sufficiently fulfilled the transformative promises articulated in the Brazilian Constitution of 1988 and the ACHR and, at times, in their own decisions, is another question.[54] Yet, what is clear in our empirical study is that both the STF and the IACtHR adhere to a conceptualization of equality as substantive and positive, embracing positive measures as a necessary tool for promoting equality and dismantling historical and structural inequalities. This conceptualization of equality and the relevance of positive measures in their jurisprudence opens spaces for judicial scrutiny of the interconnections between poverty and inequality and has had concrete impacts on Brazilian public policy.

Through multiple tools—particularly the approaches of addressing poverty and economic vulnerability as a suspect classification, as context, and as grounds for positive measures derived from equality—the two courts have been able to confront the perpetuation of poverty in Brazil. Both courts have assessed the actions of the State—including positive measures—addressing the perpetuation not only of multidimensional poverty but also monetary poverty in the country. Sociological studies and statistical data were central to identifying the evolution of poverty in Brazil and in relation to protected groups, particularly racial groups.

Through these approaches, the two courts have addressed the distributive dimension of inequalities related to poverty in Brazil, particularly in relation to the black and brown communities in the State. Notwithstanding these shared practices, important differences remain between the approaches adopted by the STF and the IACtHR, which impact their ability to assess the perpetuation of poverty cycles. These differences are the focus of section 8.1.3 below.

8.2.2 Two central differences

8.2.2.1 Poverty and the transformative dimension of equality

Chapter 6 showed that one of the strategies the STF uses for addressing poverty as a matter of equality is the consideration of economic status as a suspect

[53] Ibid.

[54] For a critical analysis concerning the STF, see Werneck Arguelhes (2020), *supra* note 5.

classification. However, this strategy has been mainly applied to disputes in which the Court is called upon to revise a public policy already implemented by the State. More resistance appears to be encountered when the Court is called upon to revise a universalist policy (ie a public policy applied to the general population in Brazil) and evaluate its impact on the poor.

The most illustrative example is probably *ADPF 541* (2018), in which the STF was asked to analyse the constitutionality of cancelling the voter registration of citizens who had not submitted their fingerprints as part of the recently implemented biometric voter registration system.[55] The Brazilian Socialist Party, acting as the applicant, observed that the electoral identity cards of at least 3.6 million voters had been cancelled as a result of this regulation. This happened in a context in which the last presidential election, which had occurred in 2014, had approximately 3.5 million votes separating the elected president and the second frontrunner. The applicant argued that the cancellation of electoral identity cards, while apparently neutral, disproportionately impacted the poorest and most socio-economically vulnerable.[56] The dispute was decided by the STF a few days before the 2018 presidential elections.

The STF disagreed with the applicant. In a vote adopted by the majority, the Justice *rapporteur*, Roberto Barroso, found that the impugned measure aimed to enhance security in the electoral process. On the one hand, he recognized that this procedure affected the poor to a higher degree. On the other hand, he concluded this also held true for a series of other bureaucratic procedures. According to the Justice, it would always be possible to argue that such a measure burdens the poorest[57] to a greater degree: 'because they have fewer resources, because it is more difficult for them to be discharged from their professional duties by their employees, because they have less access to information, or even because they face more difficulties to comprehend or tackle state bureaucracy'.[58] Justice Barroso gave as an example military enlistment. In Brazil, military enlistment (although not military service) is mandatory for men aged 18. Access to a series of services, including registration as a voter, is only accessible for a man upon proving that he presented himself for enlistment. Still, the Justice asserted, no one argues that this procedure violates the right to vote by disproportionately impacting the poor.[59] He concluded that it would only be possible to question the validity of the cancellation of electoral registration cards if the applicant had demonstrated that this procedure had

[55] STF, Judgment, *ADPF 541/DF*, 26 September 2018. Justice rapporteur: Roberto Barroso.
[56] Ibid, pp 24–25, paras 4–5.
[57] In the original language, 'hipossuficiente'.
[58] *ADPF 541/DF* (2018), *supra* note 55, pp 24–25, para 4. Translation by the author.
[59] Ibid.

been conducted to prevent specific groups of citizens from taking part in the results of the election or to suppress votes to the detriment of specific political parties.[60] The claim was held inadmissible because there was no such evidence in the case.[61]

Justice Barroso also analysed the data presented by the Socialist Party showing that 53% of the cancellations of electoral registration cards had taken place in the North and Northeast regions of Brazil, the poorest regions in the country. Only 20% of the cancellations occurred in the Southeast, the country's richest region. The Justice discussed this data by focusing on one specific case: the State of Bahia, which accounted for the largest number of cancelled electoral identity cards (583,333 cancellations). He noted that the Electoral Justice in Bahia had made announcements in several media outlets to remind the population to undertake biometric registration. Such announcements appeared in tax, energy, and water bills, and were also disseminated during football matches of Bahia's two biggest clubs, on radio and TV, and in newspapers and posters, among other platforms. A special opening time was held for biometric registration, and thirty-four additional locations to conduct the registration were established in the capital. Therefore, the Justice concluded that it could not be said that the population had not been informed of the requirement to register, under penalty of having their voter cards cancelled, nor that the State had failed to take all reasonable measures to ensure registration was accessible to all.[62] Lastly, the Justice found that the applicant had not proved that the measure was unnecessary or disproportionate in the strict sense. He asserted that summoning every person whose card would be cancelled would be too onerous and complex for the public administration.[63]

The majority of the bench adopted the vote of the *rapporteur*. Two dissenting Justices, Lewandowski and Marco Aurélio, voted in favour of the applicant. Justice Lewandowski highlighted that the great majority of the voters whose electoral cards had been cancelled lived in a situation of economic vulnerability and resided in the country's most remote areas. Furthermore, given the number of cancelled electoral cards—a number equivalent to the total number of voters in many European countries—the measure had the potential to significantly impact the elections.[64]

The equality claim presented by the Socialist Party referred to participative equality. The Party asked the Supreme Court to recognize different constraints

[60] Ibid, p 31, para 20.
[61] Ibid.
[62] Ibid, pp 31–32, para 23. Translation by the author.
[63] Ibid, pp 32–34.
[64] Ibid, pp 97–103.

faced by individuals living in poverty and socio-economic vulnerability. It also asked the Court to accommodate those differences by removing central constraints and obstacles to the realization of the right to vote. Therefore, the claim touched on transformative equality as a means for realizing participative equality. As Fredman explains, the transformative dimension of equality allows individuals to break free from constraints without imposing predetermined expectations on how they exercise their agency.[65] When the bench focuses on whether the population was informed of the need to conduct biometric registration, it focuses on the agency approach rather than the structures that might perpetuate differences based on socio-economic condition. The Justice *rapporteur* explicitly recognized the greater difficulty faced by the poor in carrying out bureaucratic procedures when these require travelling to locations far from home or work, to comply with certain formal requirements, or taking time off work to solve pending administrative matters.[66] Nonetheless, this was not recognized as disproportionate impact for the purposes of the right to equality, and thus did not warrant measures tailored to the specific disadvantages of this group.

An analysis guided by transformative equality could have led to the same outcome reached by the majority in *ADPF 541* (2018), provided it demonstrated that the State had identified the affected group's vulnerabilities and taken reasonable steps to accommodate their specific needs. However, even if the outcome of the dispute remained unchanged, explicitly engaging in such an assessment would imply recognizing the State's duty to adopt a vulnerability-sensitive approach and implement measures capable of overcoming the barriers to participation arising from the disadvantages and marginalization of the poor. It would also subject the adequacy of the State's actions—and its failure to accommodate difference—to judicial scrutiny.

ADPF 541 (2018) can be read as an indication that transformative claims, in contrast to purely distributive claims, remain unlikely to succeed in cases in which poverty alone (ie disconnected from factors of intersectionality) is the suspect classification. Future research should investigate this hypothesis further, as there are not enough cases of indirect discrimination based on economic status to identify a clear pattern in the STF's jurisprudence. In contrast, the IACtHR addresses the transformative dimension of equality when assessing positive obligations to tackle poverty or economic status as a ground of differentiation on its own, whether or not in association with intersectionality.

[65] Fredman (2011a), *supra* note 33, p 580, pp 14–15.
[66] *ADPF 541/DF* (2018), *supra* note 55.

8.2.2.2 Effectiveness under judicial scrutiny

The IACtHR's assessment of positive obligations derived from substantive equality to address poverty incorporates a strong assessment of effectiveness. The latter plays a central role in the IACtHR's analysis of positive obligations to address poverty to a degree that contrasts with the approach of the STF. To grasp the distinction between the approaches adopted by each of the two courts in assessing compliance with the positive obligations to address poverty, a comparison between the *Fireworks Factory* case and *MI 7.300* (2021) is particularly useful.

Both cases involved a context of chronic poverty and had as their object the measures the Brazilian Federal State had taken to address poverty. However, in the *Fireworks Factory* case, the IACtHR focused its analysis on the persistence of poverty within a specific municipality, without explicitly engaging with data on the reduction of poverty in Brazil more broadly. The fact that the explosion at the fireworks factory occurred in 1998 does not sufficiently explain the absence of such data in the judgment, especially given that the Court's finding regarding the persistence of poverty in the municipality relied on IBGE data from 2010.

In states with chronic poverty, it is axiomatic that poverty will persist in some municipalities even if a state implements highly effective anti-poverty public policies. If a state's obligation to address poverty in accordance with the right to equality is to be assessed simply as a matter of effective reduction of poverty in all municipalities simultaneously, two conclusions emerge. First, the notion of progressiveness in realizing the positive dimension of human rights is deprived of meaning. Second, one faces the risk of concluding that every state with chronic poverty is automatically in continuous violation of the right to equality until poverty is effectively reduced in the territory as a whole, regardless of the policies implemented in the meantime.

These consequences might impact human rights protection. First, if deterrence is considered an objective of court rulings, the focus on effectiveness separated from the consideration of progressiveness might produce a negative effect, as the deterrence argument of human rights prosecution loses its point. Deterrence is unlikely to take place if states facing chronic poverty are automatically found to be in continuous violation of the right to equality until chronic poverty can no longer be found in any municipality. Second, a focus on effectiveness that is disconnected from progressiveness may run counter to transformative constitutionalism. Even if states comply with court orders and develop socio-economic programmes targeting the development and reduction of poverty in a specific municipality, the results are still highly casuistic. State compliance with the obligation to effectively address poverty cycles in one specific municipality might take priority over a wider state policy to address poverty throughout the nation and equitably among its regions and municipalities. Such an outcome is unlikely to produce structural modifications in the historical persistence of poverty in the state and even in the region in question—as the structures that contribute to the perpetuation of poverty often transcend one single municipality—and might lead to more casuistic decisions with regard to which municipalities should be prioritized in the allocation of anti-poverty policies. Such an approach might also exacerbate marginalization, as the most vulnerable groups may face greater obstacles appearing before courts and presenting the context of their specific municipality to the Inter-American System of Human Rights.

A contrast to the focus on effectiveness disconnected from progressiveness is the STF's approach in *MI 7.300* (2021).[67] The case was taken to the Supreme Court by Alexandre da Silva Portuguez, a homeless man with moderate mental disability and epilepsy living in unemployment and receiving the *Bolsa Família*. The petitioner called upon the STF to analyse the omission of Brazil to implement the right to universal basic income.

Universal basic income was guaranteed by law in Brazil in January 2004 through a statute that provided that every Brazilian residing in the country and every foreigner residing there for five years or more would be entitled to a universal and unconditional basic income, regardless of their socio-economic condition. The statute determined that the inclusiveness of the universal basic income was to be expanded in phases, having first as its priority the most needed strata of the population. In addition, it determined that the value of the benefit should be sufficient to cover citizens' minimum expenses in terms of food, education, and health, taking into account the country's degree of development and the State's budgetary capacity.[68] However, more than seventeen years after the law was promulgated, the right to a universal basic income had still not been implemented.

The Justice *rapporteur* in *MI 7.300* (2021) was Gilmar Mendes. In a decision adopted by the majority of the bench, Justice Mendes observed that the Federal government regarded the PBF as the first stage of the universal basic income.[69] He also noted that, in its inception, the PBF poverty line was equivalent to a little over one-third of the minimum wage. However, by 2021, it was equivalent to only 16.18% of the minimum wage. This change indicated a significative downgrade of the PBF poverty line, equating to a *de facto*

[67] STF, Judgment, *MI 7.300/DF*, 27 April 2021. Justice rapporteur: Gilmar Mendes.
[68] Brazil, 'Law No. 10,835', 8 January 2004, Article 1.
[69] *MI 7.300/DF* (2021), *supra* note 67, p 45.

exclusion of millions of people who would be considered poor under international thresholds.[70] In the Justice's view, this indicated a regression in the fight against poverty in Brazil, further confirmed by the analysis of the updated *Bolsa Família* benefit values applicable in 2021. The value of the *Bolsa Família* basic benefit had remained unchanged since 2018 (see Chapter 2). While in 2004, the benefit represented 19.23% of the minimum wage, it represented only 8.09% of the minimum wage in 2021.[71]

Chapters 2 and 5 have already discussed the insufficiency of the updates of the *Bolsa Família* benefits and the PBF poverty line. Justice Mendes read this insufficiency in *MI 7.300* as evidence that individuals living below the extreme poverty line 'have lost more than half of their economic capacity to provide subsistence for themselves and their families, which increases the level of inequality between the poorest strata of the population and those who earn only a minimum wage'.[72] The Justice concluded that, despite the PBF, there was insufficient protection with regard to fighting poverty and extreme poverty in Brazil, 'especially in relation to the most vulnerable portion of the Brazilian population'.[73] To reach this conclusion, it was insufficient for the STF to be provided with data showing the persistence of poverty in the country or in its more vulnerable regions. Instead, having been asked to determine the extent to which Brazil had fulfilled its positive obligations to address poverty, the STF engaged in a detailed and thorough analysis of the policies adopted in the country. Included in its analysis was an assessment of the setbacks in Brazil's anti-poverty public policies over the years and data from the IBGE on the state of poverty in the country.

Justice Mendes asserted that cash transfer programmes fundamentally contributed to the reduction of inequality that subtracted dignity from the lives of millions of Brazilians and, consequently, inhibited 'the capacity for political engagement and the enjoyment of the most relevant constitutional rights and freedoms'.[74] He also contended that the executive and the legislature were better positioned, given their nature as majoritarian institutions, to determine which of the community's legitimate interests were to be prioritized given the scarcity of public funds. Were the Supreme Court to safeguard through judicial means the basic universal income without any regard to progressiveness and budgetary planning, it would, at once, 'exceed the limits that, over more than 20 years, have been developed by its jurisprudence in the context of

[70] Ibid, p 46.
[71] Ibid, p 51.
[72] Ibid.
[73] Ibid.
[74] Ibid, p 61. Translation by the author.

injunctions and infringe the progressiveness enunciated by the Legislature for the implementation of [this] monetary benefit'.[75]

While recognizing the unconstitutionality of the State's omission, Justice Mendes asserted that 'the implementation of public policies unilaterally by the Judiciary, replacing the political scrutiny of elected representatives, can lead to a state of affairs even more unconstitutional than the simple lack of regulatory norm'.[76] Therefore, in a vote that was adopted by the Court's majority, he found that the values of the PBF should be 'updated to adapt to the economic and social reality in the post-pandemic period'.[77] The STF called upon the legislature and the executive to adopt the necessary measures to update the *Bolsa Família* benefits and improve the cash transfer programmes in force, especially the universal basic income regulated by Law No 10,835/2004, unifying these systems if possible. Furthermore, it determined that, in the fiscal year following the judgment, the President of the Republic was to determine the value of the basic universal income benefit for the segment of the population living in socio-economic vulnerability.[78]

While the STF was not deciding an equality claim in this specific dispute, this decision highlights how a court can consider effectiveness and progressiveness as complementary concepts when assessing the state's positive obligations derived from human rights. Furthermore, while the focus of the decision was on social and economic rights, the reasoning is applicable to equality assessments.

8.3 Paths forward: addressing poverty in Brazil through judicial adjudication

This section proposes combining elements of the STF and IACtHR approaches to address poverty in Brazil and tackle its interconnections with persistent forms of inequality. More specifically, it recommends two adjustments in the courts' application of judicial strategies for addressing poverty through equality. First, a polycentric approach to distributive claims is fundamental for considering the multidimensional oppressions that reinforce poverty cycles and distributive harms associated with poverty. Second, progressiveness

75 Ibid, p 66.
76 Ibid.
77 Ibid, p 51.
78 Ibid, p 2.

should be considered when assessing compliance with the positive obligations derived from substantive equality in addressing poverty.

8.3.1 A polycentric approach to distributive claims

The empirical analysis showed that the STF and the IACtHR have an equality jurisprudence strongly focused on substantive equality. They have consistently upheld that positive obligations emanate from the right to equality and constitute its very realization by tackling *de facto* inequalities. Therefore, equality is interpreted not only as entailing an obligation not to interfere with rights based on discriminatory distinctions but also as an obligation to adopt concrete measures to promote *de facto* equality and reverse structural discrimination. Failure to do so may be subject to the judicial scrutiny of both courts.

In addition, both the STF and the IACtHR have applied a multidimensional approach to equality. This conceptualization of the right to equality has expanded the opportunities for the STF and the IACtHR to address the interlocking structural factors that perpetuate cycles of poverty in Brazil. Notably, the two courts have assessed poverty in its interconnections with race, recalling Brazil's past with slavery and recognizing the scars of the latter in the manifestations of present-day inequalities and disadvantages, including poverty, in the country. Therefore, the application of an equality approach to poverty has provided the STF and the IACtHR with a legal tool to address the intersectionalities present in the manifestation and perpetuation of poverty and the multidimensional oppressions related to poverty in Brazil.

The study shows that distributive equality remains the dimension mostly used in the jurisprudence of the STF and the IACtHR when addressing poverty. Despite this predominance, it is not unusual for both courts to address poverty through the lens of equality as a multidimensional concept. For example, a polycentric approach to distributive claims has been adopted by the STF in *ADPF 186* (2012) and *ADC 41* (2017), two leading cases concerning affirmative action for racial groups disproportionately represented among those living in monetary and multidimensional poverty in Brazil. The STF found that affirmative action was not only a distributive measure addressing individual disadvantages in opportunities but also a measure with the potential to foster interpersonal recognition and self-value, modify power structures, and incorporate diversity and plurality in institutions. As a result, institutions would be better able to understand and address processes that reproduce and perpetuate oppressions. The STF thus transcended the limits of a purely distributive analysis by assessing the dialogue between distributive remedies and the promotion of recognition. It also explicitly acknowledged the potential of affirmative action measures for promoting structural change and increasing parity in participation.

However, when poverty is argued as an independent factor of vulnerability, the STF has been more resistant to address transformative claims—for example, when assessing the claim of indirect discrimination in the case of the cancellation of electoral identity cards and the allegation that the condition of vulnerability of poor individuals should be accommodated in the procedures concerning biometric registration for electoral purposes. This book recommends expanding the application of a multidimensional equality analysis in poverty cases, including in disputes with a distributive claim as their main object.

The benefits of distributive measures will likely be curtailed when social structures that perpetuate inequalities remain unchanged. When unaccompanied by a consideration of further dimensions of inequality, the single focus on distributive harm and distributive remedies may offer partial and insufficient answers to poverty, therefore falling short of their objective of eradicating poverty and the inequalities related to poverty. Therefore, a polycentric approach to distributive claims has the potential to address the multidimensional nature of poverty more effectively and sustainably.

8.3.2 Effectiveness and progressive realization: complementary or opposing concepts?

This book also argues for caution in assessing compliance with the positive duties derived from equality through a focus on the effectiveness of the state in addressing poverty in a specific region or municipality. The assessment of effectiveness and efficiency should take place regionally when there is an indication of direct or indirect discrimination based on residency. One example is *ACO 3.359 MC-Ref* (2020), in which the STF was called upon to analyse the concentration of cuts in the PBF in the Northeast region of Brazil. The regional focus could also be applied to states with low poverty levels in which poverty is a regional rather than a national phenomenon. However, in Brazil, poverty is still a national phenomenon that particularly affects certain regions of the country (such as the North and the Northeast regions) and persists in a myriad of municipalities. In this context, the finding of a violation of equality in connection with the duty to effectively reduce poverty should not be based exclusively on evidence of the persistence of poverty in singularized municipalities. A different understanding would lead to the finding of automatic and continuous violation of the right to equality until Brazil (or other countries with similar socio-economic indicators) has completely eradicated extreme and chronic poverty from its territory.

The IACtHR's reasoning in the *Fireworks Factory* case is sound: transformative equality requires states to take measures to address the situation of structural discrimination perpetuating a condition in which certain individuals have no option but to accept precarious and often dangerous or exploitative working conditions and pay.[79] This book does not challenge the application of this transformative approach to the interpretation of the right to equality in poverty traps. What it challenges is the criteria used to evaluate whether the state has complied with this obligation, which focuses on effectiveness with little incorporation of the 'progressive realization' approach and focuses on regionalism unconnected to indications of indirect discrimination based on residency.

The consideration of progressiveness aligns with the text of the CF/88 and the ACHR in their treatment of poverty. An assessment of efficiency through the lens of progressiveness may also contribute to higher rates of compliance and deterrence by establishing achievable legal obligations and demanding a detailed analysis of the policies instituted and their effects in the country. In addition, it provides more space for manoeuvre for the legislature and the executive to formulate plans of action for addressing poverty while considering budgetary possibilities and the manifestations of poverty in society—for example, regional specificities and intersectionalities, among other factors. In this sense, courts may act as catalysts for policymaking,[80] but not as autonomous and self-sufficient policymakers in anti-poverty matters. Here, it is important to recall that progressive realization does not equate to ineffectiveness or undue and unlimited delay in addressing poverty and its interconnections with inequality.

8.4 Concluding remarks

The IACtHR and the STF have adopted a substantive conceptualization of equality, from which they have derived positive obligations for the state to

[79] For a similar analysis of poverty traps in the context of gender, see Sandra Fredman, 'Women and Poverty—A Human Rights Approach' (2016b) 24 African Journal of International and Comparative Law 494, p 500.

[80] For an analysis of the potential and limitation of courts as policymakers based on the case of the STF, see Mendes (2019), *supra* note 38.

adopt measures protecting and promoting equality in its various dimensions. The conceptualization of equality as positive equality has been central to the jurisprudence of the two courts concerning poverty and its impact on Brazil's public policies for poverty eradication and alleviation. Through this approach, both courts have been active in addressing distributive claims derived from the right to equality in a context of poverty, particularly at the interconnection between class and race in Brazil. By addressing distributive inequalities related to poverty, the IACtHR and particularly the STF have impacted public policies in Brazil on poverty alleviation, poverty eradication, and affirmative action with effects on monetary and multidimensional poverty.

In addition, the STF and the IACtHR have gone beyond distributive equality in their analysis of poverty, even though this dimension remains predominant in their case law. Both have explicitly recognized the implications of poverty for equality as participation and recognition, particularly in relation to the persistence of poverty among historically vulnerable groups. The call for structural change to accommodate the differences of individuals living in poverty has mainly focused on positive measures that address vulnerabilities arising from poverty and increase opportunities for recognition and participation in society.

In the jurisprudence of the STF, the transformative dimension is more often discussed in cases of intersectionality, in which structural change is required to reverse the perpetuation of structural poverty that disproportionately affects a vulnerable group. In the jurisprudence of the IACtHR, the transformative dimension stems from the assessment of compliance with the positive obligations derived from equality to address poverty or economic status as a ground of differentiation on its own, whether or not in association with intersectionality.

Another central difference between the two jurisdictions is the balancing between effectiveness and progressiveness in assessing the state's compliance with the positive obligation to eradicate poverty in accordance with the right to equality. While the IACtHR places a stronger focus on effectiveness and engages in limited dialogue with the public policies implemented nationally in Brazil, the STF's assessment is more connected to the principle of progressiveness. The STF brings to close scrutiny the content and scope of anti-poverty policies implemented by the State, including cash transfer programmes.

This chapter proposed combining the approaches of the two courts to increase the space for addressing the manifestations of poverty and oppressions faced by the poor. More specifically, it proposes two adjustments in the judicial strategies of the STF and the IACtHR. First, a polycentric approach to distributive claims concerning poverty. Second, balancing the progressiveness approach to the assessment of state compliance with the positive duties derived from equality to address poverty, on the one hand, and the requirement of effectiveness, on the other, in close dialogue with the content and scope of the public policies effectively implemented by the State.

9
Conclusion

> *Human rights are not just about prisoners of conscience, they are also about prisoners of poverty. Human rights are not just about torture, they are also about avoidable deaths from preventable health conditions.*
>
> **—Paul Hunt, UN Special Rapporteur**[1]

Thomas Piketty wrote that '[e]very human society must justify its inequalities: unless reasons for them are found, the whole political and social edifice stands in danger of collapse'.[2] He argues that every historical period creates contradictory discourses and ideologies designed to justify either the inequalities already present or those that certain groups believe should exist.[3] These discourses and ideologies, in turn, shape economic, social, and political rules—and, here I add, legal rules and interpretations. From the tension among these conflicting discourses—simultaneously economic, social, and political—dominant narratives emerge, which in turn reinforce and sustain the prevailing system of inequality.[4]

This book has challenged the discourses that separate poverty and inequality in law and has shown how institutions, including two Latin American courts, have built alternative narratives that recognize their interconnections. These narratives have questioned, even if only to a limited degree, the political, social, and legal edifice that sustains the unequal realization of fundamental rights based on one's economic condition alone or in intersection with other grounds of vulnerability. This analysis has centred on Brazil, situating this case study within its postcolonial and post-slavery context, which still profoundly marks the manifestations of poverty in the country at present.

This chapter presents the book's main conclusions. First, it examines the polycentric interactions between poverty and inequality and assesses whether an equality approach to poverty becomes tautological in jurisdictions where

[1] Paul Hunt, *Statement to the Panel on Maternal Mortality and the Human Rights of Women* (2008).
[2] Thomas Piketty, *Capital and Ideology* (Harvard University Press 2020), p 1.
[3] Ibid.
[4] Ibid.

Judging Poverty and Inequality in Brazil. Tainá Garcia Maia, Oxford University Press. © Tainá Garcia Maia 2026.
DOI: 10.1093/oso/9780198994022.003.0009

socio-economic rights are justiciable, such as the STF and the IACtHR (section 9.1). Next, it turns to the book's case study, summarizing the main conclusions of the empirical analysis (section 9.2). Finally, while recognizing the potential of the approaches developed by the STF and the IACtHR to address the persistent interconnections between poverty and inequality, the chapter discusses the limits of the law to promote, on its own, social change, including poverty eradication and mitigation of the persistent interconnections between poverty and inequality (section 9.3).

9.1 The equality pleonasm?

Poverty may be understood as critical lack of income, in which case one is referring to monetary poverty, and may be identified through a poverty line. It may also be defined in a multidimensional manner as deprivations of capabilities or basic needs broader than income (eg access to education and health). Furthermore, it can be defined in absolute terms through the establishment of an absolute poverty line (eg the World Bank's IPL or Brazil's Programme *Bolsa Família* (PBF) line) or be based on a relative standard, which can be monetary (such as the OECD line) or not.[5] Finally, poverty may refer to an individual's self-perception of their ability to cover daily expenses and household maintenance, personal satisfaction with the fulfilment of basic needs, or other socio-cultural aspirations.[6]

Under a multidimensional and relative conceptualization, poverty can refer to hindrances to one's capabilities to lead a socially desirable standard of living, a concept defined with reference to the parameters accepted by a given society at a given time. The notion behind this definition is that the very concept of social needs evolves with changing times and social context. For example, what is perceived today in Finland as important social needs guaranteed to every person may differ greatly from what is considered important social needs in Haiti at present. The bar of important social needs for leading a good life and participating in social and political life might be lower in the context of generalized deprivation of very basic needs. In contrast, this bar may be quite high in a society experiencing a stable economy,

[5] See Rômulo Paes-Sousa and Paulo de Martino Jannuzzi, 'Going Beyond the Eradication of Extreme Poverty: Debating the Sustainable Development Goals in Brazil' in Alberto D Cimadamore, Gabriele Koehler, and Thomas Pogge (eds), *Poverty and the Millennium Development Goals: A Critical Look Forward* (Zed Books 2016), p 114.

[6] See ibid, p 116; Niels Petersen, 'Avoiding the Common-Wisdom Fallacy: The Role of Social Sciences in Constitutional Adjudication' (2013) 11 International Journal of Constitutional Law 294, pp 316–317.

a high gross domestic product per capita, and a high median income, among other factors.

This plurality of definitions is not a problem per se, and it is not necessary—nor advisable—for scholarly work to assume any one definition as the best *a priori*. Different measurements serve different purposes. Quoting Paes-Sousa and Jannuzzi, 'a multi-sectorial strategy to overcome poverty requires a multi-dimensional perspective to evaluate its effects'.[7]

Similarly, equality can be conceptualized in different ways. If conceptualized as formal equality, it requires consistency of treatment before the law and is often represented by the Aristotelian formula of treating equals equally. However, this conceptualization is criticized for its circularity and focuses on *de jure*, not *de facto*, inequalities. It disregards past disadvantage and leaves untouched structures that perpetuate injustices (which may, at times, include even the law itself). Considering these limitations, the concept of substantive equality emerges, suggesting that granting equal treatment before the law is insufficient to realize the right to equality. Unequal treatment may be necessary to equalize individuals and groups situated in very different positions and subject to very different forms of privileges and oppressions. Since the late twentieth century and more clearly throughout the twenty-first century, the incorporation of substantive equality in human rights law can be identified in the text of international human rights treaties and the work of human rights bodies.[8]

Different theories have been proposed to delimit the content and scope of substantive equality. The latter has been interpreted as equality of opportunities, equality of results, and even as a right guided and delimited by the principle of dignity. This book adopts the conceptualization of substantive equality as a multidimensional concept addressing injustices rooted in maldistribution and misrecognition, as defined by Fraser. In addition, it adopts Sandra Fredman's analytical framework for transformative equality and recognizes that substantive equality pursues four overlapping aims: breaking cycles of disadvantage (the distributive dimension); addressing stigma, stereotyping, non-physical violence, and other manifestations of misrecognition (the

[7] Paes-Sousa and Jannuzzi (2016), *supra* note 5, p 116.

[8] eg International Convention on the Elimination of All Forms of Racial Discrimination (1965); Convention on the Elimination of All Forms of Discrimination Against Women (1979); Convention on the Rights of Persons with Disabilities (2006); UN Committee on the Elimination of All Forms of Discrimination Against Women (CEDAW), 'General recommendation No. 25 on article 4, paragraph 1, of the Convention on the Elimination of All Forms of Discrimination against Women, on temporary special measures', 2004; UN Committee on the Elimination of Racial Discrimination (CERD), 'General Recommendation no. 32, The meaning and scope of special measures in the International Convention on the Elimination of All Forms of Racial Discrimination', CERD/C/GC/32, 24 September 2009.

recognition dimension); dismantling obstacles to social and political participation (the participative dimension); and promoting structural change, including by accommodating difference where appropriate (the transformative dimension). This multidimensional understanding sheds light on the multiple interconnections between poverty and inequality.

Poverty is multifaceted and may be rooted in and reinforced by structural discrimination. Discrimination on some grounds (such as race, gender, and gender identity) may operate as a cause for the perpetuation and exacerbation of poverty that disproportionally affects certain groups. At the same time, those groups may be discriminated against not only because of their gender, race, or other social condition but also specifically on the grounds of their socio-economic vulnerability. Therefore, poverty may not only be rooted in discrimination but also function as a ground of discrimination per se. Accordingly, discrimination and poverty, as human rights issues, are interlinked concepts which often coexist and reinforce one another.

In addition to being a reinforcing factor and a root cause of poverty, equality is also interconnected with poverty as a right and principle that emanates obligations for states in the implementation of anti-poverty policies. The right to equality and non-discrimination generates negative and positive obligations for the state in creating and implementing state policies and promoting socio-economic inclusion. Furthermore, the relevance of equality to the legal assessment of poverty became increasingly apparent in the late twentieth century, when intersectionality became a key concept in international human rights law and modified how law approached discrimination. By recognizing that the intersection between vectors of oppression results in discrimination that cannot be reduced to a simple sum of their parts, intersectionality as an analytical framework requires the identification of the multiple factors that compose identities, vulnerabilities, and manifestations of oppression. Therefore, recognizing the different experiences, disadvantages, non-material oppressions, and needs faced by vulnerable groups becomes crucial in unveiling discrimination. Because poverty may be a ground of discrimination, a disadvantage suffered by a marginalized group, and an underlying factor for the manifestation and perpetuation of oppressions, it becomes relevant in the analysis of intersectional discrimination. By applying an equality approach to poverty and, therefore, unveiling inequalities that otherwise would remain invisibilized, the law acquires tools to tackle discrimination more effectively, including historical and structural discrimination interlinked with poverty cycles that disproportionately affect vulnerable groups.

Finally, equality provides a means to address poverty through law by filling gaps of protection. First, the most widely ratified international human rights treaties do not contain an explicit right to live without poverty. While poverty has often been addressed in human rights law as an issue of social, economic, and cultural rights, there is no consensus on the justiciability of these rights before international human rights courts. Second, while social, economic, and cultural rights may be protected domestically under a constitution or bill of rights, this is not always the case. Moreover, even in jurisdictions where they enjoy legal protection, they may still be interpreted as non-justiciable domestically. Hence, the right to equality may offer an alternative route through which courts can address poverty internationally and domestically.

Yet what happens in jurisdictions where socio-economic rights are safeguarded in law and are justiciable, as illustrated by cases before the STF and the IACtHR? Does the equality approach to poverty retain its added value or is it reduced to a tautology? After all, in such jurisdictions, distributive claims in disputes that affect persons living in poverty can be resolved by assessing state compliance with socio-economic rights. The focus on people's absolute levels or entitlements might make equality redundant, as such deprivations can be solved through distributive policies fulfilling one's absolute entitlements and raising the individual or group above the threshold of deprivations, as well as through social rights litigation in cases of rights violations.

Suppose poverty is conceptualized as a distributive matter only, being restricted to deprivations of absolute entitlements. In that case, it may be solved through the approach of substantive rights, that is, by assessing the obligations derived from rights, notably socio-economic rights. In addition, through the application of the *pro persona* principle, which is particularly influential in the IACtHR and requires the adoption of the most favourable interpretation of the law to the alleged victim, courts can respond to deprivations of absolute entitlements through a substantive rights approach, instead of an equality approach, without the risk of allowing for a levelling down option. One could thus argue that an equality approach to poverty becomes devoid of an added value in jurisdictions recognizing the justiciability of socio-economic rights and safeguarding a legal obligation for the state to reduce poverty. However, such a conclusion would be misleading, for three main reasons.

First, the socio-economic rights approach to poverty runs the risk of settling at a minimum level of basic needs. In turn, an equality approach plays a crucial role in rectifying disparities above the minimum. It enables courts to address the distributive dimension of poverty, not only by pushing beyond minimum thresholds of subsistence but also by tackling relative deprivations that perpetuate cycles of poverty, particularly for historically marginalized groups.

Second, and of particular importance, when a court is called upon to scrutinize action or inaction to address poverty, it is invited to transcend the limits of distributive equality and to incorporate the multiple dimensions of transformative equality into its analysis. Transformative equality entails acknowledging and rectifying misrecognition linked to poverty and various barriers that impede the equal and *de facto* participation of individuals living in poverty in political and social spheres. It also implies accommodating difference when appropriate and modifying social structures and institutions rather than solely expecting individuals to conform.[9]

Therefore, an equality approach to poverty allows courts to address further facets of exclusion and oppression related to monetary and multidimensional poverty when compared to an exclusively socio-economic rights approach. This conclusion is confirmed in this book's empirical study. Equality has amplified opportunities for the STF and the IACtHR to address poverty in Brazil through a polycentric approach (covering the redistributive, recognition, participation, and transformation fronts) and to assess poverty through the lens of intersectionality as a critical praxis. This approach challenges the division between analysing distributive harms connected to poverty, on the one hand, and equality law, on the other. As the case study of Brazil illustrates, multidimensional inequalities against historically vulnerable groups have contributed to the perpetuation of monetary and multidimensional poverty for these collectivities.

In contrast, the empirical analysis of the STF's and the IACtHR's poverty jurisprudence shows that their implementation of the social rights approach to poverty captures only a partial manifestation of the phenomenon of poverty: its manifestation as distributive harm. However, if the identification of the vulnerabilities and disadvantages related to poverty is partial, so are the responses provided through judicial protection. Therefore, a comprehensive response to poverty requires complementing social rights with an equality approach—or, in jurisdictions where social rights are not justiciable, grounding the analysis of the polycentric oppressions related to poverty in a multidimensional assessment of equality.

Third, by addressing freedom from want through a collective perspective grounded on universality, the equality approach avoids some of the pitfalls of social rights litigation. The book shows that the judicialization of poverty through the right to equality has enabled the studied courts to address poverty as unequal opportunities for the realization of rights and has provided

[9] Sandra Fredman, 'The Potential and Limits of an Equal Rights Paradigm in Addressing Poverty' (2011a) 22 Stellenbosch Law Review 566, p 569.

them with a language to require state action to modify structural pillars that maintain persistent exclusions and marginalization of vulnerable collectivities. This approach thus provides courts with tools to identify and address structural hindrances to freedom from poverty (including power relations, marginalization, and vulnerabilities linked to persistent inequalities affecting certain groups), thereby incorporating egalitarian aspirations into the analysis of freedom from want. Here, it is important to recall that the application of the law disconnected from substantial equality has, at times, reinforced the status quo and entrenched persistent inequalities in the realization of fundamental rights.[10]

In conclusion, the results of our research confirm that an equality approach to poverty retains its added value even in jurisdictions where socio-economic rights are justiciable. Yet recognizing the relevance of this approach does not clarify which strategies have been implemented in practice to address the interconnections between poverty and inequality. Answering this question requires shifting from a purely theoretical analysis of the interconnections between poverty and inequality to assessing the practice of legal institutions. This shift to practice is the object of the following sections, which turn to the book's case study.

9.2 The case of Brazil

Through an empirical analysis of the case of Brazil and the work of two courts with jurisdiction over the actions and inactions of the Brazilian State, this book investigated how law can accommodate the socio-economic concept of poverty and the role of equality in this process. In the next section, this chapter presents the main findings of this analysis. Section 9.2.1 examines the evolution of poverty in Brazil from 1988 to 2023, highlighting how intersectionality still shapes poverty in the country, and identifying key public policies implemented by the federal government to reverse the perpetuation of poverty cycles. After providing the factual and political context of the book's case study, the chapter analyses, in section 9.2.2, whether and how poverty has been incorporated into the equality jurisprudence of the STF and the IACtHR. Section 9.2.3 sets out recommendations for strengthening the

[10] See Chapter 3's analysis of the role of vagrancy laws in entrenching marginalization, as well as its analysis of the pitfalls of social rights litigation in Brazil disconnected from egalitarian premisses. For an example in a different jurisdiction, see Karen Kong, 'The Right to Food For All: Right-Based Approach to Hunger and Social Inequality' (2009) 32 Suffolk Transnational Law Review 525.

judicial responses of the two courts in addressing the complex interactions between poverty and inequality.

9.2.1 The evolution and intersectional manifestations of poverty in Brazil (1988–2023)

In 1988, 22.4% of the Brazilian population lived below the IPL, compared to 16.1% of the population in the Latin American and Caribbean region. Over the course of one decade, the poverty levels in Brazil had reduced and were virtually identical to the poverty rate in the region—by 1999, 15% and 14.7% of the population in Brazil and in Latin America and the Caribbean, respectively, lived in extreme poverty as measured by the IPL.[11]

From 1992 to 2014, Brazil went through a striking reduction in its headcount poverty ratio and its levels of multidimensional poverty in all four dimensions covered by this study (food security; health and longevity; access to education; and access to water, electricity, and sanitation). During this period, extreme poverty, measured by the IPL set at US$2.15 (2017 PPP), declined by 85.7%. Applying the PBF poverty line, monetary poverty (covering both extreme and non-extreme poverty) declined by 84%.

Poverty reduction accelerated significantly from 2003 to 2014, and Brazil became a paradigmatic case of extreme poverty reduction through the adoption of state policies addressing monetary and multidimensional poverty. The country experienced a striking decline in poverty levels, along with what Campello and Gentilli described as an unprecedented and systematic reduction in inequality levels—both in terms of income inequality and in the narrowing of gaps in the enjoyment of certain fundamental rights (eg the reduction of educational stratification).[12] Campello and Gentilli's study shows that the biggest inflection in the reduction of multidimensional inequalities in that period was the reduction of the racial gap.[13] The authors also identify a convergence in the reduction of racial inequality and the reduction of multidimensional poverty among black and brown people (from 14.9% of the black and brown population living in chronic multidimensional poverty in 2002 to 1.5% in 2015 under the IBGE's measurement of factors of chronic

[11] DataBank, 'Poverty and Equity: Brazil and Latin America & Caribbean' (World Bank) <https://databank.worldbank.org/reports.aspx?source=2&Topic=11> accessed 28 February 2023.

[12] Tereza Campello (ed), *Faces da Desigualdade no Brasil: Um olhar sobre os que ficam para trás* (CLACSO, FLACSO, agenda igualdade 2017).

[13] Ibid, p 47.

multidimensional poverty as defined by the World Bank).[14] Campello and Gentilli explain this movement as a consequence of the expansion of public policies prioritizing groups living in poverty.[15] By targeting the poor, these policies reached the great majority of the black and brown people excluded from rights and access to services and goods in the country.[16]

However, from 2015 onwards, extreme poverty and monetary poverty were again on the rise in the country. Hunger rose sharply from 2018 onwards. Between 2019 and 2021, Brazil returned to the levels of undernourishment last seen a decade earlier, according to data from FAO. By 2019, the poverty headcount ratio in Brazil, measured by the IPL and the PBF line, was similar to the country's levels in 2011 and 2012. In 2020, there was a notable decrease in the poverty rate in the country, which appears to be associated with the original configuration of the Emergency Aid benefit. However, as the threshold for eligibility for the benefit and the value of the benefit changed, the levels of monetary poverty and extreme poverty elevated once more in 2021.

In 2023, following the reinstatement of the PBF and readjustment of its benefits, Brazil reached a historical low in the percentage of its population living in extreme poverty, as measured by the IBGE using the IPL of US$2.15 at 2017 PPP (at 4%), as well as in monetary poverty, as measured by the IBGE using the World Bank's upper-middle-income poverty line of US$6.85 at 2017 PPP per day (27.4%).[17] In 2024, the country once again exited the FAO Hunger Map,[18] and its poverty levels declined further (with 3.5% of its population living under the IPL and 23.1% living under the World Bank's upper-middle-income poverty line, according to date from the IBGE).[19] By 2025, Brazil recorded its lowest unemployment rate (5.6%) since the IBGE began its historical series on unemployment in 2012.[20]

Despite these advances in reducing both monetary and multidimensional poverty, our analysis finds that poverty still has clear gender, racial, and social class dimensions in Brazil. In 2023, women earned, on average, 79% of men's earnings, even though women aged 25 or older have more years of education, on average, than men in the same age group.[21] While black people comprise

[14] Ibid, p 71.
[15] Ibid.
[16] Ibid.
[17] IBGE, 'SIS 2024, Tabelas "Padrão de vida e distribuição de rendimentos"', Table 2.18 (Pobr_Geo) (2024).
[18] FAO, 'Hunger map' <https://www.fao.org/interactive/hunger-map/en/> accessed 29 August 2025.
[19] IBGE, *Síntese de Indicadores Sociais: Uma Análise das Condições de Vida da População Brasileira 2025* (Estudos & Pesquisas Informação demográfica e socioeconômica 2025), p 62, Table 5.
[20] IBGE, 'PNADC. Séries históricas: desemprego' accessed 6 May 2023.
[21] IBGE, *Síntese de Indicadores Sociais: Uma Análise das Condições de Vida da População Brasileira 2024* (Estudos & Pesquisas Informação demográfica e socioeconômica, 2024), p 20.

approximately half of the Brazilian population, they represent approximately 70% of the individuals living in poverty.[22] They are also disproportionately represented among homeless people, heads of families in the *favelas*, unemployed people, and individuals occupying positions with low levels of specialization and prestige.[23] This group's experience of poverty is thus simultaneously a manifestation of marginalization and powerlessness as forms of oppression. Violence, another manifestation of oppression under Young's categorization, also disproportionately affects this racial group, as 70% of individuals murdered in Brazil are black.[24] Racial inequalities are also manifest in the gap between this and other racial groups in illiteracy rates and average years of education.[25]

Marginalization and exclusion based on race remain persistent features of Brazilian society and contribute to the pervasiveness of poverty among the black and brown population. Inequality sits at the root of poverty for this racial group, stemming from a historical process that dates back to slavery and its gradual, slow, and formal abolition in the country. This interconnection between racial inequality and poverty continues to manifest in Brazilian society. Moreover, poverty reinforces exclusions from the enjoyment of social rights, thereby reinforcing inequality, in a vicious cycle.

Those living among the 20% poorest in Brazil have a significantly lower rate of school attendance, a higher age-grade distortion, and a significantly reduced chance of upward social mobility.[26] Poverty is also associated with significantly lower rates of access to dentists, doctors, medical drugs, and basic sanitation, particularly waste collection, water supply, and sewage disposal through a sewerage, stormwater drainage system, or septic tank.[27] Therefore, living in poverty in Brazil entails a significant shortfall in the fulfilment of fundamental rights based on one's economic condition. Additionally, as explained above, certain vulnerable groups are disproportionately found in

[22] Ibid, p 57.

[23] IBGE, *Desigualdades Sociais por Cor ou Raça no Brasil* (Estudos e Pesquisas Informação Demográfica e Socioeconômica 2022), p 2; IPEA, *Políticas sociais: acompanhamento e análise* (2014), p 96; Tatiana Dias Silva and Josenilton Marques da Silva, *Nota Técnica. Reserva de vagas para negros em concursos públicos: uma análise a partir do Projeto de Lei 6.738/2013*, IPEA (2014).

[24] Data from 2017: Campello (2017), *supra* note 12, p 47. Data from 2025 shows that 68.2% of the victims of female homicides were black women. See IPEA and FBSP, *Atlas da Violência 2025* (2025), p 57.

[25] IBGE, *PNAD Contínua Educação 2023* (Pesquisa Nacional por Amostra de Domicílios Contínua, 2024), pp 2 and 4.

[26] IBGE, *Síntese de Indicadores Sociais: Uma Análise das Condições de Vida da População Brasileira 2020* (Estudos & Pesquisas Informação demográfica e socioeconômica, 2020), p 64, pp 90–92.

[27] IBGE, Ministério da Economia and Ministério da Saúde, *Pesquisa Nacional de Saúde 2019: Informações sobre domicílios, acesso e utilização dos serviços de saúde. Brasil, Grandes Regiões e Unidades da Federação* (2020), pp 42–47; *SIS 2020*, *supra* note 26, p 80.

a situation of poverty. This highlights the relevance of adopting an intersectionality approach to the assessment of poverty in Brazil. Hence, addressing status inequality entails addressing poverty, economic disadvantage, and the different forms of oppression that derive from the experience of poverty to which these groups are subjected.

In a paper published in 2002, Gwen Brodsky and Shelagh Day asserted that '[p]overty is a sex equality issue because women's poverty is a manifestation of persistent discrimination against women'.[28] Our analysis of statistical data on the evolution of poverty in Brazil shows that Brodsky and Day's statement holds true in the case of Brazil, where it can be expanded beyond gender. In Brazil, poverty is a status issue, as the poverty of women, black, and brown people, among other vulnerable groups, is a manifestation of historical and persistent discrimination against these groups. Simultaneously, poverty is an autonomous factor of inequality, because it carries stigmatic effects and leads to different forms of oppression that impact one's realization of fundamental rights in Brazil, aggravating vulnerabilities faced by historically marginalized groups.

Our study indicates that key measures adopted by Brazil to eradicate poverty were CCTs (notably the PBF), unconditional cash transfers (such as the BPC), valorization of the minimum wage, and distributive measures tackling inequality and the persistence of multidimensional poverty in historically marginalized groups. One example of the latter measure is the institution of quota systems for admission to public universities and to positions in the public sector, both of which have been scrutinized by the STF to assess their compatibility with the right to equality. Restrictions on access to cash transfer programmes have likewise been subject to judicial scrutiny before the STF through the lens of equality.

In conclusion, the perpetuation and manifestation of poverty in Brazil is a human rights issue interconnected with the historical perpetuation of structural discrimination in the country. However, paraphrasing Fredman, recognizing the connection between poverty and the right to equality and non-discrimination is merely the first step. More complex is determining how law—and, here I add, courts—can address poverty.[29]

[28] Gwen Brodsky and Shelagh Day, 'Beyond the Social and Economic Rights Debate: Substantive Equality Speaks to Poverty' (2002) 14 Canadian Journal of Women and the Law 184, p 188.

[29] See Sandra Fredman, 'Women and Poverty—A Human Rights Approach' (2016b) 24 African Journal of International and Comparative Law 494, pp 502–503.

9.2.2 Judicializing poverty through equality in the STF and the IACtHR

The first equality-based decisions addressing monetary or multidimensional poverty in the STF and the IACtHR were issued in 2002 and 2010, respectively.[30] Although still a recent development, poverty and socio-economic vulnerability have emerged as some of the most prominent grounds of vulnerability analysed in the equality jurisprudence of the two courts. For comparison purposes, in the IACtHR's equality jurisprudence from its creation to the end of 2020, socio-economic condition is already one of the grounds of vulnerability most often addressed by the tribunal, preceded only by gender (sixteen cases) and race or ethnic origin (twelve cases). Similarly, within the STF's equality jurisprudence from 1988 to 2020, economic condition ranked among the most frequently addressed grounds, with gender remaining the most prevalent category (thirty cases).

The incorporation of an equality-based approach to poverty and economic vulnerability in the jurisprudence of the STF and the IACtHR marks an important normative shift. During the period covered by this study, seventeen cases in the STF and ten in the IACtHR addressed poverty and socio-economic vulnerability within the framework of equality. By contrast, outside equality case law, the word 'poverty' was mentioned in only ten full bench STF decisions (1988–2020) and in six judgments of the IACtHR (1979–2020). The empirical evidence remains limited in establishing the predominance of the equality approach over others (such as the social rights approach), as courts may address deprivations related to poverty without explicitly framing them in these terms. Nonetheless, our analysis confirms the integration of poverty into the equality jurisprudence of the two courts and the added value of this approach to the assessment of poverty in Brazil.

This study finds that poverty has been integrated into the equality jurisprudence of the STF and the IACtHR both as a factor of vulnerability intersecting with other protected grounds and as a factor of vulnerability on its own. Furthermore, distributive equality claims concerning poverty, in its monetary and multidimensional conceptualization, have consistently succeeded before the two courts.

[30] STF, Judgment, *ADI 2.267-9/AM*, 7 August 2002. Justice rapporteur: Maurício Corrêa; IACtHR, Judgment (Merits, Reparations and Costs), *Xákmok Kásek Indigenous Community v Paraguay*, 24 August 2010. Series C No 214.

The STF has applied the four-prong strategies listed in Chapter 4 when addressing poverty as an equality matter. In all disputes in which poverty or economic vulnerability was a suspect classification, the STF was asked to address a distributive claim. In addition, distributive claims often succeeded when the STF was called upon to revise a positive measure or other public policy instituted to the benefit of economically disadvantaged individuals. However, when poverty or economic vulnerability alone is the suspect classification, claims based on the transformative dimension of substantive equality—denouncing inaction to accommodate the particular needs and vulnerabilities of persons living in poverty—still seem unlikely to succeed before the STF.

The IACtHR applies four strategies for addressing poverty through equality: assessing poverty and economic status as context, as a suspect classification, as the object of positive obligations derived from substantive equality, and as a factor relevant for the determination of reparations. The first three strategies have been the primary avenues the IACtHR uses to address poverty in its equality case law. Our empirical analysis shows that considering poverty as context has been a pivotal tool for the IACtHR's consideration of poverty in equality cases.

Like the STF, the IACtHR has relied on statistical data and sociological studies to identify widespread contexts of poverty. However, unlike in the equality jurisprudence of the STF, this contextual approach is not only a means of assessing the vulnerabilities of specific groups but also a tool to evaluate the effectiveness of state measures in addressing chronic poverty. When states know or should have known that groups living in poverty face structural risks and severe and systematic obstacles to fulfilling fundamental rights (such as the right to live free from slavery), the IACtHR applies a higher threshold of due diligence. The Court's exercise of judicial scrutiny to analyse compliance with this duty shifts the focus from progressiveness to effectiveness. In the Introduction, we hypothesized that a context of chronic poverty would result in an enhanced duty of due diligence by the state to prevent and reverse the perpetuation of monetary and multidimensional poverty. This hypothesis was confirmed in the jurisprudence of the IACtHR, but not in the jurisprudence of the STF.

9.2.3 Bridging judicialization and social change: paths forward

Both the STF and the IACtHR have adopted a conceptualization of equality firmly based on substantive equality and what Fredman calls the 'fourth generation' of equality. Under this equality model, states must take active measures to promote equality and non-discrimination, and state inaction is subject to judicial scrutiny. To a certain extent and with constraints, courts become second-degree policymakers. By adopting this model of conceptualization and interpretation of equality, both the STF and the IACtHR have expanded their capacity to address poverty and its manifestations in Brazil as an equality issue. *ADPF 186* (2012) and *ADC 41* (2017) are notable examples of judgments in which the STF recognized that the CF/88 imposes an obligation on the State to act towards changing structures that perpetuate historical disadvantages and oppressions, including socio-economic disadvantage and the perpetuation of poverty cycles affecting protected groups. In the jurisprudence of the IACtHR, *Hacienda Brasil Verde Workers* and *Fireworks Factory* are leading cases in which the Court exercised judicial scrutiny based on the principle of equality regarding state action and inaction to correct distributive harms related to poverty. While judicialization of poverty has not provided a sufficient solution to structural poverty, it has been an essential component of poverty alleviation and eradication in Brazil, with concrete effects on public policies that were central to the evolution of poverty in the country throughout the twenty-first century.

The STF has had an impact on Brazil's public policies addressing both monetary and multidimensional poverty. Its role has been particularly significant in confirming the constitutionality of strong distributive measures impacting multidimensional poverty, in reviewing the inclusiveness of policies aimed at reducing monetary poverty, and in imposing positive duties on the legislature and the executive derived from the right to equality and the positive obligation to reduce poverty. It has acted as a second-degree policymaker in relation to distributive claims, particularly in cases of targeted poverty, that is, poverty that disproportionately affects historically marginalized groups. At the same time, the STF and its Justices generally acknowledge the constraints to which they are subject as *subsidiary* policymakers, reaffirming that the primary responsibility and competence for designing and implementing anti-poverty policies lies with the legislature and the Public Administration. As a general rule, the Court's role is to assess the constitutionality of such measures once enacted and to review their inclusiveness and implementation (or the lack thereof) in accordance with constitutional rights and principles, including the right to equality. For example, in *MI 7.300* (2021) and *RE 500.171-7* (2008), the STF exercised its jurisdiction to review cases of state omissions in implementing public policies and in adopting positive measures to facilitate the exercise of rights by people living in poverty. However, as *MI 7300* (2021) shows, the Court considers in its analysis both the concept of progressiveness—in assessing the positive obligations related to poverty—and that of subsidiarity—in relation to its role as a policymaker in poverty eradication.

Furthermore, in assessing state compliance with the positive obligation to promote equality, the STF has consistently confirmed the compatibility *in abstracto* of affirmative action with the constitutional right to equality. It has generally upheld the constitutionality of quota systems to groups in vulnerability by considering, among other factors, a group's particular vulnerability to poverty and its historical representation among the poorest strata of the Brazilian population. It has also reviewed the requirements to access certain anti-poverty benefits and programmes, such as the BPC, and violations in their implementation, including restrictions on access to CCTs in violation of the right to equality.

In contrast, the IACtHR has not examined the content and scope of CCTs or strong distributive measures of affirmative action in Brazil. It has also not been asked to analyse impugned measures of affirmative action in its equality jurisprudence. However, it has consistently upheld an interpretation of equality as substantive equality and adopted a high threshold of effectiveness for compliance with the positive dimension of equality and the resulting duty to address poverty. Its main contribution to anti-poverty policies in Brazil resides in its examination of poverty both as a factor of discrimination requiring effective action from the State (nationally and locally) and as a vulnerability intensifying the disadvantages and oppressions faced by historically discriminated groups. In assessing Brazil's compliance with the obligation to adopt positive measures to reverse chronic poverty, the IACtHR's balance leans more towards effectiveness than progressiveness. Additionally, the Court has imposed new positive obligations on Brazil concerning the perpetuation of poverty in historically marginalized communities, with the *Fireworks Factory* case being a prominent example.

Both the STF and the IACtHR have been active in recognizing distributive claims derived from the right to equality in the context of poverty. Distributive equality remains the dimension mostly used in their jurisprudence when addressing poverty in equality cases, notably when poverty is addressed as an autonomous factor of vulnerability outside an intersectional framework of analysis. In other words, although the two courts' equality approach to poverty does extend beyond distribution, distributive arguments frequently serve as the entry point for addressing poverty in Brazil.

This book suggests that the two courts should consider further exploring the complex manifestations of poverty and the polycentric interactions of the distributive dimension with the other dimensions of transformative equality. The assessment of equality through multiple dimensions provides a venue for courts to address the various manifestations of poverty through the lens of intersectionality. Because poverty is still strongly connected to factors of intersectionality in many countries, including Brazil, adopting this multidimensional assessment of equality enhances the courts' ability to scrutinize actions and inactions of the state through an intersectional perspective that considers poverty a factor of vulnerability across multiple dimensions.

Individuals and groups living in poverty face distributive harm derived from economic structures and the perpetuation of exclusion from the enjoyment of resources and goods. The distributive harm may be rooted in unequal access to material goods and opportunities that lead to poverty. In turn, poverty may reinforce obstacles to accessing distributive goods. An essential remedy for breaking this cycle is, therefore, distributive. However, distributive injustices do not operate in isolation in poverty cycles. In addition to distributive injustices, one of the root causes of poverty may be found in non-material oppressions against historically marginalized groups, such as stereotyping, stigma, and non-physical violence preventing social and political participation and hindering social mobility. Therefore, poverty may be connected to misrecognition, hindrances to participation, and pressure for assimilation, thereby requiring remedies derived from the politics of recognition, as Fraser understands the term.

Accordingly, addressing poverty includes, but does not stop at, redistribution. Addressing injustices against persons living in poverty requires challenging cultural norms and institutionalized practices of verbal violence (the recognition dimension). It also requires addressing structures that perpetuate domination without requiring assimilation (the transformative dimension) and addressing other forms of oppression that reduce the parity of participation of persons living in poverty (the participative dimension).

Through an empirical analysis of the equality jurisprudence of the STF and the IACtHR, this book finds that both courts have addressed, to different degrees, multiple dimensions of inequality connected to poverty in their respective jurisprudences. Yet it recommends further extending the examination of the polycentric interactions of poverty and inequality, even in cases in which poverty alone constitutes a ground of vulnerability—that is, when it is not accompanied by claims of intersectionality.

The book also recommends that the assessment of effectiveness in the realization of positive duties to address poverty takes into consideration the concept of progressiveness. Tackling specifically the IACtHR's reasoning in the

Fireworks Factory case, linking the stricter duty of due diligence with the concept of effectiveness to be applied in every municipality independently of the reduction of poverty nationwide is likely to significantly reduce the weight of progressiveness in the assessment of whether a state complied with its positive obligation to protect and fulfil human rights. In the case of poverty, this approach reveals a tension between the aim of human rights institutions of establishing feasible obligations, on the one hand, and the objective of effectively protecting fundamental rights and freedoms, on the other. In *Fireworks Factory*, the Court's focus on regional effectiveness and the minimal discussion of the policies adopted by Brazil limited its assessment of the scope of the structural changes in the country's poverty levels. It also limited the Court's opportunities to assess areas of omission and deficiencies in state policy, as well as the resulting gaps that could have been addressed through judicial scrutiny.

This book argues for a balance between the progressiveness approach to the assessment of state compliance with the positive duties derived from equality to address poverty, on the one side, and the requirement of effectiveness in the implementation of these duties, on the other. Such a balance can foster deterrence, create incentives for state compliance, and contribute to the assessment of public policies implemented by the state. This balance would allow the IACtHR to act as a second-degree 'policymaker' while aiming at subsidiarity. It also avoids casuistic prioritizing of state policy based on the regions that have brought cases to the Inter-American System, a result that could impact marginalization, as the most vulnerable groups might face more difficulty appearing before courts, particularly a regional human rights court located outside their state and publishing cases in a foreign language.

9.3 Judicializing poverty: a (self-sufficient) response to a socio-political problem?

Courts can play a fundamental role in addressing poverty and its interconnections with inequalities, as shown in this book's analysis of poverty in Brazil and its judicialization before the STF and the IACtHR. However, there are limits to their capacity to promote social change. Sustainable and comprehensive modifications of entrenched patterns of oppression, exclusion, and marginalization affecting the poor and historically vulnerable communities are unlikely to happen through courts alone.

Upendra Baxi highlights the importance of discussing the limits of judicialization. He argues that courts are never tools for total societal revolution but rather, at best, instruments for incremental social change. In other words, courts, even if transformative, can never replace political action. Baxi argues that realizing this truth strengthens democratic progress in the long run.[31]

Law can be, at once, both emancipatory and an instrument for the maintenance and legitimation of the status quo—not rarely, it has even legitimized oppressions, as Chapter 3 explained in its analysis of how law has responded to poverty throughout history. In any case, even when drafted in transformative language, law and legal institutions can prove insufficient for promoting social change. The collective project of promoting social justice, including freedom from want in line with the right to equality and non-discrimination, requires identifying what is already transformative in the work of courts addressing polycentric oppressions associated with poverty, while also acknowledging the limitations of law and courts and the need to engage other agents in the transformative project, including political actors and civil society.

Recognizing the limits of courts—and indeed, of law itself—should not be confused with nihilism, nor should it lead to it. As Bhupinder S Chimni explains, legal nihilism disarms the poor and marginalized individuals and can contribute to the maintenance of the status quo.[32] Rather than amounting to legal nihilism, the recognition of the limits of courts is a reminder that, while courts can be key agents in safeguarding and even expanding rights, social challenges will generally demand a more holistic response which the court alone will not be able to provide.

While equality litigation has its pitfalls—particularly when courts detach their analysis from the concept of substantive equality[33]—this book's empirical analysis of the judicial treatment of poverty in Brazil through the right to equality demonstrates positive outcomes with transformative potential. Poverty is a complex phenomenon that originates from distributive injustices related to the economic order and from interpersonal dynamics producing non-distributive harms, including intersectional patterns of misrepresentation that hinder one's capacity and *de facto* possibilities to participate in society fully. This dynamic often transcends the interactions of identifiable agents and manifests through the perpetuation of power structures that do not eliminate,

[31] Upendra Baxi, 'The Avatars of Indian Judicial Activism: Explorations in the Geographies of [In]justice' in S K Verma and K Kusum (eds), *Fifty Years of the Supreme Court of India: Its Grasp and Reach*, vol 4 (Oxford University Press and Indian Law Institute 2001), pp 164–165.

[32] B S Chimni, 'The Past, Present and Future of international Law: A Critical Third World Approach' (2007) 8 Melbourne Journal of International Law 499, p 503.

[33] For examples from other jurisdictions, see: US Supreme Court, *Palmer v Thompson*, 403 US 217, 14 June 1971; US Supreme Court, *Kadrmas v Dickinson Public Schools*, 487 US 450, 24 June 1988; US Supreme Court, *Students for Fair Admissions, INC v President and fellows of Harvard College*, 600 US 181, 29 June 2023.

but rather constrain one's agency and personal choices when living in poverty. Judicialization of poverty through the right to equality has, to different degrees, been able to identify and address these structural hindrances and multidimensional inequalities that entrench poverty cycles. Furthermore, it has made important contributions to poverty eradication and poverty alleviation in Brazil. These contributions go beyond mere compliance with the judicial decisions studied —which, as indicated in Chapter 8, still face challenges despite being generally successful. By unveiling the interconnections between poverty and inequality and requiring positive action to address these phenomena, the equality case law of the STF and the IACtHR may impact not only legal actors but also political agents, national and regional actors, and even civil society.

In conclusion, the judicialization of poverty in Brazil has been a—albeit not *the*—fundamental response to one of the most serious and persistent human rights challenges faced by the country. However, as this book has shown, it has not operated in a socio-political vacuum. Courts hold the potential to advance the transformation of entrenched social challenges. Yet transformative projects require concerted action from a myriad of actors that include, but go beyond, law and its institutions.

References

Legislation and treaties

Brazil, 'Criminal Code of the Empire of Brazil', 16 December 1830.
Brazil, 'Law No. 2,040', 28 September 1871.
Brazil, 'Law No. 3,270', 28 September 1885.
Brazil, 'Law No. 3,353', 13 May 1888.
Brazil, 'Criminal Code', Decree No 847, 11 October 1890.
Brazil, 'Constitution of the Republic of the United States of Brazil', 16 July 1934.
Brazil, 'Constitution of the Republic of the United States of Brazil', 10 November 1937.
Brazil, 'Law on Criminal Contraventions', Law-Decree No. 3,688, 3 October 1941.
Brazil, 'Constitution of the Republic of the United States of Brazil', 18 September 1946.
Brazil, 'Constitution of the Federative Republic of Brazil of 1988', 5 October 1988.
Brazil, 'Law No. 8,742', Organic Law of Social Assistance (LOAS), 7 December 1993.
Brazil, 'Law No. 9,533', 10 December 1997.
Brazil, 'Law No. 10,836', 9 January 2004.
Brazil, 'Law No. 10,835', 8 January 2004.
Brazil, 'Decree No. 5,209', 17 September 2004.
Brazil, 'Decree No. 7,492', Plan Brazil without Extreme Poverty, 2 June 2011.
Brazil, 'Law No. 12,711', 29 August 2012.
Brazil, 'Decree No. 7,824', 11 October 2012.
Brazil, 'Constitutional Amendment No. 72', PEC das Domésticas, 2 April 2013.
Brazil, 'Law No. 12,990', 9 June 2014.
Brazil, 'Complementary Law No. 150', Lei das Domésticas, 1 June 2015.
Brazil, 'Constitutional Amendment No. 95', 15 December 2016.
Brazil, 'Law No. 13,429', 31 March 2017.
Brazil, 'Law No. 13,982', 2 April 2020.
Brazil, 'Provisional Measure No. 1,000', 2 September 2020.
Brazil, 'Decree No. 10,851', 5 November 2021.
Brazil, 'Decree No. 10,852', 8 November 2021.
Brazil, 'Law No. 14,171', 10 June 2021.
Brazil, 'Law No. 14,176', 22 June 2021.
Brazil, 'Law No. 14,284', 29 December 2021.
Brazil, 'Provisional Measure No. 1,039', 18 March 2021.
Brazil, 'Provisional Measure No. 1,061', 9 August 2021.
Brazil, 'Provisional Measure No. 1,076', 7 December 2021.
Brazil, 'Law No, 14,284', 29 December 2021.
Brazil, 'Decree No. 11,013', 29 March 2022.
Brazil, 'Law No. 14,342', 18 May 2022.
Brazil, 'Constitutional Amendment No. 123', 14 July 2022.
Brazil, 'Provisional Measure No. 1,164', 2 March 2023.
Brazil, 'Law No. 14,601', 19 June 2023.
Brazil, 'Law No. 15,142', 3 June 2025.

Communities, Council of the European, 'Council Directive 76/207/EEC on the implementation of the principle of equal treatment for men and women as regards access to employment, vocational training and promotion, and working conditions', 9 February 1976.
Diputados, México. Cámara de, 'Constitución Política de los Estados Unidos Mexicanos', Last update on 18 November 2022, 5 February 1917.
Kingdom, United, 'Equality Act', 8 April 2010.
Mexico, 'Constitution of Mexico', 5 February 1917.
Organization of American States ("OAS"), 'American Convention on Human Rights, "Pact of San Jose"', 22 November 1969.
OAS, 'Charter of the Organization of American States', 30 April 1948, amended by the Protocol of Buenos Aires of 27 February 1967.
OAS, 'Inter-American Convention on Protecting the Human Rights of Older Persons', 15 July 2015.
OAS, 'Additional Protocol to the American Convention on Human Rights in the Area of Economic, Social and Cultural Rights ("Protocol of San Salvador")', A-52, 16 November 1999.
Organization of African Unity ('OAU'), 'African Charter on Human and Peoples' Rights ('Banjul Charter')', CAB/LEG/67/3 rev 5, 21 ILM 58, 27 June 1981.
Parliament, UK, '1928 Equal Franchise Act', Parliamentary Archives, HL/PO/PU/1/1928/18&19G5c12, 2 July 1928.
Portugal, 'Livros das Leis e Posturas—Lei pela qual se reprime a vadiagem'.
Portugal, 'Lei contra a vadiagem'.
Realm, The Statutes of the, 'The Statute of Labourers', 23 Edw III, 1349.
South Africa, 'Promotion of Equality and Prevention of Unfair Discrimination Act', 2 February 2000.
UN General Assembly ('UNGA'), 'International Convention on the Elimination of All Forms of Racial Discrimination', United Nations, Treaty Series, vol 660, p 195, 21 December 1965.
UNGA, 'Universal Declaration of Human Rights', 217 A (III), 10 December 1948.
UNGA, 'International Covenant on Civil and Political Rights', United Nations, Treaty Series, vol 999, 16 December 1966.
UNGA, 'International Covenant on Economic, Social and Cultural Rights', United Nations, Treaty Series, vol 993, 16 December 1966.
UNGA, 'Convention on the Elimination of All Forms of Discrimination Against Women', United Nations, Treaty Series, vol 1249, p 13, 18 December 1979.
UNGA, 'Convention on the Rights of the Child', United Nations, Treaty Series, vol 1577, p 3, 20 November 1989.
UNGA, 'Vienna Declaration and Programme of Action', A/CONF157/23, 12 July 1993.
UNGA, 'Convention on the Rights of Persons with Disabilities', A/RES/61/106, Annex I, 13 December 2006.
Union, Council of the European, 'Council Directive 2000/78/EC establishing a general framework for equal treatment in employment and occupation', 27 November 2000.
Union, Iberian, 'Ordenações Filipinas' (1603) <https://www2.senado.leg.br/bdsf/item/id/242733> accessed 31 January 2024.

Resolutions and declarations

Assembly, UN General, 'Declaration on the Right to Development', A/RES/41/128, 4 December 1986.
Law, UN Audiovisual Library of International, 'Charter of Economic Rights and Duties of States', UNGA resolution 3281 (XXIX), 12 December 1974.
UNGA, 'Resolution 1710 (XVI)', A/RES/1710 (XVI), 19 December 1961.
UNGA, 'Resolution 3201 (S-VI)', A/RES/3201(S-VI), 1 May 1974.

UNGA, 'Resolution 3281 (XXIX)', 12 December 1974.
UNGA, 'Resolution 34/46 (1979)', A/RES/34/46, 23 November 1979.
UNGA, 'United Nations Millennium Declaration', Resolution 55/2, 8 September 2000.
Bibliothèque, Dag Hammarsjöld, 'Résolutions adoptées par l'Assemblée générale à la 47ème session' <https://research.un.org/fr/docs/ga/quick/regular/47> accessed 2 February 2024.

Judicial decisions

Colombian Constitutional Court, *C-410/94*, 15 September 1994.
Colombian Constitutional Court, *C-044/04*, 27 January 2004.
European Court of Human Rights (ECtHR), *Chapman v the United Kingdom*, App 27238/95, 18 January 2001.
ECtHR, *Stec and others v the United Kingdom*, Apps 65731/01 and 65900/01, 12 April 2006.
House of Lords, *A. v Secretary of State for the Home Department* [2004] UKHL 56 (HL), 16 December 2004.
IACtHR, Judgment (Preliminary Objections, Merits, Reparations and Costs), *'Juvenile Reeducation Institute' v Paraguay*, 2 September 2004. Series C No 112.
IACtHR, Judgment (Preliminary Objections, Merits, Reparations and Costs), *Moiwana Community v Suriname*, 15 June 2005. Series C No 145.
IACtHR, Judgment (Merits, Reparations and Costs), *Mapiripán Massacre v Colombia*, 15 September 2005. Series C No 134.
IACtHR, Judgment (Merits, Reparations and Costs), *Ximenes-Lopes v Brazil*, 4 July 2006. Series C No 149.
IACtHR, Judgment (Merits, Reparations and Costs), *Tiu Tojín v Guatemala*, 26 November 2008. Series C No 190.
IACtHR, Judgment (Merits, Reparations and Costs), *Xákmok Kásek Indigenous Community v Paraguay*, 24 August 2010. Series C No 214.
IACtHR, Judgment (Merits, Reparations and Costs), *Atala Riffo and daughters v Chile*, 24 February 2012. Series C No 239.
IACtHR, Judgment (Preliminary Objections, Merits, Reparations and Costs), *Furlan and family v Argentina*, 31 August 2012. Series C No 246.
IACtHR, Judgment (Merits and Reparations), *Uzcátegui et al v Venezuela*, 3 September 2012. Series C No 249.
IACtHR, Judgment (Preliminary Objections, Merits, Reparations and Costs), *Artavia Murillo et al. (In Vitro Fertilization) v Costa Rica*, 28 November 2012. Series C No 257.
IACtHR, Judgment (Preliminary Objections, Merits and Reparations), *Santo Domingo Massacre v Colombia*, 30 November 2012. Series No 259.
IACtHR, Judgment (Preliminary Objections, Merits, Reparations and Costs), *Afro-descendant Communities displaced from the Cacarica River Basin (Operation Genesis) v Colombia*, 20 November 2013. Series C No 270.
IACtHR, Judgment (Preliminary Objections, Merits, Reparations and Costs), *Véliz Franco et al v Guatemala*, 19 May 2014. Series C No 277.
IACtHR, Judgment (Merits, Reparations and Costs), *Norín Catrimán et al (Leaders, Members and Activist of the Mapuche Indigenous People) v Chile*, 29 May 2014. Series C No 279.
IACtHR, Judgment (Preliminary Objections, Merits, Reparations and Costs), *Expelled Dominicans and Haitians v Dominican Republic*, 28 August 2014. Series C No 282.
IACtHR, Judgment (Preliminary Objections, Merits, Reparations and Costs), *Espinoza Gonzáles and others v Peru*, 20 November 2014. Series C No 468.
IACtHR, Judgment (Preliminary Objections, Merits, Reparations and Costs), *Gonzales Lluy and others v Ecuador*, 1 September 2015. Series C No 298.

IACtHR, Judgment (Preliminary objections, merits, reparations and costs), *Duque v. Colombia*, 26 February 2016. Series C No 310.
IACtHR, Judgment (Preliminary Objection, Merits, Reparations and Costs), *Flor Freire v Ecuador*, 31 August 2016. Series C No 315.
IACtHR, Judgment (Preliminary Objections, Merits, Reparations and Costs), *Hacienda Brasil Verde Workers v Brasil*, 20 October 2016. Series C No 318.
IACtHR, Judgment (Preliminary Objections, Merits, Reparations and Costs), *IV v Bolivia*, 30 November 2016. Series C No 329.
IACtHR, Judgment (Preliminary Objections, Merits, Reparations and Costs), *Gutiérrez Hernández and others v Guatemala*, 24 August 2017. Series C No 339.
IACtHR, Judgment (Preliminary Exceptions, Merits, Reparations and Costs), *Lagos del Campo v Peru*, 31 August 2017. Series C No 340.
IACtHR, Judgment (Preliminary Objections, Merits, Reparations and Costs), *VRP, VPC et al v Nicaragua*, 8 March 2018. Series C No 350.
IACtHR, Judgment (Preliminary Objections, Merits, Reparations and Costs), *Azul Rojas Marín and other v Perú*, 12 March 2020. Series C No 402.
IACtHR, Judgment (Preliminary Objections, Merits, Reparations and Costs), *Workers of the Fireworks Factory in Santo Antônio de Jesus and their Families v Brazil*, 15 July 2020. Series C No 318.
IACtHR, Judgment (Merits, Reparations and Costs), *Guzmán Albarracín and others v Ecuador*, 24 June 2020. Series C No 434.
IACtHR, Judgment (Merits, Reparations and Costs), *Maya Kaqchikel Indigenous Peoples of Sumpango et al v Guatemala*, 6 October 2021. Series C No 440.
IACtHR, Judgment (Preliminary Objections, Merits, Reparations and Costs), *Manuela and others v El Salvador*, 02 November 2021. Series C No. 441.
STF, Judgment, *RE 218.461-3 AgR/SP*, 4 August 1998. Justice rapporteur: Sydney Sanches.
STF, Judgment, *ADI 1.946-5/DF*, 29 April 1999. Justice rapporteur: Sydney Sanches.
STF, Judgment, *ADC 19/DF*, 09 February 2001. Justice rapporteur: Marco Aurélio.
STF, Judgment, *ADI 2.267-9/AM*, 7 August 2002. Justice rapporteur: Maurício Corrêa.
STF, Judgment, *ADI 1.276-2/SP*, 29 August 2002. Justice rapporteur: Ellen Gracie.
STF, Judgment, *MS 26.310-5/DF*, 20 September 2007. Justice rapporteur: Marco Aurélio.
STF, Judgment, *ADI 2.649-6/DF*, 08 May 2008. Justice rapporteur: Carmen Lúcia.
STF, Judgment, *RE 500.171-7/GO*, 13 August 2008. Justice rapporteur: Ricardo Lewandowski.
STF, Judgment, *HC 94.009-4/SP*, 6 November 2008. Justice rapporteur: Eros Grau.
STF, Judgment, *Pet. 3.388/RR*, 19 March 2009. Justice rapporteur: Ayres Britto.
STF, Judgment, *ADPF 186/DF*, 26 April 2012. Rapporteur: Ricardo Lewandowski.
STF, Judgment, *ADI 4.424/DF*, 09 February 2012. Justice rapporteur: Marco Aurélio.
STF, Judgment, *ADI 3.330/DF*, 03 May 2012. Justice Rapporteur: Ayres Britto.
STF, Judgment, *RE 567.985/MT*, 18 April 2013. Justice rapporteur: Gilmar Mendes.
STF, Judgment, *ADPF 291/DF*, 28 October 2015. Justice rapporteur: Roberto Barroso.
STF, Judgment, *RE 581.488/RS*, 03 December 2015. Justice rapporteur: Dias Toffoli.
STF, Judgment, *RE 778.889/PE*, 10 March 2016. Justice rapporteur: Roberto Barroso.
STF, Judgment, *ADI 2.144/DF*, 02 June 2016. Justice rapporteur: Teori Zavascki.
STF, Judgment, *RE 898.450/SP*, 17 August 2016. Justice rapporteur: Luiz Fux.
STF, Judgment, *RE 587.970/SP*, 20 April 2017. Justice Rapporteur: Marco Aurélio.
STF, Judgment, *ADC 41/DF*, 08 June 2017. Justice Rapporteur: Roberto Barroso.
STF, Judgment, *ADI 5.617/DF*, 15 March 2018. Justice rapporteur: Edson Fachin.
STF, Judgment, *RE 958.252/MG*, 30 August 2018. Justice rapporteur: Luiz Fux.
STF, Judgment, *ADPF 324/DF*, 30 August 2018. Justice rapporteur: Roberto Barroso.
STF, Judgment, *ADPF 541/DF*, 26 September 2018. Justice rapporteur: Roberto Barroso.
STF, Judgment, *ADO 26/DF*, 13 June 2019. Justice rapporteur: Celso de Mello.

STF, Judgment, *ADI 3.446/DF*, 08 August 2019. Justice rapporteur: Gilmar Mendes.
STF, Judgment, *RE 494.601/RS*, 09 August 2019. Justice rapporteur: Edson Fachin.
STF, Judgment, *ADI 5.543/DF*, 11 May 2020, Justice rapporteur: Edson Fachin.
STF, Judgment, *ADI 4.868/DF*, 27 March 2020. Justice Rapporteur: Gilmar Mendes.
STF, Judgment, *ACO 3.359 MC-Ref/DF*, 05 August 2020. Justice rapporteur: Marco Aurélio.
STF, Judgment, *RE 659.424/RS*, 13 October 2020. Justice rapporteur: Celso de Mello.
STF, Judgment, *MI 7.300/DF*, 27 April 2021. Justice rapporteur: Gilmar Mendes.
STF, Judgment, *ACO 3.359/DF*, 25 April 2023. Justice rapporteur: Alexandre de Moraes.
US Supreme Court, *Palmer v Thompson*, 403 US 217, 14 June 1971.
US Supreme Court, *Kadrmas v Dickinson Public Schools*, 487 US 450, 24 June 1988.
US Supreme Court, *Students for Fair Admissions, INC v President and fellows of Harvard College*, 600 US 181, 29 June 2023.

Advisory opinions

IACtHR, Advisory Opinion, *Exceptions to the exhaustion of domestic remedies (Art. 46(1), 46(2)(a) and 46(2)(b) American Convention on Human Rights, OC-11/90*, 10 September 1990. Series A No 11.
IACtHR, Advisory Opinion, *Juridical Condition and Rights of Undocumented Migrants, OC-18/03*, 17 September 2003. Series A No 18.
IACtHR, Advisory Opinion, *The Environment and Human Rights (State obligations in relation to the environment in the context of the protection and guarantee of the rights to life and to personal integrity – interpretation and scope of Articles 4(1) and 5(1) of the American Convention on Human Rights), OC-23/2017*, 15 November 2017. Series A No 23.

Separate, concurring, and dissenting votes

Concurring Opinion of Judge Eduardo Ferrer Mac-Gregor Poisot in IACtHR, Judgment (Preliminary Exceptions, Merits, Reparations and Costs), *Suárez Peralta v Ecuador*, 21 May 2013. Series C No 261.
Concurring Opinion of Judge Eduardo Ferrer Mac-Gregor Poisot in IACtHR, Judgment (Preliminary Objections, Merits, Reparations and Costs), *Gonzales Lluy and others v Ecuador*, 1 September 2015.
Concurring opinion of Judge Eduardo Vio Grossi in IACtHR, Judgment (Preliminary Objections, Merits, Reparations and Costs), *Hacienda Brasil Verde Workers v Brasil*, 20 October 2016.
Concurring Opinion of Judge Eduardo Ferrer Mac-Gregor Poisot in IACtHR, Judgment (Preliminary exceptions, merits, reparations and costs), *Lagos del Campo v. Peru*, 31 August 2017. Series C No 340.
Concurring Opinion of Judge Humberto Antonio Sierra Porto in IACtHR, Judgment (Preliminary exceptions, merits, reparations and costs), *Lagos del Campo v. Peru*, 31 August 2017. Series C No 340.
Separate opinion of Judge Eduardo Ferrer Mac-Gregor Poisot in in IACtHR, Judgment (Preliminary Objections, Merits, Reparations and Costs), *Hacienda Brasil Verde Workers v Brasil*, 20 October 2016.
Separate opinion of Judge Eduardo Ferrer Mac-Gregor Ferrer in IACtHR, Judgment (Preliminary Objections, Merits, Reparations and Costs), *Workers of the Fireworks Factory in Santo Antônio de Jesus and their Families v Brazil*, 15 July 2020.

Vote of Justice Luiz Fux in STF, Judgment, *ADPF 186/DF*, 26 April 2012. Justice Rapporteur: Ricardo Lewandowski.
Vote of Justice Joaquim Barbosa in STF, Judgment, *ADI 3.330/DF*, 03 May 2012. Justice Rapporteur: Ayres Britto.
Vote of Justice Rosa Weber in STF, Judgment, *ADPF 324/DF*, 30 August 2018. Justice Rapporteur: Roberto Barroso.
Vote of Justice Marco Aurélio in STF, Judgment, *ADPF 324/DF*, 30 August 2018. Justice Rapporteur: Roberto Barroso.
Vote of Justice Alexandre de Moraes in STF, Judgment, *ADI 3.446/DF*, 08 August 2019. Justice rapporteur: Gilmar Mendes.
Vote of Justice Ricardo Lewandowski in STF, Judgment, *ADI 3.446/DF*, 08 August 2019. Justice rapporteur: Gilmar Mendes.
Vote of Justice Marco Aurélio in STF, Judgment, *MI 7.300/DF*, 27 April 2021. Justice rapporteur: Gilmar Mendes.

Books and book chapters

Aranha, Adriana Veiga (org), *Fome Zero: Uma História Brasileira* (MDS, Vol I, 2010).
Arguelhes, Diego Werneck, 'Transformative Constitutionalism: A View from Brazil' in Philipp Dann, Michael Riegner, and Maxim Bönnemann (eds), *The Global South and Comparative Constitutional Law* (Oxford University Press 2020).
Banik, Dan, *Poverty and Elusive Development* (Universitetsforlaget 2010).
Bantekas, Ilias and Lutz Oette, *International Human Rights Law and Practice* (2nd edn, Cambridge University Press 2016).
Baxi, Upendra, 'The Avatars of Indian Judicial Activism: Explorations in the Geographies of [In]justice' in S K Verma and K Kusum (eds), *Fifty Years of the Supreme Court of India: Its Grasp and Reach*, vol 4 (Oxford University Press and Indian Law Institute 2001).
Bobbio, Norberto, 'Igualdade e desigualdade', *Direita e Esquerda: razões e significados de uma distinção política* (UNESP 2001).
Bogdandy, Armin von, 'The Mandate of the Inter-American System: Transformative Constitutionalism by a Common Law of Human Rights' in Inter-American Court of Human Rights (ed), *Dialogue Between Regional Human Rights Courts* (IACtHR 2020).
Brinks, Daniel M, 'Social Rights Constitutionalism' in Conrado Hübner Mendes, Roberto Gargarella, and Sebastián Guidi (eds), *The Oxford Handbook of Constitutional Law in Latin America* (Oxford University Press 2022).
Brinks, Daniel and Sandra Botero, 'Inequality and the Rule of Law: Ineffective Rights in Latin American Democracies' in Daniel Brinks, Marcelo Leiras, and Scott Mainwaring (eds), *Reflections on Uneven Democracies: The Legacy of Guillermo O'Donnell* (Johns Hopkins University Press 2014).
Câmara dos Deputados, *A construção do artigo 5o da Constituição de 1988* (Obras Comemorativas, Edições Câmara 2013).
Campello, Tereza (ed), *Faces da Desigualdade no Brasil: Um olhar sobre os que ficam para trás* (CLACSO, FLACSO, agenda igualdade 2017).
Campello, Tereza, Tiago Falcão and Patrícia Vieira da Costa (org), *O Brasil sem Miséria* (MDS 2014).
Chalhoub, Sidney, *Trabalho, lar e botequim: o cotidiano dos trabalhadores no Rio de Janeiro da belle époque* (Editora da Unicamp 2012).
Coelho, Vera Schattan P and Marcelo F Dias, 'Saúde e desigualdade no Brasil' in Marta Arretche (ed), *Trajetórias das desigualdades Como o Brasil mudou nos últimos cinquenta anos* (Editora UNESP 2015).

Confucius, *Confucian Analects: The Great Learning, and the Doctrine of the Mean*, translated by James Legge (Dover Publications 1971).

Davis, Kingsley and Wilbert E Moore, 'Some Principles of Stratification' in David B Grunsky and Katherine R Weisshaar (eds), *Social Stratification: Class, Race, and Gender in Sociological Perspective* (4th edn, Routledge 2018).

Evaristo, Conceição, *Olhos d'Água* (Pallas 2016).

Ferraz, Octávio Luiz Motta, 'Substantive Equality in law and Reality' in Conrado Hübner Mendes, Roberto Gargarella, and Sebastián Guidi (eds), *The Oxford Handbook of Constitutional Law in Latin America* (Oxford University Press, 2022).

France, Anatole, *Le Lys rouge* (Calmann-Lévy 1906).

Fraser, Nancy, *Scales of Justice: Reimagining Political Space in a Globalizing World* (Columbia University Press 2009).

Fraser, Nancy and Axel Honneth, *Redistribution or Recognition? A Political-Philosophical Exchange* (Verso 2003).

Fredman, Sandra, *Discrimination Law* (2nd edn, Oxford University Press 2011b).

Frye, Marilyn, 'Oppression' in Anne Minas (ed), *Gender Basics: Feminist Perspectives on Women and Men* (2nd edn, Wadsworth 2000).

Garcia Maia, Tainá, 'Brazil' in Niels Petersen (ed), Equality's Guardians: How Courts Conceptualize Equal Protection and Non-Discrimination Guarantees (Oxford University Press 2025).

Gargarella, Roberto, *Latin American Constitutionalism, 1810-2010: The Engine Room of the Constitution* (Oxford University Press 2013).

Gonzalez, Lélia, 'Racismo e Sexismo na Cultura Brasileira' in *Revista Ciências Sociais Hoje* (Anpocs 1984).

Hadiprayitno, Irene I, 'Poverty' in OHCHR (ed), *Realizing the Right to Development* (United Nations 2017).

Haider, Asad, *Armadilha da identidade: raça e classe nos dias de hoje* (Veneta 2019).

Jannuzzi, Paulo de Martino, *Indicadores Socioeconômicos na Gestão Pública* (Universidade Federal de Santa Catarina 2009).

Jannuzzi, Paulo de Martino and Paula Montagner, 'Estado de bem-estar, políticas públicas e mobilidade social no Brasil' in Jorge Abrahão de Castro and Marcio Pochmann (eds), *Brasil: Estado de bem-estar social?: limites, possibilidades e desafios* (Fundação Perseu Abramo 2020).

Khaitan, Tarunabh, *A Theory of Discrimination Law* (Oxford University Press 2015).

Lins, Paulo, *Cidade de Deus* (2nd edn, Companhia das Letras 2002).

Mackinnon, Catharine A, *Feminism Unmodified. Discourses on Life and Law* (Harvard University Press 1987).

Marx, Karl, 'Class in Capitalism and Pre-Capitalism' in David B Grusky and Szonja Szelényi (eds), *The Inequality Reader: Contemporary and Foundational Readings in Race, Class, and Gender* (2nd edn, Routledge 2018).

Medeiros, Marcelo, *Medidas de Desigualdade e Pobreza* (EdUNB 2012).

Mendes, Gilmar, 'As cortes constitucionais e sua condição de policy-maker: análise jurisprudencial da atuação do Supremo Tribunal Federal' in Tribunal Constitucional (ed), *Estudos em homenagem ao Conselheiro Presidente Joaquim de Sousa Ribeiro*, vol II (Almedina 2019).

Moyn, Samuel, *Not Enough: Human Rights in an Unequal World* (Harvard University Press 2018).

Nieto Navia, Rafael, 'La aplicación del principio Jura Novit Curia por los órganos del sistema interamericano de derechos humanos' in Ernesto J Rey Caro and María Cristina Rodríguez de Taborda (eds), *Estudios de Derecho International en homenaje a la dra Zlata Drnas de Clément* (Advocatus 2014).

Nonet, Philippe and Philip Selznick, *Law & Society in Transition: Toward Responsive Law* (2nd edn, Routledge 2017).
Nowak, Manfred, *UN Covenant on Civil and Political Rights. CCPR Commentary* (2nd edn, NP Engel Publishers 2005).
Ocobock, Paul, 'Introduction: Vagrancy and Homelessness in Global and Historical Perspective' in A L Beier and Paul Ocobock (eds), *Cast Out: Vagrancy and Homelessness in Global and Historical Perspective* (Ohio University Press 2008).
Paes-Sousa, Rômulo and Paulo de Martino Jannuzzi, 'Going Beyond the Eradication of Extreme Poverty: Debating the Sustainable Development Goals in Brazil' in D Cimadamore Alberto, Gabriele Koehler, and Thomas Pogge (eds), *Poverty and the Millennium Development Goals: A Critical Look Forward* (Zed Books 2016).
Piketty, Thomas, *Capital and Ideology* (Harvard University Press 2020).
Pogge, Thomas W, *World Poverty and Human Rights. Cosmopolitan Responsibiltiies and Reforms* (Policy Press; Blackwell Publishers 2002).
Pogge, Thomas W, 'Poverty, Hunger, and Cosmetic Progress' in Malcolm Langford, Andy Sumner, and Alicia Ely Yamin (ed), *The Millennium Development Goals and Human Rights: Past, Present and Future* (Cambridge University Press 2013).
Schutter, Olivier de, *International Human Rights Law* (2nd edn, Cambridge University Press 2014).
Secretary-General, UN, 'The Emergence of the Right to Development' in OHCHR (ed), *Realizing the Right to Development* (United Nations 2013).
Sen, Amartya, *Inequality Reexamined* (Oxford University Press 1992).
Sen, Amartya, *Development as Freedom* (Random House 1999).
Simmons, Beth A, *Mobilizing for Human Rights: International Law in Domestic Politics* (Cambridge University Press 2009).
Sousa, Mônica Teresa Costa, *Direito e Desenvolvimento* (Juruá 2011).
Supremo Tribunal Federal, *Convenção Americana sobre Direitos Humanos: Anotada com a jurisprudência do Supremo Tribunal Federal e da Corte Interamericana de Direitos Humanos* (2nd edn, STF, Secretaria de Altos Estudos, Pesquisas e Gestão da Informação 2022).
Sweetman, Caroline, 'Editorial' in Caroline Sweetman (ed), *Gender and the Millennium Development Goals* (Oxfam GB, 2005).
Tumin, Melvin M, 'Some Principles of Stratification: A Critical Analysis' in David B Grunsky and Katherine R Weisshaar (eds), *Social Stratification: Class, Race, and Gender in Sociological Perspective* (4th edn, Routledge 2018).
Weber, Max, 'Class, Status, Party' in David B Grusky (ed), *Social Stratification: Class, Race, and Gender in Sociological Perspective* (4th edn, Westview Press 2018).
Weber, Max, 'Status Groups and Classes Social Stratification: Class, Race, and Gender in Sociological Perspective' in David B Grusky (ed), *Social Stratification: Class, Race, and Gender in Sociological Perspective* (4th edn, Westview Press 2018).
Willis, Katie, *Theories and Practices of Development* (2nd edn, Routledge 2011).
Wright, Erik Olin, 'A General Framework for the Analysis of Class Structure' in David B Grusky (ed), *Social Stratification: Class, Race, and Gender in Sociological Perspective* (4th edn, Routledge 1984).
Xun, Lu, 'The Epigrams of Lusin' in Lin Yutang (ed), *The Wisdom of China* (Michael Joseph 1944).

Journal articles

Abreu, Laurinda, 'Beggars, Vagrants and Romanies: Repression and Persecution in Portuguese Society (14th–18th Centuries)' (2007) 6 Hygiea Internationalis—An Interdisciplinary Journal for the History of Public Health 41.

Aguiar, Odaleia Barbosa de and Susana Moreira Padrão, 'Direito humano à alimentação adequada: fome, desigualdade e pobreza como obstáculos para garantir direitos sociais' (2022) 143 Serviço Social & Sociedade 121.
Albertyn, Cathi and Beth Goldblatt, 'Facing the Challenge of Transformation: Difficulties in the Development of an Indigenous Jurisprudence of Equality' (1998) 14 South African Journal on Human Rights 248.
Almeida, Danilo dos Santos and André Martins Bogossian, '"Nos Termos do Voto do Relator": considerações acerca da fundamentação coletiva nos acórdãos so STF' (2016) 2 Revista Estudos Institucionais 263.
Antunes Rocha and Cármen Lúcia, 'Ação afirmativa: O conteúdo democrático do princípio da igualdade jurídica' (1996) 33 Revista de Informação Legislativa 283.
Atrey, Shreya, 'The Intersectional Case of Poverty in Discrimination Law' (2018) 18 Human Rights Law Review 411.
Barros, Ricardo Paes de, Ricardo Henriques, and Rosane Mendonça, 'Desigualdade e Pobreza no Brasil: retrato de uma estabilidade inaceitável' (2000) 15 Revista Brasileira de Ciências Sociais 123.
Bertoncelo, Edison Ricardo, 'O espaço das classes sociais no Brasil' (2016) 28 Tempo Social 73.
Beteille, Andre, 'Poverty and Inequality' (2003) 38 Economic and Political Weekly 4455.
Biroli, Flávia and Luis Felipe Miguel, 'Gênero, raça, classe: opressões cruzadas e cconvergências na reprodução das desigualdades' (2015) 20 Mediações—Revista de Ciências Sociais 27.
Bogdandy, Armin von and René Urueña, 'International Transformative Constitutionalism in Latin America' (2020) 114 American Journal of International Law 403.
Bogdandy, Armin von and Ingo Venzke, 'On the Democratic Legitimation of International Judicial Lawmaking' (2011) 12 German Law Journal 1341.
Brodsky, Gwen and Shelagh Day, 'Beyond the Social and Economic Rights Debate: Substantive Equality Speaks to Poverty' (2002) 14 Canadian Journal of Women and the Law 184.
Brown, Wendy, 'Suffering Rights as Paradoxes' (2000) 7 Constellations 230.
Cardoso, Adalberto and Edmond Préteceille, 'Classes Médias no Brasil: Do que se Trata? Qual seu Tamanho? Como Vem Mudando?' (2017) 60 DADOS—Revista de Ciências Sociais 977.
Cepeda Espinosa, Manuel José, 'Responsive Constitutionalism' (2019) 15 Annual Review of Law and Social Science 21.
Chill, Emanuel, 'Religion and Mendicity in Seventeenth-Century France' (1962) 7 International Review of Social History 400.
Chimni, Bhupinder Singh, 'The Past, Present and Future of international Law: A Critical Third World Approach' (2007) 8 Melbourne Journal of International Law 499.
Collins, Patricia Hill, 'Intersectionality's Definitional Dilemmas' (2015) 41 Annual Review of Sociology 1.
Crenshaw, Kimberlé, 'Mapping the Margins: Identity Politics, Intersectionality, and Violence against Women' (1991) 43 Stanford Law Review 1241.
Crenshaw, Kimberlé, 'Documento para o encontro de especialistas em aspectos da discriminação racial relativos ao gênero' (2002) 10 Revista Estudos Feministas 171.
Ferraz, Octávio Luiz Motta, 'The Right to Health in the Courts of Brazil: Worsening Health Inequities?' (2009) 11 Health and Human Rights 33.
Ferraz, Octávio Luiz Motta, 'Harming the Poor Through Social Rights Litigation: Lessons from Brazil' (2011) 89 Texas Law Review 1643.
Ferraz, Octávio Luiz Motta, 'Inequality, Not Insufficiency: Making Social Rights Real in a World of Plenty' (2014) 12 The Equal Rights Review 77.
Ferraz, Octávio Luiz Motta, 'The Right to Health in the Courts of Brazil: Still Worsening Health Inequities?' (2017) 5 Revista del Centro de Estudios Constitucionales 195.
Fineman, Martha Albertson, 'The Vulnerable Subject: Anchoring Equality in the Human Condition' (2008) 20 Yale Journal of Law and Feminism 1.

Fredman, Sandra, 'The Potential and Limits of an Equal Rights Paradigm in Addressing Poverty' (2011a) 22 Stellenbosch Law Review 566.
Fredman, Sandra, 'Substantive Equality Revisited' (2016a) 14 International Journal of Constitutional Law 712.
Fredman, Sandra, 'Women and Poverty—A Human Rights Approach' (2016b) 24 African Journal of International and Comparative Law 494.
Fredman, Sandra, Jaakko Kuosmanen, and Meghan Campbell, 'Transformative Equality: Making the Sustainable Development Goals Work for Women' (2016) 30(2) Ethics & International Affairs 177.
Giarola, Flávio Raimundo, 'Trabalho e combate à vadiagem: representações da mão-de-obra nos discursos dos periódicos de São João del-Rei (1871–1888)' (2012) 4 Temporalidades 278.
Hall, Anthony, 'Brazil's Bolsa Família: A Double-Edged Sword?' (2008) 39 Development and Change 799.
Hepple, Bob, 'Discrimination and Equality of Opportunity—Northern Irish Lessons' (1990) 10 Oxford Journal of Legal Studies 408.
Hirschl, Ran, 'The Judicialization of Mega-Politics and the Rise of Political Courts' (2008) 11 Annual Review of Political Science 93.
Jannuzzi, Paulo de Martino, Enrico Moreira Martignoni, and Baiena Feijolo Souto, 'Programa Bolsa Família e sua contribuição para redução da pobreza no Brasil' (2012) 4 Revista Brasileira de Monitoramento e Avaliação 40.
Jennings, W Ivor, 'Poor Relief in Industrial Disputes' (1930) 46 Law Quarterly Review 225.
Kong, Karen, 'The Right to Food for All: Right-Based Approach to Hunger and Social Inequality' (2009) 32 Suffolk Transnational Law Review 525.
Lima, Flávia Danielle Santiago, 'Revisitando os pressupostos da juristocracia à brasileira: mobilização judicial na Assembleia Constituinte e o fortalecimento do Supremo Tribunal Federal' (2018) 63 Revista da Faculdade de Direito UFPR 145.
Louro, Guacira Lopes, 'Teoria queer—uma politica pós-identitária para a educação' (2001) 9 Estudos Feministas 541.
McCann, Michael, 'Law and Social Movements: Contemporary Perspectives' (2006) 2 Annual Review of Law and Social Science 17.
Mello, Marco Aurélio, 'Óptica constitucional: a igualdade e as ações afirmativas' (2001) 17 Revista do Tribunal Regional do Trabalho da 15ª Região 156.
Petersen, Niels, 'Avoiding the Common-Wisdom Fallacy: The Role of Social Sciences in Constitutional Adjudication' (2013) 11 International Journal of Constitutional Law 294.
Ravallion, Martin, Shaohua Chen, and Sangraula Prem, 'Dollar a Day Revisited' (2009) 2 The World Bank Economic Review 163.
Razzolini, Orsola, 'Constitutionalization of Socio-Economic Rights at the EU Level: Some Critical Notes' (2015) 98 Critical Quarterly for Legislation and Law 284.
Salata, André, 'Distribuição de renda no Brasil entre 2002 e 2013: Redução das desigualdades entre classes?' (2018a) 53 Latin American Research Review 76.
Salata, André, 'Ensino Superior no Brasil das últimas décadas: Redução nas desigualdades de acesso?' (2018b) 30 Tempo Social 219.
Terra, Paulo Cruz, 'Racismo, trabalho e ociosidade no processo de abolição: o Brasil e o Império Português numa perspectiva global (1870-1888)' (2021) 41 Revista Brasileira de História 155.
Tronco, Giordano Benites and Marília Patta Ramos, 'Linhas de pobreza no Plano Brasil Sem Miséria: análise crítica e proposta de alternativas para a medição da pobreza conforme metodologia de Sonia Rocha' (2017) 51 Revista de Administração Pública 294.
Valença, Manuela Abath, 'A Construção Social da Vadiagem nos Discursos Jurídicos do Início da Era Republicana' (2014) 1 Revista Brasileira de Sociologia do Direito 98.

Westen, Peter, 'The Empty Idea of Equality' (1982) 95 Harvard Law Review 537.
Young, Iris Marion, 'Five Faces of Oppression' (1988) 19 The Philosophical Forum 270.
Zimmermann, Clóvis Roberto, 'Os Programas Sociais sob a Ótica dos Direitos Humanos: o caso do Bolsa Família do governo Lula no Brasil' (2006) 4 SUR—International Journal on Human Rights 145.

Reports

Alfani F and others, June 2025 Update to the Poverty and Inequality Platform (PIP) (Global Poverty Monitoring Technical Note, 2025).
Berg, Janine, *Brazil. Conditional transfers as response to the Crisis: the Bolsa Família Programme* (ILO Notes on the Crisis, 2009).
Canadian Human Rights Act Review Panel, Report of the Canadian Human Rights Act Review Panel (2000).
Corte IDH. Caso Empregados da Fábrica de Fogos de Santo Antônio de Jesus e seus familiares vs. Brasil. Relatório de cumprimento, 02 June 2023.
Dias Silva, Tatiana and Marques da Silva, Josenilton, *Nota Técnica: Reserva de vagas para negros em concursos públicos: uma análise a partir do Projeto de Lei 6.738/2013* (IPEA, 2014).
Hunt, Paul, *Statement to the Panel on Maternal Mortality and the Human Rights of Women* (2008).
IBGE, *Desigualdades Sociais por Cor ou Raça no Brasil* (Estudos e Pesquisas informação Demográfica e Socioeconômica, 2019).
IBGE, *Desigualdades Sociais por Cor ou Raça no Brasil* (Estudos e Pesquisas Informação Demográfica e Socioeconômica, 2022).
IBGE, *Estatísticas do Século XX* (2006).
IBGE, *Pesquisa Nacional por Amostra de Domicílios Contínua Segundo Trimestre de 2021 (abr.-jun.)* (Indicadores IBGE, 2021).
IBGE, *PNAD 2009* (Pesquisa Nacional por Amostra de Domicílios, 2009).
IBGE, *PNAD Contínua: Características gerais dos domicílios e dos moradores 2023* (Pesquisa Nacional por Amostra de Domicílios, 2024).
IBGE, *PNAD Contínua Educação 2019* (Pesquisa Nacional por Amostra de Domicílios Contínua, 2020).
IBGE, *PNAD Contínua Educação 2022* (Pesquisa Nacional por Amostra de Domicílios Contínua, 2023).
IBGE, *PNAD Contínua Educação 2023* (Pesquisa Nacional por Amostra de Domicílios Contínua, 2024).
IBGE, *PNADC Quarto Trimestre de 2020 (out.-dez. 2020)* (Indicadores IBGE, 2021).
IBGE, *PNADC Segundo Trimestre de 2021 (abr.-jun. 2021)* (Indicadores IBGE, 2021).
IBGE, *PNADC Trimestre móvel: out-nov-dez/2021* (Indicadores IBGE, 2022).
IBGE, *Síntese de Indicadores Sociais: Uma Análise das Condições de Vida da População Brasileira 2012* (Estudos & Pesquisas Informação demográfica e socioeconômica, 2012).
IBGE, *Síntese de Indicadores Sociais: Uma Análise das Condições de Vida da População Brasileira 2013* (Estudos & Pesquisas Informação demográfica e socioeconômica, 2013).
IBGE, *Síntese de Indicadores Sociais: Uma Análise das Condições de Vida da População Brasileira 2014* (Estudos & Pesquisas Informação demográfica e socioeconômica, 2014).
IBGE, *Síntese de Indicadores Sociais: Uma Análise das Condições de Vida da População Brasileira 2015* (Estudos & Pesquisas Informação demográfica e socioeconômica, 2015).
IBGE, *Síntese de Indicadores Sociais: Uma Análise das Condições de Vida da População Brasileira 2016* (Estudos & Pesquisas Informação demográfica e socioeconômica, 2016).

IBGE, *Síntese de Indicadores Sociais: Uma Análise das Condições de Vida da População Brasileira 2017* (Estudos & Pesquisas Informação demográfica e socioeconômica, 2017).
IBGE, *Síntese de Indicadores Sociais: Uma Análise das Condições de Vida da População Brasileira 2018* (Estudos & Pesquisas Informação demográfica e socioeconômica, 2018).
IBGE, *Síntese de Indicadores Sociais 2019: Uma Análise das Condições de Vida da População Brasileira* (Estudos & Pesquisas Informação demográfica e socioeconômica, 2019).
IBGE, *Síntese de Indicadores Sociais: Uma Análise das Condições de Vida da População Brasileira 2020* (Estudos & Pesquisas Informação demográfica e socioeconômica, 2020).
IBGE, *Síntese de Indicadores Sociais: Uma Análise das Condições de Vida da População Brasileira 2021* (Estudos & Pesquisas Informação demográfica e socioeconômica, 2021).
IBGE, *Síntese de Indicadores Sociais: Uma Análise das Condições de Vida da População Brasileira 2022* (Estudos & Pesquisas Informação demográfica e socioeconômica, 2022).
IBGE, *Síntese de Indicadores Sociais: Uma Análise das Condições de Vida da População Brasileira 2023* (Estudos & Pesquisas Informação demográfica e socioeconômica, 2023).
IBGE, *Síntese de Indicadores Sociais: Uma Análise das Condições de Vida da População Brasileira 2024* (Estudos & Pesquisas Informação demográfica e socioeconômica, 2024).
IBGE, *Síntese de Indicadores Sociais: Uma Análise das Condições de Vida da População Brasileira 2025* (Estudos & Pesquisas Informação demográfica e socioeconômica, 2025).
IBGE, *Tábua completa de mortalidade para o Brasil – 2019: Breve análise da evolução da mortalidade no Brasil* (2020).
IBGE, Coordenação de Trabalho e Rendimento, *Pesquisa de orçamentos familiares 2017-2018: análise da segurança alimentar no Brasil* (2020).
IBGE, Ministério da Economia and Ministério da Saúde, *Pesquisa Nacional de Saúde 2019: Informações sobre domicílios, acesso e utilização dos serviços de saúde. Brasil, Grandes Regiões e Unidades da Federação* (2020).
IFAD, FAO, WFP, *The State of Food Insecurity in the World 2013. The multiple dimensions of food security* (2013).
International Labour Organization; ILO Office in Brazil, *Combatendo o Trabalho Escravo Contemporâneo: o exemplo do Brasil* (2010).
IPEA and FBSP, *Atlas da Violência 2025* (2025).
IPEA, *Políticas sociais: acompanhamento e análise* (2014).
IPEA and others, *Retrato das Desigualdades de raça e gênero* (2014).
Jollife, Dean and Pryds, Espen Beer, *Estimating International Poverty Lines from Comparable National Thresholds* (Policy Research Working Paper 7606, 2016).
OECD, *OECD Health at a Glance 2023 Country Note—Denmark* (2023).
OPHI, *Country Briefing: Brazil* (2010).
OPHI, *Country Briefing: Brazil* (2011).
OPHI, *Country Briefing Dec 2015: Brazil* (2015).
OPHI, *Country Briefing December 2016: Brazil* (2016).
OPHI, *Country Briefing 2017: Brazil* (2017).
OPHI, *Global MPI Country Briefing 2018: Brazil (Latin America and the Caribbean)* (2018).
OPHI, *Global MPI Country Briefing 2024: Brazil (Latin America and the Caribbean)* (2024).
Ravallion, Martin, *On Multidimensional Indeces of Poverty* (Policy Research Working Paper 5580, 2011).
Rede Nossa São Paulo, *Mapa da Desigualdade 2023* (2023).
Rede PENSSAN, *Inquérito nacional sobre insegurança alimentar no contexto da pandemia da Covid-19 no Brasil (Versão Resumida)* (2021).
UNDP, *Briefing note for countries on the 2022 Multidimensional Poverty Index: Brazil. Unpacking deprivation bundles to reduce multidimensional poverty* (2022).

UNDP and OPHI, *Global Multidimensional Poverty Index (MPI): Unpacking deprivation bundles to reduce multidimensional poverty* (2022).
World Bank, *World Development Report 1990: Poverty* (World Development Indicators, 1990).
World Bank Group, *Poverty and Shared Prosperity 2022: Correcting Course* (Poverty and Shared Prosperity, 2022).

Databases and charts

Banco Central do Brasil, 'Focus: Relatório de Mercado' (Banco Central, 2021) <https://www.bcb.gov.br/content/focus/focus/R20210924.pdf> accessed 30 September 2021.
DataBank, 'Poverty and Equity: Brazil and Latin America & Caribbean' (World Bank) <https://databank.worldbank.org/reports.aspx?source=2&Topic=11> accessed 28 February 2023.
DataBank, 'Poverty and Equity: SubSaharan Africa' (World Bank) <https://databank.worldbank.org/reports.aspx?source=poverty-and-equity-database> accessed 6 October 2021.
DataBank, 'Poverty and Equity: World' (World Bank) <https://databank.worldbank.org/reports.aspx?source=poverty-and-equity-database> accessed 6 October 2021.
FAO, 'FAOSTAT. Brazil', FAOSTAT_data_en_8-29-2025 <https://www.fao.org/faostat/en/#country/21> accessed 29 August 2025.
FAO, 'Hunger map' <https://www.fao.org/interactive/hunger-map/en/> accessed 29 August 2025.
IBGE, 'PNAD Contínua Painel' <https://painel.ibge.gov.br/pnadc/> accessed 6 May 2023.
IBGE, 'PNAD Séries históricas' <https://www.ibge.gov.br/estatisticas/multidominio/condicoes-de-vida-desigualdade-e-pobreza/9127-pesquisa-nacional-por-amostra-de-domicilios.html?=&t=series-historicas> accessed 9 September 2021.
IBGE, 'PNADC. Séries históricas: desemprego' <https://www.ibge.gov.br/estatisticas/sociais/trabalho/9173-pesquisa-nacional-por-amostra-de-domicilios-continua-trimestral.html?=&t=series-historicas&utm_source=landing&utm_medium=explica&utm_campaign=desempre> accessed 28 August 2025.
IBGE, 'SIS 2024, Tabelas "Padrão de vida e distribuição de rendimentos"', Table 2.18 (Pobr_Geo) (2024) <https://www.ibge.gov.br/estatisticas/sociais/populacao/9221-sintese-de-indicadores-sociais.html?edicao=42003&t=resultados> accessed 3 September 2025.
IBGE, 'Tábuas Completas de Mortalidade', BRASIL: Tábua Completa de Mortalidade—Ambos os Sexos—2023 (2023) <https://www.ibge.gov.br/estatisticas/sociais/populacao/9126-tabuas-completas-de-mortalidade.html> accessed 29 August 2025.
IBGE, 'Taxa de mortalidade infantil' <https://cidades.ibge.gov.br/brasil/pesquisa/39/30279> accessed 29 August 2025.
IBGEeduca, 'Conheça o Brasil—População. Educação' (IBGE, <https://educa.ibge.gov.br/jovens/conheca-o-brasil/populacao/18317-educacao.html> accessed 1 October 2021.
Inter-American Commission on Human Rights, 'B-32: American Convention on Human Rights "Pact of San José, Costa Rica"' <https://www.cidh.oas.org/basicos/english/Basic4.Amer.Conv.Ratif.htm> accessed 6 May 2023.
IPEA, 'Salário mínimo vigente' <http://www.ipeadata.gov.br/ExibeSerie.aspx?serid=1739471028> accessed 9 May 2023.
Peliano, T M Anna Maria (coord), O Mapa da Fome: Subsídios à Formulação de uma Política de Segurança Alimentar (Documento de Política No 14, IPEA, 1993).
Poverty & Inequality Platform, 'Poverty rate, % $2.15' (World Bank), <https://pip.worldbank.org/poverty-calculator> accessed 28 August 2025.

SAGI, 'Plano Brasil sem Miséria: PNAD 2013, Trajetória da Extrema *Pobreza*' (SAGI, MDS 2014).
World Bank, 'Historical MPM data', MPM-Historical-Data-AM2024-Final (World Bank) <https://documents.worldbank.org/en/publication/documents-reports/documentdetail/099109206232539968?> accessed 29 August 2025. Last update: April 2024.
World Bank, 'Individuals in households deprived in each indicator, 120 economies, circa year 2021 (2018-2024)' <https://documents1.worldbank.org/curated/en/099001206232524312/pdf/IDU-194bdd26-98c5-48f5-921c-3225b66a5716.pdf> accessed 29 August 2025. Last update: June 2025.
World Bank, 'Life expectancy at birth, total (years)—Malawi (2024)' <https://data.worldbank.org/indicator/SP.DYN.LE00.IN?locations=MW>, accessed 29 January 2024.
World Bank, 'World Bank Country and Lending Groups. Country Classification' <https://datahelpdesk.worldbank.org/knowledgebase/articles/906519> accessed 31 August 2021.
World Bank, '2023 in Nine Charts: A Growing Inequality' (2023) <https://www.worldbank.org/en/news/feature/2023/12/18/2023-in-nine-charts-a-growing-inequality?intcid=ecr_hp_headerA_2023-12-18-EndofYearCharts> accessed 6 January 2024.
World Bank, 'Poverty headcount ratio at $1.90 a day (2011 PPP) (% of population)', API_SI.POV.DDAY_DS2_en_excel_v2_2764652, <https://databank.worldbank.org/reports.aspx?source=2&country=BRA; https://data.worldbank.org/indicator/SI.POV.DDAY?view=map> accessed 2 December 2023.

Conference proceedings and meeting records

Deputados, Brazil. Câmara dos Srs, 'Annaes do Parlamento Brazileiro', vol VI, 1–31 October 1988.
Deputados, Brazil. Câmara dos Srs, 'Annaes do Parlamento Brazileiro', vol VII, 1–31 October 1988.
OAS, 'Conferencia Especializada Interamericana sobre Derechos Humanos', Actas y documentos, 7–22 November 1969.
Rights, World Conference on Human, 'Report of the World Conference on Human Rights. Report of the Secretary-General', A/CONF157/24 (Part I), 14–25 June 1993.
UN, 'Report of the United Nations Conference on Environment and Development, vol.II, Proceedings of the Conference', A/CONF151/26Rev1 (Vol II), 3–14 June 1992.
UNCTAD, 'Proceedings of the United Nations Conference on Trade and Development, Second Session', New Delhi, 1 February–29 March 1968.
UNCTAD, 'Proceedings of the United Nations Conference on Trade and Development, Third Session', Santiago del Chile, 13 April–21 May 1972.
UNGA, 'Official Records, Twenty-first Session', 1414th Plenary Meeting, 23 September 1966.
UNGA, 'Provisional Verbatim Record of the Nineth-Seventh Meeting', A/41/PV97, 4 December 1986.

Conference papers, working papers, and theses

Fraser, Nancy, *Social Justice in the Age of Identity Politics: Redistribution, Recognition, and Participation* (Stanford Univesity 1996).
Neri, Marcelo Cortes (coord), *A Nova Classe Média* (FGV 2008).
Serra, Adriana Stankiewicz, Yalonetzky, Gaston Isaias, and Belik, Walter 'Pobreza Multidimensional no Brasil, 2000/2010' (45o Encontro Nacional de Economia - ANPEC).

Teixeira, Daniel Tomazine, 'Enquadramento da Pobreza em Portugal do Baixo Medievo: Assistencialismo e Repressão Estatal (séculos XIV/XV)' (Universidade Federal Fluminense 2011).

UNGA, 'Official Records of the Twenty-Ninth Session of the UNGA', A/PV2315, 12 December 1974.

Other documents from international organizations or governments

Bolsonaro, Jair Messias, *Inauguration Address at the National Congress: 1 January 2019* (2019).

Bolsonaro, Jair Messias, *Inauguration Address at the Presidential Palace: 1 January 2019* (2019).

Cardoso, Fernando Henrique, *Inauguration Address: 1 January 1995* (1995).

CEDAW, UN Committee on the Elimination of Discrimination Against Women, 'General recommendation No. 25 on article 4, paragraph 1, of the Convention on the Elimination of All Forms of Discrimination against Women, on temporary special measures', 2004.

CERD, UN Committee on the Elimination of Racial Discrimination, 'General Recommendation no. 32, The meaning and scope of special measures in the International Convention on the Elimination of All Forms of Racial Discrimination', CERD/C/GC/32, 24 September 2009.

CESCR, United Nations, 'General Comment No.20: Non-discrimination in economic, social and cultural rights (art.2, para.2 of the International Covenant on Economic, Social and Cultural Rights)', E/C12/GC/20, 2 July 2009.

Council, Human Rights, 'Final draft of the guiding principles on extreme poverty and human rights, submitted by the Special Rapporteur on extreme poverty and human rights, Magdalena Sepúlveda Carmona', A/HRC/21/39, 18 July 2012.

Feres, Juan Carlos and Pablo Villatoro, *A viabilidade de se erradicar a pobreza: uma análise conceitual e metodológica* (Cadernos de Estudos Desenvolvimento Social em Debate 2013).

Fome, Ministério do Desenvolvimento Social e Combate à, *Questões metodológicas acerca do dimensionamento da extrema pobreza no Brasil nos anos 2000. Estudo técnico No 08/2014* (MDS 2014).

IACommHR, 'Report of the Inter-American Commission on Human Rights on the Status of Women in the Americas', OEA/SerL/V/II100 Doc 17, 13 October 1998.

IACommHR, Inter-American Commission on Human Rights, 'Considerations regarding the compatibility of affirmative action measures designed to promote the political participation of women with the principles of equality and non-discrimination', 1999.

IACommHR, 'Compendium: Equality and non-discrimination. Inter-American Standards', OEA/SerL/V/II171 Doc 31, 12 February 2019.

Ministry of Human Rights and Citizenship of, Brazil 'Pedido de Informação nº 00105.001332/2025-08 (4786717)', General Coordination of the Special Advisory Office for International Affairs, 12 March 2025.

Ministry of Social Development and Fight Against Hunger, 'Pedido de Acesso à Informação 71003.011320/2025-70', Department of Social Assistance Benefits, 25 March 2025.

Ministry of Social Development and Fight Against Hunger of Brazil, 'Pedido de Acesso à Informação 71003.011320/2025-70', SENARC/SNAS, 25 March 2025.

Sengupta, Arjun K., 'Study on the current state of progress in of the right to development submitted by Mr. Arjun K. Sengupta, independent expert, pursuant to Commission resolution 1998/72 the implementation and General Assembly resolution 53/155', E/CN4/1999/WG18/2, 13-17 September 1999.

Silva, Luis Inácio Lula da, *Inauguration Address at the National Congress: 1 January 2003* (2003).

Silva, Luis Inácio Lula da, *Inauguration Address at the National Congress: 1 January 2023* (2023).

Press releases and blogposts

FAO, 'José Graziano da Silva of Brazil elected FAO Director-General' (Issue 26 June 2011) <https://www.fao.org/news/story/pt/item/80713/icode/> accessed 6 May 2023.

Ferreira, Francisco, Dean Jolliffe, and Espen Beer Prydz, *The international poverty line has just been raised to $1.90 a day, but global poverty is basically unchanged. How is that even possible?* (World Bank Blogs 2015).

Filmer, Deon, Haishan Fu, and Luis Felipe López-Calva, *Further strengthening how we measure global poverty* (World Bank Blogs 2025).

gov.br, 'Prorrogado por mais três meses o pagamento do Auxílio Emergencial 2021' (2021) <https://www.gov.br/casacivil/pt-br/assuntos/noticias/2021/agosto/prorrogado-por-mais-tres-meses-o-pagamento-do-auxilio-emergencial-2021> accessed 7 May 2023.

gov.br, 'Mulheres são responsáveis familiares em 81% das concessões do Bolsa Família' (2023) <https://www.gov.br/planalto/pt-br/acompanhe-o-planalto/noticias/2023/03/mulheres-sao-responsaveis-familiares-em-81-das-concessoes-do-bolsa-familia> accessed 26 April 2023.

gov.br, 'Brasil sai do Mapa da Fome da ONU: conquista histórica reflete políticas públicas eficazes' (2025) <https://www.gov.br/mds/pt-br/noticias-e-conteudos/desenvolvimento-social/noticias-desenvolvimento-social/brasil-sai-do-mapa-da-fome-da-onu-conquista-historica-reflete-politicas-publicas-eficazes> accessed 22 September 2025.

Mahler, Daniel Gerszon and others, *Updated estimates of the impact of COVID-19 on global poverty: Turning the corner on the pandemic in 2021?* (2021).

Ministry of Human Rights and Citizenship of Brazil, 'Novo Plano Nacional de Erradicação do Trabalho Escravo está em fase de elaboração, após 16 anos sem atualização' (2025) <https://www.gov.br/mdh/pt-br/assuntos/noticias/2025/janeiro/novo-plano-nacional-de-erradicacao-do-trabalho-escravo-esta-em-fase-de-elaboracao-apos-16-anos-sem-atualizacao> accessed 29 March 2025.

Notícias, Agência IBGE, 'Em 2022, expectativa de vida era de 75,5 anos' (*IBGE* 2023) <https://agenciadenoticias.ibge.gov.br/agencia-sala-de-imprensa/2013-agencia-de-noticias/releases/38455-em-2022-expectativa-de-vida-era-de-75-5-anos> accessed 15 February 2024.

Rios, Marianna, '"Brazil has succeeded in overcoming extreme poverty", claims the MDS' (*World Without Poverty: Brazil Learning Initiative* 2015) <https://wwp.org.br/en/brazil-has-succeeded-in-overcoming-extreme-poverty-claims-the-mds-based-on-the-national-household-sample-survey-2014/> accessed 6 May 2023.

Schoch, Marta, Christoph Lakner, and Samuel Freije-Rodriguez, *Monitoring poverty at the US$3.20 and US$5.50 lines: differences and similarities with extreme poverty trends* (World Bank Blogs 2020).

World Bank, 'World Bank Sees Progress Against Extreme Poverty, But Flags Vulnerabilities' (Issue 29 February 2012) <https://www.worldbank.org/en/news/press-release/2012/02/29/world-bank-sees-progress-against-extreme-poverty-but-flags-vulnerabilities> accessed 29 August 2021.

World Bank, 'FAQs: Global Poverty Line Update' (Issue 30 September 2015) <https://www.worldbank.org/en/topic/poverty/brief/global-poverty-line-faq> accessed 29 August 2021.

World Bank, 'COVID-19 to Add as Many as 150 Million Extreme Poor by 2021' (Issue 7 October 2020) <https://www.worldbank.org/en/news/press-release/2020/10/07/covid-19-to-add-as-many-as-150-million-extreme-poor-by-2021> accessed 29 August 2021.

World Bank, 'How to Reduce Poverty: A New Lesson from Brazil for the World?' (*The World Bank* 2014) <https://www.worldbank.org/en/news/feature/2014/03/22/mundo-sin-pobreza-leccion-brasil-mundo-bolsa-familia> accessed 6 May 2023.

World Bank, 'Impacts of COVID-19 in Brazil: Evidence on persons with disabilities during the pandemic' (*The World Bank* 2021) <https://www.worldbank.org/en/country/brazil/brief/impactos-da-covid19-no-brasil-evidencias-sobre-pessoas-com-deficiencia-durante-a-pandemia> accessed 7 May 2023.

World Bank, 'June 2025 Update to Global Poverty Lines' (2025) <https://www.worldbank.org/en/news/factsheet/2025/06/05/june-2025-update-to-global-poverty-lines> accessed 18 August 2025.

Newspaper articles

Agência Senado, 'Congresso muda Auxílio Brasil no primeiro semestre e assegura benefício de R$ 600' *Senado Notícias* (15 July 2022) <https://www12.senado.leg.br/noticias/materias/2022/07/15/congresso-muda-auxilio-brasil-no-primeiro-semestre-e-assegura-beneficio-de-r-600> accessed 28 August 2025.

'Life in Elizabethan England' *BBC Bitesize* <https://www.bbc.co.uk/bitesize/guides/zxjgqty/revision/3> accessed 11 September 2024.

'Semana Parlamentar' *Gazeta da Tarde* (7 May 1888) <http://memoria.bn.br/pdf/226688/per226688_1888_00103.pdf> accessed 11 September 2024.

Bello, Luiz, 'Em 2023, pobreza no país cai ao menor nível desde 2012' Agência IBGE Notícias (4 December 2024) <https://agenciadenoticias.ibge.gov.br/agencia-noticias/2012-agencia-de-noticias/noticias/42043-em-2023-pobreza-no-pais-cai-ao-menor-nivel-desde-2012> accessed 3 September 2025.

Cabral, Umberlândia and Caio Belandi, 'Desemprego recua para 12,6% no terceiro trimestre e atinge 13,5 milhões de pessoas' *Agência IBGE Notícias* (29 December 2021) <https://agenciadenoticias.ibge.gov.br/agencia-noticias/2012-agencia-de-noticias/noticias/32362-desemprego-recua-para-12-6-no-terceiro-trimestre-e-atinge-13-5-milhoes-de-pessoas> accessed 8 May 2023.

Cowie, Sam, 'Brazil: Extreme poverty on the rise as elections loom' *Al Jazeera* (26 September 2018) <https://www.aljazeera.com/economy/2018/9/26/brazil-extreme-poverty-on-the-rise-as-elections-loom> accessed 13 February 2024.

Estatísticas Sociais, 'Em 2019, expectativa de vida era de 76,6 anos' *Agência IBGE Notícias* (26 November 2020) <https://agenciadenoticias.ibge.gov.br/agencia-sala-de-imprensa/2013-agencia-de-noticias/releases/29502-em-2019-expectativa-de-vida-era-de-76-6-anos> accessed 7 May 2023.

Gasnier, Annie, 'Au Brésil, 12 millions de familles mangent grâce à une bourse' *Le Monde* (14 September 2010) <https://www.lemonde.fr/planete/article/2010/09/14/au-bresil-12-millions-de-familles-mangent-grace-a-une-bourse_1411106_3244.html> accessed 6 May 2023.

Gual, Juan Royo, 'Brazil vuelve a pasar hambre' *El Mundo* (20 June 2021) <https://www.elmundo.es/internacional/2021/06/20/60ce0267fc6c83b50d8b4650.html> accessed 13 February 2024.

Kim, Jim Young, 'Brazil's Contribution to a World Free of Poverty' *Valor Economico* (24 March 2014) <https://www.worldbank.org/en/news/opinion/2014/03/24/brazil-contribution-world-without-poverty> accessed 6 May 2023.

Londoño, Ernesto and Milhorance, Flávia, 'Ravaged by Covid, Brazil Faces a Hunger Epidemic' *The New York Times* (23 April 2021) <https://www.nytimes.com/2021/04/23/world/americas/covid-brazil-hunger.html> accessed 13 February 2024.

Lowrie, Annie, 'Dire Poverty Falls Despite Global Slump, Report Finds' *New York Times* (6 March) <https://www.nytimes.com/2012/03/07/world/extreme-poverty-down-despite-recession-world-bank-data-show.html> accessed 29 August 2021.

Meyerfeld, Bruno, 'Au Brésil, « la faim est partout, et l'Etat nulle part »' *Le Monde* (29 September 2022) <https://www.lemonde.fr/economie/article/2022/09/29/au-bresil-le-retour-de-la-faim-legs-de-jair-bolsonaro_6143619_3234.html> accessed 13 February 2024.

Miranda, Tiago, 'Proposta aumenta Bolsa Família em 50% durante pandemia' *Agência Câmara de Notícias* (20 April 2020) <https://www.camara.leg.br/noticias/655130-proposta-aumenta-bolsa-familia-em-50-durante-pandemia#:~:text=O%20benefício%20médio%20pago%20a,2%20milhões%20de%20famílias%20atendidas.> accessed 7 May 2023.

Pozzebom, Elina Rodrigues, 'Aprovado pelo Congresso, auxílio emergencial deu dignidade a cidadãos durante a pandemia' *Agência Senado* (30 December 2020) <https://www12.senado.leg.br/noticias/materias/2020/12/30/aprovado-pelo-congresso-auxilio-emergencial-deu-dignidade-a-cidadaos-durante-a-pandemia> accessed 7 May 2023.

Trielli, Daniel, Prengaman, Peter, and DiLorenzo, Sarah, 'Millions return to poverty in Brazil as 'boom' decade erodes' *Seattle Times* (22 October 2017) <https://www.seattletimes.com/business/millions-return-to-poverty-in-brazil-eroding-boom-decade/> accessed 13 February 2024.

Wetzel, Deborah, 'Bolsa Família: Brazil's Quiet Revolution' *Valor Econômico* (4 November 2013) <https://www.worldbank.org/en/news/opinion/2013/11/04/bolsa-familia-Brazil-quiet-revolution> accessed 6 May 2023.

Webpages

Archives, The National, '1834 Poor Law: What did people think of the new Poor Law?' <https://cdn.nationalarchives.gov.uk/documents/education/poor-law.pdf> accessed 10 July 2022.

ba.gov.br, 'Governo da Bahia apresenta avanços na reparação às vítimas e familiares da explosão da fábrica de fogos em Santo Antônio de Jesus' (2024) <https://www.ba.gov.br/justica/noticias/2024-08/17672/governo-da-bahia-apresenta-avancos-na-reparacao-vitimas-e-familiares-da> accessed 20 March 2025.

Conselho Nacional de Segurança Alimentar e Nutricional, 'O que é o Consea?' (2017) <http://www4.planalto.gov.br/consea/acesso-a-informacao/institucional/o-que-e-o-consea> accessed 11 October 2021.

gov.br, 'Programa de Aquisição de Alimentos (PAA)' <https://www.gov.br/cidadania/pt-br/acoes-e-programas/inclusao-produtiva-rural/paa#:~:text=O%20Programa%20de%20Aquisição%20de,e%20incentivar%20a%20agricultura%20familiar.> accessed 6 May 2023.

gov.br, 'Brasil Sem Miséria' (2015) <https://www.gov.br/secretariadegoverno/pt-br/iniciativas/internacional/fsm/eixos/inclusao-social/brasil-sem-miseria> accessed 6 May 2023.

gov.br, 'Programa Cisternas' (2019) <https://www.gov.br/cidadania/pt-br/acoes-e-programas/inclusao-produtiva-rural/acesso-a-agua-1/programa-cisternas> accessed 6 May 2023.

gov.br, 'Inscrever-se no Cadastro Único' (2021) <https://www.gov.br/pt-br/servicos/inscrever-se-no-cadastro-unico-para-programas-sociais-do-governo-federal> accessed 30 August 2021.

gov.uk, 'Theresa May's equality strategy speech' (2010) <https://www.gov.uk/government/speeches/theresa-mays-equality-strategy-speech> accessed 18 March 2024.

Johnson, Lyndon B. 'Commencement Address at Howard University: "To Fulfill These Rights."' (*The American Presidency Project*,1965) <https://www.presidency.ucsb.edu/documents/commencement-address-howard-university-fulfill-these-rights> accessed 2 May 2023.

Ministério da Cidadania, 'O que é' <https://www.gov.br/cidadania/pt-br/acoes-e-programas/bolsa-familia/o-que-e> accessed 1 September 2021.

OECD, 'Poverty rate' <https://data.oecd.org/inequality/poverty-rate.htm> accessed 31 August 2021.

OPHI, 'Global Multidimensional Poverty Index' (*Oxford Poverty & Human Development Initiative*) <https://ophi.org.uk/multidimensional-poverty-index/> accessed 31 August 2021.

Secretaria de Desenvolvimento Social, 'Condicionalidades do Programa Bolsa Família' (2020) <https://www.sedes.df.gov.br/condicionalidades-bolsa-familia/> accessed 11 October 2020.

Scottish Government, 'Fairer Scotland Duty: interim guidance for public bodies' (2018) <https://www.gov.scot/publications/fairer-scotland-duty-interim-guidance-public-bodies/pages/2/> accessed 18 March 2024.

UK Parliament, '1601 Poor Law' <https://www.parliament.uk/about/living-heritage/evolutionofparliament/2015-parliament-in-the-making/get-involved1/2015-banners-exhibition/rachel-gadsden/1601-poor-law-gallery/> accessed 10 July 2022.

UK Parliament, 'Poor Law reform' <https://www.parliament.uk/about/living-heritage/transformingsociety/livinglearning/19thcentury/overview/poorlaw/> accessed 10 July 2022.

UNDP, 'Frequently Asked Questions - Multidimensional Poverty Index (MPI)' <http://hdr.undp.org/en/faq-page/multidimensional-poverty-index-mpi#t410n3222> accessed 6 September 2021.

UNDP, 'MPI 2024 FAQS' <https://hdr.undp.org/mpi-2024-faqs> accessed 18 March 2026.

Wales Centre for Public Policy, 'Implementing the Socio-economic Duty: learning from experience' (2021) <https://www.wcpp.org.uk/commentary/implementing-the-socio-economic-duty-learning-from-experience/> accessed 17 March 2024.

Welsh Government, 'Socio-economic Duty: an overview' (2020) <https://www.gov.wales/socio-economic-duty-overview> accessed 17 March 2017.

World Bank, 'Brazil. Survey Information' <https://pip.worldbank.org/country-details/BRA?pathName=Poverty%20Calculator&pathLink=%2Fpoverty-calculator> accessed 3 September 2025.

World Bank, 'Fact Sheet: An Adjustment to Global Poverty Lines' (2022) <https://www.worldbank.org/en/news/factsheet/2022/05/02/fact-sheet-an-adjustment-to-global-poverty-lines#3> accessed 13 February 2023.

World Bank, 'Multidimensional Poverty Measure' <https://www.worldbank.org/en/topic/poverty/brief/multidimensional-poverty-measure> accessed 31 August 2021.

WWP, 'What is WWP?' (*World Without Poverty. Brazil Learning Initiative*) <https://wwp.org.br/en/what-is-wwp/> accessed 1 September 2021.

Miscellaneous

IPEA, 'Diálogos com Anna Peliano—A Fome tem Pressa: Reflexões sobre o Enfrentamento da Fome no Brasil' (2021) <https://www.youtube.com/watch?v=CS5jZXXWt2I&t=19696s> accessed 3 November 2021.

PC Chief Justice of Canada, *Remarks of the Right Honourable Beverley McLachlin* (Lord Cooke Lecture in Wellington, New Zealand 2005).

Whelan, Daniel J, Mihir Kanade, and Shyami Puvimanasinghe, 'The Right to Development: Origins, History and Institutional Development' (*E-Learning Module on Operationalizing the Right to Development in Implementing the Sustainable Development Goals. OHCHR, UPEACE, UNU-IIGH* 2020) <https://www.ohchr.org/en/training-materials-online-course-right-development-and-sustainable-development-goals> accessed 2 February 2024.

Index

For the benefit of digital users, indexed terms that span two pages (e.g., 52–53) may, on occasion, appear on only one of those pages.

Tables, figures, and boxes are indicated by an italic *t*, *f*, and *b* following the page numbers.

accommodation 50–52
ADC 41 (2017) 169, 170–71, 189–91, 193, 241, 252, 261–62
Additional Protocol to the American Convention on Human Rights in the Area of Economic, Social and Cultural Rights *see* Protocol of San Salvador
ADPF 186 (2012) 168–69, 172–73, 188–89, 241, 251–52, 261–62
affirmative action 127, 143–44, 145n.123, 174–76, 175*f*, 179–80, 190–91, 192, 193, 226, 226n.116
African Charter on Human and People's Rights 76
Albertyn, Cathi 101, 107–8, 191
American Convention on Human Rights 76, 96, 202, 203–8
Arguelhes, Diego Werneck 237–39
Atrey, Shreya 95–96, 101, 102, 112

Banjul Charter *see* African Charter on Human and People's Rights
basic needs 82–84
Betinho 139
Biroli, Flávia 105
Bogdandy, Armin von 202–3, 250–51
Bolsa Família 25, 25n.43, 26–27, 26*f*, 29*f*, 123–25, 124nn.20–21, 129–30, 134–35, 135n.77, 139, 140, 185–86, 232–33, 242, 258–59
Bolsonaro, Jair Messias 131–34
Botero, Sandra 85, 237–38
Brazil Aid 26–27, 26*f*, 29*f*, 134, 135n.74
Brazil without Extreme Poverty 25, 127
Brazilian Federal Supreme Court (STF) 7, 165–201, 175*f*, 180*t*, 200*t*, 240–43, 247–56, 277–80
Brinks, Daniel M 84–85, 237–38
burden of proof 221, 221n.90

Canadian Human Rights Act 98
Campello, Tereza 144, 147–48, 273–74
capabilities 29–30, 34, 36
Cardoso, Adalberto 125–26, 130–31
Cardoso, Fernando Henrique (FHC) 117, 121–22, 139, 143–44
case selection 161–63, 209
case studies 6–7
cash transfers programmes
  Auxílio Brasil see Brazil Aid
  Auxílio Emergencial see Emergency Aid
  Continuous Cash Benefit Programme (BPC) 135, 165–66, 167–68, 183–85, 241–42
  Family Grant *see Bolsa Família*
child mortality 144–45
coding 11–12, 163–65, 210
Collins, Patricia Hill 105, 232
Colombian Constitutional Court 40, 250
conditional cash transfers (CCTs) 123–25, 156, 241, 244, 246, 276, 280
Constitution
  of 1917 (Mexico) 72–73
  of 1919 (Weimar Constitution, Germany) 28
  of 1934 (Brazil) 73
  of 1988 (CF/88, Brazil) 157, 158–61, 170–71
Convention on the Rights of the Child (CRC) 75–76
Covid-19 pandemic 35–36, 132–34, 140, 185–86, 241–42
Crenshaw, Kimberlé 4–5, 103–4, 105
criminalization of poverty 62–70

da Silva, Luiz Inácio 'Lula' *see* Lula
Dantas-Saraiva-Cotegipe Law *see* Sexagenarian Law

dignity 42, 43, 49, 49n.156, 50–51, 71, 75, 93–94, 100, 117, 207–8, 259–60
discrimination based on
  class 99, 151–53, 152*f*, 153n.161
  disabilities 106–7, 133, 186–87
  economic status 96–97, 98–99, 180–81n.80, 181–82, 205, 210–11, 217–18, 219–20
  gender 149–50, 153n.163
  poverty 91–92, 96–97, 182–83, 192, 218–19, 220–21, 221n.89, 235
  race 147*f*, 148–53, 148*f*, 168–69, 171, 172–73, 188–91
  social origin 96–97, 98, 99, 205, 217–18
due diligence 8, 224, 278

education 141–44, 142*f*, 143*f*, 147*f*, 153n.162, 153n.163
effectiveness 229–30, 231–32, 244, 246, 253–56, 260, 262–63, 281–82
electricity 145–46
Emergency Aid 132–33, 133n.61
equality dimensions
  distributive 49, 50, 111, 261–62
  participative 49–50, 111
  recognition 49, 50, 111
  transformative 49–52, 109, 111
equality of opportunities 42–43
equality of results 43
equality test 181n.81, 221n.90
European Convention on Human Rights 96, 100
European Court of Human Rights 100

FAO World Hunger Map 128, 139, 140–41, 140n.101, 141*f*
Felipe, Miguel Luis 105
Ferraz, Octávio Luiz Motta 86–87, 237–38, 239
Ferrer Mac-Gregor Poisot, Eduardo 103, 206, 216–17, 218–20, 229–30, 231–32
FHC *see* Cardoso, Fernando Henrique
Fineman, Martha Albertson 108–9
Fireworks Factory case 211–12, 213–14, 220–21, 224–25, 230–31, 232–33, 244–46, 248–49, 263
formal equality 40–41
Franco, Itamar 121, 138–39
Fraser, Nancy 43–46, 48–49, 51–52
Fredman, Sandra 38–39, 41–42, 48–54, 83–84, 95–96, 97–99, 110–11, 233–34, 235, 247–48

Gargarella, Roberto 72–73, 74
Golden Law 67–68
Goldblatt, Beth 101, 107–8, 191
Gonzales Lluy and others v Ecuador 102–3, 214

Hacienda Brasil Verde Workers v Brazil 218–20, 227–30, 246
health care 151, 153
Hirschl, Ran 94
housing 147*f*
Human Development Index 79
hunger 138–41, 141*f*

illiteracy 141–42, 150
impeachment 130
indirect discrimination 110, 256, 262–63
Inter-American Commission on Human Rights (IACommHR) 226
Inter-American Court of Human Rights (IACtHR) 7, 210–36, 222*t*, 236*t*, 244–46, 247–53, 257–60, 277, 278–79, 280
International Convention on the Elimination of All Forms of Discrimination Against Women 75–76, 268n.8
International Convention on the Elimination of All Forms of Racial Discrimination 75–76, 268n.8
International Covenant on Civil and Political Rights 96, 205
International Covenant on Economic, Social and Cultural Rights 75–76, 96
intersectionality 102–6, 113, 148–53, 220, 232, 280–81

Jannuzzi, Paulo de Martino 32, 128, 268
judicialization of mega-politics 94
judicialization of politics 94, 249
jus cogens 213
Justices
  Aurélio, Marco 167–68, 177–78, 183–86, 192, 198, 251–52
  Barbosa, Joaquim 166–67
  Barroso, Roberto 169, 170–71, 178–79, 187, 189–91, 193, 254–56
  Britto, Ayres 166, 173, 177–78, 251

Fachin, Edson 194, 243
Fux, Luiz 40, 169, 177, 193
Lewandowski, Ricardo 169, 172–73, 188–89, 192, 197, 255
Lúcia, Cármen 186–87, 252
Mendes, Gilmar 168, 169–70, 194, 195–97, 243, 258–60
Moraes, Alexandre de 197
Weber, Rosa 198

Khaitan, Tarunabh 37–38, 174–75

Labour Party (PT) 122–30
Lagos del Campo v Peru 206–7
Law of the Free Womb 64–65
legal agency 85
Lei Áurea see Golden Law
life expectancy 144–45
Lost Decade 121, 138
Lula 27, 117–18, 122–27, 134–35, 139, 140

Marx, Karl 43–44, 56
measurements of multidimensional poverty
dashboard approach 31, 138–48
Multidimensional Poverty Index (MPI, OPHI and UNDP) 30–31, 136–38, 139n.95
Multidimensional Poverty Measure (MPM, World Bank) 31, 137–38
Medeiros, Marcelo 24–26
monetary poverty
absolute monetary poverty 20, 21–24, 32, 58–59, 121–35
relative monetary poverty 22, 24, 32, 58–59
Moyn, Samuel 74, 82–83, 93–94
multidimensional poverty 29–33, 136–48

Neri, Marcelo 125–27
New International Economic Order 76, 77–78

OAS Charter 207–8
occupational mobility 125–27
oppression
cultural imperialism 57
exploitation 56
marginalization 56, 274–75
powerlessness 56–57, 191, 274–75
violence 57–58, 274–75

Pact of San José, Costa Rica *see* American Convention on Human Rights
Petersen, Niels 17
Pogge, Thomas 71, 81
positive measures *see* affirmative action
positive obligations 109–12, 191–94, 226–32
poverty lines
Bolsa Família line (PBF line, Brazil) 25–26, 26*f*, 27, 29*f*, 128–29, 129*f*, 132, 134–35, 154, 258–59
BPC line 27, 29*f*, 154, 167–68, 242–43, 243n.17
high-income countries (World Bank) 23–24, 29*f*, 129, 129*f*, 135
International Poverty line (IPL, World Bank) 21–23, 24, 26*f*, 129*f*, 132, 134–35, 135n.78, 154, 154*f*
middle-high income countries (World Bank) 23–24, 29*f*, 129, 129*f*
Organisation for Economic Co-operation and Development's poverty line 24, 29*f*
Single Register (Cadastro Único, Brazil) 28, 29*f*
Préteceille, Edmond 125–26, 130–31
Programa Fome Zero see Zero Hunger Programme
progressive realization 244, 257–58, 259–60, 262–63, 281–82
Promotion of Equality and Prevention of Unfair Discrimination Act (South Africa) 98–99
protected groups 37–40, 157–201, 180*t*, 181n.81, 221–22, 221n.90, 221n.93
Protocol of San Salvador 75–76, 206–7
PROUNI 143–44, 166, 173, 241

quota system *see* affirmative action

Rawls, John 172–73
reparations 232–34, 244–45
right to development 76–81
Rousseff, Dilma 127–30, 139, 144, 145n.122

Salata, André 126–27, 127n.35, 144n.117, 153
sanitation 145–46, 147*f*, 153
Sen, Amartya 29–30, 34–35, 36–38, 41
severe food insecurity 140, 140n.103
Sexagenarian Law 65–66
slavery 64–68, 190, 218, 220, 224, 227, 228

social justice
bivalence 44–46
participation 47–48, 52
recognition 43–44, 52
redistribution 43–44, 52, 172–73
social mobility 126, 128, 281
social rights 72–74, 75–76, 81–89, 93, 270–72
social stratification
educational stratification 147, 150–53, 152*f*, 155, 188, 189–90, 241, 273–74
occupational stratification 45–46, 149, 150, 189–91, 241
structural discrimination 193, 218, 222, 225, 227–29, 229n.133, 230, 231
stereotypes 4, 9, 12, 43–45, 49, 50–51, 52, 53–54, 57, 63, 65, 66, 68, 69–70, 83, 89, 90, 91, 98, 104, 214–15, 281
Student Financing Fund for Higher Education (FIES) 143–44
subsidiary policymaker 243, 259–60, 263
substantive equality 41–54, 109–11
Supremo Tribunal Federal see Brazilian Federal Supreme Court
suspect classification *see* protected groups

Temer, Michel 130–31
transformative constitutionalism 237–40, 249–53, 257–58, 282–84

UK Equality Act 97
UN Committee on Economic, Social and Cultural Rights (CERD Committee) 91, 205, 268n.8
UN Committee on the Elimination of All Forms of Discrimination Against Women (CEDAW Committee) 268n.8
UN Convention on the Rights of Persons with Disabilities 268n.8
unemployment 130–31, 131*f*, 133–34
Universal Declaration of Human Rights 75
Urueña, René 250–51
US Supreme Court 98, 283n.33

vagrancy laws 62–69
vulnerabilities 106–9, 181–82, 223–24, 246
vulnerable groups *see* protected groups

Weber, Max 43–44
Workers of the Fireworks Factory in Santo Antônio de Jesus and their Families v Brazil see Fireworks Factory case
World without Poverty 127–28

Young, Iris Marion 55–58, 233–34

Zero Hunger Programme 123, 129–30